DEBATING THE ATHENIAN
CULTURAL REVOLUTION

Whatever aspect of Athenian culture one examines, whether it be tragedy and comedy, philosophy, vase-painting and sculpture, oratory and rhetoric, law and politics, or social and economic life, the picture looks very different after 400 BC from before 400 BC. Scholars who have previously addressed this question have concentrated on particular areas and come up with explanations, often connected with the psychological effect of the Peloponnesian War, which are very unconvincing as explanations for the whole range of change. This book attempts to look at a wide range of evidence for cultural change at Athens and to examine the ways in which the changes may have been co-ordinated. It is a complement to the examination of the rhetoric of revolution as applied to ancient Greece in *Rethinking Revolutions through Ancient Greece* (Cambridge, 2006).

ROBIN OSBORNE is Professor of Ancient History at the University of Cambridge and a Fellow of King's College. His numerous publications include *Greece in the Making* (1996), *Archaic and Classical Greek Art* (1998), *Greek Historical Inscriptions 404–323 BC* (2003, edited with P. J. Rhodes) and *Poverty in the Roman World* (2006, edited with Margaret Atkins).

DEBATING THE ATHENIAN CULTURAL REVOLUTION

Art, literature, philosophy, and politics 430–380 BC

EDITED BY

ROBIN OSBORNE

CAMBRIDGE
UNIVERSITY PRESS

CAMBRIDGE UNIVERSITY PRESS

Cambridge, New York, Melbourne, Madrid, Cape Town, Singapore, São Paulo

Cambridge University Press
The Edinburgh Building, Cambridge CB2 8RU, UK

Published in the United States of America by Cambridge University Press, New York

www.cambridge.org
Information on this title: www.cambridge.org/9780521879163

© Cambridge University Press 2007

First published 2007

Printed in the United Kingdom at the University Press, Cambridge

A catalogue record for this publication is available from the British Library

ISBN 978-0-521-87916-3 hardback

Contents

Figures and tables

TABLES

Notes on contributors

BEN AKRIGG is Assistant Professor in Greek History at the University of Toronto. His dissertation on the demography and economy of classical Athens was written as part of the AHRB project.

ARMAND D'ANGOUR is the Fellow and Tutor in Classics at Jesus College, Oxford. His publications include articles on ancient Greek music and metre, Roman poetry, and the notions of the classic and the new. He is currently completing a book on aspects of novelty and innovation in ancient Greece.

ESTHER EIDINOW has a doctorate in ancient history from Oxford University. Her book *Risk and the Greeks: Oracles, Curses and the Negotiation of Uncertainty* was published in 2007. She currently holds a Leverhulme early career fellowship at the University of Oxford.

EDITH HALL is Professor in Classics and in Drama at Royal Holloway, University of London. Her books include an edition of Aeschylus' *Persians*, and studies of ethnicity in Greek tragedy, the reception of ancient theatrical works on the post-Renaissance stage, the ancient acting profession, and the ways in which ancient drama related to social reality. She is currently working on the cultural impact of the *Odyssey* and the evidence for ancient pantomime.

ELIZABETH IRWIN held a post-doctoral research position on the AHRB Anatomy of Cultural Revolution Project at Cambridge and is now an Assistant Professor of Classics at Columbia University. She works on archaic and classical Greek literature and politics. Her recent publications include *Solon and Early Greek Poetry: The Politics of Exhortation* (Cambridge, 2005), and 'Gods among men? The social and political dynamics of the *Hesiodic Catalogue of Women*', in *The Hesiodic Catalogue of Women: Constructions and Reconstructions*, ed. R. Hunter (Cambridge, 2005). She has co-edited a volume with Emily Greenwood, *Reading Herodotus: The Logoi of Book 5* (Cambridge, 2007) and is presently finishing a monograph on Herodotus Book 3.

ALEX LONG is a Lecturer in Classics at the University of St Andrews. His doctoral dissertation discusses Plato's view of dialectic and uses of dialogue form, and he has recently worked on Heraclitus' conception of wisdom and Lucan's Civil War. He is currently preparing translations of Plato's *Meno* and *Phaedo* for Cambridge Texts in the History of Philosophy.

KATHARINA LORENZ is Lecturer in Classical Studies at the University of Nottingham. Her interests cover Greek and Roman visual culture, especially mythological imagery and image–text interactions. She is currently completing a book on mythological imagery in the Roman domestic context.

ROBIN OSBORNE was director of the AHRB project, and is Professor of Ancient History in the University of Cambridge. With Simon Goldhill he edited *Rethinking Revolutions through Ancient Greece* (Cambridge, 2006).

PETER SCHULTZ is Assistant Professor of Art History at Concordia College. He has held advanced fellowships from the Fulbright Foundation, the A. G. Leventis Foundation, and the American School of Classical Studies, Athens. He is the editor (with Jesper Jensen, George Hinge, and Bronwen Wickkiser) of *Aspects of Ancient Greek Cult: Ritual, Context, Iconography* (2007), the editor (with Ralf von den Hoff) of *Early Hellenistic Portraiture: Image, Style, Context* (forthcoming) and the author of several articles on Attic sculpture and topography. He is currently preparing a monograph on the sculptural programme of the temple of Athena Nike in Athens.

JULIA L. SHEAR is a lecturer in Classics at the University of Glasgow. She wrote her dissertation on the Panathenaic Festival at the University of Pennsylvania and then held a post-doctoral research position on the AHRB Anatomy of Cultural Revolution Project at Cambridge at the Faculty of Classics and King's College. She is the author of several articles on Athenian religion, society, and culture, and is currently writing a book on the Athenian responses to the oligarchic revolutions at the end of the fifth century BC.

CLAIRE TAYLOR is a Leverhulme Early Career Fellow at the University of Manchester. Her doctoral dissertation examined changes in political participation in fifth- and fourth-century Athens as part of the AHRB Anatomy of Cultural Revolution project. She is interested in the social and economic history of the Greek world and is currently working on a project examining the role of wealth in fourth-century Attica.

ROBERT TORDOFF is Assistant Professor in Greek Drama at York University, Toronto. His doctoral thesis, done under the auspices of the AHRB project, and continuing research focus on Aristophanes and the politics of humour, laughter, and the comic in classical Athenian theatre.

Preface

From 2001 to 2005 the Arts and Humanities Research Board funded a research project based in the Faculty of Classics, University of Cambridge, on 'The Anatomy of Cultural Revolution: Athenian art, literature, language, philosophy and politics 430–380 BC'. The aim of the project was to look more closely at the ways in which the culture of classical Athens, with 'culture' understood in its broadest sense, changed at the end of the fifth century BC, and to consider what factors may have produced the changes and the extent to which they might be related to one another. Part of the work of the project involved consideration of how changes get constructed as revolutionary, and that work is reflected in *Rethinking Revolutions through Classical Greece* published by Cambridge University Press in 2006. This volume is concerned rather with the description and analysis of the changes themselves. The chapters here were first given as papers at a conference in Cambridge in July 2004 at which those whose research had been funded by the project, and others with close interests in the topic, explored together the nature of the changes that can be seen in Athenian political, literary, religious, and artistic culture at the end of the fifth century BC.

I am grateful to the AHRB, the Cambridge University Faculty of Classics, and King's College, Cambridge, for their support for the project and for this conference, and to Ben Akrigg, Elizabeth Irwin, Julia L. Shear, Claire Taylor, and Robert Tordoff, who carried the project through. The project discussions which helped to shape the papers given here had the advantage of input from a very large number of colleagues. In particular we are grateful to Peter Burian, Paul Cartledge, Pat Easterling, Peter Fawcett, Simon Goldhill, Josiah Ober, Peter Rhodes, Richard Seaford, Dorothy Thompson, and Stephen Todd. I am further indebted to Elizabeth Irwin for her work in consolidating the bibliographies, and to Brandon Foster for compiling the index.

September 2006   ROBIN OSBORNE

Abbreviations

Abbreviations of journal titles follow the scheme used in *L'Année philologique*. Abbreviations of classical writers' names follow the scheme used in the *Oxford Classical Dictionary*.

AP	*Palatine Anthology*
APF	Davies, J. K., *Athenian Propertied Families, 600–300* BC. Oxford, 1971.
ARV	Beazley, J. D., *Attic Red-Figure Vase-Painters*, 3 vols. Oxford, 1st edn 1942; 2nd edn 1963.
ATL	B. D. Meritt *et al.*, *Athenian Tribute Lists*, I–IV. Cambridge, Mass., and Princeton, 1939–53.
CEG	Hansen, P. A., *Carmina Epigraphica Graeca*, 2 vols. Berlin, 1983–9.
DT	Audollent, A., *Defixionum Tabellae*. Paris, 1904.
DTA	Wünsch, R., *Defixionum Tabellae Atticae, Inscr. Gr.*, III.3. Berlin, 1887.
FGrHist	Jacoby, F., *Die Fragmente der griechischen Historiker*. Berlin and Leiden, 1923– .
Gernet and Bizos	Gernet, L., and M. Bizos, eds., *Lysias: Discours: texte établi et traduit*. 2 vols. Paris, 1924–55.
ICret	Guarducci, M., ed., *Inscriptiones Creticae*, 4 vols. Rome, 1935–50.
IDélos	Dürrbach, F., ed., *Inscriptions de Délos*. Paris, 1923–37.
IG	*Inscriptiones Graecae*
K-A	Kassel, R., and C. Austin, eds., *Poetae Comici Graeci*. Berlin, 1983– .
KvA:	Curtius, E., and J. A. Kaupert, *Karten von Attika*. Berlin, 1881–1900.
LGPN	*Lexicon of Greek Personal Names*. Oxford, 1987– .

LIMC	*Lexicon Iconographicum Mythologiae Classicae.* Zurich and Munich, 1981– .
LSJ	Liddell, H. G., R. Scott, rev. H. S. Jones, *A Greek–English Lexicon.* Oxford, 1940.
ML	Meiggs, R., and D. Lewis, *A Selection of Greek Historical Inscriptions to the End of the Fifth Century.* Oxford, 1969.
NGCT	Jordan, D. R., 'New Greek curse tablets (1985–2000)', *GRBS* 41 (2000): 5–46.
Olympia V	Dittenberger, W., and K. Purgold, *Die Inschriften von Olympia.* Berlin, 1896.
Olynthus X	Robinson, D. M., *Metal and Minor Miscellaneous Finds.* Baltimore, 1941.
PA	Kirchner, J., ed., *Prosopographia Attica*, 2 vols. Berlin, 1903.
PGM	Betz, H. D., ed., *The Greek Magical Papyri in Translation.* Chicago, 1992.
PMG	Page, D. L., ed., *Poetae Melici Graeci.* Oxford, 1962.
RIB	Collingwood, R. G., R. P. Wright, and others, *The Roman Inscriptions of Britain.* Oxford, 1965.
RO	Rhodes, P. J., and R. G. Osborne, *Greek Historical Inscriptions 404–323 BC.* Oxford, 2003.
SEG	*Supplementum Epigraphicum Graecum*
SGD	Jordan, D. R., 'A survey of Greek defixiones not included in the special corpora', *GRBS* 26 (1985): 151–97.
Suppl. Mag.	Daniel, R. W., and F. Maltomini, eds., 'Supplementum Magicum', *Papyrologica Coloniensia* 16/1–2, 2 vols. Opladen, 1989–91.
TGrF	*Tragicorum Graecorum Fragmenta*

CHAPTER I

Tracing cultural revolution in classical Athens

Robin Osborne

The language of 'revolution' makes for powerful rhetoric, whether in a political realm or in the institutional politics which governs the award of academic research grants.[1] In an earlier book, *Rethinking Revolutions through Classical Greece*, published by Cambridge University Press in 2006, we have explored how the rhetoric of revolution has come to be applied to classical Greece. There is no straightforward equivalent in ancient Greek for the term 'revolution', but what happened in classical Greece has been repeatedly claimed to constitute a revolution in Western civilization. The adjective 'revolutionary' is one that can never be used as a neutral description: whenever a revolution is hailed it is hailed for ideological and political reasons. The affirmation or denial that a particular change constitutes a revolution is the affirmation or denial that what changes is something peculiarly valuable or significant. In surveying the use of the term 'revolution' with regard to classical Greece as a whole or particular features of classical Greek culture, we uncover part of the political history of classics in subsequent history.

Inevitably, the decision to devote a book, and indeed a research project, to investigating the changes in Athenian culture at the end of the fifth century itself implies that those changes were particularly significant. This book, however, is less concerned with whether or not those changes justify using the rhetoric of revolution than with analysing the changes which have made laying claim to a cultural revolution in classical Athens at least *prima facie* plausible. The book as a whole offers something of a description of the profound changes in Athenian culture at the end of the fifth century BC, and makes some preliminary attempts to understand why the changes came about and whether and how they may have been linked.

---

[1] I am grateful to Liz Irwin, Julia Shear, and the two anonymous readers for Cambridge University Press, for extremely helpful comments on this chapter.

In this introductory chapter I first discuss what is at stake in constructing history as involving continuous change or revolutionary rupture. I then essay an overview of past scholarly attempts to describe and account for the changes at the end of the fifth century in Athens as revolutionary. I conclude with an attempt to suggest ways in which we might link together, and draw some conclusions from, the separate substantive studies which follow.

THEORY

It is basic to all forms of cultural history that cultural products do not remain unchanged over long periods of time. In the case of literary culture, the temporal aspect of change is often very much subordinated in discussion to the personal aspect: we tend to think in terms of Xenophon's historical writing being different from Thucydides' historical writing because Xenophon is an individual of very different intellectual capacity, not because he is writing a quarter of a century (or whatever) later.[2] But for the archaeologist it is axiomatic that time leaves nothing unchanged: relative dating depends upon change being continuous, and, since the classical period falls at a rather flat part of the radiocarbon calibration curve, in most circumstances relative dating is the only dating that the classical Greek archaeologist has. Although it has become increasingly fashionable to decry dating on the basis of changing forms alone, and to point out that changes of place as well as changes of time can influence form and how form changes, it remains the case that within defined geographical regions instances of contemporary stylistic incoherence are remarkably hard to find. There is no evidence of any sort to suggest that there was anyone in Attica in 450 still making or dedicating *korai*, for instance, and although some potters went on using the black-figure technique to paint certain shapes of pot long after red-figure had been generally adopted, black-figure drawing did not become frozen but continued to develop.[3]

---

[2] This is not always the case, of course. Were my examples to have been Herodotus and Thucydides, or Aeschylus and Sophocles, it would not be hard to find scholars who would talk of the differences in terms of differences of generation. The case against putting Herodotus into a different intellectual generation from Thucydides is well made by comparing the context which R. Thomas 2000 (esp. chs. 2, 6, and 7) constructs for Herodotus with that which Hornblower 1987 (esp. ch. 5) constructs for Thucydides. See further below, pp. 219–21.

[3] That said, there are some cases where individual features of an artefact reproduce a form that belongs to a past era, even though the artefact as a whole could not be mistaken for one produced at an earlier period; the shape of the hawksbeak mouldings at the temple of Nemesis at Rhamnous provides one curious example of this.

But if change is a historical constant, the nature of change in any particular cultural manifestation is not for that reason uninteresting, nor are all changes equal. To stay with my sculptural example, the change in the form of the freestanding male between the *kouros* commonly known as Kroisos (Athens National Museum 3851) and Aristodicus' *kouros* (Athens National Museum 3938) raises important questions about how contemporary viewers construed these statues. In attempting to explain the change, we reach for a viewing construction which will allow both statues to satisfy the viewer's demands but will lead us to understand Aristodicus to satisfy the demands of the viewer of c. 500 BC more fully.[4] But when we view the change between Aristodicus' *kouros* and the *Discobolus* sculpted by Myron of Eleutherai, whose works were certainly displayed on the Acropolis, the attraction of thinking that the two statues are doing the same thing, but that the *Discobolus* is doing it better, is somewhat limited. The *Discobolus* seems to display a whole different set of priorities.[5] An internalist history, a history of art, conducted by comparing works of art from an aesthetic point of view – that is, the history of art elicited by double slide projection – has some claim to appropriateness in the case of explaining why Kroisos became Aristodicus. But when it comes to explaining how Aristodicus became the *Discobolus*, an internalist history seems insufficient: the break is too great. How can we compare the incomparable?[6] Whether we choose to invoke the term 'revolution', to talk of paradigm shift, or whatever, the point is that whiggish history, the history of progress towards a single goal, has become implausible.[7]

Although not, I think, usually formulated in the terms that I have just used, the argument I have just made expresses a commonly held position. It is reflected in the arguments of those who insist on reserving 'revolution' for what they see as moments of total change, like the French Revolution, and who object to more general deployment of the term. We might call this view the naïve view. It is naïve because it assumes that there can be differences in degree (from Kroisos to Aristodicus) that are not as plausibly restated as difference in kind, and that there can be differences in kind (from Aristodicus to the *Discobolus*) which are not plausibly restated as difference of degree. Part of the point of this project has been to stand

---

[4] Boardman 1978: 84 on Aristodicus' *kouros*; cf. p. 72 on Kroisos.
[5] Stewart 1990: 148: 'a period of frenzied experiment . . . culminated around 460 in the acknowledged champion among all such statues, Myron's Diskobolos'; cf. Carpenter 1960: 82–5.
[6] For the importance of doing just that, see Detienne 2000.
[7] Not that that has prevented some art historians trying to do exactly that by treating naturalism as the only dimension of art.

back from that naïve assumption and see it for what it is – that is, to see its politics. *Rethinking Revolutions through Ancient Greece* addressed itself to the politics of how moments of history get packaged up as revolutions. It was concerned with the stories that are not told, the stories that are excluded, by talk of revolution or by denial of revolution. The naïve view suggests, I have claimed, that whether we choose to invoke the *term* 'revolution' or not does not matter: there really *is* a different *sort* of change separating the *Discobolus* from Aristodicus' *kouros* from that which separates Aristodicus' *kouros* from Kroisos. The political view insists that revolutions are (also) rhetorical. If Bishop Berkeley's tree continues to be when there is no one about in the quad, revolutions, by contrast, are there only if seen by someone (other than God).

The rhetoric of revolution is undeniable, and is ignored by historians at their peril – not just because there is money to be made out of research projects and books about revolutions, but because what people believe about past continuities and discontinuities actively affects their behaviour. To accept that a revolution occurs between A and B is to expect to side with A or B and to act as if the difference between them matters; to assert that A and B are essentially the same, though different in detail, is to invite the expectation that one can hold the same attitude to A as to B. But however much we stress the significance of revolutionary rhetoric, the naïve view is not without foundation. Historical change does not happen at a uniform pace, whether we are dealing with political, social, economic, or cultural history. Even if *which* moments are marked by discontinuity is going to be dependent on the questions being asked by the observer, there can be no history *at all* without the presence of some observer or other, and the reality for observers of such moments of discontinuity is not in itself in doubt. The importance of the political view, as I have called it, is to insist that we take a self-reflexive approach to our inquiries.

APPLYING THEORY

A *prima facie* case for seeing the period of 430 to 380 as a period of discontinuity in art, literature, language, philosophy, and politics is, evidently – given that the project received funding from the AHRB – not hard to make. Paul Cartledge has summarised past scholarly views of what happened at Athens like this:

Her economy (especially the cessation of silver mining), polity (the abolition of democracy and, when democracy was restored, the spate of political trials), culture (the finger is pointed at the demise of great tragic drama), and society (in particular the trial of Socrates on charges of religious abnormality and pedagogical corruption) have all at some time been characterized as at least temporarily disabled or dysfunctional. (2001: 109)

The case I made in the original proposal to the AHRB went like this:

The late tragedies of Euripides and Sophocles differ from their earlier work not just technically, in the way verse is handled, but in their dramatic form and their concerns: plays like *Oedipus at Colonus* and *Phoenician Women* consciously revisit the themes of earlier plays re-reading the concerns of those plays in changed circumstances. Of tragedies written after 405 we generally know little beyond the titles, but they are enough to indicate a continuing change of focus. Aristophanic comedies survive from five successive decades, and a continuous process of change in theme and form is apparent; but the plays from after 400 remain notable for the absence of political engagement (still there in *Frogs*), for the focus on concerns which are less narrowly Athenian, and for the repeated emphasis on social themes which had played little role in the earlier work. Comparisons within prose literature are more difficult because of the absence of works of the same genre from before and after 400 (itself, of course, a point of major significance). But if differences between Thucydides and Xenophon may be explicable in personal terms, the differences between Antiphon and Lysias, writing words to be spoken by others, are not so susceptible to that explanation: a whole new language is forged in Lysias' works. In philosophy we see a revolution of subject-matter, of philosophical method, and of the form in which philosophy is 'written up'. Outside literature the changes are equally massive: the iconography of Athenian red-figure pottery undergoes successive revolutions in the last quarter of the fifth century and first quarter of the fourth, first with the invasion of 'Meidian' scenes, dominated by personifications and effectively anonymous female figures, and then with polychromy and a new concern for fantastic creatures as well as mythical fantasy.

Such a case might be as readily deconstructed as it is constructed. If Aristophanic politics is different in the 390s, that does not mean that there is no politics. Robert Tordoff's work (see chapter 10) has found itself emphasising continuities as well as discontinuities. Nor is the revisiting of earlier themes by tragedians much of an argument for discontinuity in a genre built, at least in part, upon revisiting epic themes. 'For sensationalism, triviality, affectation', often alleged of fourth-century tragedy, 'we ought perhaps to read', Pat Easterling has suggested (1993: 568–9), 'elegance, sophistication, refinement, clarity, naturalism, polish, professionalism – a new kind of cosmopolitan sensibility'; in changing the evaluative language, Easterling encourages us to see differences of degree rather than differences of kind. The 'whole new language' of Lysias may seem a marked break from Thucydides, but it is sufficiently little of a break from the Old Oligarch for Simon

Hornblower to canvass a 380s date for that work more normally placed in
the 420s or 410s.[8] Meidian scenes are certainly very different from those of
Polygnotus in the middle of the fifth century, but Polygnotan scenes are
themselves strikingly different in subject-matter and style from those of
Euphronios or Douris – there seem all too many candidates for revolution
in vase-painting.[9] And so we might go on – all this without invoking the
problem that in many aspects of cultural history we simply do not have
comparable evidence from the fifth and the fourth centuries: 'the fact that
extremely successful plays like Astydamas' *Hector* or Theodectes' *Alcmaeon*
failed to get through the educational filter of late antiquity and the middle ages should not cause us to brush aside a whole period of intense and
dynamic dramatic activity', to quote Easterling again (1993: 568). Paul Cartledge has judged 'soundly based' the view that Athenian popular morality
'remained substantially and consensually stable between . . . 430 and 320
BC (Cartledge 2001: 110). Even in terms of political history there is a case
for 'utopian' scenarios, as well as for the 'nightmare' scenarios which see
the end of the fifth century as the beginning of some terminal crisis of the
Greek polis (Cartledge 2001: 108–10).[10]

It is precisely the way in which the changes at the end of the fifth century
are so readily open to redescription that offers justification for this project.
In a period when so much changes, it is easy to assert or to deny the absolute
or comparative importance of any individual change. This makes it vital to
conduct a wholesale, rather than a piecemeal, investigation of the period;
focusing on cultural history and on the issue of revolution seems to be
needed. The minimum aim of the project, and of this book, then, is to
build a wigwam argument, in which arguments which are individually less
than completely compelling offer support to one another which strengthens
each of them, or to show that one cannot be built: either to bolster the claims
for changes in one field by showing that they can be better understood in the
context of changes in other fields, or to undermine the claims that particular
changes constitute a revolution by showing that there is no coherent pattern
of change. That minimum aim demands that we achieve a fuller description
of late fifth-century culture, in its individual elements and as a whole, than

---

[8] Hornblower 2000. For arguments against this position see R. Osborne 2004b, another product of
the AHRB project.
[9] On the history of fifth-century vase-painting see Robertson 1994.
[10] Alternatively it might be claimed that there was change, but it occurred at a different point. Davies
(1978/93) began the chapter entitled 'Social Change', 'The 380s are a turning point.' But reading on
into the chapter we discover that it is relations between Greek cities that Davies thinks change in
the 380s – he admits that shifts in social values (e.g. the disappearance of bawdy from old comedy
and of sexually explicit scenes from Athenian vases) and in the role and status of myth occur c. 400.

has previously been offered by other scholars, and that we set those elements in some sort of context. But that is only the minimum aim. There is a more ambitious aim. This is to move beyond co-ordination or correlation to an understanding of the reasons for, as well as the nature and scale of, any change.

WHAT IS WRONG WITH PAST TREATMENTS?

Scholars who have previously written about aspects of end-of-fifth-century cultural history have offered a variety of types of explanation. Much that has been written seeks to locate what changes in the minds of the Athenians. For Cornford, in *Before and After Socrates* of 1932, understanding the sophistic revolution was all a matter of the Greeks growing up: in Greek society after the Persian wars 'we can observe an analogous effort of the individual to detach himself from the social group' (pp. 40–1); 'In the philosophy of individual self-assertion parents will recognise something analogous to the spirit of adolescent reaction against the authority of the home' (p. 43). For Dodds, in *The Greeks and the Irrational* of 1951, trying to explain not the occurrence of but the reaction to the sophists, the key was 'wartime hysteria'. He talks of 'the regressiveness of popular religion in the Age of Enlightenment', and goes on:

The first signs of this regression appeared during the Peloponnesian War, and were doubtless in part due to the war. Under the stresses that it generated, people began to slip back from the too difficult achievement of the Periclean Age; cracks appeared in the fabric, and disagreeably primitive things poked up here and there through the cracks. When that happened there was no longer any effective check on their growth. As the intellectuals withdrew further into a world of their own, the popular mind was left increasingly defenceless, though it must be said that for several generations the comic poets continued to do their best. The loosening of the ties of civic religion began to set men free to choose their own gods, instead of simply worshipping as their fathers had done; and, left without guidance, a growing number relapsed with a sigh of relief into the pleasures and comforts of the primitive. (pp. 192–3)

Dodds then proceeds to identify as examples of regression the 'increased demand for magical healing' (p. 193) leading to the rise of Asclepius, and 'the fashion for foreign cults, mostly of a highly emotional, "orgiastic" kind, which developed with surprising suddenness during the Peloponnesian War' (p. 193). Psychological effects of the war also figure strongly in J. J. Pollitt's account of changes in art in the late fifth century in his *Art and Experience in Classical Greece* of 1972:

When compared with the Parthenon . . . the art of the late fifth century often seems . . . devoid of serious content. It shows a fascination with technique and exalts ornamental elaboration above subject matter. At the same time it seems clear that the florid style was consciously selected and developed by the artists of the period to express a particular state of mind. (p. 123)

Now the flying drapery style is obviously Gorgian in spirit, and appears to emanate from the same pressures as contemporary rhetoric. On the surface it is all elegance, but underneath it may reflect a despairing desire to retreat from the difficult intellectual and political realities of the age and to take refuge in gesture. Escapist wish-fulfillment is perhaps just as common a reaction to troubled times as overt agonizing.[11] (p. 125)

Cornford, Dodds, and Pollitt may all turn to psychological explanations, but two very different models are at work here. Psychological explanations of the Cornford type effectively redescribe the observed phenomena so that what appears to be a radical break can be understood in terms of an evolutionary coherence. Whereas Plato in *Republic* explores the workings of the city in order the better to understand the workings of the mind of the individual, Cornford uses analogies from the individual to understand the society of the city.[12] The Athenians are simply growing up, there is nothing untoward in what happens; just as every human being grows up, it is implied, so did classical Athens – it could not be otherwise.

Psychological explanations of the Dodds and Pollitt type, on the other hand, affirm that there is something to be worried about, for they look to explain radical change in culture with reference to traumatic experiences elsewhere in society. Fifth-century Athens is the healthy society, fourth-century Athens is the traumatised society. There is a notable circularity in this argument: it is only because of the episodes which Dodds takes as evidence that the trauma of war and plague caused regression that we know that the experience of war and the plague were traumatic in the first place.

There can be little doubt that the plague was in some sense traumatic, but the extent to which it cast a long shadow over the Athenian mind is more open to question: Thucydides' surprising, indeed impossible, claim about Athenian demographic recovery after the plague (6.26.2; cf. 6.12.1 (speech of Nikias)) might be taken to be some evidence that Athenians shrugged it off more lightly than Dodds would have us believe.[13] In the case of the war

---

[11] For a wholesale defence of Pollitt's approach see now Meyer and Lendon 2005.
[12] On Plato's analogy see Williams 1973.
[13] Compare Marshall 1990 for possible Thucydidean distortion of the seriousness of the plague, and Mikalson 1984 and Parker 1996: 200 (cf. pp. 150, 180) on the limited impact of the plague in Athenian religious actions.

itself, there is certainly scope for questioning its impact, whether physical or psychological. Victor Hanson (1981) convincingly demolished the case for the physical effects of invasion or the occupation of Dekeleia being devastating. And Barry Strauss has pointed out, in a paper (1997) concerned with how we periodise history and what the effects of that periodisation are, that no one at the time was aware of living through one discrete Peloponnesian War starting in 431 and going on to 404. Pausanias, writing more than half a millennium later, could observe that the Peloponnesian War 'shook Greece from her foundations like an earthquake, and afterwards Philip son of Amyntas found it already rotted and unhealthy and ruined it altogether' (3.7.11), but this passage seems primarily to be a reaction to reading Thucydides (he has just commented that it was Sthenelaidas who brought on the war against Archidamus' resistance).

Past attempts at rooting cultural change more deeply into political, social, and economic change only reveal the more clearly what has been problematic about these explanations. J. H. Finley devoted the last chapter of his *Four Stages of Greek Thought* (1966) to 'The Rational Mind'. He begins that chapter by observing that 'in the fourth century it is as if the early mist had risen to uncover no longer a world of gods but a bright mid-morning' (p. 80), and goes on: 'To the men of the fourth century the forms of rational order represented an achieved triumph' (p. 81). Turning to the question of cause he states:

Clearly no single cause suffices to explain so wide a change. The twenty-seven years of the Peloponnesian War . . . constitute what Aristotle might have judged the efficient cause. The war brought losses of men and money, loss of empire . . . loss of confidence in the promise of leaders, awareness that the state could fall apart into conflicting interests and at best hardly contained them, and – subtlest | loss – surfeit of the former dream of conquest. (pp. 81–2)

To this catalogue he then adds, 'But at least two other main forces abetted the change: the thorough-going victory of what was earlier termed a conceptual way of thought over the old mythological way, and the rise of something like an urban middle class' (p. 83), before, in concluding the chapter, reverting to a simpler choice: 'The revolution by which conceptual thinking replaced the old reliance on myth necessarily shook the brief balance of the great age. As a cause of change, the intellectual revolution far outweighs even the strain of the twenty-seven year war' (p. 107).

Finley's list of causes – financial, demographic, political, psychological – pour out in no sort of order (and with no substantiation), and their final ranking is based on no argument. It is easy, but also facile, to suggest multiple contributory factors; what is needed is some way of joining them up, of making them contribute to a single picture, not returning always to treat them as rival pictures. Rather than taking one or more aspects of cultural history, observing change, and tying that change into whatever aspect of the larger historical picture comes to mind, we need an assessment of the ways in which that larger historical picture is changing. And the larger historical picture which we paint needs to be capable of explaining the 'before' as well as the 'after'. Pat Easterling has pointed out, in the paper about fourth-century tragedy from which I have already quoted, that

if the social structure created by the democracy in the fifth century was particularly favourable to the development of tragedy, as Vernant and others have taught us to believe, then we have to explain why in the restored democracy after the Peloponnesian War these conditions no longer obtained (if it is true that they didn't), and why one should no longer expect to find tragedy questioning, criticising, challenging or redefining the structure of the *polis* as well as 'inventing' and celebrating Athens. (1993: 561)

Similarly, if we cannot explain why the *absence* of what we think developed for the first time during the period we are discussing was important for Athenian society, politics, and culture before any putative revolution, then we need to think twice about making its *presence* a salient feature of our thick description of Athens after that revolution.

AND SO TO THIS BOOK

Oswyn Murray's classic 'Cities of Reason' paper (1990) opens with Bertrand Russell's observation, with regard to experiments with monkeys and bananas, that 'animals studied by Americans rush about frantically, with an incredible display of hustle and pep, and at last achieve the desired result by chance. Animals observed by Germans sit still and think, and at last evolve the solution out of their inner consciousness.' I am happy to say that, among the scholars contributing to this book, both the American and the German are represented (literally, let alone figuratively). We bring together diverse training and dispositions, diverse expectations about how the world works. One of our key tasks is to keep in view the very question of what we are considering to count as evidence.

In a book where the question addressed is about the presence or absence of continuities and coherence, there is one sense in which it does not matter where one starts. But commitment to coherence is not the same as commitment to every item in a chain having the same causal importance, and the persuasiveness of claims of (dis)continuity will depend crucially upon the plausibility of the causal structures suggested. This volume deliberately starts, therefore, with an analysis of aspects of Athenian life which have a claim to having impinged upon all, as chapter 2 explores Athenian demography and chapters 3 and 4 Athenian politics.

Ben Akrigg, in chapter 2, establishes, more clearly and powerfully than anyone has previously done, the evidence that the Athenian population, that is, not just the citizen population, but the *total* population, was reduced in size by between a third and a half between the outbreak of the Peloponnesian War in 431 and the end of the century, going, even on a conservative estimate, from c. 300,000 to 200,000 or 150,000. He points out, partly on the basis of comparative evidence, the sorts of economic and other effects that such a population reduction will have had upon the Athenian community. Since we do not know how evenly or unevenly population loss was distributed across social classes, the political effects of the demographic change cannot be predicted simply from the population reduction itself, and scholars' attempts to do so can be shown to be based on assumptions that cannot be supported. But the economic effects are another matter. We understand enough about the Athenian economy, and the relationship between labour and both production and consumption, to be able to assess the ways in which demographic changes created opportunities on the one hand, and reduced them on the other. That understanding does not primarily depend upon the accidents of survival of literary evidence – and indeed Akrigg shows in the case of Athenian banking the problems that have resulted from assuming that absence of literary evidence for a phenomenon is good evidence for the absence of the phenomenon. Simply from the evidence of demographic change we cannot deduce which opportunities were taken and which were not, but the demographic history provides an essential backdrop against which the textual and other evidence that we have for Athenian political, economic, and social relations after the Peloponnesian War has to be read.

It is those social relations which are the concern of Esther Eidinow in chapter 3. Eidinow investigates a form of evidence which appears in Athens for the first time at the end of the fifth century. This is the curse tablet. Although curses are, predictably enough, attested from the very beginning of writing in Greece, the practice of writing a curse on lead and depositing it, normally with a recently dead body, is one for which there is no evidence at Athens until late in the fifth century. In the late fifth and fourth centuries, however, surviving evidence suggests that the Athenians were distinctly more inclined to write curses than were other

Greeks. Eidinow describes the nature of the practice and the rationale of the curses and asks why the Athenians began to curse at this particular historical moment. She emphasises cursing as an act that is individual, secret, and not likely to be undertaken by those who could achieve the same results in other ways. Although the motivation for particular curses is not always easy to discern, being reduced to cursing is itself a mark of the breakdown of normal relations of social control, both personal and civic.[14] Such a breakdown is well attested for the months surrounding the oligarchic coup of 411 by Thucydides, and by the narratives about the regime of the Thirty offered by Xenophon and in various speeches of Lysias. What the curse tablets suggest is that relations between Athenians were never returned to the 'normality' of the fifth century. Eidinow draws attention to the various curses that are directed at those involved in lawcourt cases, and in various ways cursing seems closely connected to, and a form of inversion of, lawcourt speeches. The secrecy of curse tablets contrasts with the public performance of a dispute involved in bringing it to court. If the courts make private matters public, curse tablets relating to lawcourt cases attempt to remove sanction from the public sphere. There is a particular contrast between the requirement, brought in shortly after 380, that evidence to be used in court should be written down and sealed in a container at an early stage of proceedings, to be made public in court, and the writing down and secreting not of evidence but of requests for a particular form of penalty in the curse tablet. The practice of publication of lawcourt speeches, a practice which seems to have been new in the late fifth century, prolonged the life of disputes by making permanently available the hostile sketches of each other's behaviour painted by litigants in court, seems similarly to relate to the making permanent of hostility in the written curse tablet. Both alike suggest that, in a markedly smaller and less cosmopolitan community, fourth-century relations were more faction-riven than fifth-century ones were.

If Eidinow's curse tablets illuminate ways in which private behaviour changed, Claire Taylor's examination in chapter 4 of what the prosopographic (and largely epigraphic) evidence reveals about patterns of participation in Athenian politics turns our attention to public behaviour. It has been known for some time that the distribution pattern of deme of origin of generals and of those proposing decrees was different in the fourth from in the fifth century.[15] What Taylor is able to show is that the change in

---

[14] V. J. Hunter 1994 fails to register the role of curses in social control in Athens.
[15] R. Osborne 1985: 69–71.

patterns of participation extends beyond those two groups and that it is accompanied by a decline in the degree of dominance of political activity by those who are known to be wealthy. These findings tie in with the picture created by Akrigg, where the fourth century sees less economic polarisation, and lend weight to the case for remarkably egalitarian distribution of land ownership.[16] They also suggest a picture of fourth-century politics in which Athenian citizens living outside the town of Athens itself take advantage of the opportunities created by the decline in citizen numbers, and are more, rather than less, keen to play their part in central politics. This opens up the possibility that the change in the political tone, so often detected in fourth-century democracy, may be a product not primarily of the constitutional changes which scholars have been keen to list, but rather of the political running being made by citizens of different socio-economic backgrounds.[17]

In chapter 5 Julia Shear turns our attention away from issues of who was participating to issues of where and how they participated. She traces the ways in which, both by virtue of a range of building projects and by the inscriptions and activities located there, the Athenian Agora became, in the last quarter of the fifth century, the focus of Athenian civic attention. This stands in contrast to the way in which during the sixth century, and again during the third quarter of the fifth century, at least, Athenian attention, both corporate and individual, had been primarily directed to the Acropolis. By an analysis of the inscriptions set up in the Agora, Shear is able to show the changing ways in which civic duty was mapped out in and upon the Agora, as the Athenians sought to reinforce the democracy overturned first in 411 and again in 404. The decision to display the reinscribed lawcode in the Agora is so familiar that the contrast with the display of Solon's laws on the Acropolis is often overlooked. The decision in 394/3 to add statues of Konon and Euagoras to an Agora which until this point had featured statues only of the Tyrannicides has never been emphasised in the scholarship. Even more powerfully than the decision with regard to the lawcode, this decision moved the centre of civic consciousness to the Agora, placing emphasis upon glory achieved in the eyes of the people, rather than on glory achieved in the eyes of the gods.

Both the 'civic' and the 'religious' poles of this change in the relationship between the two deserve further consideration. The republication of the lawcode was accompanied by a series of changes in how law was made and

[16] Morris 2000: 140 2, reinterpreting work by Foxhall and Osborne.
[17] Rhodes 1979–80;, Hansen 1989c.

operated. These changes reflect in part the self-scrutiny which both had helped bring about and was occasioned by the two oligarchic revolutions.[18] The most obvious change was the decision in 403/2 that, in future, laws and decrees should be distinguished, and that only decisions of particular force, not those of general significance, should be made at a single sitting of the Assembly (Andokides 1.87). This self-denying ordinance not only involved making the conceptual distinction between general rules and particular decisions, but required the Athenian people constantly to re-survey the general framework of rules within which they lived.[19] For all that Athenians increasingly stressed the rule of law, the new procedure made it clearer than ever before that it was up to the Athenians themselves to establish how they lived.[20] Other changes in legal procedure associated with the restoration of democracy (such as the invention of *paragraphē*) or adopted early in the fourth century (such as the sealing up of testimonies, mentioned above) further indicate a desire to ensure that what happened on any particular occasion conformed to the pattern which the people had laid down. The same is true of the increasing reference of all judicial or quasi-judicial matters to the court: after 362 we know of no case of *eisangelia* that is finally decided in the assembly. Emphasis on the letter of the law, there visible in the Agora, and on investing authority in those identified in the law, replaced emphasis on the spirit of the law, enshrined up there on the Acropolis.[21]

It would be possible to situate the changes which Shear discusses against the background of changes in attitudes to the gods which scholars have often alleged to be taking place in the late fifth century. The way in which the Acropolis ceases to be the prime centre of political display could be held to be parallel to the move of religious interest from such old Olympians as Athena to more 'personal' gods such as Asclepius (if not Socrates' *daimonion*). Certainly in so far as what Shear is describing is a separation of religious from civic display, it accords with it being the marginally political religious events that catch contemporaries' attention (as the Bendideia catches Plato's attention so as to become the setting for the opening of the *Republic*). But the attention which is caught in the Agora is not an exclusively secular attention: the lawcode incorporated the religious calendar, and it was that religious calendar which was argued about in the courts when Nikomachos was prosecuted (Lysias 30; Todd 1996). Although there is little evidence

---

[18] See further R. Osborne 2003 and 2004b, esp. pp. 13–14.
[19] Hansen 1978/1983 for the distinction; MacDowell (1975) for lawmaking in the fourth century.
[20] Ostwald 1986: 497–524; R. Thomas 1994.
[21] There was, of course, a backlash to this, as orators sought to counteract particular laws of which they disapproved; R. Thomas 1994 esp. p. 133.

of the Athenians intervening with the way in which major festivals were celebrated in the first half of the fourth century, the mass of legislation of the 340s and 330s, much of it associated with Lycurgos, includes measures concerned with both Panathenaia and Dionysia.[22] Arguably the change in the prominence of the Acropolis is less a matter of Athenians becoming interested in different aspects of religion, and more a matter of the Athenian people becoming increasingly conscious that they have to take day-to-day responsibility for all their alignments, political and religious. Matters which the Athenians in the fifth century assumed that they wanted to show off to the gods (and men) now become matters for their own continued contemplation and for the state archive. This accords with Taylor's findings, which suggest that a wider range of Athenians in the fourth century than in the fifth felt that they had to involve themselves in the day-to-day running of politics. Such heightened awareness of the importance of the political decisions being taken seems plausibly to display itself in the choice that decisions, once taken, should not be deposited in a sanctuary and forgotten, but should be kept before the people's eyes in the civic centre.

What is kept before the eyes, in a rather different sense, is the subject of Katharina Lorenz's discussion of the changing ways in which the scenes on Athenian pottery of the late fifth century are organised visually, and what this implies about the way in which stories are told. Lorenz borrows from narratology the concept of 'metalepsis', the merging of distinct narrative levels, and illustrates the ways in which such merging can be found in late fifth-century Athenian pots. This manner of presenting narrative is quite novel, although related both to archaic polychronous 'synoptic' narration and to classical frieze forms isolating a single moment. Lorenz emphasises the ways in which the technique of metalepsis involves the viewer, who has to intervene in order to make decisions about what he or she is seeing and has to reposition himself or herself, metaphorically at least and sometimes literally. One result of employing the technique is to raise more actively the question of mythological and allegorical meaning. This question, which is latent in many Athenian pots, can be activated by, for instance, the juxtaposition of mythological and 'real-life' scenes on different parts of a vessel. But this is also a question which was not limited to Athenian pottery, but which was raised for Athenians on a day-to-day basis as they negotiated the programmes of sculpture and painting on display on the temples of the Acropolis or in the Painted Stoa in the Agora. Reviewing mythological and allegorical meaning was one of the things involved in moving the focus

---

[22] RO 81 for Panathenaia; Humphreys 1985 and Hintzen-Bohlen 1997 for Lycurgos.

of Athenian politics from its juxtaposition to the mythological conflicts and civic ritual on display on the Parthenon to the historical conflict and political commemorations on display in the Agora.

In the face of a persistent narrative of decline in Athenian vase-painting from the heady excitement of early red-figure, Lorenz stresses the way these metaleptic scenes heighten awareness of issues of the visual and make demands on the viewer, and she suggests that we can talk of an 'iconic turn'. We might support that suggestion more generally with reference to the return to the Athenian cemetery of the sculpted grave stele. Whereas Athenians in the first generation after the Persian wars saw no figurative imagery in cemeteries and rather little in sanctuaries – with no building of temples and some reduction in the practice of dedicating sculpture – Athenians of the last thirty years of the fifth century saw increasing amounts of figurative imagery on graves to complement, if never to rival, that over-flowing abundance of sculpture on the Parthenon and on and around the temple of Athene Nike. But the 'iconic turn' involved in the invention of metalepsis is a matter not simply of introducing more imagery, but of introducing imagery that has to be more closely engaged with, and with which the viewer has more self-consciously to relate.[23] Grave stelai provided just such imagery, thrust in the face of Athenians both because they were prominently placed in cemeteries on the roads entering Athens and the villages of Attica and because their imagery regularly reflected directly on Athenian domestic and public life.

We are told that Critias, the leading figure in the Thirty, had a gravestone in which Oligarchy and Democracy were engaged in combat (Scholia on Aeschylus 1.39). This gravestone does not survive, the inscription which is supposed to have been written on it did not identify the scene shown, and we have no extant gravestone which we have reason to believe to show personifications. Critias' tomb, however, raises the possibility that Athenian tombs were regularly like many English nineteenth-century tombs, facing the viewer with allegory rather than reality – or rather, leaving them to slip metaleptically between the two. This possibility is worth entertaining not least because it draws attention to the wider politics of metalepsis. In flagging up the difficulty of distinguishing not just different times but different modes of reality (past and present, mythical and historical), meta-lepsis demands that a viewer consider the exemplarity of what they are observing. Rather than taking it for granted that all citizens have an equal

---

[23] From that point of view there is an apt comparison with the Platonic dialogue, discussed by Long in chapter 9, whose form requires that readers make up their own mind which speaker they agree with.

part to play in the democratic city, viewers who are challenged to decide on the status of the scene which they are observing must ask themselves where the action portrayed, or the particular actor who may be represented, might fit into the life of the polis.

The question of where one particular actor, the sculptor, fits into the life of the polis is the subject of the chapter by Peter Schultz. Schultz is concerned with the very possibility of the social history of art. Schultz establishes, by judicious comparisons of pairs of late fifth- and early fourth-century sculptures, the marked change in conception that can be traced in Athenian sculpture. Against the tradition, particularly associated with Bryn Mawr and with Rhys Carpenter and his pupils, which insists that artistic identities in antiquity are phantom, not just in the sense that we cannot say anything about those artistic personalities but in the sense that, since individual personalities made no impression on art, there was nothing to be said, Schultz insists that the individuality of the particular artist can be shown to be noted, and paid for, in late fifth- and early fourth-century Greece. By careful analysis first of the records of the payment of sculptors for different architectural sculptures at Epidaurus and then of what is said by a variety of classical authors about particular artists, Schultz shows that those who commissioned sculpture knew that different sculptors produced works that differed in both style and quality, and that they were prepared to pay to get pieces of a suitable style and quality for the particular location for which they needed the sculpture. In one sense, what Schultz demonstrates is hardly surprising, but his chapter not only overturns what has become unchallenged orthodoxy within classical archaeology but also serves to raise important questions about the play of individual and superindividual forces in cultural change.

Talk of cultural revolution is always in danger of resorting to vague claims about 'the spirit of the age'. On the basis of observed marked cultural change extending across a whole range of cultural products, it is tempting to think that cultural change operates as a sort of disease which spreads insidiously through a society or through all the practitioners of a particular cultural form in a society. Schultz's insistence on taking personal agency seriously is important here. His emphasis on the different products produced by different individuals points to the necessity of seeing sweeping cultural changes as the reactions of numerous individuals. However far we desire to produce a general picture of cultural revolution, that revolution can happen only if individuals take their own decisions to act differently.

It is with the decisions taken by two particular individuals working in the same cultural form that Elizabeth Irwin is concerned in the eighth chapter. Irwin takes the famous disagreement between Herodotus and Thucydides over Minos and explores its implications. Irwin looks at the role which their treatment (and Plato's) of Minos plays in each historian's overall story, and emphasises the way in which stories of the thalassocrat Minos inevitably 'read' the story of the thalassocrat Athens, at the same time as Herodotus and Thucydides also 'read' each other's history. One result of this is to raise, in a particularly powerful form, the question of the date at which Herodotus' text was composed and the priority of Thucydides to Herodotus. But a second result is to reveal the politics of Thucydidean (and Herodotean) historiography. The picture which Irwin offers of Thucydides and Herodotus composing their histories 'side by side' brings out the way in which the very emergence of historiography as we know it is linked to the particular political force which Athenian imperialism, and its resistance by Sparta and her allies, had given to the way in which the past is talked about.

Rosalind Thomas (2000) has recently put Herodotus firmly back into the context of the second half of the fifth century as a thinker, and Robert Fowler (1996) has emphasised the revolutionary nature of Herodotus citation and evaluation of source material and the distance between Herodotus and writers such as Hecataeus.[24] Comparison of Herodotus with the *logopoioi*, to whom he himself makes reference (2.134, 143), and with the sophists and authors of medical treatises, tends to suggest that Herodotean history was primarily an intellectual endeavour, part of an increasingly critical interrogation of the natural world and what men said about it. But the question of how one can come to know about the world and what happens in it was not just an intellectual but also a political matter. Cynthia Farrar showed in *The Origins of Democratic Thinking* (1988) how epistemological questions and views were bound up with political questions and views: one's views of how knowledge is attained and who can attain it affect one's views of who appropriately takes political decisions. Even if it were simply the pace of intellectual inquiry in general which prompted Herodotus and Thucydides to address themselves to the question of how one finds out about and reaches an understanding of events which have happened, one

---

[24] Note especially R. Thomas 2000: 219: 'The latter half of the fifth century saw rapid developments in the methods and habits of polemical or rhetorical argument, the refinement of techniques suitable for the lawcourts or Athenian assembly, but techniques which were also part of the atmosphere of restless controversy and polemic that lay behind this intellectual revolution, in which opponents' theories are taken up and demolished. I would like to draw Herodotus into this milieu, to see a large part of his methods and style in the *Histories* as part of this intellectual world'; and cf. R. Thomas 2000: 5 on others' acceptance 'that there are elements in Herodotus reminiscent of preoccupations of late fifth-century thinkers' without examining the implications.

would still want to ask what were the political implications of their answers to this question. But we should perhaps at least contemplate whether it was not the political importance of assessing claims about the past which provoked Herodotus' and Thucydides' inquiries in the first place. Is theirs an intellectual curiosity with political implications, or a political engagement fuelled by contemporary intellectual debate?

The form in which that intellectual debate was disseminated is the subject of Alex Long's investigation, in chapter 9, of the invention of the Socratic dialogue as a form of literary expression and philosophical inquiry. Long argues against 'essentialist' explanations of the adoption of the dialogue form by Plato. Examining in detail Plato's use of dialogue in the *Republic*, Long argues that the form and the argument are there intimately connected. We are meant, Long suggests, to entertain seriously the idea that it is the interventions of the interlocutors that determined the course of the discussion, and that without them many topics that turn out to be central would not have been broached. At least part of the responsibility for the course and conclusion of the discussion comes to rest with the interlocutors, rather than with Socrates. At the same time, however, the *Republic* shows Socrates to be very capable both of positing objections to views he himself expresses and of producing rebuttal. Philosophy at its best does require some sort of critical exchange, but the philosopher can conduct this with himself. Dialogue with others does not, for Long, have one function; it is a tool with various possible uses, and, whatever its general virtues, when Plato chooses to use it he does so because of the particular purpose in any given dialogue.[25]

Long's demonstration that Plato did not believe that philosophy had to be done in dialogue with others challenges the cultural historian to offer a non-philosophical explanation for the invention of the dialogue as a literary form. Dialogue, in the form Plato and Xenophon record it, was not a feature of the formal institutions of Athenian democracy. The Assembly did not do its business conversationally, and neither did the lawcourts (Athenian juries did not retire and discuss before voting, and although there is a little evidence for cross-examination 'everything hangs on the speech').[26] We do not know in detail how Council business was conducted, but in a body of 500 people more or less formal speeches must have formed the core of the exchanges, rather than anything seriously resembling conversation. However much the practices of civic government may have stimulated the

[25] Long's argument is essentially complementary to that offered by von Reden and Goldhill 1999.
[26] The quotation is from Todd 1993: 130. For cross-examination see Aristophanes, *Acharnians* 685–8.

rise of philosophy, as Vernant (1962) and Lloyd (1979) have insisted, it cannot have been these practices that inspired the invention of question-and-answer dialogue. Nor is it plausible that the dialogue form was brought into existence merely by Socrates' charisma. Socratic conversational practice was not a feature restricted to the last decade or so of his life; Plato's own dramatic dates for dialogues run back into the 420s, and Socrates' habits are likely to have been formed at the latest by the 430s. If it was Socrates' raising of conversation to an art form that inspired dialogue, one would expect the earliest manifestations to appear in writing decades before they do. Nor will moving the inspiration from life to literature and from Socrates to Plato help the case. Plato does indeed prove the most brilliant literary exponent of the dialogue form, but antiquity credited others with the invention of the form (Diogenes Laertius 3.48), and the evidence that we have suggests that among the Athenians a number of writers essayed the format at one and the same time.

The more convinced we are by Long that dialogue with others is not essential to the Socratic or Platonic philosopher, the more an explanation for the florescence of the dialogue in Athens in the quarter-century following the restoration of democracy in 403 needs to engage with what was peculiar to that period. The broad coincidence with curse tablets may be particularly revealing here. If curse tablets show a crisis of confidence in public and institutionalised ways of establishing justice, the publication of dialogue too might suggest a lack of confidence that public institutional debates ensure that the best arguments will prevail. One of the things dialogues do is to capture, or manufacture, on paper insights which demand too much personal application and concentrated attention from listeners ever to be conveyed in a public gathering. One cannot be a spectator, Cleon's θεατής, in a dialogue.[27] Dialogue flags up the fact that everything that is said is said from a position; as in drama, so in dialogue, there is no speaker who can claim objectivity. With its different speakers, dialogue offers a choice of viewpoints in exactly the way that the Meidian vase-painting analysed by Lorenz offered a choice of viewpoints. And just as no single viewpoint can be said to be the painter's view, so no single viewpoint can be attributed to the author of a dialogue.

Plato's own epistemological views rendered him unsympathetic to democracy, and sceptical of Protagoras' attribution to the people at large of such a sense of shame and of fairness as to formulate naturally sensible judgement. Even those not committed to the theory of Forms might find

---

[27] Thucydides 3.38.4. On spectatorship and democracy see Goldhill 1999, esp. pp. 1–10.

in the events of the last two decades of the fifth century at Athens grounds for despairing of the possibility of convincing a mass public of complex and subtle ideas. The trial of the generals after the sea battle at Arginoussai strongly undermined any confidence in the power of the public sense of shame or fairness. Readers of Thucydides' Melian Dialogue might reasonably think that if institutional politics was condemned to being a matter of spokesmen talking past each other in fundamentally profitless ways, then it was urgent to get the fruits of what could be achieved in engaged conversation recorded and disseminated.

We are reminded that the extent to which the issues discussed by the philosophers were issues also discussed by Athenians at large, and of the way in which politics and intellectual life were mixed together, by Robert Tordoff in chapter 10, in which he looks at Aristophanes' *Assembly Women* and its relationship to book 5 of Plato's *Republic*. Tordoff's interest is in the implication for our understanding of comedy of Aristophanes' engagement in this play with an intellectual idea. Against a persistent theme in the scholarship on old comedy that old comedy became politically less engaged after the end of the Peloponnesian War, Tordoff explores the possibility that Aristophanes' commitment to political discourse remains unchanged but that the style of his engagement alters. He emphasises Aristophanes' consistent commitment to 'saving the city' and the way in which Aristophanes *represents* himself, and is represented by others, and above all by Plato, as politically significant. Rather than seeing seriousness (or the comic) as immanent in the text, Tordoff argues that the very division in modern scholarship over how to understand Aristophanes' plays shows seriousness (and humour) to lie in the decision of the audience.[28]

The importance of this insight for the wider inquiry of this book lies in its opening the way to seeing the changes that occur in the manner in which Aristophanes deals with political questions as changes in what Athenian audiences might be willing to be simultaneously both serious and comic about. If we account for the election as general of the Cleon bitterly attacked in *Knights* by suggesting that the Athenian audience at the time was rather less willing than scholars have been to take Aristophanes' attack on Athenian political leaders seriously, we might wonder whether the prominence of *Clouds* in Plato's perception of what turned Athenians against Socrates might lie in Athenians coming, two decades later, to take seriously an attack which at the time of its first performance they had taken as comic. On this view, what *Assembly Women* contributes to our understanding of cultural

---

[28] For a useful discussion of previous scholarship on Aristophanes' seriousness see Silk 2000: ch. 7.

change in Athens is evidence that issues of constitution, and even of radical change to the constitution, were the sorts of things which could be taken seriously, and as a joke, in the late 390s, whereas no one thought of taking them seriously, or joking about them, in the 420s or 410s. Previous scholars have thought that the difference between the personal politics of the 420s and the social politics of *Assembly Women* and *Wealth* was a difference in Aristophanes' attitude to individual politicians; Tordoff's chapter suggests that we should rather construe it as a change from taking the constitution for granted, and thinking that what one had to be serious about, or could only be comic about, was the way in which individuals behaved within that constitution, to realising that crucial to the salvation of the city was whether or not the constitution itself deserved serious re-examination. If it was Athenian power and reactions to it that concentrated the minds of Herodotus and Thucydides upon the task of historical explanation, it was the questioning of Athenian democracy, on this view, that made Athenians entertain abstract political thought.

Tordoff's discussion of the ways in which comedy changed between 430 and 380 is paralleled by Edith Hall's discussion of the changes that occur in tragedy in these same years. Hall emphasises the different sorts of ways in which drama changes, and draws attention to the difficulty of isolating individual features of change as determinative. Changing use of music, the expansion of the amount of dramatic activity, and its exportation to a wider world, an increasing theorisation of tragedy, and changes to the repertoire, can all be traced.[29] The last of these relates directly to politics: later tragedy does seem to move away from specifically Athenian mythology, but Plato's comments in book 7 of *Laws* make it clear that for him tragedy had certainly not lost its potential political force. The very tendency towards re-performance of classic tragedies, however, itself guaranteed that, in the fourth century, tragedies did not have the same possibilities for topicality. Hall suggests that the revolution undergone by tragedy was primarily one of 'globalisation' – Aeschylus had already taken his tragedies to Sicily, but it was now increasingly professional actors who were putting on tragedy all over the Greek world and who were achieving widespread fame. This inevitably changed the focus of tragic drama, even while it left much of the form and sensibility unchanged.

The emphasis in Hall's *tour d'horizon* is very different from that of Tordoff's particular study of one comedy and its intellectual context. It is important therefore to stress what the two pictures have in common. The move from personal politics to constitutional debate in Aristophanes parallels the

---

[29] On the exportation of Athenian drama see esp. Taplin 1999.

move from details of Attic cult to more general questions of religion and metaphysics in tragedy. In both cases the concerns cease to be closely tied to Athens and become concerns with which a much wider Greek world was engaged. One way of looking at this is as a negative 'watering down' of particular Athenian concerns, but this is to miss the positive opening up of worldview that is involved. Athenian audiences are now being faced not with celebratory, or denigratory, concerns with the particular mechanisms of their religious or political practice, but with the big questions of political and theological understanding of the world.

Armand D'Angour's chapter, however, warns us that the changing aesthetic of tragedy should not be analysed as merely instrumental: just as the changes in the auditory experience of radio have made a deep impression on modern audiences, so the changes in the auditory experience of drama will have made an impression on ancient audiences. Different sounds, different melodies, different harmonies, conjure up different worlds. New sounds serve in part precisely to announce newness, and in doing so to encourage the expectation that novelty extends also to content. Expectations of sounds varies constantly, and it is hard for any period of history to distinguish what most would have regarded as a 'totally new' sound from what they would have regarded as but a new variation on a familiar sound. But we have sufficient evidence to suggest that the particular changes in sounds at the end of the fifth century signalled particular changes in expectation: the complexity of the musical effects of Euripidean drama pointed to the complexity of the ideas involved, but they also pointed to music as a matter for professionals rather than something in which all could take part. This musical distancing of the audience from the stage is parallel to, and surely related to, the distancing effected by the professionalisation of actors, and seems also to have transformed the experience of preparing or participating in dithyramb from something any set of youths from a tribe could manage to something to which very particular, and expensive, training had to be devoted. One further effect of this was to divorce music from class: if an ability to perform music, at least at the standard required at the symposium, had been expected of the Athenian elite in the early part of the fifth century, ability to perform the new music required a degree of professionalisation anathema to the wealthy. Alcibiades cannot have been the first wealthy man to look in a mirror while playing the pipes (Plutarch, *Alcibiades* 2). If the story of Marsyas made the *aulos* what divided gods from satyrs, in the late fifth century the *aulos* came to divide groups of men.[30] But if music was now something for which expertise was required, that had implications for

---

[30] Wilson 1999.

the limits of both elite and popular judgement. And those limits were a political matter. People's changing expectations of expertise and participation in music could not but raise questions for whether their expectations about expertise and participation in politics should also change.

A POLITICAL REVOLUTION?

The various explanations offered by earlier scholars for cultural change at the end of the fifth century, criticised earlier, primarily focused on 'natural development' ('growing up and growing out of myth and into rationalism') or on the trauma caused by a peculiarly long and total war. By contrast, although acknowledging as fundamental the demographic consequences which followed directly or indirectly from war, this introduction has repeatedly stressed the political significance of the various more or less blatantly revolutionary changes which the chapters of this book will explore. In some senses this was inevitable. A project which sets out to show how changes in different human activities are co-ordinated is pretty well bound to find that what co-ordinates them are the bonds which humans have between one another. Whether, to use the language of Aristotle in *Politics* book 1, we are dealing with what people do together for the sake of life (and stress economics) or with what they are doing together for the sake of the good life (and stress culture), the very act of co-ordination between human actors is a political act. In these terms, what this volume necessarily sets out from the start to illustrate is the way in which political possibilities were constrained by demographic and economic conditions, and the way in which cultural actions were embedded in political choices.

No volume could cover all the ways in which Athenians acted, and there is much that this volume has not done. It has offered only a gesture towards an economic history; it has not risen to the challenge of describing and addressing linguistic change; it has not attempted to engage directly with Dodds's claims or unravel Athenian religious history.[31] In some areas it has chosen to offer a broad survey, in others to look intensively at particular examples. In the different chapters, the reader will find some convergence of method and assumptions but no party line. What this introduction has sought to do is to suggest where coherence may be found. That suggestion succumbs to the temptation to see the Athenians as a community and to put the 'traumatic experiences' of the oligarchic revolutions of 411 and 404

---

[31] Which has been well done by Parker 1996: chs. 9–10. I have engaged with Dodds's construction of the history of ecstatic cult activity in Attica in R. Osborne 1997a.

into centre stage. It does not do so to suggest that, had Athens only avoided civil strife, fifth-century culture would have continued unchanged. Indeed, repeatedly it will have been clear that the changes in which this book is interested had begun before ever the Athenians had begun to suspect that their Sicilian expedition would be a disaster. Arguably, the oligarchic coups were enabled not simply by defeat in war but by those same changes in attitude which they then proceeded to reinforce.[32] The suggestion of the centrality of political events is made, therefore, to emphasise what Thucydides already noted – that it was very difficult to end liberty (*eleutheria*) in the hundredth year after the tyrants had been expelled (8.68.4). Athenian 'liberty' was not just the expectation that all could and would be involved in the life of the city; it was also a vision of personal freedom – the rose-tinted vision offered by Pericles, and no doubt so many others, in the Funeral Orations.[33] Whatever the Athenians had in fact in the way of freedom, they had come to believe that they were securely in possession of a style of life which combined personal autonomy with corporate power; for the loss of these, no amount of exploration of tyranny on the tragic stage could prepare an Athenian audience. To that extent, at least, J. H. Finley was, I think, right to stress the surfeit of former dreams.

Whether or not Athens was the first democracy to be established in the Greek world,[34] Athens was certainly not the first Greek city to see a popular government overthrown. But the power which democratic Athens had achieved, and the way in which it had become the exemplary representative of popular government, with which all other cities desiring themselves to be democratic identified (Thucydides 1.1.1), meant that it was easy for Athenians to imagine themselves to be different, to imagine that they were not Thebes, and delude themselves into thinking that they knew what was going on and could hunt out deviants.[35] Thucydides repeatedly drew attention to the Athenians being mistaken about what they knew (1.20; 6.1.1; 6.53; 6.60), unaware of their ignorance, and inclined to mistake opinion for knowledge, and Herodotus too draws attention to the gullibility of the Athenian assembly (1.60; 5.97.2). Talk of conspiracy in the 420s was grist to Aristophanes' comic mill; after 411 all such jokes had to be taken seriously.

The terms in which I have described the cultural changes explored in this book have often opposed a fifth century in which the community is central to a fourth century in which the place of the individual is at least always in

---

[32] So, in effect, R. Osborne 2004b: 13–14.   [33] On which Loraux 1986 remains fundamental.
[34] And this depends on what you are prepared to count as democracy. See Robinson 1997 for a particular construction.
[35] On not being Thebes see Zeitlin 1986.

question. But if we are inclined to think that what we see in the revolution effected in Athens in these years is the loss of Athenian innocence, we do well to remember the totalitarian assumptions which went with Athenian confidence in their communal ability to face down the rest of the world. The innocence of the spectator of Cleon's speech had terrifying results which fourth-century Athenians would never emulate.

CHAPTER 2

The nature and implications of Athens' changed social structure and economy

Ben Akrigg

In this chapter I am going to try to identify and explain some ways in which the society and economy of Athens were affected by the experience of and defeat in the Peloponnesian War. Clearly an account of this length cannot be exhaustive. I shall focus on the area which I believe to be of the greatest importance – the historical demography of Athens during this period. I hope to demonstrate that this is a subject which can fruitfully be studied, and that it has important implications for any study of classical Athens. More generally I want to suggest that looking at the economic history of Athens can suggest reasons for supposing that a cultural revolution really did take place over this period.

In order to do this I shall look at accounts that have been provided by modern scholars, and suggest why I think that they are more or less unsatisfactory – largely because they ignore or misconstrue the importance of demography. But I also want to make it clear right from the start that while I think demography is important and deserves more attention than it generally gets from the majority of Greek[1] historians, I am *not* claiming that it is the *only* thing that matters. Rather, it should be seen as one in a complex web of competing, complementary, and interacting factors that together gave rise to and comprised a cultural revolution in Athens.

In regard to this, there is something else that I want to make clear at this point. I think that the cultural revolution experienced by England in the late Middle Ages is a useful comparative model for classical Athens. What I want to stress here is that the usefulness of the comparison lies not just in what happened in England in the thirteenth, fourteenth, and fifteenth centuries, but also in how modern historians have approached it.[2]

---

[1] This is an area which has received a great deal of attention from scholars in *Roman* history, especially since Hopkins 1966. See Parkin 1992, and the summaries in Golden 2000 and Scheidel 2001. For a brief consideration of some of these issues as they apply to Greek history, however, see now R. Osborne 2004a: 39–54.

[2] The problems and potential of using comparative evidence for social history have been eloquently discussed with specific reference to classical antiquity by Cartledge 1985 and Golden 1992. This is

In the past, the explanatory models that have been used to explain change in the Middle Ages have taken one of three broad approaches, each with its roots in the work of theorists of the eighteenth and nineteenth centuries. One of these approaches, drawing ultimately on the work of Ricardo and Malthus, saw the relationship between population size and the scale of available resources as central. Marxist approaches instead highlighted class relations, while a third set of approaches, inspired by Adam Smith, emphasised the importance of the development of commercialised economies and the rise of markets.[3] More recently, however, medieval historians have been

not the place for a full discussion of the implications of trying to do comparative history. However, I should in the first place make it clear that I hope I have succeeded in using medieval England only as a *comparative* model for classical Athens, and not as a *predictive* one. Secondly, I ought to explain why I think that the comparison is an appropriate one. The extent to which cultural, social, economic, and political change in later medieval England can be explained by reference to the colossal demographic shock occasioned by the Black Death has long been a source of debate and controversy. Crucial questions have been raised not just for the course of English history but for historical explanation in general and for the explanation of *change* in particular. It is this latter point which makes the comparison with classical Athens interesting and important, and justifies the choice of *England* as the comparison. For it is on what happened in England – partly as a result of the relative abundance of evidence here – that many of these debates have centred in the first instance.

In the current context I should also want to stress the importance of this relative abundance of evidence. Increasingly this seems to be allowing medieval scholars to see the *complexity* of the situation, and the *variety* of effects and experiences of the demographic (and other) factors at work – effects and experiences which can seem strange and even counterintuitive in terms of what is predicted by theoretical models. Inevitably we are much less well-informed about classical Athens. But our lack of evidence should not blind us to the possibility (the likelihood, even) that similar levels of complexity obtained there too.

[3] The key texts are: Malthus's *An Essay on the Principle of Population* (1798); Ricardo's *The Principles of Political Economy* (1817); Marx's *Das Kapital* (1867–94) and the *Grundrisse* (1857–8); and Smith's *The Theory of Moral Sentiments* (1759) and *An Inquiry into the Nature and Causes of the Wealth of Nations* (1776). Since the Second World War, the most distinguished proponent of a 'population and resources' model for understanding change in the medieval English economy has been Michael Postan, whose key articles are gathered in Postan 1973a and Postan 1973b. Robert Brenner's article in 1976, written from a Marxist perspective, was enormously influential and sparked a lengthy debate in the pages of *Past and Present*, for which see Aston and Philpin 1985. For 'commercialisation'-led approaches, see e.g. Persson 1988 and Britnell 1996. For summaries and an attempt to chart new approaches, see Hatcher and Bailey 2001. In his *The Class Struggle in the Ancient Greek World* (1981), de Ste Croix cited Brenner's article with approval, criticising 'various types of "economic model-building" which try to explain long-term economic developments in pre-industrial Europe primarily in terms either of demography . . . or of the growth of trade and the market . . . disregarding class relations and exploitation as primary factors' (p. 83). My response to this has two parts. In the first instance I would simply agree that class relations and exploitation *do* have a role to play in explaining economic development. But I would also argue that a class-based model alone is not going to be any more successful than the other single-issue alternatives. It is directly relevant for the current case that by de Ste Croix's own admission there are problems in applying his model to the case of classical Athens, even if we were to accept his general picture (pp. 283–300) – his defence being the entirely reasonable observation that Athens was in no way typical. But it is perhaps worth noting that it also runs into problems in the late Roman Republic (pp. 337–44); it is significant, I think, that the greatest problems with using de Ste Croix's grand model occur precisely in the times and places where our evidence is most abundant, just as the inadequacies of the traditional 'supermodels' of medieval history have been exposed by increasingly detailed study of the available records.

turning away from debating the relative merits of large-scale single-issue models that see the end of feudalism and serfdom, or the emergence of capitalism, or the foundations of the modern English state as determined *only* by population change, or class relations, or the commercialisation of the economy, or the money supply, or war. Instead, they are inclined to argue that all these things have their own importance.

Moreover, it is increasingly stressed that the effects of all these factors will not have been felt equally by everyone, but varied considerably according to an individual's geographical, cultural, social, and economic location. For Athens our evidence is much more meagre, and such variability is much harder to trace, but the possibility that it existed should always be recalled when we look at the evidence that we do have. We should not try to fit everything we have into a single, simple model.

The point I want to make here is this: demographic models clearly cannot be used to explain *everything*, but the experience of medieval historians in the twentieth century should caution us against arguing that on that account they cannot be used to explain *anything*. Before moving on, I want to note in passing that similar points have been raised in a debate in *Roman* history concerning the likely effects of the Antonine plague, where at least one of the protagonists has also made explicit use of a comparison with the Black Death in Europe and the Middle East for his model of economic change in Roman Egypt.[4]

First, we need to establish what we (think we) know about the population of Athens and Attica during this period. The evidence is limited. We are fortunate that the single best piece of evidence that we have comes at the start of the period we are interested in. This is Thucydides 2.13.6–8, part of the speech reportedly given by Pericles to reassure the Athenians that the scale of their resources all but guaranteed them victory in the coming war with Sparta:

He added that they had 13,000 hoplites, apart from the 16,000 in garrisons or on the walls of the city. This many men were on guard at the start of the war, whenever the enemy invaded Attica; they were drawn from the oldest and youngest men, and from those metics who were equipped as hoplites. For the Phaleric Wall was 35 stades long from Phalerum to the city wall: and the guarded portion of the city wall itself was 43 stades long (the section between the Long Wall and the Phaleric Wall was unguarded). The Long Walls running down to the Piraeus were 40 stades long; only the outer wall was guarded. The whole circuit of the Piraeus and of Munychia was 60 stades long, and half of it was guarded. Pericles also pointed out

---

[4] Scheidel 2002: 100 for the comparison with the Black Death in Europe and the Middle East, drawing on Duncan-Jones 1996, with responses from Greenberg 2003 and Bruun 2003; the Black Death comparison is made also in Scheidel 2003: 120.

that there were 1,200 cavalry (counting the mounted archers), 1,600 foot-archers, and 300 seaworthy triremes.[5]

The depressing thing is that this *is* the best piece of evidence we have.[6] Trying to extract demographic data from army figures is fraught with difficulties which I do not want to minimise.[7] Mogens Hansen, whose account of fourth-century Athenian demography is the central work on the subject, has dismissed this passage as almost impossible to use as a source of useful information on the Athenian population.[8]

Hansen's pessimism is largely based on what seems to me an almost perverse reading of Thucydides' text. As army figures go, those presented in Thucydides 2.13 are actually rather good. I see no reason why they should not be given as much credence as those given by Diodorus for the Athenian military effort in the Lamian War in the 320s – figures which form an important part of Hansen's argument about the fourth century.[9]

[5] ὁπλίτας δέ τρισχιλίους καὶ μυρίους εἶναι ἄνευ τῶν ἐν τοῖς φρουρίοις καὶ τῶν παρ' ἔπαλξιν ἑξακισχιλίων καὶ μυρίων. τοσοῦτοι γάρ ἐφύλασσον τὸ πρῶτον ὁπότε οἱ πολέμιοι ἐσβάλοιεν, ἀπό τε τῶν πρεσβυτάτων καὶ τῶν νεωτάτων, καὶ μετοίκων ὅσοι ὁπλῖται ἦσαν. τοῦ τε γάρ Φαληρικοῦ τείχους στάδιοι ἦσαν πέντε καὶ τριάκοντα πρὸς τὸν κύκλον τοῦ ἄστεως, καὶ αὐτοῦ τοῦ κύκλου τὸ φυλασσόμενον τρεῖς καὶ τεσσαράκοντα (ἔστι δὲ αὐτοῦ ἃ καὶ ἀφύλακτον ἦν, τὸ μεταξὺ τοῦ τε μακροῦ και τοῦ Φαληρικοῦ), τὰ δὲ μακρὰ τείχη πρὸς τὸν Πειραιᾶ τεσσαράκοντα σταδίων, ὧν τὸ ἔξωθεν ἐτηρεῖτο· καὶ τοῦ Πειραιῶς ξὺν Μουνιχίᾳ ἑξήκοντα μὲν σταδίων ὁ ἅπας περίβολος, τὸ δ' ἐν φυλακῇ ὅν ἅμισυ τούτου. ἱππέας δὲ ἀπέφαινε διακοσίους καὶ χιλίους ξὺν ἱπποτοξόταις, ἑξακοσίους δὲ καὶ χιλίους τοξότας, καὶ τριήρεις τὰς πλωίμους τριακοσίας.

[6] There is at least one other passage in Thucydides with superficial appeal in this regard: the account of the disastrous retreat of the Athenian army on Sicily, where a figure of 'no fewer than 40,000' is quoted. The problem with this kind of text, though, is that, even if we accept its accuracy (and most of the arguments that can be used in support of 2.13 do not apply here), we do not know who is included in this figure. How many were residents of Attica before the expedition, and how many were allies or mercenaries? How many were citizens, how many metics and how many slaves (since *all* of the last had not deserted)? With no way to answer these questions, it is hard to see what use to make of this passage in the present context.

[7] As noted by Golden 2000: 24 and Scheidel 2001: 49 with n. 195 referring to Henige 1998.

[8] Hansen 1981, 1982. French 1993 and Lapini 1997 have also more recently cast doubt on the usefulness of Thucydides 2.13 for demographic purposes and on traditional interpretations of the text. See note 9 below.

[9] Hansen 1985: 36–43, 66–9, on Diodorus Siculus 18.10.2 and 18.11.3. There is no space here for a full treatment of the size of Athens' population in 431 or of the extent of the casualties which it suffered in the following three decades. However, there are two aspects of my position which demand clarification. The first is that I believe that the army figures presented by Thucydides in 2.13 can be taken seriously. I am not aware of any good reason to suspect the text at this point. The transmission of *any* numerical figures is always highly problematic. These, however, are at least not *obviously* implausible (unlike, for example, Herodotus' for Xerxes' army (7.184–6) and the examples cited by Henige). For what it is worth, they are also broadly consistent with the figures given by Diodorus – who gives 12,000 and 17,000 as the strengths of the 'field' and 'garrison' forces respectively (12.40.4) (and for the same total of hoplites as Thucydides), and may well, as Rhodes observes in his commentary on book 2 of Thucydides, be indulging in 'variation for variation's own sake' (1988: 196). It also seems to be at least plausible to suppose that Thucydides, an intelligent contemporary observer, native of Athens, and military commander in the early stages of the war, could have known, to the nearest

The figures of 2.13 can, in combination with the other scraps of information we have, and within fairly broad limits, give us some idea of the size of the Athenian population in 431. This is not the place to enter into a detailed discussion of where those limits might lie. For now, I think it reasonable, and it should be fairly uncontroversial, to take 300,000 as a figure for the total population of Attica at the start of the Peloponnesian War.[10]

I want to come back to what such a figure actually means, but I want first to look at how this population would have been affected by the events of the following decades. No one, I think, would dispute that the number of people living in Athens in 403 was significantly smaller than it had been in 431. We do not have any basis for firm figures, but we can make reasonable guesses as to the likely scale of the decrease.

There were two obvious factors at work – increased mortality and emigration. Increased mortality would have resulted primarily from the 'plague'

thousand, how many hoplites Athens had available. As army figures presented in a literary source go, these are surely rather good. Most of the problems that scholars have had with this passage seem to result from an unwillingness to accept either that the 'reserve' or the 'garrison' force could have been larger than the 'field' army – although Thucydides himself immediately goes on to stress the enormous length of the fortifications surrounding the Athens-Piraeus complex – or that there really might have been a very large number of metics in Athens, at least at the start of the war, who had access to hoplite equipment. To reject, emend, or subject to tortuous reinterpretation what Thucydides says just because it clashes with our preconceptions (as Hansen 1981, 1982, French 1993, and Lapini 1997 all seem to me to be doing) is surely to approach things the wrong way round. Scepticism about the value of this passage is not universal – see e.g. van Wees 2004: 241–3.

The second concerns the scale of casualties suffered by the Athenians as a result of the plague. Again, I believe that Thucydides 3.87.3 is meant to imply total losses of around 30 per cent, and at least 25 per cent, over the four years during which the plague afflicted Athens. Here I agree with Strauss (1986: 75–6, with p. 84 n. 33) that when Thucydides specifies that the 4,400 hoplites who died were *ek tōn taxeōn* (ἐκ τῶν τάξεων), this implies that they should be understood as being from the 13,000 'field' army alone and not from the total number of 29,000. Again, this is not the place for a full discussion, but I would like to stress the simple fact that Thucydides troubles to specify that these are a particular group of hoplites, which would not have been necessary if he really meant *all* the hoplites, and also observe that at 8.69.1 the word *taxis* (though admittedly in the singular) seems to be employed explicitly to distinguish field troops from garrison troops: *hoi men epi teixei, hoi d'en taxei*, οἱ μὲν ἐπὶ τείχει, οἱ δ' ἐν τάξει.

Three hundred *hippeis* are also supposed to have died. At 2.13 Thucydides said that there were 1,200 *hippeis*, including *hippotoxotai*. We do not know how many *hippotoxotai* there were. It is usually assumed (e.g. Spence 1993: 98) that there were 200 of them, with 1,000 citizen *hippeis*, but the basis for this is extremely slender (relying on Ar. *Knights* 225; Xen. *Cavalry Officer* 9.3 is irrelevant) and we do not know whether they are supposed to be included here – but on the simplest reading, 25 per cent of Athens' cavalry died in the plague. At Potidaea, Hagnon lost 1,150 hoplites out of a total of 4,000 (about 29 per cent) in the space of only forty days, but this was in the context of a cramped and doubtless extremely insanitary siege camp (Thucydides 2.58.3).

[10] This is the figure suggested by Rhodes 1992: 83, for example. Garnsey (1988: 90) suggests 250,000. But if, for example, Hansen (1988: 14–28) is right in suggesting that a figure of 60,000 should be seen as a realistic *minimum* for the number of citizen males over eighteen, then these kinds of figures would have to be revised upwards.

(whatever the disease actually was). Thucydides' account at 3.87.1–3 implies that it caused the deaths of between a quarter and a third of the population:

In the following winter, the plague attacked the Athenians for a second time. In fact, it had never entirely gone away, although it had almost abated. This later outbreak lasted no less than a year, and the first had lasted for two, and nothing else had such a severe effect on the Athenians or did more to damage their power. No fewer than 4,400 hoplites from the field army and 300 of the cavalry died, along with an incalculable number of common people.[11]

The exact proportion could be disputed, but Thucydides leaves no doubt that the loss of life was on a substantial scale – and that it almost certainly dwarfed any of the other causes of population loss over this period.

But these other causes were significant in their own right. It has frequently been remarked that the accounts of both Thucydides and Xenophon are littered with figures for Athenian combat casualties; it is also clear that they are not giving us the full picture of Athenian losses as a direct consequence of fighting the war. Quantifying the losses precisely is probably beyond us; the estimates provided by Barry Strauss and by Hansen are barely more than guesses.[12] But it is clear that thousands of Athenians died in battles on land and sea, and it is likely that thousands more died away from the battlefield as a consequence of the privations and squalor of armies on campaign without modern medical and logistical services.

Those who stayed at home would not have been safe either. Even if the Attic countryside was not evacuated as completely as the literary sources like to imply,[13] any increased density of population within the Athens-Piraeus fortress could have resulted in a worsened disease regime for the inhabitants (with a bigger prey population available for the disease pathogens, transmission being facilitated by, and with a greater burden placed on, both water supply and waste disposal), so that even without the plague, the 'normal' mortality of the population may have been elevated during the years when Attica was under imminent threat of invasion.[14]

Then there are the effects of migration. The bulk of Athenian citizens and their families had nowhere to go – on the contrary, the loss of Athens'

---

[11] τοῦ δ' ἐπιγιγνομένου χειμῶνος ἡ νόσος τὸ δεύτερον ἐπέπεσε τοῖς Ἀθηναίοις, ἐλιποῦσα μὲν οὐδένα χρόνον τὸ παντάπασιν, ἐγένετο δέ τις ὅμως διοκωχή. παρέμεινε δὲ τὸ μὲν ὕστερον οὐκ ἔλασσον ἐνιαυτοῦ, τὸ δὲ πρότερον καὶ δύο ἔτη, ὥστε Ἀθηναίους γε μὴ εἶναι ὅτι μᾶλλον τούτου ἐπίεσε καὶ ἐκάκωσε τὴν δύναμιν· τετρακοσίων γὰρ ὁπλιτῶν καὶ τετρακισχιλίων οὐκ ἐλάσσους ἀπέθανον ἐκ τῶν τάξεων καὶ τριακοσίων ἱππέων, τοῦ δὲ ἄλλου ὄχλου ἀνεξεύρετος ἀριθμός.

[12] B. S. Strauss 1986: 179–82; Hansen 1988: 14–20.

[13] E.g. Thucydides (2.14) and Dicaiopolis' opening speech in Ar. *Acharnians* (1–39, esp. 32). See also Hanson 1999; Foxhall 1993.

[14] Sallares 1991: 221–90; Grmek 1989: 95–9.

overseas possessions may have led to the *return* of some expatriates.[15] But they are likely to have been vastly outnumbered by the non-Athenians going the other way. We cannot know for certain, but it must be highly probable that large numbers of metics – at least the ones who had the option of somewhere better to go – will have left Athens. And Thucydides explicitly claims that large numbers of slaves were lost to Athens during the Decelean War.[16] The figure he gives, of 'more than 20,000', has, unlike those at 2.13, no claim to be taken seriously, but it is clearly meant to imply 'a lot'. And these losses are on top of the slaves who must have died at least in proportion to the citizens as a result of both disease and warfare.[17]

I conclude from all of this that the population of Athens immediately after the war's end was no more than two-thirds its pre-war size, and perhaps it had been reduced by as much as half.

Well, so what? It is my impression that, in so far as they think about it at all, the response of many people today to that question is that it made the Athenians feel quite sad and led them to contemplate their own mortality a little more, as perhaps is shown by the reappearance of sculpted grave stelai in the last third of the fifth century and by the pessimism evident in some of Aristophanes' plays of the 420s. I am not saying that these things did not happen; quite the reverse. But there must have been more to it than that.

Thucydides, for one, was in no doubt: for him, the casualties inflicted by the plague were the greatest blow to Athens' power that the city suffered during the war (3.87.2 above). This rather striking comment does not get the attention it deserves – partly, no doubt, because the fact that the Athenians managed to keep on fighting, often successfully, for another twenty years suggests that their *dunamis* was not *fatally* compromised. But that does not mean that Thucydides' judgement was wrong. In terms of the sheer numbers of men who died, he must have been right – even the bloodiest battles of the war could not have caused that level of casualties among the citizen body.[18] But still it is true that the plague cannot be claimed as the proximate cause of Athens' military defeat.

Those modern scholars who *have* been interested in the population of classical Athens have been primarily, and often solely, concerned with the

---

[15] On the numbers involved: A. H. M. Jones 1957: 167–76 on colonies and cleruchies, expressing scepticism as to how many cleruchs actually went abroad; also Hansen 1988: 22.

[16] Thuc. 7.27.4–5. On this passage see Hanson 1992. Hanson is prepared to go further than I am on the significance of the figure (at least as evidence for Athenian perceptions of the numbers of slaves in Attica), but I agree with him that Thucydides does seem to have *agricultural* slaves in mind.

[17] That slaves *were* directly involved in Greek warfare as combatants, as well as providing logistical support for their masters, on land as well as at sea, is now beyond doubt; see esp. Hunt 1998, but also van Wees 2004: 68–71.

[18] This is made starkly apparent by the tables in Hansen 1988: 22, 27.

political implications of the numbers of citizens. This is understandable, given the nature of Athens' democracy and the importance of questions of participation.[19] The problem has been that this is precisely one of those areas where there are difficulties in comparing the fifth and fourth centuries. Hansen's *Demography and Democracy* is the best treatment, but he had already excluded Thucydides as a useful source and is interested only in the fourth century, where the picture he draws is an essentially static one.[20] The most recent account of the fifth-century citizen population is Cynthia Patterson's – but because she was interested only in the immediate context of the citizenship law of 451/0, she did not need to go any later than 431 (1981: 40–81). So the period when Athens suffered a major demographic shock gets neglected.

There is one exception: Strauss's (1986) account of Athens 'after the Peloponnesian War'. Again, his primary interest here is in *political* history. But he rightly saw that the politics of postwar Athens can be understood only in their social and economic context. An important part of his argument was demographic. The trouble is that his arguments about population losses do not work.

In summary, what he wants his demographic argument to do is to help explain why the amnesty declared after the restoration of democracy actually worked reasonably well, and why there was not a prolonged and violent counter-revolution of the sort that might have been expected in the light of what happened in other Greek cities like Corcyra. He does this by saying that the poorer Athenian citizens (whom he is happy to label 'thetes') suffered disproportionately heavy casualties compared to their richer countrymen ('hoplites'), and especially towards the end of the war. If they had not died in such great numbers, they would have been more politically assertive in the immediate postwar period and would have exacted a more violent revenge on the supporters of oligarchy. As it was, they were weak, demoralised, and leaderless.[21]

---

[19] Made explicit by Gomme 1933: 1 – 'the most interesting question' about the Athenian population relates to the operation of the democratic constitution, although Gomme was interested in other issues too. Hansen 1986 is of course concerned with nothing else.

[20] Hansen 1986; on Thucydides see Hansen 1981, 1982. Hansen 1988: 14–28 does consider Thucydides 2.13 again, but is mainly concerned in fact to argue that Thucydides' claims are consistent with his picture of the fourth century, rather than assessing them again in their own right. His final sentence (p. 28) is revealing: 'In conclusion: 30,000 Athenians in ca. 350–322 pre-supposes a minimum of 25,000 Athenians in ca. 400, which again pre-supposes some 60,000 Athenians in 431, if we accept the severe losses reported by Thoukydides and Xenophon; *and this figure is perfectly compatible with Thoukydides' account of Athenian manpower in 431*' (my emphasis).

[21] B. S. Strauss 1986: 42–86. His conclusions are summarised at pp. 80–1: 'By 405, a good part of the political class was at the bottom of the Aegean. It is small wonder then that *hoi polloi* were no more assertive after the restoration of democracy in 403.'

The 'thetes' are supposed to have been those Athenians who were too poor to afford hoplite equipment, and are assumed to have fulfilled their military obligations primarily by serving in the fleet. This in itself requires some slightly dubious assumptions,[22] but the real trouble is that we do not actually know how many citizens like this there were before the war, or how many there were after the war, or how many of them died during the war, or when. We can *guess* within broad limits – but Strauss's argument demands a level of precision about all these things that we cannot hope to attain. And even if we could, we still would not actually know what the political views of these men really were.

Rather than pursuing Strauss's line any further, I want instead to look briefly at two other accounts of Athenian economy and society that conspicuously fail, or refuse, to consider demography.

First there is William Loomis's *Wages, Welfare Costs and Inflation in Classical Athens* (1998). I find this a problematic book for a number of reasons, but in the present context the striking thing about it is Loomis's overwhelming preoccupation with explaining all the things in his title in terms of the available money supply. Assuming that he is right in his identification of wage movements in Athens, then his explanation of a rise in wages between 450 and 432 in terms of increased revenues from the empire seems perfectly reasonable.[23] Some of his other claims are more dubious, however. For example, it is hard to accept that the abolition of pay for public office during the period of the oligarchic regime of the Four Hundred in 411, which is a substantial part of his argument that we should see major cuts in wages between 412 and 403, should be seen *solely* as a reflection of Athens no longer having the cash to support wages as a result of the Sicilian disaster and the Spartan occupation of Decelea. Yet this is what Loomis suggests, with no hint that the political ideology of an oligarchic regime might have prompted the change (1998: 244–5).

More seriously, his explanation of an increase in wages between 403 and 330 as 'very slight and gradual inflation during a long period of sustained prosperity and growth in the silver supply' (p. 257) is question-begging, and no explanation at all. Even if ultimately he would dismiss the idea, it would have been appropriate to have at least some consideration of the idea that wage movements might have something to do with the demand

[22] Gabrielsen 2002.

[23] Loomis 1998, 243: 'The increasing amount and circulation of this money, in the context of a (presumably) less rapidly increasing labor supply, would have been the cause of the wage increases in this period [i.e. the later fifth century].' It is tempting to ask why commercial activity, which he cites as a factor in the gradual increase in wages which he traces through the fourth century, was not a factor worth considering – unless, of course, as Cohen 1992 implies it is, he thinks that commercial activity was a novelty in fourth-century Athens.

for and supply of *labour* as well as the money supply and 'the expansion of commercial and banking activity' (p. 247) – and that the available labour force in the fourth century was rather smaller than it had been in the fifth. But Loomis is almost silent on the issue.

I would argue too that Loomis's determination to look only at wages is giving us only part of the story, and a part that is very difficult to understand in isolation. Wage levels on their own tell us very little; they acquire meaning and interest only in relation to *prices* – what could Athenian wage-earners buy with their money?[24] Loomis is quite right to observe that it is much harder to talk about prices, compare them, and track their movements in antiquity than it is to do the same with wages.[25] But even if we cannot quantify wages, we should at least think about the likely pressures that would have acted on them – otherwise the whole notion of talking about wages and inflation becomes rather pointless. In short, I think that Loomis's account of the economy of Athens is an excellent example of the dangers of adopting monocausal explanatory models.

The other modern account that I want to mention is Edward Cohen's *Athenian Economy and Society; A Banking Perspective* (1992). There is rather more that is valuable in this book – although I find it frustrating that Cohen seems determined to perpetuate a debate about the nature of the Athenian economy in terms of whether it was 'primitive' or 'modern', and traduces Finley's *The Ancient Economy* as a primitivist contribution, rather than as an attempt to move beyond this sterile argument.[26]

But leaving that aside, Cohen starts his book by making a very strong claim, which he never really argues for, namely that

the fourth century at Athens witnessed two startling, and perhaps interrelated innovations: the transition to an economy governed (in Aristotle's words) by 'monetary acquisition' rather than by traditional social motivations, and the development of the world's first private businesses ('banks', *trapezai*) which accepted from various sources funds ('deposits') for which they had an absolute obligation of repayment while being free to profit from, or even lose, these monies in their own loan and investment activities. (1992: 1)

Clearly there is a certain amount of scope for taking issue with Cohen's claim that these things happened in the way he describes at all. But that is

---

[24] Loomis 1998: 250 does (very briefly) raise the possibility of increased prices in 450–432.
[25] Loomis 1998: 1–2, although it seems to me that Loomis has blurred his own boundaries, especially in his use of figures for payments to 'Doctors, Lawyers and Professors' (pp. 62–75) and 'Prostitutes and Pimps' (pp. 166–85).
[26] See Morris's foreword to the 1999 edition of *The Ancient Economy* for an attitude towards Finley's work that makes it more interesting than Cohen's interpretation allows.

not my primary concern here; instead, what I want to question is Cohen's unproven assumption that it was the fourth century that saw the changes he describes. It is true that almost all the direct evidence for banking operations is fourth-century in date, but that is not the same thing.[27] Cohen provides no coherent account of why the fourth century should be different from the fifth, or why it was only *after* the Peloponnesian War that banks emerged as important institutions in the Athenian economy, and that the economy began to be governed more than previously by 'monetary acquisition'. I would argue that what we know or can reasonably infer about fifth-century Athens and the likely mechanisms of change that operated during the war provides no obstacle to pushing such developments back into the 400s. I also think Cohen may have hit on *something* important happening in fourth-century Athens – not the 'startling' appearance of a free-market economy, as he sees it, but a culturally determined response to the particular shocks experienced during the last decades of the fifth century.

To try to persuade readers of this, I want now to talk about what I think are the important things going on at this time. I start by returning to the absolute size of the Athenian population in 431 – about 300,000. Now on its own that is just a number, and as Robert Sallares was at such pains to point out in *The Ecology of the Ancient Greek World*, total population figures in isolation are not very interesting or useful.[28] But fortunately we do know some other things about Athens and its history, so we can put this figure into some kind of context. In short, this is a lot of people: more than had ever lived in Attica in the past and almost certainly more than would live there again until well into the nineteenth century.[29] It is a big population, densely settled. And *that* is potentially very interesting.

What are the implications of a population like that? One is something that would clearly be recognised by Thucydides (and Plato[30]) – a big population can provide military power. Scheidel (2001: 67) recently pointed out that if military power were *straightforwardly* linked to population, then we should all be talking Chinese. But when the institutions that allow the mobilisation of military manpower are comparable – as they were in

---

[27] And in fact there is a case for believing that the bank later run by Pasion was founded in the fifth century. It was already a going concern when Pasion took it over from Archestratus and Antisthenes (Demosthenes 36.43), and *may* possibly have already been in operation in the 420s: Trevett 1992: 2 n. 2.

[28] Sallares 1991: 48, where he makes 'the elementary but fundamental point that numbers only become significant if set in a structural framework which explains the interplay of forces that regulate the numbers and their effects on other bodies'.

[29] Garnsey 1988: 90–1; Gallant 2001: 75–115 on the demography of Greece after independence and the (rather peculiar) role played there by the city of Athens in social change in the nineteenth century.

[30] *Laws* 737d, 740b1–741a5.

the Aegean world of the fifth century – then numbers do count, and they helped to lay the basis for Athens' military prominence.

But there are many other implications too, not all of them so positive. A couple of negative ones are obvious. A big, dense population is vulnerable to a whole new set of diseases that could not gain a foothold in smaller, scattered populations – as graphically demonstrated by the plague of Athens.

And again, a big population can be difficult to feed. The productive capacity of Athenian agriculture may have been seriously underestimated in the past, at least before Peter Garnsey's work on the subject, but even on the most optimistic estimates a population of 300,000 in Attica will have needed to import large quantities of food, even in good years, just to maintain subsistence.[31]

Of course, outstripping the carrying capacity of one's land is only a problem if one cannot get food from anywhere else. Fifth-century Athens does not seem to have had any serious problems in this respect. Revenues from silver-mining and the empire meant that Athens as a whole could afford to pay for imports. Providing pay for jurors, building workers, and the men who built, crewed, and maintained the fleet will have ensured that many of the ordinary inhabitants of Attica will actually have been able to buy food when necessary – and also, crucially, that there was a ready market available to anyone with food to sell.

This term 'market' raises a number of other issues. When we think about markets – in the sense of actual physical locations for exchanges rather than anything more abstract – the temptation is to visualise the Piraeus or the agora in the centre of Athens. And of course we are not *wrong* to do so, for a number of reasons. The city of Athens, with the Piraeus, even in the fifth century, must have been home to a substantial fraction of the population – at least some of whom will have had to buy at least some of their food in a market. The Piraeus was Attica's major port now, and the easiest place to buy and sell imported goods will have been within the urban complex. Attica is not so big that anyone would have been really remote from that urban centre, if they needed to use it.

But it is also worth bearing in mind that the rest of Attica must also have been densely settled – even if the exact pattern of settlement is a question that will never quite go away.[32] Density of settlement facilitates the movements of more than just disease, and would have eased exchange

---

[31] Garnsey 1988: 89–106; also Hansen 1988: 12–13.
[32] R. Osborne 1985: 15–46 and Lohmann 1993 (for example) present rather different pictures (although see R. Osborne 1997b: 246).

at more local levels too. Put very crudely, if there are lots of people living nearby, it is much easier to find someone with whom to exchange things, and those things do not need to be transported very far – in other words, transaction and information costs are low. This can be an important factor if one is trying to explain the commercialisation of an economy,[33] and it may have tended to create a fifth-century Attica that was full of local markets and economic activity other than agriculture (and silver-mining).

Any account of market exchange and commercialisation in classical Athens has to mention Aristophanes' *Acharnians*.[34] There is little I want to add here, so I shall be brief. Dicaiopolis' opening speech (lines 1–39), taken in isolation, *could* be used to imply that market exchanges were confined to the urban centre (although incidentally it does also seem to indicate that 'monetary acquisition' was alive and well already in the 420s) – but then what do we find Dicaiopolis doing when he has made his private peace? He sets up a market (lines 719–28). It is interesting to note that, although numerous references are made to money, Dicaiopolis remains resistant to selling things for money, and concern about monetary acquisition runs throughout the play – clearly we do not have to go as late as Aristotle to find this anxiety. I would not claim that this proves my point – although I do not think that it does it any harm – but it might leave Cohen with some explaining to do.

Probably we ought to hope that I am right, though. With a population this large, there was not going to be much decent agricultural land to go around. This is bad for Athens overall for the reason given earlier: that it was going to be difficult, if not impossible, to feed the population from Attica's own resources. But the situation is even grimmer if we consider the position of the individual ordinary citizen. For the rich, of course, the news was much better.

All other things being equal, if there are lots of people within a fixed area, labour is going to be abundant and cheap. Land, on the other hand, is going to be scarce, and expensive. This is bad news for those who rely for part or all of their subsistence on wages of some form, whether in cash or in kind. Loomis may or may not be right to identify an upwards movement in wages in the decades before the outbreak of war, but there must have been severe downward pressure on their real value. The almost inevitable result will be a trend towards an increasingly polarised distribution of wealth and low average standards of living.

[33] As has been recognised, again, in accounts of fourteenth-century England. See e.g. Persson 1988: 65–7, 88.
[34] E.g. M. I. Finley 1973: 107; von Reden 1995: 131–5.

For the fortunate few this is good news – provided that the social tensions that this might cause do not land them with some deeply unpleasant consequences. Now in fifth-century Athens the profits of empire, the existence of strong local associations beyond the household, and a prevailing ideology of citizen equality may have mitigated the most extreme consequences.[35] But still, for many people much of the time, some source of subsistence other than what they could produce on such land as they had would have been necessary, and this would effectively have forced them to engage in other forms of economic activity. If local markets existed, this would have been easier; the need for them might also have been a powerful stimulus to the 'commercialisation' of the economy.

In short, my point is that I see no reason to believe in Cohen's startling innovation in the fourth century. All the indications are that the Athenian economy would have been becoming increasingly 'commercialised' (if that is what was happening) already in the fifth century. And given that Athens' import trade must have been at least as great in the fifth century as in the fourth – and in all probability greater – there is no reason not to believe that the banks that Cohen sees as crucial to facilitating this trade in the fourth century did not already exist too – and if his picture of the fourth century is right, surely every reason to believe that they *did*.[36]

But other things were going on too. Even if the institutions of empire and democracy shielded the inhabitants of Attica from the worst consequences of the economic situation, inequalities in the distribution of wealth would still have been increasing, and increasingly obvious. The rich elite were still able to get richer, albeit at the expense of other groups, whether the citizens of other cities or slaves in the silver mines of Laurion.

All of this derives essentially from the observation that Athens' population in 431 was around 300,000. Take away maybe half those people and we should expect the picture to be shaken up quite substantially. The Athenians probably *were* unhappy that so many of their friends and relations had died. Their military power would never be the same again. But that is not the whole picture – and some parts of it were a little less bleak, even if it would have been hard to appreciate this at the time.

The land of Attica now had to be distributed among fewer people; in theory the survivors should have been better off, on average, in material terms. And as labour became scarcer and more valuable relative to land, the value of wages should have risen, leading to an improved average standard

---

[35] See Gallant 1991: esp. 194–6 for a rather bleak assessment of the prospects for Greek peasants in general.

[36] And see n. 27 above.

of living, and acting, if not to reverse, then at least to retard the polarisation of wealth distribution (and remember that those among the wealthy whose riches derived from overseas possessions or silver-mining will have lost those sources of revenue by the end of the war[37]). It is here that the comparison with Europe and especially England after the Black Death is most obviously useful as suggesting that such a picture has at least some claim to plausibility, and that, crudely, is the use to which Scheidel puts it in his article on the Antonine plague (2000: 2).

So far, though, I have considered only the overall *size* of the population. But I think it is worth at least speculating about the possible consequences for the *structure* of the population. There are a number of different ways that the events of the years 431–403 could have affected this. First of all there is age structure. As this is an area prone to considerable controversy, I shall talk only in fairly general terms.

It is agreed that the population in 431 was greater than it had been at the start of the fifth century. Some of the growth would have been the result of immigration, but so far as we can tell, the citizen population was growing 'naturally' too – by which I mean just that more citizens were being born than were dying (cf. C. Patterson 1981: 40–81). Growing populations tend to have a high proportion of young people, for fairly obvious reasons. But we cannot assume that the proportion was the same in the fourth century, after a period when the population had declined drastically, and as a result of phenomena with age-specific effects. Again, so what?

Of course, I am presenting an oversimplified case here, not least by talking only about mortality and not fertility. This is partly because we have no direct evidence for fertility rates, and we have no idea what happened to them in the aftermath of the plague or indeed at any other time. It is possible that the responses both to the plague and to cessations of hostilities would have been an increase in fertility, or a kind of 'baby boom'. On the other hand it is also possible that fertility was depressed as a result of the hardship and uncertainty of the war years, which would have seriously retarded a recovery in population numbers. But whatever happened, mortality overall was raised to such a level that no amount of reproduction could compensate in the short term.

---

[37] And the wealthiest men we know about in the fifth century, like Oionias with his property worth 81$\frac{3}{4}$ talents on Euboea (*IG* i³ 422.217–8, 375–8), or Nicias with his 1,000 slaves in the silver mines (according to Xen. *Ways and Means* 4.14) had their fortunes in these areas. Fine 1951: esp. 200–8 made what is in some ways a more radical suggestion, that the land of Attica became alienable only as a result of the strains of the Peloponnesian War. While I think I would resist his conclusion, it seems clear that there was considerable dislocation of land tenure over this period.

But in the short term that was not necessarily an entirely bad thing. Fewer children means fewer dependants. In the long term this would be a problem for people who grew old with no one to support them. In the short term, however, it might have meant that a household would have more labour available and fewer drains on its resources. And that is only to see the situation in crude economic terms; the potential for wider social implications is obvious.[38]

Speaking of households, it is also worth noting that highly elevated levels of mortality will have resulted in more families than usual being left without heirs, or dying out altogether. This cannot explain why any particular known family disappears into obscurity, but it must have been a real phenomenon, with real consequences for the distribution of wealth and for social mobility within the citizen body. The traditional *oikos* may have been under threat from an increasingly commercialised world, as Cohen (1992: 5–6) wants to stress, but many actual *oikoi* were probably more immediately threatened by a risk of extinction.

Finally on population structure, I want to consider briefly the question of slaves. There must have been far fewer slaves in Athens in 403 than in 431 – not only absolutely, but also relative to the free population. Not only were they exposed to the same risks of heightened mortality as the free, but they were running away or otherwise being lost as well. And in late and postwar Athens the cash needed to replace them would have been in short supply.[39] What this adds up to is the likelihood of a real change in the position of slaves in Athenian society. Political, social, and economic upheaval internally; military defeat externally; a scarcity of labour: any of these things individually would present challenges to slave-owners; together they must have put severe pressure on their ability to keep hold of and control their slaves.[40] It is hardly surprising, then, that it is in the fourth century that we start to see evidence for manumission and for (some) slaves gaining increased status, responsibility, and, exceptionally, citizenship.[41] And it is here that Cohen seems to be making real and important observations about

---

[38] It is curious, in the light of the kind of argument presented in B. S. Strauss 1986, that B. S. Strauss 1993 makes no attempt to consider the possibility that the age structure of Athenian society might have changed over the period in which he is primarily interested (450–350 BC), as it would surely have been relevant and might provide support for his picture.

[39] As far as it is possible to tell, the breeding of slaves within households seems not to have been a major source of new slaves in classical Athens; Garlan 1988: 52–3; Fisher 1993b: 36–7; Pomeroy 1989, and Pomeroy 1994: 297–300 on Xen. *Economics* 9.5 – a key text for this issue.

[40] O. Patterson 1982: esp. 285–96.

[41] For a summary of the evidence (such as it is) see Fisher 1993b: 67–70, and at slightly greater length Garlan 1988: 73–84.

the growing importance of slaves[42] in the banking sector. But in ascribing this growing importance to the emergence in the fourth century of a market economy, he has, I think, mistaken both the causes and the significance of the phenomenon.

Population change caused a major dislocation in Athenian economy and society, whose significance I have barely begun to explore. I have highlighted, very briefly, some issues that are clearly of wider interest, but there is far more to be said, especially in the realm of production – agricultural and otherwise. Population change cannot explain *everything* – even without the plague, for example, fourth-century Athens would have been a different place from fifth-century Athens – but if we want to get to grips with the nature and timing of change, then we would be foolish to ignore a factor which has, potentially, such great explanatory power.

---

[42] And perhaps of wives too. Cohen 1992: 61–110.

CHAPTER 3

Why the Athenians began to curse

Esther Eidinow

When we talk about cursing, we usually have in mind the conditional model: 'If a certain offence is committed, then may a certain punishment follow.' The curses that form the subject of this chapter – so-called *katadesmoi*, or *defixiones*, or 'binding curses'[1] – are a whole different breed. They seldom ask for a punishment; they rarely threaten a horrible end. Instead, their self-confessed intention is to 'bind' or 'immobilise' their victims.[2] They were written, I believe, by men and women who hoped to limit the inevitable risks of a dangerous situation.

The relevance of these texts to a consideration of cultural change in Athens during the fifth to fourth centuries BC lies in their timing. By far the majority of the curses that have been dated to the classical period have been found in Attica, the first tablets appearing in Athens towards the end of the fifth century BC or early decades of the fourth. Of course, we have to take into account the particular foci of modern archaeology and the uncertainty inherent in dating these tablets. Nevertheless, as it stands, the evidence suggests a marked shift in Athenian behaviour and beliefs, which

---

This chapter became the basis for chapter 7 of my book *Oracles, Curses, and Risk among the Ancient Greeks* (Oxford, 2007). My thanks to Robin Osborne and the anonymous readers for Cambridge University Press, whose suggestions have been extremely helpful.

[1] Contemporary scholars usually use the term *defixio* (from *defigo*, 'to nail down' or 'transfix'), although (Ogden 1999: 5) it is found only in a bilingual gloss, see LSJ s.v. ii 40. (Other possible Latin terms discussed in Tomlin 1988: 59 (*execratio*, 'curse'; *devotio*, 'dedication/curse/spell'; *commonitorium*, 'memorandum'; *petitio*, 'petition', and *donatio*, meaning 'dedication/giving') are particularly relevant for Romano-British curses, which mostly concern thefts and the consigning of the thief or the stolen property to divine protection.) In Greek curse texts of the archaic and classical periods, the tablet is referred to as 'the lead' (see *DTA* 55, side A, line 16). Other terms: κατάδεσμον, 'a binding' (*DT* 85, side B, line 3) read by Ziebarth 1934: 1040–1, no. 23 and ἀπορίαν or 'blocking spell' (*DT* 85, side A, line 13, trans. Gager 1992: 8); εὐχά, 'a prayer or boast' (*SGD* 91; but others have read this as τύχη, an invocation to the goddess of luck or chance, of a kind often found at the beginning of public documents, cf. *SGD* 19 and *DTA* 158).

[2] From this period, *SGD* 89; threats of horrible ends appear more frequently in later tablets (e.g. *DT* 93 and 129).

may be considered as part of a larger cultural revolution, although by this I mean a significant change, not one that was startlingly speedy or sudden.[3] As I will hope to show in this chapter, the practice of writing binding curses is likely to have been the result of many different influences and cultural developments; indeed, binding curses may have existed in another form, before finding this particular mode of expression.

Most binding curses dating to the sixth to first centuries BC are found inscribed on small sheets of lead or lead alloys. For a long time, scholars believed that this was because lead's physical qualities meant that curse-writers thought it particularly suitable for writing letters to the dead, but it is more likely that it was because lead was cheap and available. Besides, although they have not physically survived, there is evidence that other materials – bronze, wax, and papyrus, among others – were also used.[4] Once the curse had been inscribed, the lead strip was folded, sometimes pierced with a bronze or iron nail, and then buried underground. Popular locations included wells, the sanctuaries of chthonic deities (gods associated with the underworld), and graves, where curse tablets have been found placed in the hands of the corpse itself.[5]

When we compare them again to the conditional form of curse, we find very different patterns of use. Conditional curses are usually intended to afford some kind of protection from potential wrongdoers. They are powerful precisely because they are uttered or inscribed out in the open, intended to be read or heard, and feared. As such, we find them 'standing guard' over a variety of objects, including gravestones, and playing an admonitory role in certain civic events. The evidence suggests that this conditional form of curse probably has a long history: as early as the eighth century BC, it appears, the formula was so familiar that it could be turned around to become the basis for a joke, as in the jovial graffito that appears

---

[3] Not an unusual use: see Brunt 1988: 10, who describes how 'the word "revolution" is customarily employed in English . . . to denote any momentous change, even one accomplished gradually like the Industrial Revolution'.

[4] For lead as appropriate for writing to the dead, see *DTA* pp. ii–iii, a view now revised in the light of evidence that other materials were used (see Graf 1997: 131 and Gager 1992: 31 n. 5 for examples of curses written on a variety of materials, including copper, tin, ostraca, limestone, talc, papyrus, and gemstones). Among the curse collections: *DT* 196 is made from bronze; *DTA* 55 describes the creation of tablets in lead and wax. The *Greek Magical Papyri* include recipes using gold or silver (*PGM* x nos. 24–35) or iron (*PGM* IV nos. 2145ff.); *Suppl. Mag.* 44 is written on a scrap of linen. Plato (*Laws* 933a–c) mentions moulded images of wax left at crossroads or in graveyards. For lead as cheap and available, see Jordan 1980: 226–9 for an overview of ancient Greek texts inscribed on lead tablets, including private letters and financial documents.

[5] See *SGD* 1 and 2.

on the 'Cup of Nestor': 'Whoever drinks from this cup, may desire for fair-crowned Aphrodite seize him.'[6]

In contrast, neither the formulae nor the creation of binding curses seems to have entered the public realm. In fact, up to and including the classical period, the existence of these curses is barely even acknowledged in ancient literature. The fullest descriptions are found in two passages of Plato, which also provide the most reliable Greek terminology for this practice. In the *Republic*, binding curses (Plato calls them κατάδεσμοι), are one of the services touted by travelling salesmen who knock on the doors of the wealthy offering to expiate current and ancestral sins, or cause harm to an enemy. In the *Laws*, Plato cites them (here he calls them καταδέσεις), alongside sorceries and incantations, as one of the ways to harm someone by supernatural methods, in contrast to poisons that are administered physically, causing harm κατά φύσιν, 'according to nature'.[7]

This lack of literary evidence is made up for by the archaeological material, which has provided over 1,600 curse tablets from all over the Graeco-Roman world. The earliest tablets date to the early fifth or late sixth century BC and were found in the Greek city of Selinus, Sicily. By the mid fifth century, tablets are beginning to appear in Attica and possibly Olbia by the Black Sea. A century or so later, the evidence suggests the practice of curse-writing is spreading across the rest of the Graeco-Roman world, and it continues to flourish well into the eighth century AD.[8] However, while

[6] Objects: for example, Middle Proto-Corinthian II aryballos, 675–650 BC inscribed 'I am the lekythos of Tataoa; whoever steals me shall become blind' (London, BM 1185.6–13.1 [A 1054], in Oakley 2004: 234 n. 38); in Greek epitaphs of Asia Minor, found on grave stelai from the fourth century BC (see Strubbe 1991). Civic language: at the beginning of meetings of the Athenian assembly against any misdirecting speaker: Dem. 19.70, Din. 2.16; by plaintiffs against themselves before they enter the homicide courts of the Areopagus (Dem. 23.67–68) or Palladion (Dem. 23.71, although Aesch. 2.87 describes an oath being taken by the winner of the case, after its successful conclusion); Aesch. I.114 implies that curses might be taken before other courtcases. Faraone argues for the use of conditional curses, especially in military circumstances, reinforced with rituals of sympathetic magic, e.g. Xen. *Anabasis* 2.4; Hdt. 8.132.2; Aesch. *Septem* 43–54, parodied by Ar. *Lys.* 189. The citizens of Teos publicly cursed anyone who might wish them harm (c. 470 BC; ML 30); curses apparently made at Cyrene's foundation to protect the settlement agreements were reported by the fourth-century Theran embassy to Cyrene (ML 5). Nestor's cup (late Geometric; ML 1 / *CEG* I. 454); see R. Osborne 1996: 116ff. For an argument that this inscription is a serious magical spell, see Faraone 1996. For the early date of conditional curses, and evidence for their being part of the drift of religious technology from the East into Greece, see Faraone 1993, Johnston 2004: 349ff.

[7] Pl. *Republic* 364c; *Laws* 933a (μαγγανείαις τέ τισιν καὶ ἐπῳδαῖς καὶ καταδέσεσι λεγομέναις, 'by means of sorceries and incantations and curses, as they are called'). In addition to these two references, there is also an indirectly attested mention by the orator Dinarchus (in Harpocration's *Lexicon of the Ten Orators*, entry under καταδεδέσθαι; my thanks to Simon Hornblower for this).

[8] Most of the 1,600 curse tablets are written in Greek, although there are ongoing discoveries of large numbers of late Latin *defixiones*, especially in Britain. These numbers are from Ogden 1999: 4 and Faraone 1991: 22. There are some problems of identification: for example, the 436 inscribed lead

recording these timings as the generally accepted facts, it is also essential to emphasise how difficult it is to date these texts accurately. The criteria – including letter-forms, textual formulae and the context of discovery – are, in most cases, highly uncertain. As a result, these tablets tend to be dated very generally and, even then, dates can vary widely between scholars. Moreover, a number of the earliest excavated curse tablets have now disappeared, so they cannot be redated using modern methods.

It may well be an accident of the historical record, but, as noted already, in this early period of curse-writing (fifth to first centuries BC), the great majority of curse tablets hail from Attica. I have located twelve curse tablets that date to the fifth to fourth centuries BC, and full texts are included as an appendix. This chapter sets out to explore why ancient Athenian men and women may have started to employ written binding curses in this period.

CURSING: FORMULAE AND PERSONNEL

I will start with some more general information about the language of curse texts, and the identity and intention of their creators. For the most part, across the corpus, curse-writers remain anonymous.[9] In fact, most of our information about the kinds of people who might be writing curses draws on what can be gathered from the texts about their targets. Across the corpus, the accursed encompass all parts of society, including women, children, and

tablets listed by Audollent as *DT* 45 each contain a different single name; they show little sign of manipulation or any nail holes. Although Audollent included them in his collection, other scholars believe they were probably used for counting or registration of some kind, and are not curse tablets. Of the Greek material, *DTA* has 220 examples (all Attic Greek); *DT* contains 166 tablets (and 137 in languages other than Greek); while *SGD* lists another 189 published examples and reports the existence of a further 461 tablets which have not yet been published; *NGCT* lists 122.

9 There are a few texts in which the writer identifies himself or herself: 'Pausanias' names himself on a tablet from Akanthos, Macedonia (see Jordan 1999: no. 3); Phila on a curse found in Pella, Macedonia (see Voutiras 1998); in *DT* 5, Prosodion curses the unnamed woman who has seduced her husband; Onesime may have written *DTA* 100, a curse text from fourth-century Attica. Wünsch in *DTA* thought so and Versnel 1991: 65 agrees, but this is debated, as Parker 2005: 126 n. 42 describes. A number of judicial tablets seem to mention the names of those who wrote them – or at least, of those who are facing legal difficulties, e.g. *DTA* 88, *SGD* 6 (in the appendix to this chapter), and *DT* 44. The author and the writer of a curse may not be the same person: caches of curse tablets probably written by the same hand have been found; *DT* 18–21 are four of some sixty fragmentary Greek inscriptions inscribed on talc found at Hagios Tychonas (ancient Amathous in Cyprus) that seem to show the same formulae and share a writer; for a further 200 fragmentary tablets (of which sixteen have been published, erroneously ascribed to Kourion but actually from Amathous), see Aupert and Jordan 1981: 184, who date the tablets to the second century AD. For further examples see Jordan 1985 (tablets) and 1988 (dolls apparently shaped by the same hand). In contrast, lower-quality scribing or lack of literacy (e.g. *DT* 85, *SGD* 48, *SGD* 173), or more individual expressions (e.g. the curse by Phila from Pella, Macedonia, or the eclectic choice of targets in *DT* 86) may indicate cases in which people tried to write curses without the help of a professional.

neighbours, husbands, wives, and lovers, pimps and sex workers, soldiers, slaves, politicians, litigants, and craftsmen.[10]

The targets of the earliest of the Athenian tablets appear only as a name or list of names in the nominative. However, a highly formulaic idiom quickly develops. Three basic spell types can be identified, although these are not chronologically sequential, and all three types of spell frequently appear at the same time, sometimes on a single tablet.[11]

The first type usually uses a verb of binding or restraining, which is often repeated, sometimes many times; καταδῶ, 'I bind' is the most frequently used. Alongside we also find other verbs such as καταδεσμεύω, meaning 'I bind up', and κατέχω, 'I immobilise or restrain'.[12] The idea of 'binding' may be related to the ritual nailing or piercing of the tablet itself, but it cannot be limited to this meaning. Nailing the tablet was surely a symbolic action, intended to reinforce the writer's attempt to impose a restraint on something he or she perceived to be a threat.[13] The targets of binding may include people, sometimes singling out specific parts of their body (including, sometimes, the 'spirit'), and/or their words and deeds (a common formula); occasionally, the locations they work in and the tools they use; events or circumstances, such as marriage; and even their thoughts and hopes.[14]

Other verbs found among the tablets add further nuances to this idea of binding. Some use compounds of γράφω, meaning something like 'I register';[15] we also find compound verbs of τίθημι and δίδωμι, which seem

---

[10] Political figures: *DTA* 11, 24, 30, 42, 47–50, 57, 65, 84; litigants: *DTA* 39, 66, 94, etc.; actor: *DTA* 45; chorus members, chorus leaders, and trainers: *DTA* 33, 34; doctors: *SGD* 124, *NGCT* 24; neighbours: *DTA* 25; lovers: *SGD* 57; children: *DT* 47; sex workers: *DTA* 86, *SGD* 48; soldiers: *DTA* 55; slaves: *DTA* 75; craftsmen: *SGD* 44 (potters), *SGD* 3, 4 (silver bellows-workers), *SGD* 72 (a seamstress), *SGD* 170 (a ship's pilot), *DTA* 69 (a helmet-maker and his gold-worker wife), *DTA* 87 (a cloth-maker and what may be a wooden-frame-maker or a rope-maker), *DTA* 55 (a pipe-maker and a carpenter); *DTA* 68 provides a selection of professions including a pimp, sex workers of various kinds, a boxer, and a miller; numerous tablets mention innkeepers, e.g. *DTA* 30, 68, 87; *SGD* 11.

[11] Faraone 1991; this is a simplification of his own four categories, which are, in turn, a simplification of Kagarow's five categories (1929: 44–9). Faraone (1991: 5) notes that Attic curses that mention only the name of the intended victim steadily decrease in frequency until they disappear in the first century AD, while complex formulae become more popular in later periods. However, the opposite appears to be the case with the older curse tablets from Selinus, Sicily, where lists of names become more common towards the end of the fifth century, while more complex formulae appear earlier (see Curbera 1999: 165).

[12] καταδίδημι, *DTA* 42, 55, 74, 84; καταδεσμεύω, *NGCT* 24; καταδηνύω, *DTA* 75; κατέχω, *DTA* 109.

[13] Wünsch, *DTA*, p. iii: καταδῶ, short for καταδῶ ἥλοις, I fix with nails (cf. Pindar, *Pyth.* 4.71); noted by Faraone 1991: 24 n. 24. See the discussion on nailing and its use in later tablets in Graf 1997: 135ff.

[14] Names and body parts *passim*; 'workshop' in *DTA* 68, 75 (and *emporion*), and *SGD* 124; tools in *DT* 52, 73; 'marriage' in the curse of Phila, from Pella, Macedonia (*supra*); 'thoughts' in *DT* 52; 'hopes' in *DT* 73.

[15] These verbs are most usually found in early Sicilian tablets and only occasionally in Attic tablets.

to mean something like 'I consign'.[16] In these cases, the victim is sometimes registered or consigned πρός certain gods or the dead. Πρός is used in fifth-century BC legal and business transactions to mean 'in the presence of', and these verbs may show the writers drawing on public and legal language, perhaps to add authority to their request.[17]

Πρός is also used to invoke the presence of a god in formulae that use the verb καταδῶ. For example, an Attic tablet dated to the third century BC (*DTA* 81) binds its victims 'before Hermes'; while *DT* 68, an early fourth-century Attic text, binds its victims in the presence of Hermes of the underworld ('Chthonios'), the dead, and Tethys (in mythology, the daughter of Gaia and Heaven; see below for further discussion of this tablet). Alternatively, texts call on the gods in the vocative and then use the passive third-person singular perfect imperative, to request that their target 'be bound' – a plea perhaps, rather than an order, to the gods to perform an act of binding. For example, *DTA* 105, a third-century text from Attica, repeatedly asks, 'O Hermes of the underworld, let so-and-so be bound in the presence of Hermes of the underworld and Hekate' for a number of different targets; *DTA* 106 repeats the 'let so-and-so be bound in the presence of . . .' formula, although it does not call explicitly on a god.

In formulae that invoke the gods using the verb κατέχω, 'I immobilize', the imperative is balder. *DTA* 88, a curse from Attica dating to the third century BC, begins by addressing Hermes the binder ('Katochos'), and continues, κάτεχε φρένας γλῶτ(τ)αν (τοῦ Καλλίου·) 'bind Kallias' mind, tongue'. In *DT* 50, a fourth-century curse from Athens, both Hermes and Persephone are invoked to bind the target, a woman called Myrrine, and her body, spirit, tongue, feet, deeds, and wishes until she goes down into Hades, wasting away (κατέχετε Μυρρίνης . . . σῶ[μα καὶ ψυχὴν καὶ γλῶτταν καὶ πό]δας καὶ ἔργα καὶ βουλὰς ἕως ἂν εἰς Ἅιδου καταβῆι . . .] φθίνουσα). κατέχω is rarely found in the first person, as the action of the agent of a curse. The exception is *DTA* 109, which starts Μανῆν καταδῶ καὶ κατέχω, 'I bind and immobilise Manes.'

The second of the three styles of binding spell consists of appeals directly or indirectly to the gods or other supernatural powers for their assistance.

---

[16] These do not appear in judicial tablets of this period. Graf (1997: 124) also notes among later Greek tablets verbs meaning 'to adjure', ὁρκίζω and ἐξορκίζω (a rare early appearance in *SGD* 81?), and, among tablets in Latin, the derivative *ligare*, *alligare*, and *obligare* ('to bind'), and the verbs *dedicare* and *demandare*, 'to dedicate', and *adiurare*, 'to entreat'.

[17] Gordon 1999b: 257. A further example of this echoing of public documents is the use of the phrase Θεοὶ ἀγαθῆι τύχη, which is regularly used in public inscriptions and opens at least one curse tablet (e.g. *SGD* 18).

It appears as early as the fifth century, becoming much more common by the early fourth century, when it is found frequently in Attic curse tablets. Of these tablets, some, as already noted, directly address gods, usually those with underworld associations, including Hermes the binder, Persephone, Hekate, and Ge; others invoke them only as witnesses or overseers; some do both simultaneously.

There are a number of tablets that mention the dead. Two, possibly three, tablets appear to address the corpse with which the tablet is buried. As mentioned above, *DTA* 100 may address the dead by name, although an alternative reading takes this as the name of the writer of the curse. More clearly, in a curse from Pella, Macedonia, Phila, the woman who wrote the curse, entrusts her intentions to Makron – who is presumably the person in whose grave the curse was buried – and the *daimones*. However, later in the curse, when she pleads for pity – pity that she hopes will lead to the carrying out of the curse – Phila addresses only the *daimones*.[18] *DT* 43 calls on one Pasianax and reads: 'Whenever you, O Pasianax, read this letter – but neither will you, O Pasianax, ever read this letter . . .' It is as if the writer, having first asked Pasianax to read the curse, then realises that he/she/it cannot do this. This would seem an appropriate way to treat Pasianax if indeed he was a corpse. But this is not certain: it may be that this Pasianax is some other kind of supernatural entity. 'Pasianax' is attested as an epithet of Zeus, while Wünsch suggested that Pasianax was a name belonging to Pluto, which, once transferred to a corpse, also carried power.[19] Voutiras has suggested that 'euphemistic appellations' like Pasianax may actually have been intended to soothe the anger of the dead with whom the curse was buried, lest it be turned on the curse-maker. He argues that later, similarly phrased curses suggest that its use is likely to be formulaic, but also points out that in at least one later text the formula is used to call on the more familiar demon *Abrasax*.[20] But whichever way we read it, the curse hardly suggests Pasianax's power to carry out the act of binding. On the contrary, it focuses on his lack of capacity: having made it clear that Pasianax is unable to read, it goes on to draw an analogy between this weakness and the way in which it is hoped that the target of the curse, the man bringing the lawsuit, will be unable to take action.[21]

[18] Voutiras 1998.   [19] Gager 1992: 131 n. 35; Voutiras 1999.
[20] Voutiras 1999: 78. *DT* 44 uses much the same formula – and the same corpse – to target another legal team; later text *SEG* 40.919.
[21] However, Voutiras argues that 'although they [the writers of these curses] treat them as lifeless corpses for the purpose of sympathetic magic that will render the *defixi* powerless, the operants must have felt that the souls of the dead could become powerful and are potentially dangerous *daimones* of the nether world'.

Two, possibly three, curses invoke the dead in general. The uncertain example is *SGD* 20, found in the Athenian Agora, and dated to the fourth century. It binds its targets πρὸς τοὺς κάτω, 'in the presence of those below', a phrase which might be intended to describe either the dead or the underworld gods. More explicit is *DT* 52, a late fourth-century Attic text, which binds its victims 'before those who died before marriage' (παρὰ τοῖς ἠϊθέοις) and describes their reading the curse, although the instruction to restrain or bind, i.e. to carry out the intention of the curse, is given to Hermes.

When the writer of *DT* 68 asks to bind its victim πρὸς [το(ὺ)ς] ἀτελ[έ]σ[το(υ)ς] he or she may be thinking along the same lines, since 'unmarried' is just one of the many meanings proposed as a translation of the word ἀτέλεστος. Whether we plump for 'unmarried', 'uninitiated', or 'unfulfilled' as the final translation, this word is likely to belong to a cluster of terms that indicate 'the dead who are, in some way, incomplete', and this curse is likely to contain what seems to be the earliest appeal of this kind to the dead.[22] The curse is against a woman called Theodora, its use of ἀτέλεστοι echoing its plea that everything to do with her be ἀτέλεστα, just as the corpse with which the curse is buried is ἀτελής. This play on a family of words may be the earliest example of analogical magic among the curses.[23] Even if the exact meaning of each term is not clear, the intention behind the curse is manifest: Theodora is to experience a lack of success in both her business and her relationships (or, possibly, the business of her relationships, if she is a *hetaira*).[24]

---

[22] Various translations given: Audollent 1904 has 'the uninitiated'; Graf 1997: 150–1 and Gager 1992: 90 (though some nuances are given in n. 26) have 'unmarried' (which Johnston 1999: 78 n. 12 observes is not found elsewhere). Jameson *et al.* 1993: 131 suggest it means those dead who have not received proper funeral rites, τέλη, from the living after their death. Cf. Soph. *Antigone* 998–1032; Hom. *Odyssey* 11.72–6; and a fourth-century gold tablet which assures the dead woman in whose grave it was found that 'you will expect beneath the earth what τέλεα the other blessed (dead) expect' (see Jordan 1989: 129–30).

Would these graves have been identifiable? Johnson (1999: 78 n. 12) argues that, although Graf 1994: 153 observes that the graves of the uninitiated would not have been marked, neither would the graves of the untimely dead. However, it can be argued in turn that the graves of unmarried men and women may have been marked with *loutrophoroi* (see e.g. Oakley 2004: 27 (Athens National Museum 1975) and 74 (Museum of Fine Arts, Boston, 03.800) for images on white-ground lekythoi that depict such a use of this vessel), or with a stele inscribed with an appropriate poem (e.g. a young woman called Thersis is commemorated in a poem composed by Anyte, *AP* 7.649, which is likely to have been inscribed on the tomb; see Snyder 1989: 68; cf. *AP* 7.486, 490, 646; for Attic grave-markers for women from the late fifth century onwards, see R. Osborne 1998: 195ff.). Local knowledge may have provided information for a curse-writer or salesman about graves suitable for curse burial.

[23] Earliest form of analogical magic: Jameson *et al.* 1993: 130. Earliest appeal to the dead in curse tablets: noted by Johnston 1999: 73. ἀτελής also found in *DTA* 98, *SGD* 99.

[24] Theodora as *hetaira* cursed by a rival courtesan: Dickie 2000: 576.

So, during this period, across the curse corpus, the dead – both the corpse in the grave and the pale ranks thronging the underworld – are invoked, on occasion, as witnesses, sometimes even expected to read the curse. They are in a few cases described as being, in some way, dead 'before their time'. However, the texts do not yet show the concentrated focus on invoking 'the untimely dead' that we find in later spells and formularies.[25] Nor is it certain that the tablets were usually buried with those who had died young.[26] In the texts of this period, there is no tablet that directly addresses the dead – a particular corpse or those below – and asks them to carry out the instructions of the curse, as found in later material.

The curse against Theodora, *DT* 68, mentioned above, brings us to the third and final style of spell: this comprises a wish that the target take on the characteristics of something involved in the binding ritual – a so-called *similia similibus* formula. For example, *DTA* 67 (an Attic text, dated to the third or fourth centuries) asks that the target be as cold (ψυχρά) as the lead tablet on which the curse is written. Three Attic curses, *DTA* 105, *DTA* 106 and *DTA* 107 (dated to the fourth century), all ask that the victims and their doings resemble the lead of the curse tablet. *DTA* 105 requests that the words and tongues of his victims become as cold (ψυχρός) and faint-hearted (ἄθυμος) as the lead tablet; *DTA* 106 asks that the words and deeds of the target become as useless (ἄχρηστα) as the lead tablet; while *DTA* 107 describes the lead of the tablet as dishonoured and cold (ἄτιμος καὶ ψυχρός), and asks that the doings of his victim be the same.[27]

In some cases, these analogies are expressed in physical ways: twisting or scrambling the text may reflect what the author hopes for his victim.

[25] See, e.g., the erotic spells collected in *Suppl. Mag*, many of which begin by invoking a soul of the dead, or *nekuodaimon*, to do their bidding; alongside chthonic gods and daemons, no. 45 calls on the 'untimely dead youths'; no. 46 invokes 'men and women who suffered an untimely death, youths, and maidens'.

[26] Jordan 1988: 273 does say that 'in every period of antiquity when we have been able to estimate the ages of the dead who have curse tablets in their graves . . . those ages have proved to be young', but elsewhere (1985: 152) he draws attention to the fact that 'in only a very few cases, however, has it been possible to test this theory, for the ages of skeletons with which *defixiones* have been found are seldom reported and the burials are seldom adequately described'. (This point is also made by Parker 2005: 128 n. 48.) Plato (*Laws* 933b2–3) describes how people are disturbed by seeing wax figurines left on the graves of their ancestors, which might suggest that some of the graves involved were of those who had lived long enough to have children (this point is also noted by Johnston 1999: 75 n. 118).

[27] Moraux turned to the philosophical/scientific literature of ancient Greece to examine the significance of coldness, finding that it represented fear and lack of vitality rather than death (1960: 49): 'c'est également pour annihiler l'ardeur combattive de l'adversaire et le purer de ses moyens d'attaque que l'on prie les dieux de lui "refroider"'.

For example, *DTA* 67 asks not only that the target's words be cold, but also that they resemble the way the curse is written – some of the words appear in the text backwards. The writer of *SGD* 99, an early fifth-century text from Selinus, written on a round tablet, asked that the tongue of his victim be twisted to the point of uselessness, and composed this part of the curse in a spiral.[28] In *DTA* 65, a third-century Attic curse, no particular desire is expressed in the text, but the letters of the victim's name are twice written upside down at the end of the spell. In some cases, these wishes are expressed in the very shape of the tablet. Some of the Sicilian curse tablets may have been intended to represent the part of the body – a foot or a tongue – at which they were aimed.[29] Similar analogical magic may be the reason why some curse tablets are more elaborately shaped. For example, tiny flat figurines or 'voodoo dolls' have been found, sometimes buried in what look like miniature coffins. In some cases, the doll's limbs are bound, its head, feet, or torso twisted. The curse may be written on the doll or inscribed on a surface of the box.[30]

Confronted with a curse shaped like a coffin, complete with corpse, it is hard not to conclude that curse-writers had deadly ambitions for their victims; indeed, some scholars have argued for a fatal subtext lurking beneath these *similia similibus* formulae. However, this is yet another aspect that distinguishes binding curses from conditional curses. The latter tend to seek the wholehearted destruction of the wrongdoer. In contrast, looking across the corpus of binding curses for this period, the evidence of the texts suggests that 'binding' was essentially a pre-emptive practice, intended to neutralise a threat, rather than eliminate it utterly. The fact that the idiom of binding curses consistently draws our attention to the underworld – whether it is through the nature of the tablets' burial, or the character of the supernatural personnel they invoke – is neither because curse-writers wanted to add to the ranks of the dead, by killing their victims, nor because they thought the dead could carry out their wishes. They wanted their victims to be like the dead – that is, as texts across the corpus repeatedly emphasise, they wanted them to be cold and useless. In these tablets, the dead may be called on as witnesses, but curse-writers invoke the powerful gods to fulfil their instructions.

[28] *SGD* 100, also from Selinus, is very fragmentary, but appears to have a similar shape and content (Gàbrici 1927: no. 13).

[29] Text written on a tablet shaped like a foot on *SGD* 87; on a tablet possibly shaped like a tongue, *SGD* 86. Example of scrambled text on *SGD* 95; letters written backwards on *DT* 60.

[30] Doll and coffin sets include: *SGD* 9 from the Kerameikos in Athens, dated to the early fourth century; the doll has its arms bound behind its back; *NGCT* 11, 12, 13, Athens, early fourth century.

CURSING IN ATHENS

Let us turn now to the more specific question of why Athenians started to curse. The precedent of Sicilian practice provides a first response. Curse tablets dating to the sixth/fifth centuries BC have been found in Selinus, and, like the earliest Athenian tablets, most of them appear to be judicial in character.[31] The fifth century was a period of particular political turbulence in Sicily, and it makes sense that participants in legal cases, threatened by the skills of their opponents, might have turned to cursing to manipulate the legal system.[32] There is some force in the argument that the Athenians simply adopted this practice from the Sicilians, perhaps along with the arts of rhetoric.[33]

But although this may identify one factor, it still raises the question of what cultural developments made such a transmission feasible. There can, of course, be no precise answer, only an assembly of conjectures intended to raise some idea of the complex influences that might have played a part. This chapter presents a selection of these, exploring how, why, and when the practice of written cursing may have started in Athens.

How? Technologies and beliefs

First, the question of how the practice of curse-writing spread: I think we have to consider not only particular technologies, but also the beliefs that meant that those technologies were relevant. A passage of Aeschylus' *Eumenides* sheds useful light on both aspects: at lines 306ff., the *Erinyes* or Furies, acting as the prosecution, are charging Orestes, who is, in this context, in the role of the defence. The *Erinyes* say: οὐδ' ἀντιφωνεῖς, ἀλλ'

---

[31] Examples include: *SGD* 95, which has been dated to the sixth century BC (Dubois 1989; Brugnone 1976 dates it to the end of that century), to 500, and to post-500 BC (*SGD*); *SGD* 96, dated by some to the end of the sixth century (Brugnone 1976, *SGD*, Dubois 1989) and by others (Arena 1989) to the beginning of the fifth century; also *SGD* 99–101, all dated between the end of the sixth century and the first half of the fifth century BC.

[32] Other evidence may suggest contemporary anxiety about the manipulation of the angry dead: the *Lex Sacra* from Selinus, which dates approximately to the decade before 450 BC, provides detailed prescriptions for purification rites and the treatment of dangerous spirits. This evidence of civic concern in Selinous about the manipulation of *miasma* ('pollution') arising from violent deaths suggests there may have been some kind of conflict in the city (see Jameson *et al.* 1993: 131).

[33] For the widespread belief in antiquity that the study of the arts of rhetoric originated in Sicily (beginning with Corax and Tisias, then Empedocles, who taught Gorgias) and subsequently appeared in Athens, see Radermacher 1951: 11–27; also Kennedy 1994: 11ff.

ἀποπτύεις λόγους ('You do not reply, but spurn [my?] words?'[34]) and go on (306): ὕμνον δ' ἀκούσηι τόνδε δέσμιον σέθεν ('You will listen to my song by which I will bind you'). The Scholia Vetera offer this explanation: οὐκ ἀποκρίνη. ἢ ἀντὶ τοῦ οὐδέ ἀντιφωνήσεις μοι ἀλλὰ σοῦ βουλομένον λαλεῖν τὸ φθέγμα δεθήσεται ('You do not reply. Or in place of this: you will not reply to me, although you want to speak, your voice will be bound'). If the Scholia are right, although the first performance of the *Oresteia* antedates the first appearance of Attic judicial curses by more than half a century, this ὕμνος δέσμιος or 'binding song' of Aeschylus' *Eumenides* may be meant to represent the creation of an oral binding curse, suggesting that this was already a familiar practice in Athens.[35]

If this is the case, then it may be that the archaeological record preserves a gradual shift in practice, a move towards the creation of written texts, in addition to an existing oral practice. As we have noted earlier, some of the verbs used to 'hand over' the victim to the will of the god recall the language of business transactions.[36] For example: *DTA* 102 describes itself as a letter (to the *daimones* and Persephone) conveying (κομίσας) the victim, Tibitis; similarly, *DTA* 103 starts, 'I am sending this letter to Hermes and Persephone.'[37] Since similar developments are happening in public, business, and legal communications in Athens at this time, it is possible that the development of curses in written form happened along-side, and was influenced by, the growing use of writing for commercial

---

[34] In some editions, lines 303–4 are printed as a question, in others as a declarative sentence (see Faraone 1985: 152 n. 14). It seems as if the Furies are describing Orestes' contempt for their words, but the Scholia Vetera suggest that it may be words in general that Orestes will be unable to use (cf. Faraone 1985: 152).

[35] Faraone 1985 suggests that it represents either an early form of written binding curse, or an oral type of a sort that existed prior to the written versions. I would suggest that, as with the development of the use of writing in other areas of life, it is likely that oral and written practice coexisted (as R. Thomas 1992: 45ff.). There may be support for this in the instructions for the creation and deposition of curse tablets found throughout the Greek Magical Papyri (e.g. *PGM* IV 296–466), in which the practitioner is told to intone certain words as he or she deposits a curse tablet.

[36] Versnel 1991: 73 compares the use of verbs of similar sense on the Cnidian tablets (*DT* 1–13); Faraone 1991: 10 finds parallels in the inscriptions on two Attic grave stelai (*IG* II² 13209–10) that hand over the two markers to the control of the underworld gods, and in a Cretan tablet, dated to the imperial period, that also places a nearby gravestone under the gods' control (*ICret* II (17) 28). A tablet from Alexandria, Egypt, dating to the third century AD (Daniel and Maltomini 1992: 15, no. 54, esp. notes to lines 21–2, p. 22; *DT* 38) presents its targets to the supernatural powers using, as the editors observe, the language of orders for arrest and delivery recorded in the documentary papyri (*P Hib.* I 54, 20–2; *P Abinn.* 51, 15f.).

[37] See also *SGD* 54, location unknown, undated, which mentions a gift – it may be, as interpreted by Faraone (1991: 24 n. 15), that the victim is being offered to the gods of the underworld as a gift, or that the gift is intended to persuade the gods to do the agent's bidding. *SGD* 109, from Lilybaion, Sicily, second century BC, uses a similar gift formula, but (as Jordan says of *SGD* 177) its significance is not clear from the published text.

purposes.[38] The use of written business and legal contracts in Athenian life may have shaped ideas about how best to make an effective arrangement even with the supernatural.[39]

This shift in practice is accompanied by some subtle shifts in belief: in particular, those concerning the relationship between the living and the dead. For example, the passage from the *Eumenides* shows the *Erinyes*, terrible creatures usually invoked by those seeking vengeance, especially members of the dead who were angry at the living, resorting to a type of incantation that was used by the living – probably even by some audience members of the original production.[40] This passage is part of a swathe of evidence that suggests that, during the period in which curse-writing took hold, beliefs about the relationship between the living and the realm of the dead were slowly changing. The perceived gap between the two realms was gradually narrowing; its denizens could be depicted as using familiar practices.[41] The curse-writers of this period may not yet have achieved the direct and easy interaction with the underworld powers that we see in later materials, but the underworld was no longer so remote. These texts show the dead called as witnesses, their distinctive qualities invoked by curse-writers to express their intentions for their targets.

In conclusion, at least two significant and related trends seem to have played a part in influencing 'how' written binding curses appear in Athens: first, a growing belief in the power of the living to reach out to the underworld, and simultaneously, the spread of the use of writing, especially for legal and business contracts. Together, these may have prompted both the development of cursing from an existing oral tradition into a written form, and new ideas about how mortals might best interact with the dead, including the creation of contracts with supernatural entities.

---

[38] Athens' first city archive was built at the end of the fifth century, probably to organise the accumulated documents and inscriptions of the democracy. Evidence for the first written contract (Isoc. 17.20) dates from the first decade of the fourth century. In the courts, changes in terminology indicate that complaints at the preliminary hearing (*anakrisis*) that were originally made orally were, by the time of Demosthenes, being made by the litigant himself, in writing; the earliest evidence for the reading out of written testimony in court dates to around the late 390s (Isaeus 5.2); see R. Thomas 1992: 41–5).

[39] For the idea that alphabetic literacy is not a neutral skill that transforms a society, but is used to support cultural practice, see R. Thomas 1992: 26. She also argues (p. 31) that, from as early as the archaic period, there was likely to have been a strong cultural association between public documents and communication with the gods (e.g. temple dedications and sacred laws). On commercial letters, see R. Thomas 1992: 73.

[40] Johnston 1999: 285.

[41] See Johnston 1999: 27–8 for further evidence for changes in ancient Greek attitudes to the dead during the fifth century.

Why? Motivations and circumstances

In looking for the social role that cursing played, scholars are gradually abandoning the temptation to describe this activity simply as evidence for black-magical practices – partly, no doubt, because of the widely acknowledged difficulties of defining magic at all.[42] Instead, more functional explanations have emerged: for example, that the tablets should be viewed as weapons in situations of rivalry and competition between individuals, providing vivid illustrations of the agonistic nature of ancient society; or that they were a way for people to regain the initiative when they were otherwise essentially powerless.[43] Likely contexts of competition provide the following headings for categorising the curses: judicial, theatrical, commercial, and love curses – and a fifth category that combines prayers for justice with cursing (called 'border-area' by Versnel).[44] These explanations and categories may manage to account for the content of a number of tablets. However, in many cases, the information in a text is far from easy to interpret, and it is hard to make a straightforward diagnosis of the circumstances in which it was written. I will offer a few brief examples of the ambiguity of the data from across the categories.

First, commercial curses: it is usually assumed that the curses in this category demonstrate the extent of economic competition among the businessmen of antiquity.[45] Many of these curses do identify the particular professions of their targets, and a number extend the remit of binding to include his or her workplace, labour, products, and income. However, none of this professional detail ever relates to the writer of the curse, only ever to the target. This undermines the argument that any curse was composed because its writer was motivated by a sense of economic competition. After all, anyone who feels enmity towards someone may curse his or her work; he or she need not be a business rival. As an example, *SGD* 3 and 4 (see appendix to this chapter) are two curses apparently aimed at the same

---

[42] For a useful summary of the development of anthropological approaches to magic see Luhrmann 1989: 345ff. Much has now been written on the difficulties of defining 'magic' in the ancient world; see, e.g., Meyer and Mirecki 1995, Gordon 1999a, Johnston 2005.

[43] Agonistic: Faraone 1991. Powerlessness: Faraone 1991: 20 argues that they were likely to have been a last defence of the 'perennial underdog . . . protecting himself against otherwise insurmountable odds', but himself admits there is no proof of this; see also Graf 1997: 157.

[44] Faraone 1991: 10; Versnel 1991: 64.

[45] E.g. Faraone 1991: 11: 'Tradesmen (and innkeepers as well), in their efforts to stay ahead of the competition, employed *defixiones* to inhibit the success and profit of their rivals'; Gager 1992: 152: 'We should not be surprised to find individuals who were prepared to seek an advantage for themselves by cursing or binding the affairs of their nearby competitors.' Ogden 1999: 32 states: 'Trade curses appear to have been generally made between rival tradesmen.'

blower from a silverworks.[46] They identify him by his profession and curse whatever work he produces. However, they also mention other aspects of his life, including his wife and possessions.[47] An explanation of business rivalry is plausible, but it is also quite conceivable that the agent of this curse was anxious to ruin the blower in a number of ways, and included detail about his profession simply in order to help the gods to identify him correctly.[48]

This explanation of a more general hostility would also make sense of those tablets that list a myriad individuals in a wide range of professions. Straightforward business rivalry seems an unlikely motivation for the writing of a curse that targets shopkeepers, a miller, and a boxer, as well as a number of prostitutes.[49] Either there is some connection between these people that we are not told about (for example, there has been some kind of neighbourhood disagreement, or the writer is the disgruntled member of a club or society cursing its other members[50]) or the curse-writer has taken the opportunity of putting stylus to lead to curse a number of people for whom, for various different reasons, he feels some hostility (a sort of 'saturation cursing').

The commercial detail of *DT* 68 adds a further economic dimension to what otherwise seems to be a curse intended to destroy the relationships of its target, Theodora.[51] This curse offers another example of the rich, and often bewildering, details that make it so difficult to decide the circumstances and motivations behind the writing of many *katadesmoi*. Some scholars have given this curse a commercial basis, deducing that the writer of this curse was a rival courtesan, jealous of Theodora's successful trade.[52] However, other explanations also fit the evidence: for example, the writer may have been a wife frightened that Theodora might seduce away her husband. Alternatively, since there is no element of the text that indicates

---

[46] Gager 1992: 151ff. and Ogden 1999: 34 include *SGD* 3 as commercial; López Jimeno 1991 adds *SGD* 4.

[47] Gager 1992: 163: 'probably a worker of bellows in a silver shop'.

[48] *DT*/*DTA* 70 does include mention of one of the target's profession and does mention τὰς ἐργασίας, but the consistent binding of ἅπαντα suggests that the curse's author intended his attack to effect more than just the commercial activities of his targets.

[49] *DTA* 68; see also *SGD* 11 and 48.

[50] Such as members of dining groups, burial associations, cults, organisations, kinship groups, trade alliances, etc. See Gaius, *Dig.* 47.22.4 for a law of Solon's that lists various sacred and secular groups in Athens in the early sixth century (cf. Fisher 1988).

[51] Faraone 1991: 13 and 28 n. 59; Gager 1992: 90, no. 22.

[52] ἐργασία is used of a courtesan's trade: Hdt. 2.135; Dem. 18.129; and of sexual intercourse: Arist. [*Problems*] 876a.39; Dickie 2000: 576.

the gender of the creator of the curse, it is also possible that the writer was male, and motivated by desire for Charias.[53]

Finally, a couple of judicial curses: *SGD* 9 and *NGCT* 13, both in the appendix to this chapter, are two of a number of curses categorised as judicial on the basis of the identity of their targets.[54] The case of *SGD* 9 seems quite straightforward: its target Mnesimachos has been identified as a *choregos* and a defendant in a lawsuit in which Lysias wrote the speech for the plaintiff.[55] Moreover, the text includes the phrase καὶ ἔ τις ἄλλος μετ' ἐκένο ξύνδικός ἐστι ἔ μάρτυς ('and anyone else on his team, a fellow litigant or witness'). In contrast, the text of *NGCT* 13 comprises only a list of names, including that of Theozotides, a comparatively rare name, also belonging to a man who, we know, took part in a court case in the fifth century.[56] Scraps of a speech written against him by Lysias reveal an attack on two fronts: first, for trying to restrict state stipends for orphans to legitimate sons and excluding illegitimate and adopted (the future tense of the speech suggests that this proposal has not yet been carried); and secondly, for adjusting the pay of the *Hippotoxotai*.[57]

It may be that *NGCT* 13 was written against this Theozotides, perhaps even in preparation for the very lawsuit for which Lysias wrote his speech. However, even if we accept that it is the same man, it is also possible that it was written in a non-judicial context of hostility. The two decrees described in the speech above, along with the speech itself, suggest that this

---

[53] This theory would also explain the curse's request to make Charias forget his desire for Theodora (side B, lines 10–11).

[54] *NGCT* 11 and 13 were found alongside *NGCT* 5. From the same find: *NGCT* 10 (a tablet without any terminology that helps to identify the circumstances of its writing, and a list of names that lack both patronymics and demotics) and *NGCT* 12, a doll and coffin set which almost certainly comprises a judicial curse, since its text refers to καὶ οἱ ἄλλοι ἀντίδικοι. See Schlörb-Vierneisel 1964; Jordan 1988. *NGCT* 10–13 are in the appendix to this chapter.

[55] Identified by Trumpf 1958: *choregos*, *IG* II² 3092; Lys. fr. 182 Baiter/Sauppe; see Jordan 1988: 275.

[56] This identification was made by Jordan 1988: 276. Five persons named Theozotides are listed in *LGPN* II, of whom numbers (2) and possibly (1) are the Theozotides found on the stele and in Lysias' speech: (2) c. 450–400 BC. Pl. *Apology* 33e; K–A IV. 330 fr. 489; Poll. 8.46 (= *PA* 6914; 6913); *SEG* 28.46.3; *IG* II² 5 + *SEG* 14.36.3.11; Lys. fr. 59; *P Hib.* 14, 28, etc.; cf. *APF* 6915); (1) fifth/fourth century BC *P Oxy.* 1606, 249, etc. (Θεοζοτίδης – pap.), which Stroud 1971: 297 argues is likely to be the same Theozotides. The other three listed are: (3) mid fourth century BC, Dem 21.59; *IG* II² 1927, 39; 12 (5) 542, 35; *SEG* 28.190 (deme) (*PA/APF* 6915) – Theozotides' grandson; (4) Teithras, fifth/fourth century BC, *AAA* 7 (1974): 191 no. 1 = *IG* I³ 1510; and (5) Athens?: 400 BC, Immerwahr 1990: 876.

[57] On the speech, see Davies 1971: 222–3; information found in part of a papyrus (*P Hib.* 14), discovered in 1902 by the Egypt Exploration Society, which contained part of an oration by Lysias concerning a decree regarding state stipends, proposed in 403/2. In 1970, a stele was discovered inscribed with this decree; see Stroud 1971: 280–301. *Hippotoxotai* were mounted bowmen used as police at Athens.

Theozotides exercised views that were likely to have made him enemies.[58] As this suggests, the identification of known political figures among a curse's targets may indicate 'judicial' circumstances, but they may also point to a wider context of civic hostility. This is, of course, particularly true of those tablets that do not include forensic terminology or show only a list of names (cf. *DTA* 24, *NGCT* 11 – see the appendix to this chapter).[59] The binding of a target's tongue, sometimes taken to indicate that the curse was written before a court case, would also be an appropriate action for a situation of political danger, or one in which the writer feared the effects of gossip.[60]

From this brief exploration, we can see that although detail does sometimes allow the identification of a plausible context for the creation of the curse, in many cases caution needs to be exercised in imputing motivations or fixing identities to the writers of these texts. For many curses in the corpus it is impossible to pin down a single (or in some cases any) clear motivation or context for their creation. Admittedly frustrating, this ambiguity may also be useful and stimulating, provoking us to go beyond our first assumptions about the relationships and institutions of the ancient city. In fact, the confusion we feel as we read some of these curse texts may evoke something of the agitated feelings and circumstances that prompted their writers to compose them in the first place.

---

[58] Opinions differ as to whether Theozotides raised or cut the pay of the *Hippotoxotai* (for the former, see Stroud 1971: 298–9; further references in Loomis 1995: 232 n.11; for the latter, see Loomis 1995). Either measure can be interpreted as overtly pro-democratic. His success in reducing the pay of the *Hippeis* would be a blatantly hostile measure taken against a group that had supported the Thirty during their period in power in Athens. The decree to support the orphans of those Athenians who had fought at Phyle meant, in effect, providing for them as if their fathers had died in a foreign war rather than in a civil war. Moreover, by stressing the fact that support would go not to νόθοι and ποιητοί (as the speech tells us), but to the sons of (explicitly) Athenians (this from the stele), Theozotides seems to have been showing support for the idea of limiting citizenship – which was surely a subject for debate in the months following the restoration of the democracy. However, Loomis argues that Theozotides was attempting to reduce the city's costs during a time of 'acute financial emergency' (1995: 236). Either way, what matters to the argument of this chapter is that Theozotides' political activities were likely to have generated controversy and hostility.

[59] The names of renowned orators and politicians appear on a number of Attic curses – and the question of how to categorise these curses has been raised many times before. For example, Preisendanz (1972: 9) recognised the need for a 'political' category, but also recognised that the fact that so many court cases in Athens were in fact political in nature would make it difficult to separate judicial from political curse categories.

[60] Wilhelm (1904: 115–22) argued that *DTA* 24 (see the appendix to this chapter) and *DTA* 47–50 and 57 were created between warring political factions in Attica during the early fourth century.

When? The historical context

As the chapters in this book demonstrate, relatively ample evidence – economic, political, cultural – means that we can construct a coherent picture of many aspects of life in Athens during the late fifth and early fourth centuries. The corpus of curse tablets adds yet another aspect, suggesting that, for some Athenians, this was a time when anxieties compelled them to turn to supernatural forces for help, particularly in confrontations with their fellow citizens. Can what we know about contemporary events help us understand what might encourage such behaviour?

It was certainly a turbulent period: the Peloponnesian War draining the city of men and resources, military defeat prompting anger and confusion about Athens' systems of leadership and raising the question of what the victors would choose to do with the city.[61] Against this backdrop of political turmoil and surely sometimes terror, the collapse of the empire had diminished the prosperity of the city and the livelihoods of many. The evacuations from Attica to Athens probably meant that there was a higher concentration of people in the city, each struggling to find the wherewithal for survival. Even if the population had dropped by the end of the war, it may still have been the case that there were too many people in Athens to be comfortably fed and employed.[62] No doubt economic hardship helped to foster differences and resentments.

Meanwhile, on the political front, the oligarchic underground had risen in 411, and although they had managed to stay in power for only a matter of months, in 404 they returned under the aegis of the Spartans, with attendant political, emotional, and physical horrors. These events revealed the flaws in the democratic ideal, the fractures dividing the citizen body. It is easy to imagine how such events bred an atmosphere of suspicion, nurturing existing feelings of hostility. Thucydides says of Athens under the oligarchic coup of 411 BC, 'It was impossible for anyone who felt himself ill-treated to complain of it to someone else so as to take measures in his own defence; he would either have had to speak to someone he did not know or to someone he knew but could not rely upon.'[63] In this context,

---

[61] For example, the Sicilian defeat was blamed on the advisors and oracle-mongers (Thuc. 8.1.1); this resulted in the appointment of the *probouloi* (Thuc. 8.1.3), whose exact function is unclear, but who were likely to have been 'part of an effort by the democracy to impose self-restraint, and this has been rightly described as having a "quasi-oligarchic flavour"' (Hornblower 2004: 173, quoting Gomme *et al.* (1945–81), v, Book 8: 6f.).

[62] Thuc. 2.14ff. See Hornblower 2004: 146, 184, and the suggestion that a larger, recently uprooted and distressed civic population may be one explanation why Athenian oratory and politics grew more aggressive during this period.

[63] Thuc. 8.54, 63 and esp. 66 (trans. Warner).

in which men and women were isolated, vulnerable, and terrified, curses would have offered a means of self-protection when it was impossible to be sure of anyone else's support.[64]

If this is a correct view of current events, then curses can illuminate something of the detail of daily life, offering fragmentary glimpses of the experiences and responses of individuals and the operation of certain Athenian institutions. I will offer a brief example using the evidence of the judicial curse texts. These challenge a number of current assumptions about the workings of the Athenian lawcourts.

The most familiar model of Athenian litigation is as an arena of competition for the Athenian elite, battling it out in one-on-one legal duels.[65] However, the curse texts reveal a different pattern: teams of people, involved in prosecution or defence, in a range of different litigious situations (for example, both *graphai* and *dikai*, by those about to serve a legal summons or in the polemarch's court), seeking supernatural intervention to increase their side's chances of success.[66] In addition to the teams of people directly involved in court events, some of these texts bind more intriguing figures, for example, οἱ συμπαρόντας, 'those standing around' (*DTA* 79); τοὺς μετ' ἐκείνο[υ σ]υνεστάκειν, 'those standing about with him' (*DT* 67); παρατηροῦσι, 'observers' (*SGD* 176).[67] The fact that such people were considered significant enough to be cursed raises the question of the power of the spectator in the Athenian courts.

The curse texts raise further challenges to our assumptions. As is well known, it was highly unlikely that a woman would be physically present in an Athenian court. Litigants would even go to some lengths to avoid mentioning respectable women's names.[68] Yet there are a number of judicial

---

[64] Thanks to Robin Osborne for drawing this to my attention.

[65] For this model of the lawcourts see Todd 1993, also Cartledge 1990, Christ 1998: 35–7, Garner 1987, Ober 1989, 1994, and Wilson 1991. Many attested and identifiable litigants were politically active and wealthy; see Hansen 1989: 34–72.

[66] For the most part, because we do not know the kinds of cases that were involved, we cannot estimate what was at stake. The fact that penalties imposed on convicted defendants in *graphai* were more severe than those convicted in *dikai*, and that an individual who prosecuted a *graphē* and failed to obtain one-fifth of the votes faced (at least, in some cases) a substantial fine, might suggest that curse tablets were more likely to be written in fear of the penalties of *graphai*, but there is no hard evidence for this. About to serve a summons: *SGD* 82. Polemarch's court: *NGCT* 9.

[67] Chaniotis 1992: 69–73 argues that the παρατηροῦντες (*SGD* 176) were in fact supporters brought to court by the litigant in order to influence the judges with their reactions or merely with their presence. Lanni 1997: 183 has also argued for the crucial role played by the spectators (οἱ περιεστηκότες) who stood at the edges of the courtrooms in Athens (and indeed at other key political venues), watching and listening to the cases and having 'an important effect both on the litigants' arguments and on the jurors' decisions'.

[68] It appears to have been acceptable to mention the names of the dead, of prostitutes, slaves, or female relatives of opponents. On naming female defendants, see Schaps 1977: 323–30 and Sealey 1990.

tablets that include women among their targets, cursed with the same emphasis and level of detail as the accompanying male names.[69] This is something of a surprise: women's lives were certainly shaped by events in the lawcourts, but the fact that they turn up as targets on these curse tablets suggests that these women were considered to be, somehow, dangerously active in this arena.

Challenging our expectations, a review of the forensic corpus reveals how, although women might not be considered legal entities, they could and did also influence events in the Athenian courts in a variety of ways. Some of the roles they played were sanctioned by the system: for example, a few are named as defendants; others seem to have provided evidence, which could be presented to the court via a male citizen in a number of different ways.[70] Beyond these more official channels, Foxhall points out how women may have been in the background or even at the heart of a number of legal cases.[71] Less directly, women might still exercise influence over the course of a case, for example by preventing their husbands from

---

Just 1989: 112 points out that, although 'it is stated . . . that a commonplace tactic of Athenian law-court pleading was for the accused to present his wife, children, and friends to the jury' so as to provoke their pity and support, there are only two examples where those placed before the jury include women: in one, the female is a little girl, and in the other, they are the aged mothers of the defendants (Ar. *Wasps.* 568ff. and Dem. 25, 84ff.). It seems likely that women who were exhibited tended to be in these categories, rather than those who were, as Just 1989:112 puts it, 'possessed of their full sexuality'.

[69] *DT* 50 includes an attack on two men, two women, and a slave (it appears to be two couples and the slave of one of the couples), in which the tongues of all the targets are bound. *DT* 61 and *NGCT* 50 target women in phrases that describe them as part of (or that have them leading) groups 'with so-and-so', which is a formulation used in other tablets for those allied (officially or unofficially, we cannot tell) in a litigious team. *DTA* 39, 67, 68 (fragmentary, and half of the key legal term, μαρτύρας, in line 10, is supplied by the editor), and 106, and *DT* 87, include women in curses which include legal terminology and seem to name them as targets.

[70] Women could be sued only in cases for which they could pay the penalty. Because they (officially) did not own property, this meant that they could not appear as defendants in cases where the penalty was a fine or the payment of damages. However, they could still be executed or sold into slavery, e.g. [Dem.] 59, a *graphe xenias* against the *hetaira* Neaira, as an example of the latter, and Antiph. 1, a homicide case (*dike phonou*) against the plaintiff's stepmother for the murder of his father, as an example of the former. Although there is no evidence that women ever took evidentiary oaths in court, it does seem clear that a woman could, if challenged to do so, swear an evidentiary oath in an arbitration, which could then be proffered by a male litigant as evidence in court; see Dem. 39, in which Plangon tricks the politician Mantias by taking up his challenge to swear to the paternity of her children (see Foxhall 1996: 144; Todd 1990b: 35). One method of introducing evidence from a woman was just to incorporate it into a speech, demonstrating that the woman was in a position to know the facts; see e.g. Lys. 32; Dem. 55.27. See Just 1989: 33–9.

[71] Foxhall 1996: 141ff. Women prompt or exacerbate court cases: Lys. 1; Dem. 41; 55.23–5, 27; Isae. 3, [Dem.] 48; Demosthenes' recovery of his patrimony, encouraged by his mother Cleoboule (Dem. 27–30); see also the role of the mother of the orphans who are fighting for their inheritance in Lys. 32 (Todd 1993. 203).

giving false evidence, and their reaction to a verdict was important enough to the jurors for it to be brought up in forensic argument.[72] The evidence suggests that women from different contexts in Athens interacted with the law and its institutions in a variety of significant ways, beyond the more obvious social divisions of legitimate and illegitimate status.

With the support of evidence from the forensic corpus, the range of targets appearing on judicial curse tablets suggests that legal processes were only one stage of ongoing conflicts or alliances that were being played out in other civic arenas, such as the *oikos*, by men and women, family members, groups of friends, and enemies. They suggest that the dangers a litigant faced not only arose from the behaviour of a single opponent in an elite competition, or even just from events that occurred within the confines of the court, but were affected by his standing in his networks of relationships that extended into the larger community.

Of course, the evidence of the tablets is far too scanty a foundation on which to try to build a detailed understanding of the workings of Athenian society, or a particular institution within it. Nor am I prescribing that the brief glimpses these texts provide of the behaviour of some members of Athenian society should stand as a comprehensive description for that of all. However, even with the broad brush that historical distance imposes, the sentiments these texts express – the naked suspicion, resentment, and fear – all seem to indicate a troubled society, one in which one's fellow citizens could pose a significant risk.

How, why, and when Athenians started to curse

Bringing together even these few answers to the questions of how, why, and when Athenians started to curse, suggests that the appearance of curse tablets in Attica in the late fifth and early fourth centuries should be attributed not merely to the chance survival of evidence, but to a particular confluence of precedent, developments in certain technologies and beliefs, and events, which, together, provided a suitable context.

A brief overview of the curse texts suggests that competition, although a helpful explanation for some, does not provide a satisfactory account of them all. For example, it is difficult to describe those who cursed women or bystanders in court as competing with their targets, although they clearly perceived them as posing a danger. The same observation must be true of those who cursed long lists of people in different professions: these were not their commercial rivals, although they obviously perceived them as being

---

[72] Isae. 12.5; Dem. 59.110–11.

threatening in some way. Besides, if the motivation was simply competition, then why do curse tablets written against athletes take so long to emerge in the historical record?[73] Why are there not curses against rival cities?

I want to suggest instead that Athenian men and women used curses, among other techniques that invited supernatural intervention, in an attempt to control risks. This draws on Mary Douglas's theory of the social construction of risk, which posits that, depending on its cultural structures and beliefs, a society will designate certain aspects of life as posing greater danger to its members than others; these then become the foci of anxiety for individuals within that culture.[74]

Bringing this approach to bear on this body of texts illuminates the motivations behind individual texts. For example, it helps to resolve some of the problems of ambiguity discussed above, when a curse is clearly dripping with hostility, but there is no obvious prize for which agent and target must be competing. It also helps us to understand curse-writing and the culture that practised it. The notion of 'risk' draws attention to the web of socio-cultural values and beliefs that underpinned the practice of writing curses. The fact that much of this material can be grouped according to context suggests that perceptions of danger – and alongside this, notions of authority, responsibility, misfortune, and blame – were generated and shared within and across society, informing the creation and operation of institutions and relationships in the ancient city.[75]

The florescence of cursing in late fifth-century Athens seems inextricably intertwined with the loss of self-confidence and increase in bitter inter-citizen relations evidenced by events like the mutilation of the Herms and the profanation of the Mysteries in 415, and the oligarchic coups of 411 and 404 BC.

The affairs of the Herms and Mysteries may be particularly relevant in this instance, showing anxieties and tensions expressed through attitudes to religion; indeed, this may have been a time when religion itself was a cause for concern.[76] These curses offer an index of circumstances in which people in the city confronted their fear of each other, and, at the same time, provide valuable insights into the institutions and activities of civic life, and

---

[73] Athletic curses start to appear around the second century AD.

[74] See, in particular, Douglas and Wildavsky 1982.

[75] Although it is outside the remit of this chapter, it is worth observing that over the centuries the contexts in which cursing occurs change, reflecting shifting socio-cultural concerns.

[76] For scepticism about widespread attacks on religious dissenters and intellectuals at the end of the fifth century see Dover 1988 and Wallace 1994. But Parker 1996: 210 concedes that in this period 'speculative thought was perceived by some as a threat'. See Rubel 2000: 178–232 and Graf 2000 for convincing arguments that the affairs of the Herms and the Mysteries were indications of a growing Athenian anxiety about religious matters. Janko (1997, 2001, 2006) provides insights on the outlawing of Diagoras in 415 BC relevant to this case (also mentioned by Graf 2000: 125ff.).

the values and beliefs that shaped and were shaped by them. Together, they convey a vivid, albeit fragmentary, glimpse of what it was like to live in Athens at this time.

APPENDIX: LATE FIFTH AND EARLY FOURTH-CENTURY CURSE TEXTS (LISTED BY DATE OF PUBLICATION)

DTA 24

Provenance: Greece, Attica, Halai
Dated: Early fourth century BC (Wilhelm 1904)
Text: Wünsch

Side A
   Φυκίων Ἐργοκράτης
   Τρυ]φ(ε)ρός Ἀριστοκράτης

Side B
   Μ]ήδεια Πιστοκλέης
   Νικο[μ]ένης Εὐθήμων Σ[ύ]ρα.

DTA 38

Provenance: Greece, Attica, Piraeus; a grave
Dated: Early fourth century BC (Wünsch); fifth century BC (Wilhelm 1904)
Text: Wünsch
1. Φιλιππίδης
2. Εὐθύκριτος
3. Κλεάγορος
4. Μενέτιμος
5. καὶ το(ὺ)ς ἄλλο(υ)ς πάντας
6. ἢ ὅσοι συν[ήγο–
7. ροι αὐτο[ῖς

DT 68

Provenance: Greece, Attica
Dated: Early fourth century BC (Jordan in Jameson *et al.* 1993: 130)
Text: Audollent except for an improved reading of the first eight lines of side B by Jordan in Jameson *et al.* 1993: 130

Side A

1. [κα]ταδῶ Θε[ο]δώρα[ν] πρὸς [τ]ἠ–
2. ν] παρὰ Φε[ρρε]φάττηι καὶ πρὸς
3. [το(ὺ)ς] ἀτελ[έ]σ[το(υ)ς]· ἀτελὴς [ε]ἴ[η] α[ὑτὴ
4. κα]ὶ ὅτι ἂμ πρὸς Καλλίαν διαλ[έγειν] μέλ–
5. [ληι καὶ πρ]ὸς Χαρίαν ὅτι ἂν διαλ[έγειν] μέλλη
6. καὶ ἔ]ργα καὶ ἔπη καὶ ἐ ργασίας· .α   πρ
7. ἔπη λόγον ὃν ἂμ πο[τε] καὶ λέ[γηι · καταδῶ (?)
8. Θεο]δώραν πρὸς Χαρίαν ἀτελῆ αὐτὴ(ν) ε[ἶν]αι
9. [καὶ ἐπι]λαθέσθαι Χαρίαν Θεοδώρα[ς] καὶ το[ῦ π]α[ι–
10. δί]ο(υ) τοῦ Θεοδώρας ἐπιλαθέσ[θ]αι Χαρί[α]ν
11. [καὶ τῆς] κοίτης τῆς [π]ρὸς Θε[οδ]ώρα[ν.]

Jordan in Jameson *et al.* 1993: the opening of side A ([κα]ταδῶ Θε[ο]δώρα[ν] πρὸς [τ]ἠ[ν] παρὰ Φε[ρρε]φάττηι καὶ πρὸς [το(ὺ)ς] ἀτελ[έ]σ[το(υ)ς]·) is no longer tenable.

Side B

1. [ὡς] οὗτος [ἐ]ντ[α]ῦ[θ]α ἀτε[λ]ὴς κ[εῖται, οὔ–]
2. [τως] ἀτέλεστα εἶναι Θεοδώρ[ας πάντα]
3. [κα]ὶ ἔπη καὶ ἔργα τὰ πρὸς Χαρίαν καὶ
4. [πρ]ὸς ἄλλος ἀνθρώπος· καταδ[ῶ Θεόδω–]
5. [ρον π]ρὸς τὸν Ἑρμῆν τὸ<γ> χθόνιον κα[ὶ πρὸς]
6. τὸς ἀ]τελέστος καὶ πρὸς τὴν Τῆθυν. ἀ[τέλεστ–]
7. [α κ]αὶ ἔργα τά πρὸς Χαρίαν καὶ τὸς ἄλλος
8. [ἀνθ]ρώπος καὶ [τὴν] κοίτην τὴν π[ρ]ὸς Χαρίαν
9. [ἐπι]λαθέσ[θ]αι Χαρίαν τῆς κ[οί]της· [Χ]αρ[ίαν]
10. καὶ. το(ῦ) παιδίο(υ) [Θ]ε[οδ]ώ[ρας ἐπιλαθέ –
11. σθαι ἦσ]π[ερ] ἐρᾶ[ι] ἐκε[ῖνος]
12.   γ   ο

SGD 3

Provenance: Greece, Athens, Kerameikos
Dated: Second half of fifth century BC (Peek 1941: 89) or middle of fourth century BC (Jeffery 1955)
Text: Peek 1941: 89–90, no. 1

1. Λυσανίας ἐκ τõ ἀργυ
2. ροκοπίο φυσε͂τέ ς
3. καὶ αὐτὸς καὶ ἑ̄ γυνὲ καί
4. τὰ χρέματα καὶ hότι ἐργά
5. ζεται καὶ τὰ χρέματα

6. καὶ χε͂ρες καὶ πόδε[ς] κα[ὶ νο͂]ς
7. κεφαλε͂ ῥὶν ἀνθεμ . . . ν .
8. γε͂ς hιερᾶς·

SGD 4

Provenance: Greece, Athens, Kerameikos
Dated: Second half of fifth century BC (Peek 1941: 89); middle of fourth
century BC (Jeffery 1955)
Text: Peek 1941: 89–90, no. 2
1. [Λ]υσαν[ίας]
2. [ἐ]κ το͂ ἀργυροκοπ[ί]
3. [ο κ]αὶ γυνε͂ αὐτο͂ [κα]
4. [τα] δὲω καὶ hότι
5. [ἐρ]γάζεται καὶ hότι
6. [πρ]άσει καὶ hότι διαχ[ει]
7. [ρί]ζεται καὶ hό[τι – –]
8. . . . . ι καὶ . . . . ιν – –
9. – – –

SGD 6

Location: Greece, Athens, Kerameikos Museum
Provenance: Greece, Athens, Kerameikos; a disturbed fill of the fourth
century BC in the area of the grave plots of the Potamians and of Hegeso
Dated: Later fifth century / early fourth century BC (Jordan 1985); early
fourth century BC (Peek 1941: 94)
Text: Peek 1941: 94
1. Πυθέας
2. Πύθιππος
3. Ἡγέστρατος
4. Σμιδυρίδης
5. ὁπόσοί ἰσιν
6. ἀντίδικοι
7. Εὐόπηι
8. μετὰ Πυθέο

SGD 9

Location: Greece, Athens, Kerameikos Museum
Provenance: Greece, Athens, Kerameikos; grave 40 near the plot of Antidosis, daughter of Iatrokles

Dated: Early fourth century BC (Jordan 1985)
Text: Trumpf 1958: 94–102
1. Βαρβυριτίδης Ξώφυγος
2. Νικόμαχος Οἰνοκλῆς
3. Μνησίμαχος
4. Χαμαῖος Τεισωνίδης
5. Χαρίσανδρος
6. Δημοκλῆς
7. καὶ ἔ τις ἄλλος μετ' ἐκένοιν
8. ξύνδικός ἐστι ἔ μάρτυς

NGCT 10

Location: Greece, Athens, Kerameikos Museum, inv. JB 6
Provenance: Greece, Athens, Kerameikos; above graves of Eupheros and Lissos
Dated: Early fourth century BC (Jordan)
Text: Costabile 2000: 91

Side A
1. ἐπλυ(σίη) at right angles to the rest of the text, in the middle of the tablet
2. γυναῖκα at right angles to the rest of the text, to the left of the tablet
3. Σ Ε
4. Τελέ{σ}στης
5. Μενεκλῆς
6. Πυρ[ρία]ς Πύρρος ὁ <ὠ>|μησ|τής the last three words upside-down and written right to left

Side B
1. Εὔθυμ[ο]ς
2. ἀν<έ>θεμεν (κ?)αὶ
3. Τιμοκράτης
4. σύνδικ(οι)
5. ἐ<ξ> Ξυπεθῆς
6. Εὔθυμ[ο]ς ὁ
7. Λεπτ[ίνου]

NGCT 11

Location: Greece, Athens, Kerameikos Museum, inv. JB 4

Provenance: Greece, Athens, Kerameikos; above graves of Eupheros and Lissos
Dated: Early fourth century BC (Costabile 2000)
Text: Costabile 2000: 113
Doll: no inscription
Box: Inner side of hinged lid
  Μικίνης
  Καλλίας Ἀντιφάν̣[ης?
  Πεδιεύς ῎Ανδριππος

NGCT 12

Location: Greece, Athens, Kerameikos Museum, inv. JB 4
Provenance: Greece, Athens, Kerameikos; above graves of Eupheros and Lissos
Dated: Early fourth century BC (Costabile 2000)
Text: Costabile 2000: 108
Inner side of base of box inscribed
  Θ̣εοχάρης ὁ κηδεστὴς ὁ Θ<ε>οχάρο(υ)ς
  Σωσί·στρατος, Φιλοχάρης,
  Διοκλῆς καὶ οἱ ἄλλοι ἀντίδικοι.
Right arm of the doll: ΘΥ
Left arm of the doll (Jordan 2000): Θοχάρης (Θ<ε>ο<χ>άρης: Costabile)

NGCT 13

Location: Greece, Athens, Kerameikos Museum, inv. JB 5
Provenance: Greece, Athens, Kerameikos; above graves of Eupheros and Lissos
Dated: Early fourth century BC (Costabile 2000)
Text: Costabile 2000: 101
Inner side of base of box inscribed
1. Θεοζοτίδης
2. Διοφάνης
3. Διόδ<ω>ρος
4. Κ<η>φισοφ<ῶ>ν
Left arm and also outer side of right leg of doll: Θεοζοτίδης
Right arm: Διόδω<ρο>ς
Neck and shoulders from back of head: Δ̣ιόδῳ<ρος>

Outer side of right leg: Διοφάνης
Back and left leg: Κ<η>φισοφ<ῶ>ν

NGCT 24

Location: England, Oxford, Ashmolean Museum, inv. G 514.3
Provenance: Greece, Attica
Dated: Very early fourth century BC (Jordan 1999)
Text: Jordan 1999: 115–17

Side A
1. Εἴ τις ἐμὲ κατέδεσεν
2. ἒ γυνὴ ἢ <ἀ>νὴρ ἒ δ<ο>ῦλος ἒ ἐ̂–
3. λεύθερος ἒ ξένος ἒ ἀσ–
4. ὄ τος ἒ οἰκεῖος ἒ ἀλλώτ–
5. ρτος ἒ ἐπὶ φθόνον τὸν
6. ἐμῖι ἐργασίαι ἒ ἔργοις,
7. εἴ τις ἐμὲ κατέδεσ–
8. εν πρὸς τὸν Ἑρμῆν τὸ–
9. ν ἐριόνιον ἒ πρὸ̀ς τὸν
10. κάτοχον ἒ πρὸς τὸν δό–
11. λιον ἒ ἄλλοθί πο, ἀντι–
12. καταδέσμεύω τὸς ἐχ̣ρ̣θ̣–
13. ὸς ἅπαντας.

Side B
1. Καταδεσμεύω ἀὐτίδικον Δί–
2. ωνα καὶ Γράνικον μὲ ΑΠ[.] Δ?. Ε–
3. ΣΤΑΙ αὐτὸν τοῦ ἐ̣λά[τον]ο (?) μέ–
4. ρος πλείονος ἒ ἐγὼ ἀνεδόμεν.

CHAPTER 4

A new political world

Claire Taylor

This chapter documents and discusses some of the changes in Athenian politics in the fifth and fourth centuries BC: in particular, the changes in political participation. Although questions about participation in democracy have often been asked, scholars have rarely considered whether participation in fourth-century democracy was similar to, or different from, fifth-century democracy. This is partly due to the constraints of the literary evidence – the main focus of historians interested in this question – which have limited discussion to the social composition of a specific institution, or the ideology of participation.[1] This chapter, however, argues that change in political participation not only should be expected during the period of democracy, but also is detectable. Why should participation remain static when there were considerable changes, not only in the institutional setting of democracy, such as pay for office, codification of laws, or organisation of institutions, but also in Athenian society?[2] Social change can be seen in a number of spheres: from changes in funerary culture, or the construction of private houses, to changes in attitudes to wealth and the organisation and payment of liturgies.[3] In addition, demographic decline almost halved the citizen population.[4] It would perhaps be more surprising if these changes did not affect participation in politics to some degree. If the focus is widened

---

[1] See, for example, discussions of the social composition of juries: A. H. M. Jones 1957: 124 (suggesting change between the fifth century and the fourth, but with methodological difficulties); Todd 1990a: 164–7; Markle 1985: 267–71; R. K. Sinclair 1988: 55–60. Ideological constraints are discussed by Carter 1986, but see also the criticisms of this by Cartledge 1987.

[2] For institutional changes in fourth-century democracy, see Rhodes 1979–80: 305–23. Political pay: compare *Ath. Pol.* 24.3 (fifth century) with *Ath. Pol.* 62.2 (fourth century); for juries: *Ath. Pol.* 27.3 (after 462/1); Assembly: *Ath. Pol.* 41.3 (390s). *Nomothetai, nomoi,* and *psephismata*: Lys. 30.2, 25; Andoc. 1.87. Organisational changes in the *boule* (fifty *prutaneis* replaced by nine *proedroi*): *IG* II² 43 (late 390s–379/378); specific duties for *strategoi* created: *Ath. Pol.* 61.1, etc.

[3] For discussion of these phenomena see Morris 1998: 64–70; Rhodes 1993: 551 (on *Ath. Pol.* 47.1 and the decreased usefulness of property qualifications); Davies 1981: 17–24; Gabrielsen 1994: 173–213.

[4] Hansen 1985; B. S. Strauss 1986: 70–86; Akrigg, chapter 2 in this volume.

to include non-literary evidence, it is clear that significant changes did, in fact, occur.

However, assessing change between the fifth century and the fourth is complicated by the nature of the source material and the difficulties of comparing different types of evidence clustered in a limited chronological period. Nonetheless, it should be stressed that there is a large body of evidence concerned with political activity surviving from both centuries which is generally ignored. Prosopographical evidence of those who were politically active under the democracy can reveal much of interest about Athenian society and politics, but is almost completely unexploited in this context. An examination of the citizens who were recorded as politically active reveals that there *are* fundamental changes in the sociology of politics from the fifth century to the fourth.

This article, therefore, examines this prosopographical material. A sample of 2,183 politically active citizens has been analysed for changes in wealth and deme origin between 480 and 322. The sample includes a wide range of activities – office-holders as well as those politically active in other contexts – namely *strategoi, tamiai, bouleutai,* decree-proposers, archons, phylarchs, hipparchs, dikasts, and other (unknown) officials recorded on *pinakia*.[5] These are chosen as they cover a variety of different kinds of political activities in all institutions of public life (i.e. office-holding, Assembly, *boulē,* lawcourts), there is reasonably good evidence for each group, and most groups are represented in both the fifth and the fourth century.[6]

I have chosen to focus on two areas of analysis: the wealth and the deme origin of politically active citizens, because of the relatively large body of evidence for these topics. In both of these areas it is possible to distinguish change, which raises further questions about the role of wealth and regional patterns within Athenian politics. I will briefly outline these changes, before evaluating the historical implications of this evidence.

[5] Develin 1989 provides most prosopographical information on office-holders and decree-proposers (but see reviews by Mattingly (1988/1996–7) for the fifth century and Hansen (1992) for the fourth century). This is supplemented by Kroll 1972 for dikasts and unknown magistrates recorded on *pinakia*. Davies 1981: 151–66 has a convenient list of military officials, and Hansen 1989d lists *rhetores* and *strategoi* of the fourth century.

[6] All except dikasts and the magistrates known from *pinakia* are recorded in both the fifth and fourth centuries. It is important to include these two groups, especially dikasts, to cover the range of political activity. There is no reason to expect a difference in the patterns shown if dikasts are removed: in fact, removal has no effect on the general pattern (minor differences will be highlighted as appropriate). This is in itself interesting: it might be expected that dikasts, who spent between 175 and 225 days a year in court, would be more heavily city-biased than magistrates, who served for a year (Hansen 1999: 186). The opposite, in fact, seems to be the case. Of course, the nature of the magistrates' offices is unknown (it could involve a large volume of work in the city itself).

Table 4.1 *Wealth and political activity in fifth- and fourth-century Athens (n = 2,183).*

Date	Politically active citizens	Wealthy politically active citizens	Wealthy politically active citizens (%)
Fifth century	445 *(445)*	84 *(84)*	19% *(19%)*
Fourth century	1,729 *(1,612)*	184 *(181)*	11% *(11%)*
Undated	9 *(9)*	3 *(3)*	
Total	2,183 *(2,066)*	271 *(268)*	12% *(13%)*

Numbers in brackets show the data excluding dikasts and magistrates recorded on *pinakia*.

Table 4.1 shows the proportion of attested wealthy citizens who are also known to be politically active from both the fifth and fourth centuries. These citizens were recorded in (at least) one of the political activities defined above (although they are only counted once, at their first appearance in the historical record), and are also recorded as belonging to the liturgical class (referred to throughout as 'the wealthy').[7] Taken on its own, Table 4.1 suggests that there were fewer wealthy citizens involved in fourth-century politics compared with fifth-century politics.[8] However, the evidence for wealthy fourth-century citizens is much greater than that for fifth-century citizens (e.g. lists naming trierarchs, lawcourt speeches in inheritance cases); indeed, there is generally more relevant prosopographical evidence from the fourth century than from the fifth (e.g. prytany lists, decrees). Should the smaller proportion of fourth-century wealthy citizens who were politically active therefore be interpreted as a change in the nature of the evidence, or can it be seen as a change in the pattern of participation?

Before this question is discussed further, I want to highlight another possible indication of change. Examination of the demotics of this group

[7] Following Davies's definition of the liturgical class, with a few addenda, such as cavalry members: *APF* xx–xxvii. See also Davies 1981: vi; Spence 1993: 287.

[8] This pattern occurs for most political activities if analysed separately, as well as for the overall pattern. *Strategoi* alone do not show a decrease in the proportion of wealthy citizens in office from the fifth to the fourth century, but an increase (from 34 per cent to 40 per cent). The sample is admittedly small (83 fourth-century *strategoi*, compared with 121 fourth-century decree-proposers and 147 fourth-century *tamiai*), but large enough for the failure to match the general pattern to be significant. The wealthy were likely to have been particularly attracted to the *strategia* in all periods (see Ps. Xen. *Ath. Pol.* 1.3), and a large proportion of citizens recorded as performing multiple trierarchies are also known to have been *strategoi*, implying that the super-rich were attracted to this office. See Gabrielsen 1994: 214–15. Removing the *strategoi* from the sample only makes the change for others who are politically active more striking.

Table 4.2 *Wealthy citizens involved in political activity
recorded in each area in the fifth and fourth centuries.*

	Zone 1	Zone 2	Zone 3	Total
Fifth century	38 *(30.9)*	19 *(14.2)*	19 *(8.2)*	76
% recorded as wealthy (5C)	58%	27%	15%	
Fourth century	42 *(31.4)*	57 *(42.5)*	74 *(31.9)*	173
% recorded as wealthy (4C)	31%	40%	29%	

Numbers in brackets show the data adjusted: see n. 10.

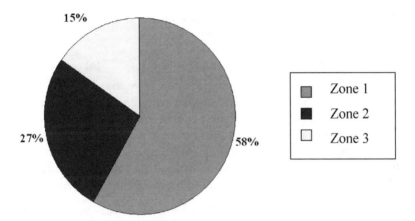

Figure 4.1: Graph showing wealthy citizens involved in political activity in
the fifth century.

of wealthy citizens suggests that there is some kind of regional dimension to participation (the nature of this will be discussed further below).
Table 4.2 (see also Figures 4.1 and 4.2) shows the proportion of wealthy
citizens engaged in political activity in the fifth and fourth centuries with
demotics from three different areas of Attica. Following Hansen 1989b, but
with some modifications, Attica has been divided into three sections: the
city and demes within a couple of hours' walk of the city (called here 'zone
1'); demes within approximately four hours' walk of the city (zone 2); and
demes further away, which take longer than four hours to reach the city

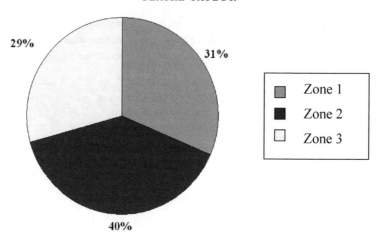

Figure 4.2: Graph showing wealthy citizens involved in political activity in the fourth century.

(zone 3).[9] The first two zones are similar in geographical size and, assuming that bouleutic quotas imitate the distribution of the citizen population across demes, they are similar in citizen population: zone 1 has an aggregate bouleutic quota of 123, and zone 2 has 134, whereas zone 3 has 232. Likewise, demes from zones 1 and 2 record similar numbers of funerary inscriptions which record demotics (429 and 475 respectively), whereas many more are known from demes in zone 3 (776).[10] Table 4.2 (see also Figure 4.1) shows that, in the fifth century, over half of the attested wealthy citizens involved

[9] See Hansen 1989b: 87–8. In his preliminary study, Hansen measured deme distance 'as the crow flies'. I have attempted to take into account terrain, and – as much as possible – road routes. Since there is no comprehensive work on ancient roads, in practice this means measuring distance from the *Karten von Attika* series, a detailed nineteenth-century map, depicting fewer modern-engineered roads than more recent maps. This is obviously not ideal, but, given current knowledge of ancient roads, is a practicable solution. Traill (in the Barrington Atlas) noted that 'modern roads . . . [tend] to follow the course of their ancient predecessors'. This is not always the case, however, and modern routes for motor vehicles (e.g. Vouliagmeni Avenue, which also appears on *KvA*) cannot take advantage of the mountain passes accessible to walkers, e.g. the Panari pass linking southern Attica with the city over Mount Hymettos (see Korres and Tomlinson 2002). For sections of roads in Attica see the articles in Goette 2002; also Petropoulakou and Pentazos 1973, Ober 1985, Vanderpool 1978, and Young 1955. Further discussion of this methodology in C. Taylor 2005.

[10] Where assessable, it seems reasonable to assume that bouleutic quotas are a rough approximation of deme membership and that this bears some relation to the citizen population of a deme. See Gomme 1933: 49–66; Rhodes 1972: 11–12; Whitehead 1986: 22–3; Traill 1975: 56. Bouleutic quota per zone has therefore been used as an adjustment to take into account the relative size of each area. For this reason, when the adjustment is made, the data will be presented both with and without *bouleutai* to avoid double-counting of data. That bouleutic quotas are an acceptable, albeit rough, guide to population distribution across Attica is supported by the close correlation of the number of fourth-century funerary inscriptions recording demotic with bouleutic quotas of individual demes.

in political activity came from demes near the city (zone 1). This is in marked contrast with the fourth century (Figure 4.2): many more citizens from non-city demes can be seen to be politically active. This implies that, within the sample of wealthy citizens, the proportion of those who were politically active and had demotics from, or near, the city decreases from the fifth century to the fourth, while the proportion of those with demotics from outside the city area increases.

The prosopographical evidence, therefore, appears to suggest that a smaller proportion of wealthy citizens was involved in politics in the fourth century than had previously been the case, and that a smaller proportion of the wealthy who were involved in politics had demotics from the city area. On the face of it, this implies that a city-based elite were over-represented in politics in the fifth century, and that citizens from a wider selection of Attic demes were more visibly involved in fourth-century politics. This would represent a substantial change in the sociology of political activity and the practice of politics in the two centuries, but how far can this evidence be used in this way? We can ask the same question as was asked in respect to changes in patterns of wealth: are these patterns simply a product of the changing nature of the evidence from the fifth century to the fourth? Or do these patterns imply real change in democratic society and politics?

WEALTH, POLITICS, AND PROSOPOGRAPHICAL PROBLEMS

Using prosopographical evidence in this way requires some evaluation, and it is necessary to discuss the nature of our sample. First, it is important to state that more prosopographical information survives from the fourth century than from the fifth, so more citizens – politically active or otherwise – are known from this time (compare Tables 4.1 and 4.2). This reflects the increase in epigraphic evidence dating to the period, from which most (although not all) prosopographical records are obtained.[11] However, this is not the whole story: within the data collected there is a varied chronological distribution of different kinds of political activities. Although the fourth century (particularly the second half of it) provides many records, it is by no

Arguably, however, this is the case only for the fourth century, the period from which the quotas survive. This means that it is impossible to extrapolate the surviving quotas back to the fifth century, without suggesting some kind of reorganisation (Hansen *et al.* 1990: 44 n. 25 suggests 403 as a likely option). It must be noted that there is no direct evidence for such a reorganisation, but arguably none would be expected; it is only through the epigraphic evidence of the late fourth century that we know of the reorganisation of 307, and few prytany lists survive before the early fourth century. See Traill 1975: 25–9.

[11] See Hedrick 1999: 400–4; also Oliver 2000b: 15–18.

means the best-attested period for all the different types of political activity examined here. *Tamiai* and *strategoi*, for example, are much better attested in the fifth century than in the fourth, whereas *bouleutai* and decree proposers are better attested in the fourth century than in the fifth. This is due to the types of records which survive from both centuries (schematically, treasury accounts and peace treaties from the fifth century; prytany lists and decrees from the fourth). So even though, in the overall distribution, there are more fourth-century records than fifth-century records, within the sample there are some types of political activities which are better attested in the fifth century than in the fourth; we should not be overly dismissive of the fifth-century material.

The chronological distribution of the sample is important for comparing my sample of politically active citizens with the wealthy citizens recorded in *APF*. The increase in epigraphic evidence in the second half of the fourth century results in an increase, not only of prosopographic information about these politically active citizens, but also of attested liturgists (i.e. all wealthy citizens, not just those recorded as being politically active): approximately 65 per cent of the entries in *APF* are, broadly speaking, from the second half of the fourth century.[12] That there is an increase in absolute terms in the number of attested wealthy citizens in the fourth century, which does not seem to carry over into wealthy citizens who are also politically active, at least demonstrates that there is sufficient reason to investigate further.

THE CHANGING ROLE OF WEALTH IN ATHENIAN POLITICS

The increase in the number of attested wealthy citizens is closely paralleled by an increase in the number of politically active citizens, suggesting that the survival of evidence is not the only factor involved in the patterns highlighted here.[13] But if the pattern shown by the evidence presented in Table 4.1 is to be taken seriously, it must be viewed within the context of changes in the role of wealth in Athenian society. To what extent are these related to the changes in prosopographical evidence highlighted above?

There are numerous hints in our sources that there were various changes in attitudes to wealth and political activity in this period. For example, *Ath. Pol.* 47.1 states that property qualifications were no longer used to

---

[12] See Davies 1981: 28–34.
[13] Comparison of the percentage of my sample with that of *APF* in a specific time period (here using the *APF* generations E–I (466–301)) shows that both sets of data are well correlated: the chronological distribution of my sample closely mirrors that of *APF*.

limit access to office by the end of the fourth century: *tamiai* were no longer confined to the ranks of the *pentakosiomedimnoi*, although the law that required them to be *pentakosiomedimnoi* remained in force.[14] This presumably indicates that property qualifications had fallen out of line with economic realities, and so were no longer deemed to be an important indicator of wealth or political ability. But this is not the only indicator of change. From c. 420, and throughout the fourth century, there is an increase in the number and grandeur of grave monuments erected in Athens and Attica. Since funerary monuments for private individuals were uncommon in the fifth century, this should be considered to be a change, not only in the funerary culture of Attica, but also in the spending habits of fourth-century citizens.[15] Additionally, citizens in the fourth century were increasingly encouraged by demes to use their wealth for the benefit of the community: sponsoring choruses, building bridges, repairing public buildings, etc.[16] A change in the language of donation is discernable epigraphically c. 350, encouraging competition among liturgists to give to their deme through honorific titles and decrees awarding *philotimia*.[17]

These examples demonstrate that the role of wealth in fourth-century society was undergoing certain changes, and this is also implied by the prosopographical evidence. This prosopographical evidence, collated in Table 4.1, suggests that proportionally fewer wealthy citizens were involved in politics in the fourth century than in the fifth. To explore this further, we must ask whether the fifth-century wealthy were no longer wealthy in the fourth century, but were still politically active, or whether they remained wealthy but played a reduced role in politics.

CHANGES IN THE DISTRIBUTION OF WEALTH?

Davies observed that many prominent fifth-century families are unheard of in the fourth century: there is little evidence for the continuation of fifth-century political dynasties, such as the families of Pericles, Cimon, or Andocides in the fourth century, and it is usually presumed that they had died off.[18] Other families are known still to exist but seem to play

---

[14] See Rhodes 1993: 551, 603.   [15] Morris 1998: 64–70, Meyer 1993: 105, Stears 2000: 45–52.

[16] *IG* ii² 1198 (*choregia* at Aixone); *IG* ii² 1191 (bridge at Eleusis); Vanderpool 1969: 6–7 (repairing *palaistra* at Kephisia). See Whitehead 1986: 234–51.

[17] Whitehead 1983: 63. See also R. Osborne 1990: 276–7; Whitehead 1993: 72–3.

[18] *APF* 460, 311, 31 respectively; Davies 1981: 84–5. However, the family of Cimon does reappear in the late fourth century: Miltiades (VII) of Lakiadai, presumably a descendant of the fifth-century family, is known as an *oikistēs* to the Adriatic in 324 (*IG* ii² 1629: Rhodes and Osborne 2003: no. 100). That

no role in politics, such as the family of Alcibiades.[19] The reasons for the disappearance of these families is uncertain, but it is likely that some would have been destroyed: the losses of plague and war would have hit some families hard. Even so, individual families may have avoided complete disappearance by making opportune marriage alliances or adopting heirs.[20] Davies observes that marriages between politically prominent families (such as those between Alcibiades and Hipparete, or Cimon and Isodice) are regular in the fifth century, but almost unknown in the fourth, though this may, in part, reflect the differing concerns of the source material, as Cox points out.[21] However, these differences should not be overstated: marriage strategies were certainly used in the fourth century, as well as in the fifth, as is demonstrated by the lengthy family disputes recorded in forensic oratory. The family of Dicaiogenes, for example, demonstrates that political as well as economic factors influenced marriage decisions over a number of generations.[22]

Marriage and adoption, therefore, could have been used to keep alive family interests – to ensure that property was inherited. Although such strategies would not have been able to circumvent all possible disasters within the life-cycle of any particular family (for example, if many members of one family were affected by disease at the same time), their use implies that families would have at least tried to ensure that their *oikos* did not cease to exist and that their property was passed on.[23] The suggestion that many wealthy families died off at the end of the fifth century should then be questioned: the fact that families are not heard of again in the fourth century does not necessarily mean that they did not exist. There may be other possible reasons for the disappearance of these families from the

the family was still considered of a high social class (if not wealthy) must be demonstrated by the marriages of Miltiades' daughter Euthydice, first to Ophellas, the later tyrant of Cyrene, and then to Demetrios Poliorcetes. However, as Davies points out 'not a single *leitourgōn* is securely identifiable within the family' in the fourth century. See Davies 1971: 309–11.

[19] Attested descendants: Alcibiades' granddaughter Hipparete (II) married Phanocles (I), son of Andromachos of Leukonoion (recorded on gravestones *IG* ii² 7400, 6746). Alcibiades, son of Phanocles of Leukonoion, recorded on *IG* ii² 6719, is likely to be their son, as is Aristion (*IG* ii² 6723). The son of Aristion is also commemorated on a grave-marker, although his name is lost (*IG* ii² 6722). However, he could be the Phanocles (II) recorded on *IG* ii² 5434 as the husband of Cleo (daughter of Cleoneos of Aixone). All of the above grave-markers were found in the Kerameikos. Nothing further is known about any of them. See *APF* 21–2.

[20] See Rubinstein 1993: 62–4; 1999: 55–61.

[21] Davies 1981: 119–20, Cox 1998: 216–29. See also Humphreys 1993: 25–6. For the incredibly complex world of intermarriage between fifth-century politically prominent citizens see *APF* table 1.

[22] Isae. 5. For discussion see Cox 1998: 10–15.

[23] Rubinstein 1999: 48–9. For the political effects of adoption (in a Roman Republican context) see Hopkins and Burton 1983: 48–50, 70–4, 103–7.

record. Aristotle, *Rhetoric* 1390b29–31, mentions the degeneration of certain aristocratic families 'into maniacs . . . fools and dullards' (εἰς μανικώτερα ἤθη . . . εἰς ἀβελτερίαν καὶ νωθρότητα), which may perhaps imply that the families of Pericles and Cimon lasted longer than the source material behind *APF* can account for.

It is plausible, therefore, to suggest that some families may have decided not to be involved in politics; others may have no longer been able to contribute financially to the polis and so are undetectable as being members of the wealthy elite. The descendants of Alcibiades, for example, could fall into either category. Known only through their grave-markers (see n. 19), they may have been prevented from pursuing a political career through association with their discredited ancestor. On the other hand, the level of their family wealth may not have been as high as it had been in the fifth century: Lysias 14.31 and Isocrates 16.46 hint at financial difficulties.[24] Though Alcibiades may be thought of as an exceptional character, what we know of his later family history does suggest that there can be a range of possibilities for the disappearance of wealthy fifth-century political families from our sources in the fourth century.

If fifth-century wealthy families were still politically active in the fourth century, but were no longer contributing to the polis through liturgies, this may suggest that significant changes in wealth distribution occurred during the fourth century. It is impossible to test this directly on individual families, but comparative evidence of the effects of demographic change is worth considering in this context because such studies demonstrate some of the ways in which intense population decline (e.g. that which occurred at the end of the fifth century) can affect the remaining population. However, instead of heralding a crisis in agriculture, society, or politics, demographic decline can bring benefits for survivors.[25] One such benefit may be a change in the distribution of wealth: for example, a significant proportion of land coming into different ownership, perhaps even a more egalitarian distribution of wealth with a higher percentage of the surviving population able to own some land. Studies of the patterns of land-holding in fourth-century Attica by Osborne and Foxhall, reinterpreted by Morris, suggest that the distribution of land was remarkably egalitarian in comparison with other ancient Mediterranean societies (such as in Roman Egypt).[26]

---

[24] Although Lysias 14.7–8 demonstrates that Alcibiades' son (also Alcibiades) was wealthy enough to be in the cavalry in c. 395. See *APF* 21.

[25] See Akrigg, chapter 2 in this volume.

[26] Foxhall 1992: 156–9; R. Osborne 1992: 23–4. See also Foxhall 2002: 211; Morris 2000: 140–1.

In an ideal world it would be useful to assess whether land-ownership in fourth-century Athens was more egalitarian than in the fifth century, but this is very difficult due to the constraints of the evidence, and the problems of comparing similar types of economic transaction in both time periods. However, there are indications that there was a change in wealth distribution at this time, at least at the top of the social scale: estimates of the size of the liturgy-paying class show that the increase of liable citizens from the fifth century to the fourth (from approximately 700 to between 1,200 and 1,500) was accompanied by a decrease in the amount that individual citizens paid (from a talent per year in the fifth century to 3,000 drachmas in the fourth).[27] Therefore, the levels of wealth required for paying liturgies had halved, but the number of people eligible to pay had doubled, implying that fewer citizens could afford – or chose – to pay fifth-century levels. On the one hand, this may, of course, be hiding a significant number of liturgy-avoiders: the fourth-century legislation concerned with liturgies repeatedly attempts to define who should be paying, implying that this was a controversial issue among the wealthy and the *demos* at large.[28] However, it may also indicate that the rich were experiencing changes in their relative levels of wealth: they were less well-off than their fifth-century (great-)grandfathers.[29]

Another area which was affected by change was land ownership abroad: the wealth of Athenian citizens was potentially seriously affected by the closing off of opportunities for owning land overseas at the end of the fifth century. The loss of empire and of Athenian control of the Aegean would necessarily have reduced Athenian ability to invest in, and exploit, land outside Attica. On the one hand, the wealthy in particular would have been affected by such a measure: the surviving evidence points to extensive exploitation of overseas land by wealthy citizens, such as Oionias or Diodotos.[30] However, all Athenians could own land abroad; the lot was certainly used to distribute land in cleruchies, though presumably

---

[27] Gabrielsen 1994: 177–82, 215; *APF* xxix; Davies 1981: 24.

[28] For the reforms of the trierarchy proposed by Periandros in 358/7 and Demosthenes in 340, see Gabrielsen 1994: 182–212. For liturgy-avoiders, see Gabrielsen 1987; Christ 1990.

[29] Davies 1981: 100–5, 167–8, observes a sharp decline in the number of Athenian competitors in chariot races after the end of the fifth century. He suggests that chariot-racing no longer brought with it the political rewards that it had done in earlier periods, but it may also be because fewer wealthy citizens had the massive resources to pay for it. However, it is arguable that Alcibiades' well-publicised victories somewhat inflate the peak at the end of the fifth century; if he is removed from the sample, the decline does not appear quite so strong.

[30] *IG* i³ 422; Lys. 32. Oionias is not alone among those recorded on the Attic stelai owning land overseas: Adeimantos had land in Thasos (*IG* i³ 426, lines 45–6), and property in Abydos belonging to an unknown owner was also sold (*IG* i³ 427, line 78). See further Cargill 1994: 192–6; Figueira 1991: 57–62; Schmitz 1988: 84–92.

additional land – perhaps that lying outside of the allotted area – could be bought by individual citizens, which, of course, would enable wealthy citizens to enrich themselves further.[31]

THE POLITICAL INACTIVITY OF THE WEALTHY?

Socio-economic changes in Attica are clearly important, but they need not be the only factor behind the changes revealed by the prosopographical evidence. If fifth-century citizens retained their wealth into the fourth century, but were no longer politically active, an explanation related to politics may be more appropriate. Forensic oratory argues for a culture of quietism or non-participation among certain sections of the wealthy. The wealthy are portrayed as generous liturgy-payers who mind their own business and do not meddle in politics (e.g. Lysias 19.55–8). Although this is certainly a *topos*, it does show that such a *topos* was an acceptable and effective characterisation. The motivation for such spending was not, as these wealthy citizens argue, political gain, but to head off malicious prosecution and to stand the citizen in good stead with the *demos* (Lysias 25.13); that is, they are doing their duty as wealthy citizens in society.[32] The regularity of this *topos* suggests that it was effective, and implies that non-participation in politics by the wealthy was, to some extent, acceptable to the *demos*. However, it is difficult to distinguish how widespread such a practice was from its appearance in lawcourt speeches.

Quietism is most detectable in the extant source material in the early fourth century, and it should be asked whether there is a link between the non-participation of the wealthy in fourth-century politics and the stasis at the end of the Peloponnesian War. Were wealthy citizens opting out of fourth-century democracy (at least early fourth-century democracy) because they did not want to participate; or were they, in effect, opted out, because they were politically unable to participate? The association of the cavalry with the Thirty, and the men of the Piraeus with the democrats (Xenophon *Hellenica* 2.4.10, 24), hints at political division along social or

---

[31] E.g. Lalonde *et al.* 1991: P4, concerned with the selling of land on Lemnos. See Cargill 1994: 194–6. It is difficult to know how to interpret Eutheros, the returning cleruch (Xen. *Socratic Memoirs* 2.8.1–6). Xenophon portrays him as being reluctant to work as a farm bailiff, although advised by Socrates to do so, and he is normally thought of as poverty-stricken. But was poverty the reason for his departure from Athens in the first place? He says he received no inheritance from his father, but was this because of poverty, or part of an arrangement which saw Eutheros taking up land in a cleruchy, designed to prevent the splitting of the estate among many sons? Eutheros may represent an influx of poor citizens returning to Attica after the Peloponnesian War, but the passage is notoriously slippery and this is certainly not necessary

[32] Carter 1986: 110–13, but see Cartledge 1987: 63, who suggests that the reason for this is to avoid being cast as anti-democratic.

class lines at the end of the fifth century, and certain sections of wealthy society may have been viewed with distrust or suspicion after the restoration of democracy.[33] These citizens may have become alienated, either because they themselves no longer wanted to play a role, or because their previous behaviour – despite the amnesty – prevented them from doing so: the suitability of Leodamas for archon was questioned because he had supported the Thirty; furthermore, his replacement, Euandros, was similarly accused, although he managed to pass his *dokimasia*.[34]

There is considerable evidence, therefore, for changes in the role of wealth in Athenian society from the fifth century to the fourth, and the prosopographical evidence fits into this framework (Table 4.1). But this is not the only conclusion to be drawn: Tables 4.1–4.2 and Figures 4.1–4.2 show that there is also a change in the deme origins of the politically active wealthy, which raises questions about migration and the impact of democracy on the Attic countryside.

REGIONAL PATTERNS? DEME MEMBERSHIP, DEMOTICS, AND MIGRATION

One of the most striking changes in fourth-century politics is the apparent increase in wealthy, politically active citizens with non-city demotics. In the fifth century, a substantial proportion of these citizens were from demes within the city area: over half of those recorded in the fifth century (Figure 4.1). This shows that a city elite was over-represented in fifth-century politics. Other evidence supports this: if the demotics of citizens named on ostraka (by definition a fifth-century activity) are compared, a similar pattern can be seen. Figure 4.3 shows (again assuming that bouleutic quotas imitate the distribution of the citizen population across demes) that over half of the citizens named on ostraka are from demes in or near the city, whereas those from demes further away received proportionally fewer votes. The citizens recorded here can almost certainly be considered politically prominent, for although some votes may have been cast for 'non-political' reasons, the vast majority must have been for citizens who made some kind of political impact. That over half of these prominent citizens came from the city area also implies that a city elite was over-represented in politics.

Figure 4.2, on the other hand, shows a larger proportion of wealthy, politically active citizens with demotics from outside of the city in the fourth century. Approximately two-thirds of these citizens have demotics

---

[33] The cavalry for instance. See Spence 1993: 216–24; Low 2002: 102–22.
[34] Lys. 26.10–15; Arist. *Rhetoric* 1400a 32–6. See also Pl. *Epinomis* 7.325e.

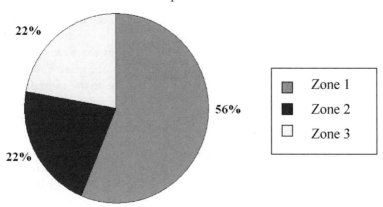

22%

22%

56%

Zone 1
Zone 2
Zone 3

Figure 4.3: Graph showing the distribution of demotics of candidates for ostracism.

from demes in zones 2 or 3. Does this mean that citizens from non-city demes had replaced the city-based elite of the fifth century in politics in the fourth century?

Not necessarily. The most simple explanation for a change in the deme origins of politically active citizens would be migration, that citizens had moved to Athens after their ancestors had been allocated to a deme under Cleisthenes, perhaps in great numbers during the Peloponnesian War (Thucydides 2.14–16). Because deme membership was hereditary, citizens kept the demotic of their fathers wherever in Attica they lived, meaning that demotics potentially indicate nothing about place of residence.[35] However, assessing residence patterns is complicated, and the evidence of funerary inscriptions should not be over-interpreted. Their geographical distribution may be more connected with excavation patterns, or with the ideology of display, than with widespread migration in itself.[36] Motivations for commemoration may vary, and choosing the right type of display seems to have been important. Demes such as Rhamnous and Kephale, for example, have very different commemoration practices, perhaps related to the relative numbers of non-deme members visiting these places: Rhamnous had a garrison, harbour, and temple; Kephale did not.[37] Moreover, commemoration does not give direct information about the place of residence, permanency of residence, or even place of death of the deceased; these have to be suggested based on a number of factors (Are the demotics local? How many generations of family are recorded on the monument? etc.). It is,

[35] Unless they are found in a specific context (most often a funerary context), where they are sometimes taken to demonstrate migration from (usually) deme to city, see Gomme 1933: 44–5; Damsgaard-Madsen 1988: 60–3; Hansen 1989b: 80–1.
[36] Meyer 1993: 115–16; Whitehead 1986: 353–5.   [37] R. Osborne 1991: 239–46.

therefore, difficult to determine how long (if at all) a citizen lived in the vicinity of his grave monument, or even whether he died there. Highly visible, and therefore prestigious cemeteries, such as the Kerameikos, are likely to attract certain types of display, meaning that the grave monuments found here, in particular, do not necessarily represent the mortality patterns of the local population: Dexileos of Thorikos (to give a well-known example) certainly did not die in Athens, yet his monument is prominently displayed in the Kerameikos on the junction of two roads. Of course, it is unknown whether he lived in Athens or Thorikos (or even elsewhere).

Using grave-markers as a test of migratory patterns can therefore be problematic, but other factors suggest that there was no desertion of the countryside in the fourth century. Demes continued in their political, cultural, and religious importance; indeed, the evidence for deme life is more abundant in the fourth century than in the fifth.[38] Fourth-century *choregoi* chose to celebrate their victories in city competitions in their own demes, implying that the deme was considered an important arena for such display.[39] Moreover, wealthy citizens in particular could afford to maintain strong links with the city and their deme. Owning property in both places was probably common for the wealthy.[40] The population of Attica was, in all likelihood, fairly mobile, but citizens also retained close contact with their deme (Demosthenes 57.10); being a representative on the *boulē*, for example, presumably required near permanent residence in the city for a year if the office was to be seriously performed (although see Demosthenes 22.35–7 or *Ath. Pol.* 30.6 for hints that this was not always the case), but it also promoted personal links with the deme, and provided a connection between the political life of the city and that of the demes.

Migration, though significant, cannot be the only explanation for the pattern of political participation which appears in the fourth century (Figure 4.2). Mass permanent migration, as is the impression given from uncritical observation of the funerary evidence, would require massive socioeconomic change in Athenian life and, furthermore, raises questions about the economic activities of the migrants. There is no evidence to suggest that fourth-century citizens were no longer, or less, involved in agricultural activity after they had moved to the city: the opposite in fact seems to be

---

[38] See Whitehead 1986: 41.
[39] *IG* ii² 3101. See Whitehead 1986: 234–5; Wilson 2000: 244–52. However, N. Jones 2004: 155–6 questions whether this was always the case (i.e. that *IG* ii² 3091, from Aixone, is an exception).
[40] E.g. Demosthenes of Paiania (Din. 1.69); Timotheus of Anaphlystos: Piraeus (Dem. 49.22); Timarchus of Sphettos: a house near the Acropolis (Aeschin. 1.97); Themistocles of Phrearrhioi: Melite. See Gomme 1933: 39 n. 4; Hansen 1989b: 80; Travlos 1988: 121.

the case, with evidence of agricultural practices spreading to marginal areas in the fourth century.[41] Nor can the migrants be seen to be increasingly involved in city-based economic activities. A model which requires a great degree of urbanisation does not fit well with the agrarian nature of Attic society, where citizens had strong ties to their ancestral deme. Nevertheless, migration may play some role in the pattern shown by the prosopographical evidence. Migration from the country to the city did occur and the citizen population was mobile: why else would the deme assembly of Halimous be held in Athens, if it could not attract a reasonable number of deme members there? But even here, most (*hoi pleistoi*) of the demesmen lived in Halimous itself, and so left the meeting before the business was complete to return there (Demosthenes 57.10).

Even if migration was a major feature of fourth-century Athenian life, the increased proportion of citizens from demes outside the city area during this period can still be seen as a significant change. If they had all moved to Athens, if they were all residents of the city, Figures 4.1 and 4.2 would still imply that a different set of citizens was involved in fourth-century politics. Citizens from all over Attica were always involved in political activity: in the fifth century this was true to some extent, but in the fourth century a higher proportion of citizens from non-city demes was involved in politics than had previously been the case.

THE DECLINE OF THE CITY ELITE?

The prosopographical evidence therefore raises a number of issues. It describes the sociology of political activity in the fourth century as significantly different from that of the fifth, where fewer wealthy citizens are recorded as politically active and a greater proportion of citizens with non-city demotics were politically active. Fifth-century politics seems to be dominated by a prominent city-based elite which is simply not detectable in the fourth century.

The reasons for the appearance of a city elite are important for understanding why there is a change. The prominence of a fifth-century city elite may not necessarily be due to a deliberate control of politics at the expense of other citizens, despite the attempts of the Thirty to reduce the franchise to just those wealthy city-based citizens (Xenophon, *Hellenica* 2.3.51). The fourth-century widening of participation away from this group may be, in part, a reaction to the oligarchy, but other factors which would have

[41] Terracing on Hymettos and Atene: Bradford 1957: 31–4 and plate 8; Lohmann 1993: 226–9.

promoted a city elite should be considered. Candidates for certain types of office, for example, may have been more likely to come from demes in or near the city. Comparison of offices which were elected with those selected by lot indicates that candidates with demotics from in or near the city outnumber those with demotics from other areas of Attica in elected offices, but not in sortitive offices. This implies that the process of being elected may have favoured candidates from certain areas, perhaps because members of the city elite were more likely to put themselves forward as candidates in elections. Furthermore, voters from city demes may be more likely to outnumber those from other demes, and they may have voted for candidates prominent in their deme or prominent in the city itself. Whatever the reasons behind the difference, it is clear that the use of the lot opened up politics to a wider group than those who were members of the city elite.

MORE NON-WEALTHY CITIZENS IN POLITICS?

If the fourth century saw a decline in the political dominance of the city elite, and proportionally fewer wealthy citizens involved in politics, it follows that increasing numbers of non-wealthy citizens were politically active. However, it is impossible to focus directly on non-wealthy citizens due to the lack of positive evidence for this group: presence of wealth is demonstrable, if dependent on the survival of source material, but absence of wealth is impossible to demonstrate prosopographically. The surviving documentation of liturgy-payers is simply not sufficiently comprehensive to enable us to claim that if there is no positive evidence for a citizen's being a liturgist, he is not a liturgist.[42] And that is even before any attempts to assess other claims, or accusations, of poverty are made, such as those found in forensic oratory (e.g. Demosthenes 18.126–31). However, the prosopographical evidence has the potential to enable questions about non-wealthy citizens to be asked. A name on a prytany list at least gives a geographical origin (if it survives with demotic), a political function (as a member of the *boulē*), or a social context (having been voted honours). It may be impossible to distinguish the wealth status of individuals from such limited information, but equally, all known politically active citizens cannot be wealthy. Wealth status is more likely to be attested in the fourth century than in the fifth, which suggests that a high degree of significance should be placed

---

[42] *Contra* Reed 2003, who assumes that the absence of evidence for wealth of maritime traders means they are consistently poor.

on the observation that fewer wealthy citizens are known to be politically active. Although absolute proportions of wealthy citizens involved in politics are unobtainable, the evidence implies that more non-wealthy citizens are involved in politics in the fourth century than had previously been the case. According to the prosopographic evidence, non-wealthy citizens played an increasingly active role in democratic politics. This is a highly significant observation, and has important implications for interpreting fourth-century society and politics.

A NEW POLITICAL WORLD?

There may be a connection between the decrease in the proportion of wealthy citizens visible in politics and a greater degree of non-wealthy citizens participating. Wealthy citizens may have considered certain types of political activity debased by the involvement of more non-wealthy citizens, such as may have occurred with the office of *tamias* (*Ath. Pol.* 47.1).[43] However, the decrease in the proportion of wealthy citizens involved in politics should not be overstated: 11 per cent of the sample of politically active citizens in the fourth century are known to be wealthy (see Table 4.1), which may be approaching three times as many wealthy citizens as in the population as a whole.[44] Although the wealthy are less politically active in the fourth century than in the fifth century, they still play a disproportionately large role in fourth-century politics.

Even if this is the case, the larger proportion of non-wealthy citizens involved in political activity in the fourth century demonstrates that Athenian democracy of this period was able not only to appeal to, but positively to include, a whole range of citizens who did not participate in the fifth century (or, at least, not in large numbers). The fourth-century democracy was in this way fundamentally different from that of the fifth century. There is a real possibility that the size and improved economic position of the fourth-century population prompted a higher percentage of the citizen population to participate in political life.

The fourth-century increase in political activity of citizens from the whole of Attica was a counter to the city-based elite of the fifth century, breaking down their hold on fifth-century politics. The fourth-century democracy was, by contrast, much more inclusive. Examining the sociology

---

[43] Additionally, the social composition of *tamiai* may have been affected by the creation of new financial offices. See Aeschin. 3.25; Mitchel 1973: 190–2; Humphreys 1985: 201–14.

[44] If 1,200–1,500 liturgists were needed each year for the system to function in a citizen population of 30,000, approximately 4 per cent of the population can be considered wealthy.

of the *demos* through the prosopographical evidence allows the study of Athenian democracy to be shifted in focus. Previous assessments of the institutional context of democracy have suggested that the fourth-century political system was more moderate, 'tempered . . . with efficiency', somehow less democratic.[45] Analysis of the personnel of political activity, by contrast, suggests that the fourth-century democracy was, in terms of the participation of its citizens, more 'radical' than fifth-century democracy, with a wider cross-section of the citizenry involved.

Furthermore, it may even be possible to connect the changing sociology of the *demos* with changes in decision-making. Fourth-century military policy, for example, arguably concentrated on the defence of the Attic countryside, with border forts, watchtowers, and signal relay stations being built, alongside changes in the leadership, training, and recruitment of the army.[46] It would not be implausible to suggest that citizens with demotics from the Attic countryside, who were increasingly involved in politics in the fourth century, had an effect on policy and decision-making in the democracy, at least in this instance. The prosopographical evidence shows that fundamental changes occurred in fourth-century democracy. Participation in politics was not static, but dynamic, affected by a range of social, economic, and political factors. The fifth-century democracy was dominated by a city elite, but this city elite was much less visible in the fourth century, enabling a larger proportion of non-wealthy citizens, and those from non-city demes, to be politically involved. In comparison with the democracy of the fifth century, fourth-century Attica was a new political world.

[45] Rhodes 1979–1980: 314. See also Ostwald 1986: 509–24; Hansen 1999: 297–304. Discussed by Ober 1989b: 22 and, in a broader context, Davies 1995: 29–36.

[46] E.g. *Ath. Pol.* 61, 42.3–5. Ober 1985: 89–100, 195–203. See also Harding 1988, with reply from Ober 1989a.

CHAPTER 5

Cultural change, space, and the politics of commemoration in Athens

Julia L. Shear

For much of the fifth century, the Acropolis, visible from all over Athens, remained the very centre of the city: her most important sanctuary, the location for displaying decrees, laws, and lists of offerings and tribute, the prime place for erecting a large dedication but also for making a simple one, a good spot for a public war memorial, and the particular focus of the city's most important festival, the Panathenaia. Other areas had more limited functions: for example, the Sanctuary of Dionysus as sacred space, the *Demosion Sema* as burial ground for the war dead and other notables, and the Pnyx as home of the *ekklesia*. The Agora, meanwhile, remained a multipurpose public space: the location of the *boulē* and the *archons*, but also of the city's market, its racetrack, and a building commemorating victories over the Persians and other enemies. Despite all this activity, the Agora was default public space and not the focus of attention. This situation changed dramatically between 410 and 390 BC. At that time, the market square suddenly became the focus of attention and was remade into the space of the democratic citizen as one part of the democrats' larger process of responding to the oligarchic revolutions of the Four Hundred and the Thirty. This remaking of the Agora was also accompanied by a revolution in the city's practices of commemoration. The emphasis ceased to be on the Athenians as a corporate group and, instead, highly successful individual leaders were now the focus of commemoration. With this change came also a new type of

This essay has developed out of my larger work on the Athenians' reactions to the oligarchic regimes at the end of the fifth century. For much help and advice, I am indebted to the other members of the AHRB Anatomy of Cultural Revolution Project: R. Osborne, S. D. Goldhill, E. K. Irwin, B. Akrigg, C. Taylor, and R. Tordoff. Thanks are also due to the participants in the conference 'The Anatomy of Cultural Revolution in Athens' as well as to S. D. Lambert. For permission to study material in their care, I would like to thank Ch. Kritzas, the emeritus director of the Epigraphical Museum in Athens, his assistant Ch. Karapa-Molizani, and J. Jordan, the secretary of the Agora Excavations. The Faculty of Classics, University of Cambridge, and King's College, Cambridge, together provided a wonderful place in which to do the work leading to this essay. Any remaining mistakes are, of course, my own.

statue, the honorary portrait, and a new place for erecting such statues, the Agora. Despite the importance of these processes for our understanding of the development of the market square, scholars have not previously focused on this sharp shift in patterns of use and commemoration, nor have they connected it with the Athenians' responses to oligarchy. In this chapter, I focus on one aspect of this larger project of restoring democracy after oligarchy, the changes in the politics of space and commemoration in the Agora between 410 and 390. By the end of this period, the market square was made into a new and heavily civic space, changes which then set the pattern for the area's subsequent development in the fourth century and the Hellenistic period.

ATHENS BETWEEN 430 AND 420 BC

The extent of these changes in the Athenian cityscape is most clear if we look at its development at two points: first between 430 and 420 and then in 390. In 430, just after the start of the Peloponnesian War, the city was at the end of an intense period of construction focused on the Acropolis and its immediate slopes (Figure 5.1).[1] On the Acropolis, the Parthenon had just been finished; it was dedicated in 438 and its pediments were finished in 433/2.[2] There was no need yet for any repairs or alterations. The Propylaia was also in use, even though work had stopped in 433/2 and the final detailing would never be done.[3] Contemporary with the Propylaia project were the enlargement and sheathing of the Nike Bastion to the west and the construction of the foundations for the marble Ionic temple.[4] Work had evidently progressed far enough on the Bastion for the decree authorising the temple and other construction to be set in place against the west face of the double anta located at the northwest corner of the Propylaia's southwest wing.[5] To the east of the Propylaia, the Bronze Athena by Phidias, better known to modern scholars as the 'Athena Promachus', was not more than thirty years old and had been under construction in the

---

[1] For the bibliography of the monuments on the Acropolis and the south slope, see Travlos 1971 with Hurwit 1999: 313–18.

[2] *IG* i³ 436–51, 453–60; Philoch. *FGrHist* 328 F121.

[3] *IG* i³ 462–6; Plut. *Pericles* 13.12; Heliod. *FGrHist* 373 F1 and Philoch. *FGrHist* 328 F36, both cited by Harp., s.v. προπύλαια ταῦτα.

[4] The northwest corner of the temple was bonded into the masonry sheathing of the bastion, and the western and northern foundations of the temple match the courses of the bastion; Miles 1980: 323–4. The temple must have been designed before the foundations could be laid.

[5] *IG* i³ 35; I. M. Shear 1999: 123–4; W. B. Dinsmoor 1923: 320–1.

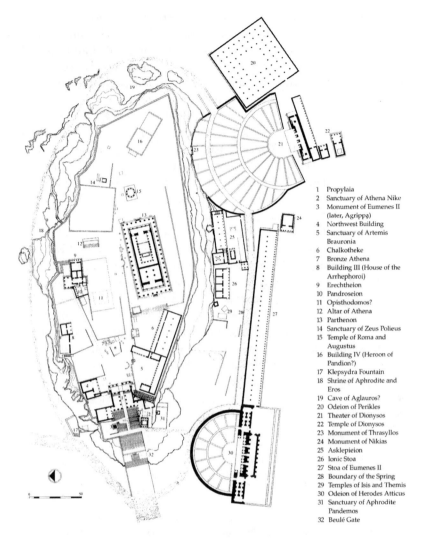

1   Propylaia
2   Sanctuary of Athena Nike
3   Monument of Eumenes II
    (later, Agrippa)
4   Northwest Building
5   Sanctuary of Artemis
    Brauronia
6   Chalkotheke
7   Bronze Athena
8   Building III (House of the
    Arrhephoroi)
9   Erechtheion
10 Pandroseion
11 Opisthodomos?
12 Altar of Athena
13 Parthenon
14 Sanctuary of Zeus Polieus
15 Temple of Roma and
    Augustus
16 Building IV (Heroon of
    Pandion?)
17 Klepsydra Fountain
18 Shrine of Aphrodite and
    Eros
19 Cave of Aglauros?
20 Odeion of Perikles
21 Theater of Dionysos
22 Temple of Dionysos
23 Monument of Thrasyllos
24 Monument of Nikias
25 Asklepieion
26 Ionic Stoa
27 Stoa of Eumenes II
28 Boundary of the Spring
29 Temples of Isis and Themis
30 Odeion of Herodes Atticus
31 Sanctuary of Aphrodite
    Pandemos
32 Beulé Gate

Figure 5.1: Restored plan of the Athenian Acropolis.

450s.[6] Additional work may have been going on in the Brauronion.[7] The Acropolis had also accumulated a vast number of inscriptions including

---

[6] *IG* I³ 435; Tracy 1984: 281–2; on the statue generally, see Harrison 1996: 28–34 and Hurwit 1999: 151–3, both with further bibliography.
[7] Hurwit 19991 197 8, 313.

tribute lists, treaties, and decrees as well as private dedicatory statues and other monuments, both public and private. Of the major fifth-century buildings, only the Erechtheion did not yet exist and had almost certainly not even been planned.[8] On the south slope of the Acropolis, the Odeion of Pericles next to the Sanctuary and Theatre of Dionysus had recently been completed.[9] In the Agora, there had been much less recent activity. Various civic buildings, the Stoa Poikile, the Stoa Basileios, the Old Bouleuterion, and the Tholos, as well as several other structures, including the Southeast Fountain House and the Aiakeion, had been in place since the end of the 460s at the latest (Figure 5.2).[10] Only the Hephaisteion was still under construction in 430.[11] Absent from the Agora were inscriptions and any statues other than the Tyrannicides and probably a statue dedicated by Leagrus to the Twelve Gods.[12]

The Agora in the 420s continued to be a location for considerable building activity. Both the Stoa of Zeus and South Stoa I belong to this decade and their multipurpose form reflects the varied ways in which the public space of the market square was used at this time: for gossiping, buying and selling, and waiting for the *ekklesia* to start, among other activities.[13] The rooms in South Stoa I were evidently intended and used for dining, but excavation has also produced large numbers of small bronze coins, a certain indication in excavated contexts in the Agora of significant commercial activity.[14] This same decade also witnessed a considerable concern for the shrines and altars in the area. The Altar of Aphrodite Ourania, damaged during the Persian sack of 479, was repaired, and the rock outcropping of the Crossroads Enclosure received its parapet barrier.[15] It is very likely that the enclosure wall of the Triangular Hieron southwest of the square

---

[8] The Erechtheion certainly does not follow the alignment of the Parthenon, the Propylaia, and the Nike Temple, and so it is very unlikely that it was planned as part of this project. The Caryatids are generally agreed to date to c. 420 and so construction must have begun by this date; see e.g. Boardman 1985: 148; Stewart 1990: 167; Hurwit 1999: 206; on the date, see also J. L. Shear 2001: 797–9.

[9] Plut. *Pericles* 13.9–10; Miller 1997: 219–23; Hurwit 1999: 216, 317.

[10] Stoa Poikile: Shear, Jr 1984: 13–14; Stoa Basileios: Shear, Jr 1993: 427–9; 1994: 240; Old Bouleuterion: Shear, Jr 1993: 418–24, 426–7, 429; Tholos: Thompson 1940: 126–8; Shear, Jr 1993: 429; Southeast Fountain House: Thompson and Wycherley 1972: 197–200; Aiakeion: Stroud 1998: 93–7.

[11] The decree of 421/20 on the Hephaisteia should mark the completion of the temple, and the cult statues were under construction between 421/20 and 416/15; *IG* I³ 82, 472.1–20; Camp 1986: 87.

[12] Leagrus: *IG* I³ 951; Gadbery 1992: 472–4.

[13] Stoa of Zeus: Thompson and Wycherley 1972: 100; South Stoa I: Thompson 1968: 53. Activity in the Agora: e.g. Ar. *Acharnians* 21–2 and perhaps 547–51; *Knights* 624–82, 1245–6; *Wasps* 488–99. For further discussion of activities in the Agora, see Millett 1998: 211–28, but note that his account is synchronic rather than diachronic.

[14] Thompson 1968: 49–53; Thompson and Wycherley 1972: 76–7.

[15] Aphrodite Ourania: Shear, Jr 1984: 28–32; Crossroads Enclosure: Shear, Jr 1973: 364, 366, 369.

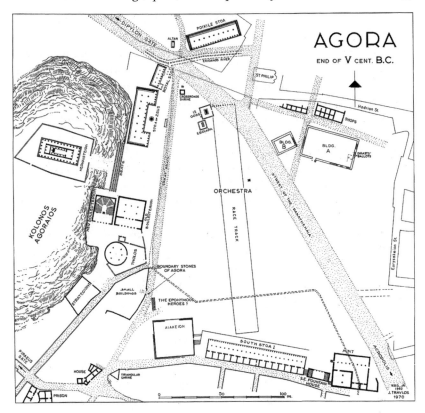

Figure 5.2: Restored plan of the Athenian Agora in c. 400 BC. The statues of the Tyrannicides were located on the base between the racetrack and the Panathenaic Way.

and the renovation of the Altar of the Twelve Gods and its enclosure, both archaeologically datable to some time in the last thirty years of the fifth century, also belong to the 420s.[16] The Athenians' concern for the care of sacred space and its proper demarcation is not limited to these four shrines in the Agora. The decree of 418/7 concerning the sanctuary of Codrus, Neleus, and Basile specifies that the *temenos* is to be enclosed, the contract for the enclosure is to be let out, and the *horistai* are to mark out the boundaries of the shrines in the *temenos*.[17] In the decree concerning firstfruits for Eleusis from perhaps 422, Lampon's amendment requires the *basileus* to

---

[16] Triangular Hieron: Lalonde 1968: 128–32; Shear, Jr 1973: 369 n. 30; Twelve Gods: Gadbery 1992: 466, 470–4.
[17] *IG* I³ 84.1–11

mark out the boundaries of the shrines in the Pelargicon and specifies that
altars are not to be erected in the future without the approval of the *boulē*
and the *demos*.[18] That the shrines and sanctuaries were under pressure in
the 420s is further attested by Thucydides, who reports that, at the start
of the war, the displaced people from the country took up residence in the
shrines, the sanctuaries of the heroes, and the Pelargicon, as well as in all
the empty spaces in the city.[19] In the face of this influx and the plague, the
Athenians were evidently taking especial care of their religious spaces. A
concern for regulating and strengthening the city's religious life in the 420s
also explains both the decision to begin work on a new temple for Athena
Polias on the Acropolis (the Erechtheion) and the erection of a statue of
Zeus in front of his contemporary stoa in the Agora.[20] This figure forms
an important parallel for the statues of the Eponymous Heroes set up soon
after 430 in the southwest corner of the market square;[21] it suggests that
the Heroes were important in their religious guise, as the 'founders' of the
ten Cleisthenic tribes, and not merely as images of the democracy. These
ten statues, accordingly, should belong to the class of religious figure and
not of honorary statue.

ATHENS IN 390 BC

In 390 BC, the situation was significantly different. On the Acropolis, the
only new building was the Erechtheion, begun in the second half of the 420s
and finished only under the restored democracy between 409/8 and 406/5
(Figure 5.1).[22] The sanctuary continued to be the prime location for erecting inscriptions and continued to receive statues and other dedications,
as it had in the period before 430. In contrast, the Agora had changed
significantly because, after the completion of the projects in the 420s
and, by 421/20, of the Hephaisteion, construction continued in the market. Between 410 and 405, the New Bouleuterion and the wings for the
Stoa Basileios were built and, around 400, the Mint and the first dedicated
court structures, Buildings A and B (Figure 5.2). In 394/3, bronze statues of
the Athenian general Conon and Euagoras of Cypriot Salamis were erected
in front of the Stoa of Zeus; for the first time, individual living men were

---

[18] *IG* i³ 78a.54–7.   [19] Thuc. 2.17.1–3.
[20] Thompson and Wycherley 1972: 101. For a general discussion of the situation in both Athens and
Attica, see Miles 1989: 227–34.
[21] Shear, Jr 1970: 203–22; *contra*: Kron 1976: 229–32; N. Robertson 1990: 50–2. The first certain
reference to the monument is in 421 in Ar. *Peace* 1183–4; Ar. *Knights* 977–80 may conceal a slightly
earlier reference.
[22] *IG* i³ 474 + *SEG* 33.22; *IG* i³ 475 + *SEG* 33.22; *IG* i³ 476–9.

honoured in the Agora with statues. We know of only two inscriptions set up in the Agora before 410; between 410 and 390, a significant group of documents was erected in this area.

INSCRIPTIONS AND CHANGING PATTERNS OF USE

The changes between 430 and 390 were not merely limited to a shift in the primary focus of building work from the Acropolis to the Agora. The ways in which these spaces were used were also transformed and the new patterns of use were played out in the city's topography. As Peter Liddel's study of the places of publication of Athenian state decrees shows, before 430 BC such inscriptions were erected on the Acropolis or, if they concerned sacred matters, in the relevant sanctuary.[23] The archaeological evidence for inscriptions which do not indicate the place of publication or do not preserve the place of publication seems to bear out this pattern. For the period before 430, the one exception proves the rule: a proxeny decree of about 450/49 was erected at the Bouleuterion.[24] As the publication clause makes clear, however, the stele in the Agora was a second copy; the first copy was erected, as we would expect, on the Acropolis. Subsequently, this pattern continues in the years between 430 and 411, again with one exception: two copies of the great tribute reassessment of 425/4 were erected, one on the Acropolis and a second again in the Agora at the Bouleuterion.[25] In both of these anomalous cases, the Agora inscription is a second copy of an inscription also erected on the Acropolis, and, as such, they do not ignore the general convention which places state decrees on the Acropolis. That the Acropolis rather than the Agora was the appropriate place for the publication of state decrees is also suggested by the decree concerning firstfruits for Eleusis: while the original decree specified that *pinakia* with the amounts of grain were to be placed in the Eleusinion at Eleusis and in the Bouleuterion, Lampon's amendment required the decree and the *xungraphai* to be inscribed on two marble stelai and to be set up in the sanctuary at Eleusis and on the Acropolis.[26] In perhaps 422, documents on wooden tablets could be placed in the Bouleuterion, but stone stelai belonged on the Acropolis.

---

[23] Liddel 2003. The stelai with Ephialtes' and Archestratus' laws about the Areopagus Council, which the Thirty took down from the Areopagus, might seem like an exception to this rule; [Arist.] *Ath. Pol.* 35.2. This Council, however, seems to have met either in or next to the sanctuary of the Semnai Theai, and so these inscriptions, in fact, fall into the category of stelai erected in sacred places; for the Areopagus and the Semnai Theai, see Wallace 1989: 215–18; Vanderpool 1950: 35–7.

[24] *IG* i³ 27 7–10.   [25] *IG* i³ 71.23 5.   [26] *IG* i³ /8a.26–30, 48–51.

Table 5.1 *The distribution of Agora inscriptions before 393 BC.*

	In front of Bouleuterion	In front of and in Stoa Basileios	In front of Stoa of Zeus
before 430	*IG* I³ 27 (+ Acropolis) (c. 450/49)		
430–411	*IG* I³ 71 (+ Acropolis) (425/4)		
410–404	Demophantus' Decree (And. 1.96–98) (410/9) Probably Documents concerning the *boule* (*IG* I³ 105) (c. 409)	Dracon's Law (*IG* I³ 104) (409/8) Laws (completed by 404)	
403–395	Honours for the Athenians returning from Phyle (*SEG* 28.45) (403/2) Probably Sale of Property of Thirty (*SEG* 32.161) (402/1)	Laws (403–399) Probably Theozotides' Decree (*SEG* 28.46) (403/2)	
394/3			Honours for Conon (Dem. 20.69–70) (394/3) Honours for Euagoras (RO 11) (394/3)

This pattern changed distinctly after the removal of the Four Hundred (Table 5.1). In the first prytany of 410/9, the *boulē* and the *demos* passed the decree and accompanying oath that was moved by a certain Demophantus and that mandated how the Athenians should behave if the democracy were to be overthrown in the future.[27] The resulting inscription was set up in front of the Bouleuterion (Figure 5.2).[28] In the following years, additional inscriptions were erected in the Agora: the reinscription of Dracon's law on homicide was put up in front of the Stoa Basileios in 409/8, while the stele with documents concerning the *boulē* was probably erected in front of the Bouleuterion at about the same time; then, the re-publication of the laws, both secular and sacred, involved their display in the two new annexes of the Stoa Basileios, as well as the erection of stelai with the

[27] Andoc. 1.96–98. The date is based on comparison with *IG* I³ 375.1–3.
[28] Andoc. 1.95; Lycurg. *Against Leocrates* 124, 126.

sacrificial calendar in front of the stoa, a project completed by 404.[29] These two areas received further documents in the years immediately after the return of the democrats in 403: the honours for the Athenians returning from Phyle were put up in front of the Bouleuterion in 403/2, and the laws were repositioned and re-displayed in the Stoa Basileios between 403 and 399.[30] Since epigraphical activity is focused specifically in these two areas of the Agora, it is very likely that two further documents belong in them. In 402/1, the stelai documenting the confiscation and sale of the property of the Thirty by the *poletai* were probably set up in front of the Bouleuterion, where the documents produced by the fourth-century *poletai* would be displayed.[31] The decree of Theozotides honouring the legitimate sons of the Athenians killed fighting the Thirty was probably set up in front of the Stoa Basileios in (probably) 403/2, hence its discovery in the wall of the nearby section of the Great Drain.[32] Then, in 394/3, honorary inscriptions for Conon and Euagoras, the king of Cypriot Salamis, were erected next to their statues and the statue of Zeus Eleutherios in front of the Stoa of Zeus.[33]

In contrast to the two earlier inscriptions, these stelai set up after 411 are not second copies, but originals, and they concern laws and honours for citizens, matters which previously either belonged in a sanctuary context or were apparently not inscribed at all.[34] Contemporary honours for

---

[29] Dracon's law: *IG* i³ 104. Documents concerning the *boulē*: *IG* i³ 105. Other laws: *IG* i³ 236, 237; for new texts of the sacrificial calendar, see Lambert 2002. *IG* i³ 105 is related to the other laws, but the fragments were found on the Acropolis, an unlikely setting divorced from the other laws and the *boulē* on which the text focuses. For these reasons, the inscription was more probably set up in front of the Bouleuterion; so also N. Robertson 1990: 58–9; *contra*: Lewis 1967: 132. For a security *horos* which must have travelled *up* to the Acropolis, see *IG* ii² 2720 with Lambert 1996: 110 n. 3. For the dates of the reorganisation of the laws, see Rhodes 1991: 88–9; Todd 1996: 102–11. I discuss the relationship of the laws and the sacrificial calendar to the Stoa Basileios in detail in J. L. Shear: in preparation.

[30] Honours for Phyle: *SEG* 28.45 with Aeschin. 3.187–91. I am not convinced by Taylor's arguments that this document also honoured non-Athenians; M. C. Taylor 2002. Such a reconstruction implausibly requires some non-Athenians to have been honoured twice: once in this document and then later in RO 4 = M. J. Osborne 1981–2: 1. D6; see further J. L. Shear: in preparation. Laws: J. L. Shear: in preparation.

[31] *SEG* 32.161. Fourth-century documents: Lalonde *et al.* 1991: 66–7, 74.

[32] *SEG* 28.46; Stroud 1971: 280.

[33] Conon: Dem. 20.69–70; cf. Wycherley 1957: 213 no. 261; Euagoras: Rhodes and Osborne 2003: 11.20–2 with Lewis and Stroud 1979: 191–3; *contra*: Lawton 1995: 122 no. 84. For the statues of both men, see the discussion below.

[34] Sanctuary context: *IG* i³ 231, 232, 234 and perhaps *IG* i³ 3. Not inscribed: The earliest examples of inscribed honorary decrees for Athenians seem to belong to 403/2 and the years immediately following: *SEG* 28.45, 46; Dem. 20.69–70. Honours for Athenians, such as Cleon's *sitesis* and *proedria*, must certainly have been passed in the fifth century, but there is no evidence that they were

non-citizens, however, continued to be erected in Athena's sanctuary: the decree for Thrasyboulus, the assassin of the oligarch Phrynichus, in 410/9, the original honours and citizenship for Euagoras of Cypriot Salamis perhaps early in 407, and the honours for the non-Athenians returning from Phyle in 401/400, among other documents, all belonged on the Acropolis, not in the Agora.[35] This distinction emphasises that the Agora inscriptions specifically concerned Athenian citizens; their location in this particular setting, consequently, was especially appropriate because, as one of the city's civic centres, it housed most of its governmental structures.

The emphasis on citizens is picked up in a number of the texts of the inscriptions. The decree of Demophantus indicates that it is every good citizen's duty as a male democrat to kill tyrants and oligarchs.[36] If he dies in the process, he will receive the Tyrannicides' benefits: for himself, a bronze statue in the Agora and a hero cult as a 'founder' of democracy; for his sons, *sitesis* in the Prytaneion, *proedria*, and perhaps *ateleia* from liturgies, military service, and certain other duties.[37] The honours for the Athenians returning from Phyle and the decree of Theozotides reward those men who freed the city from the oligarchs and brought back the democracy. On the stele for the returning Athenians, their names are listed in official tribal order with patronymics and demotics, and the epigram indicates that they were crowned by the Athenian *demos*.[38] In Theozotides' decree, the fathers are described as 'Athenians', a term which signals their citizen status. Their sons must be legitimate, hence the examination mentioned in line 15, and the surviving names of the sons include both patronymic and demotic, again markers of their position as citizens of the city.[39] In these texts, these citizens are all closely linked with the democracy itself. The rule of the

---

inscribed, perhaps because of the ideological problems of singling out one member of the *demos* from the rest; cf. Whitehead 1993: 47; for Cleon's honours, see Ar. *Knights* 573–6 with 280–1, 702–9, 766, 1404–5; Gauthier 1985: 95–6.

[35] Thrasyboulus: *IG* I³ 102; Euagoras: *IG* I³ 113; for the date, see M. J. Osborne 1981–2: II. 22–4; non-Athenians: RO 4 = M. J. Osborne 1981–2: 1 D6; other honours for non-citizens: e.g. *IG* I³ 103, 106, 110, 114, 116, 117, 125, 126, 127; *IG* II² 6, 9, 13, 17, 22, 24.

[36] For further discussion of these dynamics, see J. L. Shear: forthcoming.

[37] Tyrannicides' cult: M. W. Taylor 1991: 5–9; Parker 1996: 123, 136–7. Sons: *sitesis*: *IG* I³ 131.1–9; cf. Isaeus 5.47; *proedria* and *ateleia*: Isae 5.47; cf. Dem. 20.18, 127–130. Since Cleon requested and obtained both *sitesis* and *proedria* after his victory at Sphacteria, these two honours must have been awarded to the descendants of Harmodius and Aristogeiton before 425; above n. 34. That Conon received *ateleia* along with his bronze statue after Cnidus suggests that this benefit had already been awarded to the descendents of the Tyrannicides by 394/3 and before it is mentioned by Isaeus in c. 389; Dem. 20.70; Gauthier 1985: 96–7. For the exemptions conferred by *ateleia*, see MacDowell 2004: 127–9.

[38] For the epigram, see *SEG* 28.45.73–76 with Aeschin. 3.190.

[39] The legitimacy of the sons is clear from Lys. fr. 6.2 (Gernet and Bizos); see also Stroud 1971: 291–2, 299–301.

demos was made possible by the city's laws, now prominently displayed on stelai in and around the Stoa Basileios.[40] Oligarchs do not use such laws, as the epigram on the stele for the returning Athenians makes clear: the Thirty are described as ruling with 'unjust statutes' (ἀδίκοις θεσμοῖς).

The association of citizen, democracy, and law in the texts was reinforced by erecting these documents in the Agora, the 'home', as it were, of the rule of the *demos*. If these inscriptions had been placed on the Acropolis, they would have been lost among many other documents pertaining to all sorts of different subjects, some of concern to Athenians, but others, like the tribute lists and honorary decrees for foreigners, of concern also to non-Athenians. These documents stood out in the Agora because there were no other inscriptions. The square housed the *boulē* and the *archons* and, from it, citizens ruled the city.[41] These activities, in turn, reinforced the stress in the inscriptions on citizenship and on democracy. At the same time, the Agora also displayed the Tyrannicides, the 'founders' of the democratic city and the Eponymous Heroes, the 'founders' of the democratic tribes through which all citizens participated in Athenian civic life. While the statues of the Eponymoi were comparatively new, their role was not; it had been established about one hundred years before by Cleisthenes. Both Harmodius and Aristogeiton and the heroes provided models for the proper Athenian, and emphasised that he supported the rule of the *demos*, a point also made by Demophantus' decree. In contrast, the Acropolis had no such democratic connections and, in this setting, the messages of the inscriptions would have been muted and lost. To present this particular image required the inscriptions to be erected in the Agora and nowhere else.

SPACE, USE, AND THE AGORA

Changes in the Agora were not limited to setting up inscriptions there rather than on the Acropolis. The location of these inscriptions was also important. They clustered in three particular areas and so emphasised them:

---

[40] Compare Dem. 20.107: at Athens, 'there are curses (*arai*), laws, and safeguards (*phulakai*) in order that no one else will have power over' the *demos*.

[41] I am not suggesting that Athenians did not go to the Agora for other purposes, such as shopping and gossiping; indeed, these activities have been carefully documented by Millett 1998: 211–28. His focus, however, is not on civic activities, which receive short shrift in his discussion. For him, the Agora is a 'neutral stage' upon which individuals appeared (p. 220). While this description may be correct for the period before 411, it is certainly not true for the years after 411. That shopping was not as important as civic activities is indicated by the topography: shopping occurred in temporary structures, but civic duties took place in permanent structures which remained after the market was finished and were continually visible.

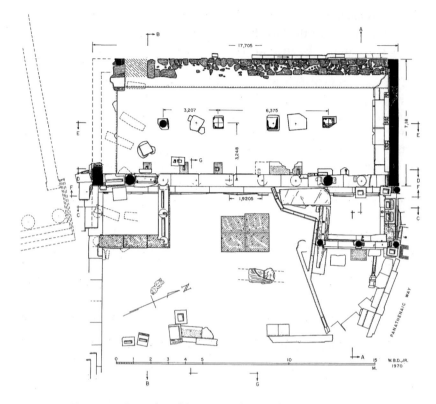

Figure 5.3: State plan of the Stoa Basileios in the Athenian Agora.

in front of the Bouleuterion, in front of and in the Stoa Basileios, and in
front of the Stoa of Zeus (Table 5.1 and Figure 5.2). The Stoa Basileios
and the Bouleuterion were both closely connected with the democracy and
they were also the sites of important construction. The two wings added
to the Stoa Basileios between 410 and 404 seem to have been specifically
designed to display great marble stelai on which were inscribed the city's
laws, newly collected and organised (Figure 5.3).[42] Solon's *kurbeis* had been
kept in the stoa from at least 461, but the inscription of the laws on stelai
made them available in a familiar modern medium and, in their reorganised
form, they could easily be consulted by anyone who wished to do so.[43] The
basileus worked partially in their presence and the *archons* swore annually

[42] Wings: Shear, Jr 1971: 250–2.
[43] Solon's *kurbeis*: Stroud 1979: 11–17, 41–4; Shear, Jr 1994: 240–1; *contra*: e.g. Rhodes 1981: 131–4; Sealey
      1987: 140–5; Rhodes 1991: 91 with n. 23.

to uphold the laws on the *lithos*, the oath-stone, where they were flanked by the laws. These juxtapositions indicated that the democratic officials both followed the laws and depended on them for their authority. Both the ritual itself and the display in the stoa emphasised that democracy depended on and was safeguarded by the law; the two were, accordingly, intimately connected.[44]

The Stoa Basileios was not the only location in the Agora in which laws became available for consultation at this time. The building of the New Bouleuterion between 410 and 405 gave the *boulē* a new home and the city's archives, collected in one place for the first time, were installed in what we must now refer to as the Old Bouleuterion (Figure 5.2).[45] In this archive, the laws and the decrees of the *demos* and the *boulē* seem to have been kept in separate sections.[46] On a practical level, these documents were conveniently at hand for the *boulē* to consult. The juxtaposition between the neighbouring structures also linked the *boulē* with the laws of the city and located the current deliberations and actions of the Council in relationship to its past decisions. The choice of the Old Bouleuterion as the location for the city's archives must be understood in the context of the way in which the Four Hundred had used the building. One of the oligarchs' first acts was to pay off the democratically elected *bouleutai* and take over the Bouleuterion for their own use as the centre of their power.[47] In the years after 411, the Four Hundred were replaced, not with the democratic *boulē*, but with the laws themselves, the very documents which made the rule of the *demos* possible and the rule of anyone else impossible. This decision powerfully erased the oligarchic presence and emphasised that democracy had been re-established. The idea of situating the *boulē* in relationship to the laws mirrored what was going on in the Stoa Basileios. These two buildings with the laws now anchored the west side of the Agora, and their importance was further marked by the erection of inscriptions only in these two areas. They were the space, *par excellence*, of the *demos*, whose rule depended on and was supported by the laws.

In about 400, a third area was also associated with the *demos*: the northeast corner where the first permanent court facilities were constructed, Buildings A and B (Figure 5.2).[48] The courts ensured that the laws were

---

[44] For similar sentiments, cf. Dem. 20.107.   [45] Shear, Jr 1995: 178–89; Sickinger 1999: 105–13.
[46] Sickinger 1999: 105, 147–59.
[47] Thuc. 8.69–70.1; [Arist.] *Ath. Pol.* 32.3.
[48] Townsend 1995: 24–30, 40–9; apparently accepted by Blanshard 1999: 38–41. In the Agora Excavations, finds of dikastic equipment are concentrated in two areas: around the Tholos, the home of the *prutaneis*, and the area of the later Square Peristyle; Townsend 1995: 42–3, table 1 and illustration

actually followed and so they were appropriately situated across from the display of the laws in the Stoa Basileios. At the same time, the citizen *dikastai* coming out of Building A could look across at the Tyrannicides on whom the decree of Demophantus indicates that they were supposed to model their behaviour. The installation of the courts in the Agora must have significantly changed the patterns of use because now large numbers of citizens came here specifically for court activities. In contrast, in the fifth century, courts met variously in different locations around the city, as Alastair Blanshard has shown, but there is no evidence that they were ever held in the Agora before about 400.[49] At that time, the democratic activities in the marketplace were no longer confined to the *archons* and the *bouleutai*; now, a large section of the *demos* itself was formally included in the ordering of the city's life and the protection of its system of rule. By constructing these permanent, purpose-built facilities, the courts themselves were put on permanent display in the Agora. This decision was particularly significant because one of the Thirty's first acts had been to curtail the courts severely;[50] these new facilities clearly demonstrated the reversal of that policy. The overall appearance of the market square, in turn, suggested that the courts were just as important a part of the system as the *boulē* and the *archons*.

The contemporary construction of the Mint in the southeast corner of the Agora provided one last major structure connected with the democracy (Figure 5.2).[51] The archaeological remains show that production in this building was limited to bronze working, and silver coinage was never minted at this location; the silver mint and the relevant decrees and laws must be

---

2. This distribution is both distinctive and significant, and points to the use of the buildings under the Square Peristyle by the city's courts. Any attempt to disassociate the courts from these structures must provide a convincing explanation for this distribution of material.

[49] Blanshard 1999: 18–59, 221–2, esp. 41–2, 47, but note that the chronological distinctions are mine rather than his. The earliest references to lawcourts in the area of the Agora date to the middle of the fourth century and concern courts meeting in the Stoa Poikile, a chronological distinction overlooked by Blanshard; Dem. 45.17; *IG* II² 1641.25–33; Blanshard 1999: 33–5, 47–53. Stroud's recent identification of the rectangular *peribolos* at the southwest corner of the Agora as the Aiakeion means that we cannot locate the *Heliaia* or any other court here; Stroud 1998: 85–104. The general absence of dikastic equipment in this area also tells against this identification. Although the *poros* steps north of the New Bouleuterion have been identified by Boegehold as the meeting place of a court in the fifth century, no dikastic equipment has been found in this area; Boegehold 1967; 1995: 13–14, 95; apparently accepted by Blanshard 1999: 37–8, 53–4. This absence again suggests that no court ever met here.

[50] R. Osborne 2003: 262–4.

[51] Camp and Kroll 2001: 127–45. Since the latest pottery in the construction fill belongs to c. 400 (e.g. olpai of the type *Agora* XII, no. 273), the building cannot have been constructed in the last decade of the century, where Camp and Kroll would evidently like to place it; Camp and Kroll 2001: 142 n. 9, 144–5.

located elsewhere and outside of the market square.[52] Between the fourth and the first century, the building certainly served as the city's mint for bronze coinage; it now appears that bronze coins first began to be minted in Athens about 400 BC, and so it is very likely that the building was intended as the city's mint from its initial construction.[53] Alternatively, it may originally have been intended for the manufacture of public weights, tokens, and measures.[54] In either case, this building was producing items necessary for the proper functioning of the (democratic) city. The Agora was not necessarily an obvious place in which to construct this industrial structure, and its function contrasts with the neighbouring buildings; siting it here required a deliberate decision of the Athenians. Its location would have made it easily accessible to the *boulē* and the *archons* and it suggests the possibility of a distinct degree of transparency in its operations. Located on the square, the building was associated with the other structures of the democracy so that its connection with the *demos* was emphasised. As such, it anchored the southeast corner of the Agora and complemented the court structures to the north and the buildings on the west side. Now, buildings firmly connected with the rule of the *demos* marked the major boundaries of the market and identified the area as the civic heart of the city.

COMMEMORATION AND THE INDIVIDUAL

The changes in the Agora were not limited to the erection of stelai and the construction of these buildings. The ways of celebrating military victory won by the *demos* were also altered. Two of the stelai not only recorded documents, but also memorialised both the living democrats, who returned from Phyle, and the dead democrats who did not; the sons of the latter were also celebrated in the same document as their deceased fathers. As monuments to Athenian military success, they represent a new pattern of commemoration, and led to greater changes, the commemoration of individual citizens. Athenian victories had been celebrated outside the Acropolis before 403/2. After the success at Eion in 476/5, the *demos* voted to set up three herms somewhere north and west of the Agora; their epigrams honoured the entire Athenian force, and no particular individual was specifically mentioned.[55] The late 460s and the 450s saw the erection in the Agora of the Stoa Poikile with its painting cycle commemorating

---

[52] Camp and Kroll 2001: 133–60.   [53] Camp and Kroll 2001: 144–5.   [54] Camp and Kroll 2001: 145.
[55] Aeschin. 3.183–5; Plut. *Cimon* 7.4–8.1. Aeschines particularly stresses that the names of the generals were omitted and only the *demos* was mentioned.

the Athenian victories over the Persians and Spartans (Figure 5.2).[56] In both monuments, the achievements of the Athenian *demos* as a corporate group were celebrated and no individual was singled out. Individual honours were accorded only to the Tyrannicides, now safely dead and heroised. This pattern continued in the 420s: in the Stoa Poikile, the shields taken from the Spartans on Sphacteria and from the Scioneans and their allies were from the Athenians as a group.[57]

In 403/2, in contrast, the Athenians honoured only a part of their number: the citizens who returned from Phyle. It was undoubtedly the 'right' part of the Athenians, that is the members of the *demos* who fought against the tyrants, but it was, nevertheless, only a part. The way in which these men were honoured is also striking. The living men were given money for a sacrifice and dedications, and olive crowns; the dead were buried in the *Demosion Sema* and were honoured through their sons, who were assimilated to the war orphans and so were presented to the Athenians in the theatre at the Dionysia.[58] In both cases, the honours were rituals and the inscriptions themselves. These rewards contrast both with the Stoa Poikile and Eion Herms and with the specifications of Demophantus' decree which prescribed the Tyrannicides' honours for dead democrats and their sons.[59] Buried with those killed in war, the dead Athenians got their cult, but not the bronze statues erected for Harmodius and Aristogeiton. Through their burial, the dead were assimilated to the war dead, just as the sons were assimilated to the war orphans. Consequently, the Thirty became external enemies of the city, not citizens, and the divisions between the Athenians were de-emphasised. The dead democrats' role as the opponent of external enemies will have been further stressed by the rituals of their burial in the *Demosion Sema*. If, as A. W. Gomme and Nicole Loraux have suggested, the procession at the burial of the war dead conveyed their bones from the Agora to the cemetery, then the process will have linked Theozotides' decree with the tomb and will have reinforced the text's stress on the external nature of the conflict.[60]

The setting of the inscriptions in the Agora is also important because it juxtaposed the Athenian democrats with the Tyrannicides and with Demophantus' decree: the victors over external enemies were contrasted with the killers of (internal) Athenian tyrants and potential Athenian tyrants and

[56] Paus. 1.15.1–3.   [57] Paus. 1.15.4; *IG* I³ 522.
[58] Living: Aeschin. 3.187; *SEG* 28.45. Dead: Lys. 2.64 and cf. 2.66; Loraux 1986: 35–6, 200; sons: *SEG* 28.46; Lys. fr. 6.2 (Gernet and Bizos).
[59] Above, n. 37.
[60] Procession: Gomme *et al.* 1945–81: 11.102; Loraux 1986: 20; *contra*: Stupperich 1977: 32; Clairmont 1983: 3.

oligarchs. At the same time, the relationships between the monuments invited viewers to compare the memorials and to make the connections not made in the texts, that the democrats from Phyle had also freed Athens from tyrants just as the Tyrannicides and the Athenians who followed Demophantus' decree had. The setting further situated the monuments for the men from Phyle in relationship to the Stoa Poikile so that their victory over external enemies was added to the series of successes against the Persians and the Spartans and their allies, which this building celebrated. That the achievements of the returning Athenians were seen as part of this series of external victories is made clear by Aeschines' description of the monuments in 330 BC. He describes first the Eion Herms, then the Marathon painting in the Stoa Poikile, and finally the stele with the rewards for the Athenians returning from Phyle.[61] This sequence presupposes that all three events were victories over external enemies and that the return from Phyle was on a par with the battles of Eion and Marathon. Situating the stelai with Theozotides' decree and with the honours for the returning democrats in relationship to the Stoa Poikile and its paintings and shields again suggested that the unified Athenians had fought against the Thirty just as they had against their earlier enemies.

While the monuments for the democrats from Phyle mark a new development in Athenian practices of memorialisation, a more striking change occurred some ten years later in 394/3, when the first honorary statues for individual living men were erected. In this year, bronze statues of Conon, the victor of the naval battle at Cnidus, and Euagoras, the king of Cypriot Salamis, were set up in front of the Stoa of Zeus Eleutherios and near the statue of Zeus Soter (Figure 5.2).[62] Demosthenes reports that Conon's honorary decree specified uniquely that the honours were voted 'because Conon freed the allies of Athens', and Euagoras' decree indicated that the king had acted as a Hellene on behalf of Hellas, a phrase apparently used in the proclamation of his honours.[63] Their decrees, as I noted earlier, seem to have been set up next to the figures and so also in front of the Stoa of Zeus. The decrees, the statues, and their location combined to emphasise that these two men were the liberators of Athens and the bringers of freedom. Placing these monuments in the Agora emphasised the connections between the democracy which had authorised the rewards and the honorands whose democratic credentials were displayed in this way. Erected in front of the stoa, the statues were also juxtaposed with the figures of the Tyrannicides, the only other non-sacred statues in the Agora; Conon

[61] Aeschin. 3.183 191.   [62] Isoc. 9.56–7; Dem. 20.69–70; Paus. 1.3.2–3.
[63] Dem. 20.69; RO 11.14–19; Lewis and Stroud 1979: 190–1.

and Euagoras, consequently, were also figured as the slayers of a tyrant. In Euagoras' case, Pausanias' stress on his Athenian citizenship suggests that this information was included on the monument's base, now no longer preserved. The honorands, accordingly, were clearly identified as democratic Athenians who had imitated the earlier Tyrannicides and had subsequently been suitably honoured. They would then serve as models for future generations of (democratic) citizens.

Demosthenes stresses that Conon was the first man after the Tyrannicides to be voted a bronze statue, and both he and Aeschines emphasise that fifth-century military leaders did not receive bronze statues from the *demos*; these generals' known statues on the Acropolis all seem to have been private dedications and so uncontrolled by the city.[64] Had Conon's and Euagoras' figures been set up on the Acropolis, they would not have stood out visually and they could have been read as private dedications.[65] In order for them to be read as democratic saviours and 'tyrannicides' honoured by the city, the statues could only have been placed in the Agora near the Stoa of Zeus and Harmodius and Aristogeiton. This location emphasised that the figures were public honorary statues voted by the *demos*, and not private dedications. The placement of the authorising inscriptions near the statues ensured that there could be no ambiguity about what sort of monument they were, a necessary precaution given their novelty. The two statues introduce a new type, the public honorary statue, and a new place for their erection, the Agora. This setting also contrasted the statues with the less elaborate monuments for Phyle, and emphasised that they celebrated the achievements of the whole polis and not just the committed democrats. At the same time, the dynamics de-emphasised the Spartan identity of the defeated enemy and the Persian fleet which made the victory possible.[66] Celebrating these successes together, the unified Athenians could ignore both their own lack of power and their dependence on their barbarian enemy of the fifth century.

The ways in which the Athenians chose to honour Conon and Euagoras contrast strongly with the various honours given to Lysander after the

---

[64] Aeschin. 3.181–2; Dem. 23.196–8. Generals on the Acropolis: e.g. Diitrephes: Krumeich 1997: no. A 15; Pericles: Krumeich 1997: nos. A 37, A 38 = *IG* I³ 884; Phormion: Krumeich 1997: no. A 42; Tolmides: Krumeich 1997: no. A 58; Xanthippus: Krumeich 1997: no. A 59; more generally, see Krumeich 1997: 214–15, 218–20.

[65] This distinction is clearly brought out by the slightly later statues of Conon and Timotheus on the Acropolis: we now know that they were private dedications made by Conon and Timotheus and not honorary figures; *IG* II² 3774 + *SEG* 36.246 = Löhr 2000: no. 86. As such, they joined the ranks of similar figures populating the sanctuary.

[66] For these dynamics in Euagoras' honorary decree, see the comments of Lewis and Stroud 1979: 191.

battle of Aigospotamoi.[67] His statues were also erected: by the Samians at Olympia, by the Ephesians in their sanctuary of Artemis, and by the Lacedaimonians at Delphi, where the figure was part of a much larger group known as the 'Monument of the *Nauarchoi*', which commemorated the naval victory.[68] Our testimonia indicate that these figures of Lysander were all dedications in sacred spaces, a traditional form expected in sanctuaries. The memorial at Delphi also celebrated victory in battle, another well-established type of monument. The neighbouring group set up by the Athenians to commemorate the battle of Marathon provides a good parallel for the Spartan dedication because it, too, contained a statue of the human Miltiades, as well as gods and heroes.[69] In the crowded sanctuary at Delphi, the Spartan memorial would not have stood out as particularly unusual. The novelty of the statues in the Athenian Agora is further brought out by the Samians' and the Ephesians' later actions: after Cnidos, both cities set up statues of Conon and Timotheus in their respective main sanctuaries.[70] Strikingly, these figures were not placed in these cities' *agorai* and, indeed, it is difficult to find examples of public statues erected in such settings before Conon and Euagoras at Athens.[71] The best example is the archaic statue of the pankratiast Arrachion at Phigalia, but, since he died winning at Olympia, he may have been the recipient of a cult.[72] If this inference is correct, then his figure represents another traditional type, the athlete who receives a cult; Theogenes of Thasos with his cult and statue in the Agora is perhaps the best known example.[73] Such rites were certainly not among the honours awarded by the Athenians to Conon and Euagoras and this absence would have stressed the unusual nature of their public honorary statues in the Agora: a novel type invented for a place and purpose specific to this polis.

[67] For a summary, see Bommelaer 1981: 7–23.

[68] Samians: Paus. 6.3.14–15; Ephesians: 6.3.15; Lacedaemonians: Paus. 10.9.7–11; Plut. *Lysander* 18.1; ML 95; Jacquemin 1999: 338 no. 322 with further bibliography. On the various statues, see Bommelaer 1981: 13–16, 20–3.

[69] Paus. 10.10.1–2; Jacquemin 1999: 315 no. 078 with further bibliography.   [70] Paus. 6.3.16.

[71] Krumeich includes no certain examples in his catalogue: 1997: 223–50.

[72] Arrachion: Paus. 8.40.1–2; Krumeich 1997: 202–3 with further bibliography.

[73] Heroisation of athletes: Currie 2005: 120–57. Theogenes: Paus. 6.11.2–9; Grandjean and Salviat 2000: 73–6 and Currie 2005: 120–1, both with further bibliography. Note that Currie 2005: 147 states that 'athletes could also be voted a public statue in their hometown, often in the agora', but he provides no specific examples, much less fifth-century figures not connected with cult; perhaps they are properly a fourth-century phenomenon. By 330 BC, Lycurgus could construct a contrast between the Agora at Athens with its statues of good generals and the Tyrannicides and the marketplaces of other poleis with their statues of athletes; Lycurg. *Leocrates* 51.

COMMEMORATION AFTER CONON AND EUAGORAS

As well as providing a new way of commemorating generals' achievements, the figures of Conon and Euagoras also had important ramifications for the future development of the Agora. In the twenty or so years after 394/3, the Athenians honoured three more generals with bronze statues: Chabrias because of his naval victory at Naxos in 376, Iphicrates because he destroyed a Spartan division near Corinth in 390, and Timotheus because of his cruise around the Peloponnese to Corcyra in 375.[74] In all three cases, the monuments seem to have been set up not long after the event, as Philippe Gauthier argues.[75] Timotheus' and Chabrias' statues certainly stood in the Agora.[76] Since Iphicrates' memorial is regularly mentioned together with them and honorary statues were not yet being erected on the Acropolis, it is very likely that Iphicrates' figure also stood in the marketplace, perhaps not far from the monuments for the other generals.[77] Pausanias provides further details about Timotheus' figure: it was set up next to the images of his father and Euagoras in front of the Stoa of Zeus (Figure 5.2); like both of them, he was identified as a saviour and bringer of freedom, roles which he fulfilled, not by killing a tyrant, but by his military success.

Chabrias' monument was rather more complicated and points towards future developments. The fragments of its base show that it was decorated with citations and carved olive crowns voted by various groups, including soldiers campaigning at Syros, Naxos, Abydos, Mytilene, and the Aianteion in the Hellespont, and the *demos* of Mytilene.[78] This reference to Naxos identifies the honorand as Chabrias and requires the restoration of a crown voted by the Athenian *demos*, the honour mentioned by the literary sources.[79] Chabrias' victory at Naxos belongs in 376, but his activities in

---

[74] Aeschin. 3.243; Dem. 23.196–8; [Dem.] 13.21–22; cf. Dem. 20.75–86.

[75] Gauthier 1985: 97–103, 177–80; also Krumeich 1997: 208–9. Against an early date for Iphicrates' honours, see e.g. Davies 1971: 477–8; Pritchett 1974: 70 n. 52; cf. Dover 1968: 45–6, 193; Burnett and Edmondson 1961: 89. To Gauthier's arguments, we should add that Dem. 20.85 indicates that Chabrias' honours must have been awarded after those of Iphicrates and Timotheus. The epigraphical evidence for Chabrias' statue, *SEG* 19.204, to be discussed below, indicates that it was erected in 375 or 374.

[76] Timotheus: Paus. 1.3.2–3; Nepos, *Timoth.* 2.3. Chabrias: Nepos, *Chab.* 1.2–3; the fragments of the figure's base were also found in the Agora; Burnett and Edmondson 1961.

[77] Iphicrates' statue is also attested by Dem. 23.130. There is no reason why this figure should be identified with the one seen by Pausanias in the Parthenon, and the latter's location suggests that it was dedicatory rather than honorary; Paus. 1.24.7. Krumeich 1997: 208 also places Iphicrates' honorary statue in the Agora.

[78] *SEG* 19.204.

[79] Burnett and Edmondson 1961: 80–7, 90–1. For Chabrias' crown, see Dem. 24.180 and cf. the references in n. 74.

the Hellespont and on Lesbos seem to belong in 375.[80] The overall effect is to provide a partial history of the honorand's career. This sense must have been enhanced by the statue which showed the general in a pose associated with a land campaign in 378/7 in Boeotia: the figure stood at ease with its spear upright and its shield leaning against one knee.[81] This decidedly martial image contrasted with that of the Tyrannicides, and stressed the highlights of Chabrias' career. It looks ahead to the period after 330 when honorary statues commemorated a man's whole career, not just one battle.[82]

Since the authorising inscriptions for Conon's and Euagoras' honours seem to have been erected near their statues, it seems likely that the parallel decrees for Iphicrates, Timotheus, and Chabrias were also set up near or next to their figures. Certainly, some later honorary decrees were set up in the Agora next to the statue which they authorised.[83] Some of these men, such as Callias and Phaidrus of Sphettos and Philippides of Paiania, were the recipients of the greatest honours which the city could bestow; their statues, their inscriptions, and their honours develop out of the practices which began with the awards for Conon and Euagoras.

The erection of their statues led not only to an Agora with statues of good generals and the Tyrannicides, as it was famously described by Lycurgus in 330, but also to the development of the Stoa of Zeus as a place for commemorating military victory.[84] In the middle of the fourth century, the paintings installed in the building included depictions of Theseus with *Demokratia* and *Demos*, and a cavalry engagement fought at Mantineia in 362.[85] This combination stressed that that victory was won by the democratic city. The connection between freedom and the building also continued into the early third century, when shields borne by men killed fighting the Macedonians and the Gauls were dedicated here; in the case of Leocritus, who died in combat with the Macedonians, the dedication was made by the Athenians.[86] Following the pattern set by the monuments for the early fourth-century generals, these honours again commemorated the individual as a bringer of freedom to the democratic city. Like the Stoa Poikile, the Stoa of Zeus became a place for celebrating the multiple victories of the *demos*, a process

---

[80] Burnett and Edmondson 1961: 80–7.
[81] Diod. Sic. 15.32.5, 33.4; Polyaenus 2.1.2; Nep. *Chabrias* 1.2–3; J. K. Anderson 1963; Buckler 1972.
[82] Gauthier 1985: 103–12.
[83] *IG* ii² 682.87–9 (Phaidrus of Sphettos); *SEG* 28.60.106–7 (Callias of Sphettos); 45.101.44–5, 48–50 (Philippides of Paiania); *Agora* 16.291.38–41 (Calliphanes of Phyle); 310.50–2 (Z/Menodorus of Trinemea); and perhaps 240.13–15.
[84] Lycurg. *Leocrates* 51, where he notes that other cities set up statues of athletes in their *agorai*.
[85] Paus. 1.3.3–4.
[86] Leocritus killed fighting the Macedonians in 287: Paus. 1.26.2. Cydias killed fighting the Gauls in 279: Paus. 10.21.5–6. His shield was dedicated by his family.

begun with the erection of the statues of Conon and Euagoras in front of the building.

The decision to set up these two monuments introduced a new pattern of commemoration which was evidently not limited to public honours voted by the *demos* and the *boulē*. Victories won in the tribal contests of the Panathenaia and the Olympieia began to be memorialised in the Agora in the first half of the fourth century. The earliest known monument celebrates the success of [K]rat[e]s of Peiraieus in the apobatic race of the Panathenaia.[87] The cuttings on the top surface of the base show that it did not support a bronze statue, and I have argued elsewhere that it carried a marble pillar and a prize Panathenaic amphora. The overall structure was of a completely different order of magnitude from that of the figures of Conon and Euagoras, but it represents a similar desire to commemorate the achievements of a single man in a civic setting. The victory was won in the apobatic race, a contest with a pronounced military flavour, in which participation was limited to Athenian citizens. The monument proclaims [K]rat[e]s' status as an Athenian and his 'military' achievements and, consequently, reflects many of the dynamics of Conon's and Euagoras' statues. If these figures together with the Tyrannicides and the Stoa Poikile delineated the proper behaviour for the Athenian on the field of battle, then [K]rat[e]s' monument emphasised that this same citizen ought to display his status and prowess by competing in Athena's games.

Other memorials in the Agora commemorated the victories of tribal teams in the *anthippasia*. As in the apobatic race, only Athenian citizens could take part in this contest and their participation allowed them to display their status. Since the event was a mock cavalry fight, the teams probably consisted of the tribes' *hippeis*; the connections between actual military victory and success in the competition will have been closer than they were in the apobatic race. Participation in the *anthippasia*, accordingly, displayed both a man's citizenship and his military prowess. In the Agora, the known fourth-century monuments for Panathenaic victories seem to have consisted of a base supporting a pillar and a relief, while the extant structures for success in the Olympieia, and probably in both festivals, displayed the prize tripod from the games for Zeus.[88] The one preserved

---

[87] *SEG* 21.695 with J. L. Shear 2003: 170–2, 176. In this publication, I followed the traditional date of c. 400 BC for the base. In view of the monument's relationship to the statues of Conon and Euagoras, this date is very probably slightly too early, and the base more likely belongs shortly after 390.

[88] Panathenaia: Agora Excavations, Athens, I 7167 and I 7515: J. L. Shear 2003: 170–2, 177–8. Olympieia: *IG* II² 3130 = Löhr 2000: no. 108. Probably both festivals: Agora Excavations, Athens, I 3495: Vanderpool 1974: 313 no. 2. Agora Excavations, Athens, I 882 (Meritt 1946: 176–7 no. 24) probably also

relief, that of the tribe Leontis, showed a file of cavalry, but apparently no opponents.[89] From the depiction alone, it is impossible to tell whether the occasion was a contest or a battle, a problem also evident with the cavalrymen on the base for a victory of the tribe Antiochis.[90] The form of the monuments for the *anthippasia*, consequently, elided the distinctions between successes in the games and in war. Stressing military victory, but not the festival context, allowed the memorials to take part in the relationships created by the generals' statues, the Tyrannicides, the Stoa Poikile, and the Stoa of Zeus. These connections were strengthened by the probable location of the monuments; most of their remains have been found in the northwest corner of the Agora and, with the exception of [K]rat[e]s' base discovered in the southeast corner, it is likely that they were set up in this area.[91] This location juxtaposed them physically with the existing victory monuments for military success and so reinforced the identification of the Agora as the primary place for celebrating the city's military exploits. At the same time, this setting also emphasised the importance of celebrating the (martial) exploits of individual citizens. In time, the stress on the military nature of citizens' deeds was lost and, by the second century BC, athletic accomplishments of such citizens as Menodorus the wrestler and pancratiast were celebrated with a bronze statue.[92] Despite Menodorus' (apparent) lack of military achievement, his monument was placed in the Agora in the company of Conon and Euagoras and the memorials for the city's military victories.

SPACE, COMMEMORATION, AND POLITICS

Our evidence brings out very clearly how significantly Athenian space changed between 430 and 390 BC. During this period, the Acropolis ceased to be the primary space for displaying decrees, statues, and other monuments, and stopped being the major focus of construction activity. The only large-scale project in the sanctuary, the Erechtheion, was in some ways a

commemorated a victory in the *anthippasia*. Monuments celebrating victories in the *anthippasia* have been found outside the Agora: *IG* II² 3079; Epigraphical Museum, Athens, EM 13367: Vanderpool 1974: 312–13 no. 1. For the tripod as the prize at the Olympieia, see *Agora* XVI 203.1–4 from the mid third century BC.

[89] Agora Excavations, Athens, I 7167: above, n. 88. In my earlier discussion of this relief, I followed previous scholars in dating it to c. 400; like [K]rat[e]s' base, the relief more probably belongs shortly after 390.

[90] Agora Excavations, Athens, I 7515: above, n. 88.   [91] J. L. Shear 2003: 172 with n. 42.

[92] *IG* II² 3147 + 3149a + 3150 + 3154 + *Agora* I 1315: Dow 1935: 81–90 no. 38 with Meritt 1960: 56 no. 81, cf. *IDélos* 1957.

leftover from the Periclean period, particularly in terms of its material (marble) and decoration (elaborate sculpture), even though it was not part of the design for the Periclean Acropolis. The initial impetus for its construction seems to have been the Athenians' general concern to strengthen their religious life during the 420s. As such, the building is only one aspect of a phenomenon visible throughout the city. In contrast to the situation on the Acropolis, the focus of display and construction shifted to the Agora during this period. The projects of the 420s, however, do not yet represent the new square: the Hephaisteion had been begun in the middle of the century, while the Stoa of Zeus and South Stoa I repeat the organising effects of the earlier Stoa Poikile on the west and south sides of the Agora. In contrast, the changes after 411 are of a different order of magnitude and resulted in the creation of a very different space for the *demos*, one which was no longer a default public area. Now, it was firmly identified as the sphere of the citizen and, within this space, the democracy itself and its actions and the deeds of the democratic citizen were emphasised through display and commemoration. The inscriptions, representing proper democratic practices, wrote the control of the *demos* directly on to the marketplace. Together with the display of the laws, they emphasised that the democracy was a stable and permanent form of rule. In commemorating military achievements, both the overthrow of the Thirty and even more so the victory at Cnidus, the democracy was again emphasised and the individuals celebrated were identified as democratic saviours and 'tyrant slayers' on whom future citizens should model themselves.

The causes leading to these radical changes are to be found in the political situation in the years immediately after the oligarchies of the Four Hundred and the Thirty. In 411, the ease with which the oligarchs overthrew the democracy indicated clearly that the Athenians could not simply rely on the existing default mechanisms to protect the rule of the *demos*. They clearly did not work, and the assumption that democracy was the automatic *politeia* for the city was no longer valid. If democracy was to exist in the future, it would have to be re-established and set on a firm footing both literally and figuratively. The actions of the Four Hundred also set up oligarchy in opposition to democracy; as a result, democratic self-consciousness was greatly enhanced, if not actually born, in opposition to the events of 411. In 410, the problem facing the democrats was not only to make democracy work, but also to demonstrate visibly that it was viable; in 403, the democrats again faced a very similar situation. In both cases, democracy and its products had to be displayed and the city had to be made visibly democratic again.

For these purposes, the Agora proved to be ideal: the multiple uses made of this public space meant that it was associated with no single ideology before 411. At the same time, the Four Hundred's use of the Bouleuterion as the seat of their power indicated their desire to remake the area into their own (oligarchic) space. Similarly, the Thirty also used the Bouleuterion and attempted to dismantle the democratic *politeia* by repealing the laws of Ephialtes and some parts of the laws of Solon, the very foundations of the democracy, as well as curtailing the courts.[93] In 410 and in 403, these actions required the democrats to take back the Agora for the *demos* and to erase the oligarchs' presence from the topography. These actions of the oligarchs explain the democrats' focus on the Bouleuterion, the laws, and the lawcourts, and why they were made into monuments of the rule of the *demos*. To prevent such anti-democratic behaviour in the future, proper models of behaviour needed to be devised, hence the emphasis on displaying and rewarding the deeds of the good democratic citizen, who was expected to slay tyrants and save the city.

This remade Agora brought out the importance of the individual Athenian, who now came here not only to shop, gossip, and stroll, but also and more importantly to act as a democratic citizen in a space dedicated to this function. When he merely came to do his marketing (in temporary, not permanent facilities) and to pass some idle time, he now did so in an Agora overtly identified as democratic space and against the backdrop of permanent icons proclaiming the importance of doing one's civic duty. Their message was simple: anyone could go shopping, but only Athenian citizens could take part in political life in the democratic city. From now on, the Agora would remain the civic heart of Athens, with its honorary statues, decrees, and political public structures.

---

[93] Bouleuterion: Xen. *Hellenica* 2.3.54–6; Lys. 13.38; cf. Xen. *Hellenica* 2.3.11–12, 23; [Arist.] *Ath. Pol.* 35.1, 37.1; Lys. 13.20, 35–7, 74. The Thirty also used the Agora for their own purposes: Xen. *Hellenica* 2.3.20. Laws and courts: [Arist.] *Ath. Pol.* 35.2–3; scholia on Aeschin. 1.39; R. Osborne 2003: 263–4.

CHAPTER 6

The anatomy of metalepsis: visuality turns around on late fifth-century pots

Katharina Lorenz

Visual storytelling on pots of the later fifth century is different from the way stories are designed in earlier vase-painting. The stories depicted appear less dynamic or action-packed, the scenes are composed on multiple ground lines, and the number of labelled characters as well as abstract personifications rises considerably.[1] But even though these shifts carry the potential to signal an iconic turn which could also mark essential changes in general perception, this period has largely remained untouched in the intense research on storytelling in classical vase-painting, as for instance in the work of Wulf Raeck, Alan Shapiro, or Mark Stansbury-O'Donnell.[2] And even in those studies which focus on later fifth-century vase-painting, only two strands of interpretation for this period prevail: the pictures transmit peaceful and pleasant concepts of escapism which cater for a war-ridden Athenian population but at the same time are free of narrative and already signal the decline of vase-painting in general;[3] or the pictures are designed to provide stimulation for the audience of a newly developed culture of writing, an audience used to read stories line by line and on their own, with the vase-paintings solely providing illustrations of stories generated in other media.[4]

These two positions provide some of the co-ordinates which seem to be unavoidable when dealing with late fifth-century visual narrative: the end of Athenian vase-painting towards the middle of the fourth century, the Peloponnesian War, and the interdependence of literary and artistic media within Athenian culture. While the doomed end of a genre fails to

My warmest thanks go to the Fritz-Thyssen-Stiftung who funded the initial research for this study with a generous grant. Robin Osborne and Ivana Petrovic read and commented on earlier drafts, and I am indebted to them for their great expertise and their constant help.
[1] On personifications in Greek art: Shapiro 1993; Borg 2002.
[2] Raeck 1984; Shapiro 1994; Stansbury-O'Donnell 1999.
[3] Hahland 1930; Real 1973; Strocka 1975; Burn 1987; Burn 1989; Söldner 1999. A more diversified analysis: Borbein 1995.
[4] Giuliani 2003: 261.

function sufficiently as an argument against its originality or inventiveness, and while there is still the need to disentangle in detail the actual impact of the Peloponnesian War on Athenian artistic production, thinking about the specific qualities of transmission used in the single media, the literary and the artistic, opens a path for reassessing vase-painting in the later fifth century.

In the following, I will analyse storytelling in vase-painting with the help of an approach adapted from literary theory, focusing on narrative strategies, and specifically that of *metalepsis*, a term introduced by Gerard Genette to characterise situations in which actually distinct narrative levels are merged with each other.

My aim is to test if and in what ways a category used to describe a specific narrative strategy of a text helps to pin down the communicative potential of pictures and can account for what exactly makes vase-painting special on the verge from the fifth to the fourth century BC. This use of a category employed to characterise texts also serves a further purpose: to test Luca Giuliani's assumption that the later fifth century is the period in which visual storytelling becomes dependent on storytelling in written texts and tries to re-enact it to cater for the audience's new attitude of perception. In assessing the specific power of visual storytelling in the later fifth century through a literary category, it becomes possible to reassess this postulated relation of texts and images in this period.

VISUALISING METALEPSIS

What state is defined by metalepsis? And in what ways can a category developed to characterise texts be used to do the same for pictures? When Gerard Genette explains its functioning, he uses a short story by Julio Cortazar in which the protagonist is killed by a character from the book he is reading;[5] a fictitious character takes control of the realm of its (equally fictitious) recipient. Following Genette, metalepsis marks situations in which the boundaries between distinct narrative levels are crossed or even annihilated, an action performed by narrative agents stepping above or below their specific narrative level, via either a specific action or a speech act, and either within the text or even from text to recipient, as for instance when a character in a book directly addresses the readers and advises them to do something.[6]

---

[5] Genette 1980: 234–7; Cortazar 1977.   [6] Melina 2002; Jahn 2003: 2.3.5.

The quality and impact of metalepsis derive from breaking down one normally clearly separated level of narrative into another, or even into the reality the recipient occupies. Thus metalepsis denotes the transgression of narrative levels, with a disturbing effect on the recipients' anticipation, since the muddling of otherwise distinct levels of narrative and/or reality is not part of the general author–reader agreement. Yet, the effect on the shell-shocked readers is one of a more intense relation to the narrative(s): they need to reconfigure their anticipation, and they can even become part of the story, reacting to the demands posed on them by characters within the narrative. It is especially this last aspect which is generated because metalepsis as a narrative tool is more than just transgressing narrative levels and confusing recipients: by blending different levels of a narrative it constructs a mode of storytelling in which in some situations narrator, internal narrative, and external audience can meet face to face on the same narrative level. Thus, by manipulating the recipients' perception, metalepsis ties narration and audience closer together, letting the narrative take hold of or incorporate the readers who are originally external to the narrative, and thus extending its narrative impact.

In this sense, metalepsis characterises narrative situations which are already fuelled by visual qualities – as soon as a fictitious character steps into the world of another, hierarchically separated figure, the character gains a different quality of existence, and when a figure steps into that of the external recipients he gains a material existence; and as soon as the recipients feel the urge to react to the text they materialise themselves within it. The potential to be used for analysing pictures thus seems to be already inherent in metalepsis. Yet, from the perspective of visual art, the situation presents itself as more problematic. The key category, the narrative agent – such as a narrator – who defines and regulates the starting level from which the narrative hierarchy is derived, is hard to identify, if he can be identified at all: one could start from the protagonists of a scene if a picture features any, but just as a narrative text does not necessarily rely on its story's protagonists as narrative agents, this could also apply to the setup of a narrative picture, so the search for a protagonist could be in vain. Another vital difference between the media is that in visual art it is to be anticipated that the crossing of narrative boundaries will generally work through actions and not speech acts, at least in those cases which do not feature a mix of media within the piece of visual art itself.

Considering these co-ordinates as regards metalepsis in visual art, constructing such an effect in the visual appears to be an intellectual affair, and most of the modern pictures which create a situation of metalepsis are

Figure 6.1: 'The Eavesdropper', by Nicolas Maes.

immensely self-reflexive on their own status as visual monuments to create such an effect, as is, for instance, Nicolas Maes's *Eavesdropper*.[7] There, a maid standing behind a door, a short distance away from a man and a woman interacting, looks out of the picture on to the external spectators,

[7] Nicolas Maes, *The Eavesdropper* (1655). Collection of Harold Samuel, London.

and by putting her finger over her mouth indicates to them to remain quiet. In this way, the maid becomes the narrative agent who, skipping the narrative level by which she is separated from the external recipients, not only draws them into the same narrative level as herself – eavesdropping on a third party – but even regulates their specific attitude of perception, through an action which works as a silent speech act and transgresses the confined space of the picture frame. Whatever the basic hierarchy of narrative levels intended in the picture's inner narrative – Is the maid the narrative agent of the first order? Could the couples in the background possess the qualities of narrative agents? – the action of the maid creates its own hierarchy in relation to the external recipients in which her eavesdropping occupies the first level, and the couple the second.

These interacting spectator figures form a special case of visual narrative, and their morphing abilities make them seem only natural as a gateway through which another category from literary theory entered visual studies: reception aesthetics.[8]

The case of *The Eavesdropper* exemplifies that narrative in pictures can acquire the vital ingredients for a metaleptic situation: a hierarchy of narrative agents, as well as the crossing of narrative levels, through actions as well as through speech acts, which in their visual form remain of course silent. But how about metalepsis outside the world of spectator figures, and specifically in Greek antiquity?

While metalepsis forms a narrative reality in texts as early as Homer, who sometimes lets his auctorial voice address one of his characters directly,[9] transgressive narrative agents like the maid do not appear in pictures. What are more common from early on are figures who transgress the pictorial space confined to them: figures who look out of the picture or even figures who reach outside the picture frames on pots or in architectural sculpture. The most striking such situation is probably the giant in the frieze of the Pergamon Altar, whose knee rests on the steps of the altar's stairs.[10] This physically surmounting the pictorial space, especially, appears as a visual version of the crossing of narrative boundaries, such as between a narrative agent within a text and an external recipient: the character from the story materialises within the sphere of the recipient, neglecting his narrative's frame as defined by the pictorial space and thus violating any intradiegetic or extradiegetic mode of storytelling. In his seminal work on fourth-century sculpture, Adolf Borbein (1973: 43–61) has demonstrated

---

[8] Kemp 1998.   [9] E.g. *Iliad* 16.692–3. De Jong 2002: esp. 16.
[10] Northern projection of the Great Frieze; Berlin, Pergamon Museum. Zanker 2004: 103–12.

how such a reaching into the external viewer's sphere traceable in sculpture in the round can become an aesthetically defining element of a certain period.

The *Eavesdropper* gives an example of equivalent strategies of pictorial narrative in constructing a metaleptic situation – the composition of the figures and their interaction, the use of speech acts or speech-act-like actions. Yet there is one aspect not important for this picture but crucial for ancient visual art, and specifically for ancient vase-painting: the bodily presence of the material carrier. In vase-painting, this body is not just the surface around which the pictorial space is positioned; it also has another, doubled function: it both regulates the pictorial space and at the same time is a vital element of it, and above all it has the power to regulate hierarchies of narrative. As a 'body of narrative' the material carrier can achieve the role of an (extradiegetic) agent of narrative, opening or closing perspectives on to the story, emphasising or combining certain elements, and also helping to cross the boundaries of the narrative hierarchies it itself helps to regulate. This is where the text differs from the picture, and also where vase-painting, perceived within (and through) its material context, differs from flat-panel paintings or from productions on stage.

In what follows, these two aspects – the composition and the body of narrative – will form the co-ordinates within which I am aiming to calibrate the category 'metalepsis' for the visual to extract strategies of visual storytelling, and specifically of vase-painting in the later fifth century.

DOUBLED NARRATIVE? THE NICIAS PAINTER

A hydria by the Nicias Painter from the later fifth century presents the Judgement of Paris, a very popular subject in vase-painting as well as on the theatre stage in this period.[11] The vessel is decorated in an area which reaches from the shoulder down to the lower third of the body, and it offers three areas of action which are differentiated by their position as well as by the size of their figures, which is increased towards the outer layers: a central picture field, a figure between the attachments of each side handle and thus partly covered by the handle, and a figure to each of the further ends of the side handles.

The narrative is generated by ten characters. The Trojan prince Paris is presented in oriental dress and with a Phrygian cap. He is positioned left

---

[11] Hydria by the Nicias Painter, once Cancello; from Suessula. Von Duhn 1887: pl. 12; *ARV*² 1334.28; *LIMC* VII (1994), s.v. 'Priamos' no. 13 (J. Neils). On the myth in Greek vase-painting: *LIMC* VII (1994) s.v. 'Paridis Iuridicum' (A. Kossatz-Delssmann); also Raab 1972; Raeck 1984; Lorenz 2006.

Figure 6.2: Hydria, by the Nicias Painter. Once Cancello. Courtesy of the German
Archaeological Institute, Rome.

of the central picture axis and depicted in conversation with Hermes, who
stands right in front of him. Underneath the prince lies a bull or cow, only
its bust and forelegs visible as if hidden in a shelter. To the right of Hermes
stands Athena, facing the two men. Behind her sits a second goddess,
as indicated by the lotus-topped sceptre she holds. She is equally looking
towards the two men, and she has raised her right hand as if waving, with her
index finger extended. Considering her dress, posture, and even attributes –
a partridge is sitting underneath her – she is probably Aphrodite. Such an
identification is also supported by the little winged Eros who is aiming
for her, floating between Hermes and Athena, and who carries a garland
as if to indicate her victory. So the outcome of the judgement is already
anticipated in the hydria's design.

The other five characters on the pot are more difficult to name. The
goddess Hera is still missing from the band of goddesses, and since she
appears in all pictorial versions of the story from this period she can be
expected to be present.[12] Left of Paris stands a woman dressed in a richly
ornamented peplos who carries a lotus-topped sceptre. She closely resembles
Aphrodite, who sits on the other side, but in contrast to her this woman
on the left is not focused on Paris and Hermes but looks outside of the
central picture field to the left. Her sceptre supports her identification as a
goddess, and her similarity with Aphrodite would not necessarily contradict

[12] Raab 1972: 37–41, 80–91.

Figure 6.2 (*cont.*).

the identification as Hera, since the two goddesses frequently look similar in the scenes of the Judgement.[13] What is more remarkable is that she is not interacting with the central scene, neither with Paris nor with her fellow goddesses.

In this respect, a character from the second pictorial layer outside the central picture field would fit an identification as Hera much better, even though she is bigger than the figures in the central picture field: between the handle attachments on the right stands a woman who has raised her heavy, unadorned garment in the modest *aidos* motif and looks towards the group of Paris, thus continuing the line Athena and Aphrodite have established. At the same time, her position between the handles as well as her size relate her to the male in oriental dress who stands between the handle attachments on the left side of the vessel: he looks almost exactly like Paris, and he carries two spears, as the prince does. He is about to move towards the left, but has turned his head towards the right, looking back to the central scene as well as to the woman between the handle attachments on the other side, and he has raised his right hand as if to wave or even to articulate a lack of interest.

The third layer is established by an old man with a beard, who, on the far right of the vessel, leans on a sceptre, and who is dressed in a mantle

---

[13] Raab 1972: 88 9.

and wears a fillet in his hair. He is mirrored on the far left by a woman in dress and mantle with a cap covering most of her hair.

To pin down the specific story, the identification of characters is the central issue, but there are no decisive clues offered apart from the figures themselves. This is noticeable since the vessel comes from a period in which labelling characters is both absolutely normal and necessary, since this is also a period in which personifications flood the images who otherwise could not be identified.[14] Here however, the use of script is confined to deliver strings of letter-like yet meaningless forms above the heads of the characters from Paris to Aphrodite.

Depending on the identity of the enigmatic characters, the actions on the hydria from Suessula can be broken down into three levels of narrative. The first level is the one of the actual judgement scene, of which Paris and Hermes as well as Eros, Athena, and Aphrodite inside the central picture field form a part. The woman left of Paris, earlier identified as Hera, is physically present only in this first level of narrative, but not in regard to her action, since she is interacting with the Phrygian between the handles on the left.

The second level of narrative is generated by the figures within the handle zone: on the left the Phrygian, on the right the woman with the aidos gesture. If seen next to each other, they appear as a generic scene of a soldier's farewell: the man carries his weapons and waves goodbye, the woman presents herself in the attire of a modest wife. It is this similarity to farewell pictures which has led interpreters to identify the woman as the nymph Oinone, who is, in the literary versions of the myth, left by Paris to abduct Helen, Aphrodite's reward for his judgement. This would mean that Paris is depicted twice on the vessel. But it is questionable if this layer's characters need to be identified as specifically as this, especially since there is a tendency to name anonymous female figures within judgement scenes on Attic pots as Oinone even though no evidence exists for such identification. Though the character is named for the first time in the later fifth century by Hellanicos,[15] labelled scenes which show her and Paris together appear only in the first century AD, and probably as a response to Ovid's *Heroides* 5.[16] So on the hydria, the two could equally well present a Trojan couple whose male partner has to leave to enter war. In the context of the judgement scene, one could assume the reason for the parting to be the Trojan War, which ultimately follows from Paris' decision, and thus

---

[14] On labelling personifications, see Shapiro 1993; Borg 2002; R. Osborne 2000.
[15] *FGrHist* 4 F29.
[16] For the myth: *LIMC* VII (1994), s.v. 'Oinone' nos. 23–6 (L. Kahil).

this second compositional layer would transmit a second level of narrative which follows sequentially from the judgement episode.

The third compositional layer, outside the handles, works slightly differently. Because of the specific royal attributes of the male, the two figures depicted here can be taken to represent Priam and Hecuba, the parents of Paris. They would not necessarily form a further sequence of the narrative which starts from the judgement and ultimately ends with the Trojan War, but rather a detached instance which explains Paris' existence and equally heralds the impact which his judgement will have on his family. This is a kind of sequential layering in a composition which can be found on hydriai as early as the Vivenzio hydria by the Kleophrades Painter depicting the Fall of Troy, where a further narrative is heralded by a group at each end of the multi-event picture, leading the picture field into a new future: Aeneas to the left, Aithra to the right.[17] Likewise, a hydria by the Coghill Painter which depicts the binding of Andromeda is complemented to the right-hand side by the depiction of Perseus, who already foreshadows Andromeda's later rescue.[18]

But this naming of the mythological characters can only partly account for the compositional dynamics of the vessel. It rather seems that the composition and especially the threefold vertical layering of the figures introduce a doubling and even an ambiguity of identification into the scene which the figures in their visual characterisation do not support, and into which they are forced solely by the compositional design. These dynamics are generated by the female figure left of the seated Paris as well as by the second oriental.

What the composition does for the myth becomes apparent in the farewell scene on layer 2. The difference from generic farewell scenes is that the recipients need to turn the vessel considerably to find the counterpart of both of these handle characters. The path of understanding thus leads the eye via the scene in the central picture field, and it is thus that these two levels of narrative – nicely constructed through composition as well as through the size and characterisation of the figures – are again deconstructed. When turning from left to right, the first mirror of the Phrygian's action is the woman with the sceptre, who was identified as Hera. It is here that narrative levels 1 and 2 collapse into each other. The goddess enters a narrative level below her own; the man – by leaving for the one above his own level of narrative – again marks the permeability of narrative levels.

---

[17] Hydria by the Kleophrades Painter ('Vivenzio Hydria'): Naples, Museo Nazionale Archeologico 2422, from Nola. *ARV* 189.74.

[18] Hydria by the Coghill Painter: London, British Museum E169, from Vulci. *ARV* 1062.

In this sense, both characters perform an act of metalepsis. At the same time, not only does this arrangement perform a common act of metalepsis, but, by crossing the narrative borders, the characters depicted also seem to change their identity. The oriental signals or waves to the goddess, an action which raises anticipation, especially as regards the identity of the one signalling as well as the one receiving the signal. What would a generic Trojan signal to a goddess, and to which goddess? The two Trojans who have a more intense relationship with a goddess are Anchises and Paris, and in both cases the goddess is Aphrodite. Given the iconographic similarities between the seated Paris and this man, it is justifiable to identify him again as Paris, appearing twice on the same vessel. The same applies to the goddess whose iconographical parallels to Aphrodite were already mentioned. Thus re-identified, this narrative-transgressing group would explicitly articulate the aftermath of the judgement, Paris's choice as well as his leaving for Helen.

When continuing to turn to the right, another re-identification comes up: the woman between the right handle attachments automatically becomes part of the band of goddesses within the central picture field, since she shares their focal point, the seated Paris, and in raising her veil she also performs an action very similar to those that Hera generally performs. Thus the woman, who on the second compositional layer mirrors the action of the Trojan who corresponds to her between the other handle attachments, thus also crosses her narrative level, and, becoming the goddess Hera, she materialises in the one above her own, the Judgement scene, which at the same time changes her identification.[19]

As already mentioned, the third level of narrative is formed by the bearded king and the elderly woman who stand outside the handles. Again they mark situations of transgressing the narrative levels, since the woman is not only a mirror of the king on the other side, but equally forms the destination to which the Phrygian between the handles is striving. In this way, she forms a typical character of a farewell scene – one of the parents who are present when their son leaves – and thus she again enters narrative level 2. At the same time, both of the distant characters take part not only in the action between the handle attachments but also in the judgement scene in the centre, in which they function as spectator figures. As such, there is another double crossing of narrative levels.

[19] For a parallel composition in which Hera is shown between the handle attachments, compare a hydria by the Modica Painter: Syracuse, Museo Archeologico Regionale Paolo Orsi 38031, from Modica. ARV^2 1340.1.

Here, it is important to note that the picture demands a redefinition of narrative 'level', and this again marks a modification of metalepsis for visual analysis. In narratological terms all the characters depicted on the level would belong to the same narrative level, and only to different stages of the story. Yet, for the visual, a different principle of application seems to be necessary, since here the stages are not just different points along a line. They are, rather, distinctly used to reflect and comment on each other, as with Priam and Hecuba, who have no clear place in this line. Also, some of the characters can change their identity while moving from one level to another, and this is not a simple proleptic change of narrative stages, but a crucial modification, even a creation of new narrative. As such, they not only signal different points of reflection and abstraction, but also can generate differing narrative options, and subsequently need to be defined as distinct narrative levels.

With its different narrative levels and their interweaving, the vessel's decoration not only tells the story of Paris' judgement but also – in a specific as well as a generalising way – points towards its future course, visualising Paris' decision and departure as well as the impact on his family and on the generic Trojan. This anticipation of later events has the characteristics of a prolepsis in narratological terms,[20] which here gains further importance because the chronologically distinct levels are again metaleptically linked. Yet the proleptic and metaleptic elements of the visual narrative are not a direct part of the picture field, but are pushed towards its edges or even outside its boundaries, which are formed by the handles. Approaching the vessel frontally, these figures cannot be clearly perceived. They only come into play when moving the eye to the right or to the left – a possible viewer action at least stimulated by the goddess left of the seated Paris being oriented to the left and away from the central scene. By moving the eye, the viewer then also moves in narrative time and complexity, having to bridge the gaps as regards both content and temporal and narrative relations between the judgement scene and the four figures around the handles.

When considering the hydria in use, the dynamics go even further. One could take it by the two side handles, and thus exactly on the level of those figures – the Trojan-alias-Paris and the woman-alias-Hera – which (a) introduce a generalising element into the mythological cast, (b) construct proleptically different temporal stages, and (c) form a vital part of the metaleptic cracks within the picture's composition. Handling the

<hr />

[20] Genette 1980: 33–85

vessel, these characters are partly covered by the user's hands and – being thus invisible – could drop out of the picture, which would thus be relieved of many of its narrative frills. On the other hand, it is exactly this possibility of taking hold of the vessel in this specific place which invites the recipient to become literally part of the figure, substituting its body when grasping the handle. Such a direct contact with the scene's cast again creates a situation of metalepsis, in this case one that works between internal narration and external recipient. Again, as with the metaleptic situations inside the pictorial frame, this is generated not through a speech act but by requesting an action through the material carrier's design.

FRAMING REVOLUTION: THE VISUALITY OF ATHENIAN VASE-PAINTING

The example of the Nicias Painter's hydria brings up anew what exactly makes up for the specific ways of storytelling postulated here for the later fifth century: by simultaneously referring to different points of narrative (polychronous storytelling) as well as hinting at the future outcome (proleptic storytelling), it employs ways of storytelling which can already be found on vessels from the sixth or early fifth century onwards respectively, such as the Vivenzio hydria or the hydria by the Coghill Painter; and the feature of putting figures in between the handle attachments, so crucial for constructing interaction with recipients, also appears before the later fifth century, for instance on a stamnos in London by the Berlin Painter from the first third of the century.[21] In what ways does storytelling on late fifth-century vases differ from these earlier pictorial conceptions, and how was their special narrative potential developed? What is the visual corpus from which they emerge?

When browsing pots from the middle of the sixth down to the fifth century, the most notable feature is that figures are composed in frieze form, standing on a single, clearly defined ground-line, frequently acting within individual groups of twos or threes if not in a continuous movement in one direction. It is only with scenes from the second half of the sixth century that bystanders fill the picture fields, who primarily react to the action on display in the central scene.[22] This specific strategy of displaying figurative scenes is significantly altered only towards the middle of the fifth century with the designs of the Niobid Painter and his followers. While they still sport the

---

[21] Stamnos by the Berlin Painter: London, British Museum E444, from Vulci, *ARV²* 208.149.
[22] E.g. belly amphora by Lydos: Berlin, Staatliche Museen 1685, from Vulci. *ARV* 109.24.

traditional frieze compositions,[23] they are also the first to introduce designs in which the figures are spread in a random manner over the picture field, occupying different ground levels and thus interacting with each other from multiple angles. The most notable example is the Niobid Painter's name vase, a calyx-krater in Paris depicting Apollo and Artemis slaying the Niobids.[24] This tendency of spatial composition has frequently been connected with large-scale wall-painting, which, on the basis of later literary description, is presumed to have featured similar strategies of spreading figures in space, as in the Athenian Stoa Poikile. Whatever the influence of the other genre, many of the more influential vase-painters of the third quarter of the fifth century, the Polygnotos Painter and his group and the Cleophon Painter primarily adhered to frieze compositions. It is only with the Dinos, Eretria, and Meidias Painters and their followers that the spatial composition gains popularity again.

Next to the spatial placing of figures, the way the figures who form a picture's cast are characterised and brought into interaction with each other in a temporal perspective is a vital element in how vase pictures transmit stories. As frequently noted, the general narrative tendencies from the sixth to the fifth century change from the anachronic merging of different points in the narrative into one, synoptic scene towards compositions which focus on only one specific moment of the story,[25] or – as Giuliani (2003: 162–3) puts it – the trend goes from polychronous to monochronous pictures.

With regard to characterisation, earlier research is more divided. Wulf Raeck, who focuses on scenes of the Judgement of Paris, differentiates between how the individual figures and the scenes of action are characterised:[26] for him, the most elemental trend in fifth-century vase-painting is the emphasis on personal characterisation of single figures, which also becomes apparent in labelling figures, and not using standardised types. Giuliani – based on a critical discussion of Gotthold Ephraim Lessing's Laokoon terminology – works from a different set of parameters, and differentiates between descriptive (*deskriptiv*) and narrative (*narrativ*) elements in pictures, as well as between figures who are used 'as attribute' (*attributiv*) and those who work 'as situation' (*situativ*).[27]

Giuliani claims that there is a trend in the fifth century for the cast to operate more and more on the *attributiv* level, an observation which could

[23] Calyx-krater with two friezes (Pandora, satyrs): London, British Museum E467, from Altamura, *ARV* 601.23; calyx-krater with two friezes (Gigantomachy, Dionysus): Ferrara 2891 (T. 313), from Spina. *ARV* 602.24.
[24] Calyx-crater: Paris, Louvre G 431, from Orvieto. *ARV* 601.22.
[25] Robert 1881; Raeck 1984; Giuliani 2002; Giuliani 2003.
[26] Himmelmann 1967; Förtsch 1997; Raeck 1984; Stansbury-O'Donnell 1999; Giuliani 2002, 2003.
[27] Giuliani 2003: 35, 283, 285–6 (*narrativ*); 36, 222–4 (*deskriptiv*); 160 (*attributiv*); 161 (*situativ*).

be put in parallel with Raeck's observation on the emphasis on personal characterisation, extending the picture's content from one primarily based on transmitting a 'pure' story ('narrative' in Giuliani's sense) to one in which the narrative is lifted to a more generalised level, which not only tells a good story but also serves further purposes of describing global conditions of life and offers points of identification which reach beyond the mythological level. As an example for this, Giuliani brings forward the Vivenzio hydria with its broad depiction of the cruelty of war, not just the transmission of a particular epic episode.

From the late fifth century – Giuliani claims – there is then a certain trend to narrow the narrative-cum-descriptive scope of the pictures to tell single episodes from literary narrative. It is this that enables painters now to refer to written texts and to an 'exact' storyline and not just to oraliture, the corpus of texts heard only as spoken word from a poet, which through its constant repetition gains a literary feel, but still one in which storylines can be altered and episodes are interchangeable.

Placing the Nicias hydria in the context of these trends, it becomes apparent that its basic frieze style design is rather conservative, and its employment of polychronous as well as proleptic elements is in a sense old-fashioned because it reaches back to developments already apparent in the middle of the sixth century. At the same time it employs them in completely new form. In the first place, these elements – via the scene's cast – are merged into each other further to specify the central scene, and at the same time also to create a collapsing but dense narrative which is driven by its metaleptic structure and as such has an intense effect on its viewers. The picture works like a hologram, which, as one moves the surface, changes its appearance, while the overall content is always there even if not visible. In this way, the well-known elements of pictorial storytelling are employed to create a new narrative situation, one in which also the attributive characters can gain narrative potential. The second formal innovation lies in its specific design. The decorated vessel surmounts one of the focal problems of visual storytelling, which is the question of how an image or picture can guide or control the recipient's gaze.[28] This is solved here through creating different layers of framed situations which can only be viewed from different perspectives: the central pictorial frame, the handle frame, the back area. Not all of these frames offer an actual narrative individually, but they do so in relation to each other, and that narrative crosses the borders of the single frames. And it is here that the novelty in pictorial design can

[28] Giuliani 2003: 286–7.

Figure 6.3: Hydria, by the Meidias Painter.

be located, a pictorial design which in its ambivalence, depending on the viewer's perspective, creates a narrative in the visual and one that only the visual could create.

LABELLING AND SPACING: THE MEIDIAS PAINTER

A hydria in London helps further to disentangle strategies of storytelling in late fifth-century vase painting, again in respect of contextual movement

and with regard to the use of labels for characters. It is the name vase of
the Meidias Painter, one of the most influential vase-painters in the later
fifth century, whose name is derived from the potter's signature, 'Meidias
epoiesen', on the neck of this hydria in London. The general design of
the hydria is more complex than that by the Nicias Painter. Earlier hydriai
had a shoulder frieze and a large picture field on the body of the vessel.[29]
On the London hydria, what normally would be the shoulder frieze is
stretched down to a level underneath the handles, thus creating a large,
fairly trapezoid upper picture. Underneath is space for a frieze running
around the whole vessel.

The two picture areas of the pot – the field above and the frieze below –
have to be looked at differently. The upper field works as a panorama picture
that can be fully perceived from above in an angle of about 15°. The frieze
below can only properly be seen from a much lower viewpoint. Also, the
frieze is no panorama picture but enfolds a narrative that has to be followed
around the vessel. The linkage between upper and lower picture field is
thus primarily restricted to the central part of the frieze just underneath
the upper field.

If the viewers are to appreciate the complete decoration, they necessarily
have to engage in some activity, by turning the vessel or by shifting their
point of view. But they need to do more than simply turn it through 180°,
which is sufficient for many Greek pots, where there is a picture on the
front and another on the back. On the London hydria there are not two
but multiple options of perceiving, and they merge into one another. They
are equal, in that none of them offers a complete view of both of the picture
areas. The decoration can be perceived only in single clippings, and thus
the design of the vessel is constituted between opening and covering the
single parts of the vessel.

The hydria shows the rape of the Leucippides in the upper picture field,
and in the lower frieze Heracles in the Garden of the Hesperides, accompanied by a set of Athenian tribal heroes. Identification of characters is
no problem here, since all are provided with name labels. As well as the
vessel's general design, the choice of stories is remarkable. The Rape of the
Spartan Leucippides by the Dioscuroi almost never appears in Athenian
vase-painting.[30] Close to the neck, two chariots are spread to either side.
The one on the left has Polydeuces racing away with Elera; in the chariot
on the right stands Chrysippus, who holds the reins, waiting for the other

[29] On this pot shape in general, see Diehl 1964: esp. 61–8.
[30] The only further evidence for pictures of this story in classical Athens is Pausanias, who talks about
a painting of the wedding of the Leucippides in the Anakeion on the Athenian Agora (1 18.1).

pair, Castor and Eriphyle, who are just about to fly up from underneath. Between the two chariots is positioned an archaising statue, probably of Aphrodite, as indicated by the goddess herself sitting underneath next to an altar.[31] Aphrodite looks at the flying pair, as do most of the other figures in the picture: on the left Zeus, Agave, and Chryseis, on the right Peitho.

Lucilla Burn (1987: 15) called the composition 'centrifugal and cohesive', both at the same time. One reason for this impression is that an area close to the actual centre of the picture field is left empty, with single groups of figures arranged in a circle around it. At the same time, the scene is focused on Castor and Eriphyle, with at least five figures looking at them. The composition unfolds along two diagonal lines crossing each other in the group of Castor and Eriphyle. Thus a closely knit cross of action is created, with one line reaching from Aphrodite to Chrysippus, and the other from Peitho to the chariot of Polydeuces and Elera. Yet, with the action building up towards the end of almost each line (Polydeuces and Elera in the chariot are racing away, Peitho is running away, Chrysippus' chariot faces outwards) there is also a strong centrifugal element introduced that puts tension on the closely knit compositional centre. The composition is based on a central nucleus, but there are also dynamic forces guiding the eye away from it. Furthermore, this notion of dynamic is underlined by certain asymmetrical elements: the central figure group is not in the centre of the picture; and there is the group of Zeus, Agave, and Chryseis to the left, who do not directly belong to the closely knit cross-composition but react to it.

As to mythological identification, the name labels clearly identify both the Dioscuroi: Polydeuces as the character in the disappearing chariot, and Castor as the man in the central group. Yet the Leucippides feature under unusual labels. They are called Elera and Eriphyle, whereas normally in the literary sources they are called Hilaeira and Phoebe.[32] Whereas 'Elera' could be derived from 'Hilaeira', no straightforward connection between 'Eriphyle' and 'Phoebe' seems to exist. On the contrary, Eriphyle is one of the chief characters of a completely unconnected mythological story: she is bribed by Polyneices with Harmonia's necklace to talk her husband Amphiaraus into joining the Seven against Thebes, though he knows he will meet his death there. Eriphyle features as the role model of the greedy, untrustworthy wife.[33] Given that, Castor would have made a very bad

---

[31] Burn 1987: 22.
[32] On the myth, see *LIMC* III, s.v. 'Dioskuroi' (A. Hermary). The inscription PHOIBE appears on a black-figure vase fragment: Reggio Calabria, Mus. Naz. 1027–8 (*LIMC* III, 1986 s.v. 'Dioskuroi', no. 194).
[33] On the myth *LIMC* III, s.v. 'Eriphyle' (A. Lezzl-Hafter).

choice in abducting her. Since the Meidias Painter is generally reliable in his labelling, what appears at first sight as a mistake could be a case of mythological allusion. In this way the artist could provide the group of Castor and Eriphyle with an attributive story element in regard to the potential course of their relationship otherwise not inherent in the myth. Such an allusion would not be unusual in this period, as Christine Sourvinou-Inwood has shown in her analysis of a cup-tondo by the Codrus Painter.[34]

With Chryseis and Agave, the two women left of the altar, more descriptive-cum-narrative elements enter the scene: these are 'speaking names': Chryseis is the golden, Agave the noble and brilliant. Both could bring in further mythological echoes, the first featuring in another case of abduction as Agamemnon's booty in the *Iliad*, the second as mother of Pentheus, who will slay her son, and is thus again not exactly the woman you would want to abduct.[35] On the other side of the altar appears Peitho, who personifies persuasion.

These figures all provide the scene with further narrative lines and even with a commenting counter-reading of the central scene of action. The abduction of the Leucippides appears remarkably harmonious compared with other scenes of rape: Elera stands in the chariot not fighting off Polydeuces but, rather, elaborately presenting herself in a motif typical of contemporary pictures of Aphrodite, thus underlining her beauty. The same applies for Eriphyle, who has taken a gracious position that seems fit for a dancer, floating in the air. Aphrodite, the goddess of love, and Zeus, the father of the Dioscuroi, further underline this jolly harmony by looking up to the pair, not disapprovingly, and so does Chryseis. It is only persuasion and nobility, Peitho and Agave, running away from this sight of harmonious rape. Despite the overall peaceful abduction, their running away seems to indicate that the scene is still a forceful rape, in which persuasion and nobility have no place.

In all, the strategies concerning the overall handling of the material carrier are also extended to the inner narrative structure of the panoramic field, requiring the recipients constantly to reposition themselves. The figures are linked to each other in a highly dynamic way: the separate actions are not presented discretely, but individual figures merge into or dissolve from particular interactive relations depending on the focus of the viewer's gaze. Also, the figures are connected to each other on multiple levels of meaning – situative in the case of the figures belonging to the same mythological story,

[34] Apparently his name-piece: Sourvinou-Inwood 1990.
[35] On the myth, see *LIMC* VII, s.v. 'Pentheus' (J. Bazant and G. Berger-Doer).

Figure 6.4: Hydria, by the Meidias Painter.

and attributive in the case of the personifications and those figures that do not belong to the inner circle of the Leucippid story but here act in it via the metaphorical or mythological content that floats in the background.[36] In the end, the viewers get both: men and women gracefully pairing off and just a hint of a real, forceful rape picture.

The design of the upper pictorial field is very much in contrast with what is depicted in the lower frieze. Except for the frontal part of the frieze, which depicts Heracles in the Garden of the Hesperids,[37] the figures are set in traditionally composed three-figure groups, and the men are not dressed in elaborate clothing, as the Dioscuroi above are, but rather appear undressed, carrying a mantle and spears. Again, it is the name labels that help to identify the characters; a necessity, since the visual characterisation of the cast is in most cases rather generic. The focus in the central part is towards the right on the seated Heracles, who looks on to the Hesperid Lipara. Standing in front of him, she displays her beauty in a similar way to

---

[36] On similar narrative strategies in theatre plays, see Zeitlin 1990, 1994.
[37] On Hesperides in general, see *LIMC* v, s.v. 'Hesperides' (I. McPhee); also Brommer 1942.

the two Leucippides above. To the left, behind the apple tree, three women and a man watch this scene, and behind Heracles stands Iolaus, who is about to move to the right but looks back.

Moving to the right, underneath the side handle, a group of three women follows. Arniope and Elera frame Medea, who – unlike all the other women on the pot – is dressed in oriental garments and carries a casket. Further to the right follows a group of two: Philoctetes, facing the old, seated Acamas, one of the Athenian tribal heroes. Another three-figure group follows, consisting of another two tribal heroes, Antiochus and Hypothous/Hippothon, as well as Clymenus. Underneath the left side handle the last three-figure group is positioned, formed by Oineus, Damophon, and Chryseis.

It is unclear in what sense the scene in the garden is connected with the cocktail of primarily Athenian characters, especially since some of the names given to the figures are so general that it is difficult to connect them to a specific storyline. Only the double appearance of Elera and Chryseis, who were already on display in the upper picture field, might indicate some connection between the two story fields.

Earlier interpretations have variously claimed an escapist or a political meaning for the frieze and its combination with the upper pictorial field, and sometimes both these diametrically opposed explanatory strategies have been combined.[38] When seen from a structuralist point of view, the central part of the frieze, as well as the upper picture field, both show scenes of heterosexual courtship which differ in the reaction they receive from their spectators: no one in the lower frieze is running away. They are rather calmly focusing on Heracles and Lipara. So while the set of two mythological stories on the vessel could cater for an interest in heterosexual relationships and how they are established, the remaining figures in the frieze are more difficult to pin down because they contradict various schemes: with the closed-off groups they work against the concept of centrifugal and open design so characteristic for the other parts of the pot, and they do not present a clearly identifiable story but rather feature a cast which is descriptively connected to Athens – four tribal heroes, a king, a son of Theseus, and Medea – but not completely, since some of the names are, again, rather generic names that could belong to personifications (Clymenos, Chryseis).

The easiest explanation of this scene in the lower frieze is that this compositionally clearly distinguished part of the vessel also tells us something different, and in this case not a narrative but a description of Athenian heritage, in which Medea is not so much an evil sorceress as an equal part

[38] Burn 1987: 21.

among the rather loose set of kings and heroes. In combination with the other two pictorial areas, this establishes two distinct areas of transmission, one of narrative and one of description, with the former being spread across both the areas on the front of the vessel, and the latter confined to the back area of the hydria. Through the similarities in composition a case of spatial metalepsis is generated which links the Leucippid and Hesperid stories and – crossing the borders of mythological narrative – associatively draws the latter into the former, an act which happens in the external spectator's mind through the device of comparison. But this is not the only level of metaleptic action: even the compositionally distinct back part of the frieze, which lacks the vital ingredients of a narrative, also crosses the border into the upper picture field, doing so not through narrative layers but through modes of transmission, from the descriptive into the narrative, again established through comparison as manifest in the repetition of characters' names, Elera and Chryseis, and thus their potential double appearance in the groups which frame the paratactic back part of the frieze.

This form of modal metalepsis, between the narrative and the descriptive, again brings into focus the functions of the material carrier of the pictorial frames, the vessel: while the turning needed to experience the single areas further underlines the borders between the distinct modal areas, on the front of the vessel between the two areas of narrative, and from the front to the back, between the narrative and the descriptive, it is the compositions that – through parallel compositional postures as well as name labels – cross these borders again and force the viewers to move back and up. In this way the metaleptic values of the objects on display are not just confined to the mental experience of the recipients but are generated and become corporeal on and through the narrative body of the vessel: the crossing of different layers of transmission is a crossing of different areas of the pot.

With all this, the London hydria makes great demands on its viewers: by requesting a turning of the vessel, the arrangement of the pictorial areas leads to a continuous alteration of the modes of transmission. The viewers have constantly to reposition themselves, and this repositioning offers them, or shuts them off from, single insights into the scenes' content. By applying these visual strategies on the vessel, a way of storytelling is established which can be characterised by the simultaneousness of different modes of transmission and media (visual and textual). This design feeds on communicative options of constructing a text, but at the same time, by organising them in combination as well as by exploiting the potential for creating metaleptic suspense which the hydria as the material carrier offers, this design enables a refreshed and strictly visual transmission of content.

THE BIRTH OF ERICHTHONIUS — MULTISTABILITY V. ESCAPISM

The example of a squat lekythos by the Meidias Painter in Cleveland offers the chance to explore further two aspects of visual storytelling in the later fifth century: the identifiability of characters and escapism,[39] the latter being the main argument for the pots to be free of narrative.

The vessel displays the Birth of Erichthonius, the first king of Athens.[40] This subject appears throughout the fifth century on pots, and in the later fifth century fits in well with the general rise of topics related to Athens. It has generally been considered a particularly patriotic theme that underlines the autochthony of the Athenian people as well as their noble divine roots; it also features in Euripides' *Ion* to stress exactly this fact.[41] The Meidian squat lekythos performs a noticeable twist on the common patriotic outline, generated by the way the figures are identified.

A three-figure group shows a seated woman, identified as Ge, handing a baby, identified as Erichthonius, to Athena, who stands in front of her. This is just one group among others on the vessel, and it is nothing like a central group, since the three are positioned slightly off-centre to the right. By contrast to other versions of the story, the chthonic goddess Ge is neither half hidden in the ground nor crowned, but rather sits fully visible, very much like any other ordinary woman.[42] This simple fact is remarkable, since all the other figures in the scene are also women: five to the left of the group; four to the right, and three above it. Some of these women watch the three-figure group; others are engaged with each other. In their composition, they help to generate a spatial effect in the picture as well as to establish multiple links of visual and actual communication between the single figures, as is typical for Meidian scenes. Yet, quite unusually, none of them is named.

Attempts have frequently been made to label them as the personifications which appear so frequently on other vessels, or even as certain mythological figures who foreshadow the further stages of the Erichthonius myth. Jenifer Neils (1983) identified the women in the upper level as the three Kekriopidai to whom Athena will hand Erichthonius. But such an explicit identification

---

[39] Squat lekythos: Cleveland, County Museum of Art 82.142.
[40] On the myth, see *LIMC* IV, s.v. 'Erechtheus' (U. Kron).
[41] See Burn 1987: 21–2; Walsh 1978; Neils 1983, with identification of the female figures.
[42] On the myth, see *LIMC* IV, s.v. 'Ge' (M. D. Moore).

Figure 6.5: Squat lekythos, by the Meidias Painter.

is not necessary to make sense of the scene; even the woman handing over the baby does not have to be the goddess Ge. If she is rather a generic Athenian woman passing her baby to Athena, this would become a truly and all-embracing patriotic image, and one in which such an action is only one kind of female behaviour, shown among others, and not in a central position. Viewed in this way, the visual structures adopted from other presentations of the Birth of Erichthonius – especially the handing of a baby boy to Athena – are employed to present a not necessarily mythological version of giving birth to male offspring and putting them in the hands of Athens. As such, this forms an example of patriotic ideology and provides a female audience with behavioural ideals.

Just like the back part of the Meidias Painter's hydria, the squat lekythos's decoration transmits a rather descriptive gathering of women, and one in which anonymity is a key issue, since it is only Athena who can be clearly identified through her disposition. The scene gains narrative potential only in the handing over of the baby, which raises various questions about the reasons for and consequences of this act. Again, narrative and descriptive parts are blended into each other on this vessel and here help to generalise the narrative sequence and allow it to gain universal meaning.

This oscillation between mythological and more general ideological meaning creates a situation of multistability, an ambiguity between mytho-logical and allegorical meaning. This is generally a feature very characteristic of Athenian vase-painting, where there is frequently a narrative and ideo-logical tension – the characters could be mythological or generic, or both at the same time, as is also true for the hydria by the Nicias Painter. In this respect, vessels like the London hydria reduce the suspense because they provide labels. There, a tension fuelled by ambiguity enters only through the back door, with the mythological characters known from other stories. Especially regarding the frequency of name labels on other vessels by the Meidias Painter, the lack of them on the Cleveland lekythos demands an explanation, which here appears to be the marketing of patriotic imagery which wants its audience to identify directly with the cast.

This is a vessel whose decoration crosses the borders between differ-ent layers of transmission, and in this case those between mythological and generic/allegorical narrative or even description. And as before, this transgressive energy is produced not only through the characters and their action, but also through the vessel's design in which – again – a central representation is avoided, and the recipient is guided through the various groups on display. In its marketing ideology in a descriptive way, the deco-ration is marked by elements of non-narrative. But this lack of storytelling does not create an escapist situation, even though the general theme – a congregation of women engaged in idle, female tasks among flowers and bushes – could at first sight fit in with notions of escapism. In play, however, the scene is anything but escapist; it is a bold ideological statement to produce Athenian offspring, and thus fits in very well with common wartime propaganda.[43]

CONCLUDING METALEPSIS: EVIDENCE FOR AN ICONIC TURN?

The three examples show that applying a descriptive term like metalepsis, drawn from literary theory, to visual analysis of vase-painting demands a redefinition of this term for this special purpose. First of all, the role of the narrative agents is primarily defined by the composition and interaction of the figures, as well as by speech acts or speech-act-like actions, but also to a large extent by the pot on which the figures are positioned. In vase-painting, it is the pot that can serve as the 'body of narrative' which takes the role of an (extradiegetic) agent of narrative which guides the recipient. At the same time, the definition of narrative levels needs reconsideration when faced with a pictorial narrative. As the case of the Nicias hydria has shown, narrative stages on a pot can become narrative levels, or can be both simultaneously through the help of their material carrier. This can create proleptic-cum-metaleptic situations which in a text would be only proleptic, reaching from one narrative stage into the next. On the hydria, however, this can equally well become a clash of different narrative spheres which turn the figures' identification upside down and thus generate a metaleptic whirl as the vessel is turned.

Yet the pots are designed metaleptically not only as regards the narrative levels of their cast, but also as regards their modes of transmission, a case of *modal metalepsis*. In narratologic terms, this is probably rather a phenomenon characterised as a change of perspective or of transmitting voice. The case of the Meidias hydria, however, exemplifies that in the interplay of the material carrier as body of narrative with the composition and name labels, structures can be generated which are equivalent to the crossing of narrative levels characteristic for metalepsis. They emanate from the physical crossing of borders on the vessel, the body of narrative, which equates distinct levels of transmission, and they occur between the narrative and descriptive areas, as well as between attributive and situative elements.

---

[43] Given this, it could be worth reconsidering female scenes on pots of the Meidian circle, which, after all, account for 70 per cent of the approximately 200 vessels extant.

It is here, in redefining metalepsis for visual analysis, that the specific qualities of late fifth-century vase-painting also become apparent. As discussed earlier, many strategies employed on these vessels stem from the standard corpus of storytelling in Greek vase-painting; and some are even rather old-fashioned, such as the employment of polychronous and proleptic elements as well as the play with the ambiguity of characters. And yet the employment of these elements is rather eclectic and clearly functionalised to reach or support a specific quality: the corporealisation of the material carrier and its narrative potential. The shape of the pot is now exploited as narrative engine, something it always has been to a certain extent, but certainly never as fully realised. The pot's surface becomes a holographic foil, gaining its qualities from the fact that it can be moved around sideways as well as up and down, a quality which especially applies to the hydriai. These hologram pots bear a corpus of content, but can subsequently open or close it to the viewers and thus guide the viewers' gaze, a crucial achievement for visual matter. And it is only through guiding the gaze that these pots are able to create metalepsis, either between different narrative levels in the picture field, or between the different pictorial frames on their surface which, because the pot is also a narrative level, appear equally well as different levels of transmitting information.

Applying metalepsis underlines that the strategies employed on these vessels are anything but free of narrative. Neither do the topics depicted support an escapist interpretation, especially because they force the recipients constantly to reposition themselves between different kinds of transmission – mythological, allegorical, real-life – and subsequently between different kinds of identification with the picture presented. Similarly, through the lens of metalepsis it becomes apparent that these pots deliver a pictorial design which in its ambivalence depending on the viewer's perspective creates a narrative in the visual, one that could only be created in the visual. Through the turning of the vessel, viewer–object relations and with them situations of metalepsis are created which a text could not generate, unless it had a material carrier which simultaneously operated as (extradiegetic) narrative agent. So while the design of these vessels, with their labels and different narrative stages, feeds on the strategies of constructing a text, the corporeality of the 'body of narrative' establishes the crucial difference between a text and this kind of pot.

While the impact of a culture of reading on fourth-century vases from South Italy has been clearly established by Luca Giuliani, it does not apply to the Athenian vase-painting of the later fifth century, nor do these pots offer a link to later developments in the West. On the contrary, they exemplify a period of heightened awareness for issues of the visual and of how to guide recipients. The painters of the pots discussed here certainly take account of how texts can work, even though these texts need not be corporeal, as in a scroll, but could equally well be oraliture. But they use this knowledge, not to cater for readers, but to explore new ways of the visual, and they do so by relying on the most basic visual feature of their genre, the storyscapes offered by the pots. By doing so the pictures created surmount the confines of their flat and stationary surface, and with it also those of their medium. And in making the recipients turn the vessel, vase-painters in the later fifth century also signal an iconic turn.

CHAPTER 7

Style and agency in an age of transition
Peter Schultz

This chapter examines some stylistic changes in Greek sculpture that took place between 430 and 380 BC. It also investigates how these changes in style may have been viewed, understood, and appreciated in Athens and in other Greek communities during the late fifth and early fourth centuries. Finally, this chapter explores the idea of personal styles in Attic sculpture and attempts to situate some ancient sculptors, and the stylistic changes that they mediated, within the changing contexts of late fifth- and early fourth-century Athenian society.

To address these three topics, I have divided this chapter into three parts. In the first, 'Styles', we will examine some evidence for stylistic change in the sculpture of late classical Athens and Greece. Here, our objective will be to examine and to interpret a set of stylistic transitions that took place in the late fifth and early fourth centuries and to discuss some ways in which these transitions reflected, or helped create, a new set of aesthetic interests in Athenian art. In the second part, 'Agencies', we will test our interpretation of these stylistic developments against some specific archaeological and epigraphical evidence. Here, our objective will be to investigate some hierarchies of value within which late classical sculptors and their styles can be situated and to suggest some ways in which these hierarchies may have

I am grateful to the State Scholarship Foundation of Greece for supporting the initial research on this topic in the spring of 2004. A Tytus Summer Fellowship from the Department of Classics at the University of Cincinnati and a generous grant from the Hendrickson Fine Arts Endowment of Concordia College, Moorhead, facilitated the composition of this chapter in the summer of 2006. This chapter was written in the Carl W. Blegen Library at the University of Cincinnati and at the Carl B. Ylvisaker Library at Concordia College; I am happy to thank Jacquelene Riley, Mike Braunlin, and David Ball at UC and Amy Soma at Concordia for their generous (and patient!) assistance during the course of its composition. It is also a pleasure to thank the following friends and colleagues who have discussed various aspects of this project with me: Mark Atwood, Judy Barringer, George Connell, Craig Hardiman, Catherine Keesling, Lauren Kinnee, Eddie Schmoll, Kris Seaman, Olin Storvick, Jeremy Tanner, and Bronwen Wickkiser. I owe special thanks to David Boggs for his fine drawings. I am especially grateful to Ralf von den Hoff, Robin Osborne, Andrew Stewart, and Petros Themelis for their frank criticisms of the argument and much helpful advice. All mistakes are mine.

framed and influenced the stylistic changes discussed in the first part. In the final part, 'Contexts', we will place the arguments developed in the first two parts within a larger frame of late classical Athenian experience. Here, our objective will be to explore the way in which sculptors and painters may have been seen by the Athenian elite and how this ancient view of Greek art might facilitate a fuller understanding of these artists and their changing styles.

STYLES

Students of Greek sculpture have been using stylistic analyses to support a variety of interpretative arguments for the last 200 years.[1] For example, stylistic analyses have been, and continue to be, used as standard diagnostic tools for determining a sculpture's date. If, it is assumed, the style of Greek sculpture evolved consistently over time, then stylistic variation can be interpreted as a chronological indicator.[2] Stylistic analyses have also been used by students of Greek sculpture to track patterns of contact and influence between geographical regions. Since the sculptors of different cities often produced sculpture of different styles, the argument goes, these variations can be interpreted as evidence for the existence of regional schools and for various levels of artistic contact between *poleis*.[3] Stylistic analysis has also been the basis for the identification of individual sculptors. Here style has been used to reconstruct the oeuvres of Greek masters, most often those mentioned in Greek and Roman literary sources. If we believe that these sculptors were distinct individuals with unique artistic personalities,

---

[1] *Style* is here defined as the distinct combination of physical and formal characteristics – scale, mass, shape, colour, line, and texture – evident in a given set of objects. In general terms, the arguments that sustain the use of stylistic analysis as a tool for investigating social and cultural meaning were first formulated by Winckelmann and then refined by Arnold Houser (1951), Meyer Schapiro (1953) and Ludger Alscher (1956, 1957). For the importance of style specifically in archaeological theory and practice, see Shanks and Tilley 1992: 137–71 and Hodder and Hudson 2003: 59–65, both with bibliographies. For socio-stylistic analysis of material culture, see Borbein 1973; Barnard 2001: 115–42, 168–93; Hölscher 2002; Elsner 2003; and now Bol (2004), all with bibliographies. Recent case studies by Shanks and Tilley (1992: 172–240), Neer (2002), and T. Olson (2002: 137–162) have re-established the significance of this traditional type of analysis for contextual archaeologists and art historians.

[2] Recent case studies in which the model is applied to Attic sculpture: Harrison 1988; Brouskari 1999: 16–52; Touloupa 2002: 68–76; and Bol 2004, among innumerable others. General critique of the 'normative model': Shanks and Tilley 1992: 138–9. Specific critique of the model applied to Attic sculpture: Ridgway, e.g. 1997: 364–6; 2004: 539–56, 627–39, Keesling 2003: 36–62, and Schultz 2003b: 2004.

[3] Recent case studies in which the model is applied to Greek sculpture: Palagia and Coulson 1998, with comprehensive bibliographies. General critique of the 'regional interaction' model: Shanks and Tilley 1992: 140–1. Specific critiques of the model applied to Greek sculpture: Jockey 1998; Mattusch 1998; Ridgway 1997: 241–7; Pollitt 2000.

it is understood, then the physical remains of their work, or copies of their work, should reflect the touch of their particular hands.[4]

More important for us here, however, is the interpretative tradition that posits sculptural style as the material correlate of a socially situated *Zeitgeist*: a *Zeitstil*. In analyses of this type, the sculpture of ancient Greece is considered a cultural product and is interpreted in so far as it conforms to a set of cultural norms already considered to be 'present' in the literatures, religions, and philosophies of the period whence it came. Since, it is suggested, the style of a piece is inseparable from its cultural context, stylistic analysis can support interpretative arguments about any number of preoccupations, issues and agendas that may have permeated Greek society.[5]

But interpretative arguments that connect culture and style can be problematic, especially when we are looking at style as evidence for cultural change. One of the most troublesome problems is the often subjective nature of stylistic comparisons – specifically, the choice of objects that are compared – that can often lead to foregone (rhetorical) conclusions. Here Osborne's earlier discussion of the formal differences between Aristodicos and Myron's *Discobolus* is fundamental, especially his insistence that choosing these particular pieces of sculpture and interpreting their stylistic differences in a particular way constitute political and rhetorical acts.[6] Indeed, since the potential for both change *and* continuity is always simultaneously present within any given historical moment and/or any cultural system, discussions of particular changes *or* continuities should probably be seen for what they are: the results of our own interpretative decisions. That Osborne easily could have chosen to compare Aristodicos with, say, the Critius Boy and thereby discussed a far less remarkable, although no less noteworthy, formal change within an argument regarding cultural continuity seems to prove the point.

Keeping this in mind, I have chosen three pairs of objects that I think exemplify some of the most important stylistic changes that took place in Greek sculpture between about 430 and 380. These stylistic changes, I believe, reflect and helped generate a new set of aesthetic interests in

---

[4] Classic case studies of the model applied to Attic sculpture: Kjellberg 1926, Carpenter 1929, and Schuchhardt 1930. Recent examples of the same: Brouskari 1999: 57–71; Symeonoglou 2004; and Harrison 2005. Personal styles in Greek sculpture: Pollitt and Palagia 1996, with comprehensive bibliographies. General critique of the 'motor habit variation model': Shanks and Tilley 1992: 141. Specific critique of the model applied to Greek sculpture: Carpenter 1960, and Ridgway, e.g. 1981: 5–8, 159–91; 1997: 237–320.

[5] Early case studies of the model applied to Greek sculpture: Krahmer 1923/4, Pfuhl 1930, Buschor 1947/71, and Alscher 1956, 1957, *et al.* Recent examples of the same with various refinements in theory and practice: Pollitt 1972, 1986, Whitley 1991, Neer 2002, Hölscher 2002, von den Hoff: 2007, among many others.

[6] See Osborne, p. 3 above.

late classical Athens. These pairs consist of two freestanding, nude youths (Polyclitus' *Doryphorus* and the Louvre/Munich 'Narcissus', reflections of which show up in Athens by the last quarter of the fifth century), two relief sculptures associated with cult statue bases (from the temple of Nemesis in the Attic deme of Rhamnous and the temple of Dionysus in Athens), and two mythologico-narrative groups (Alcamenes' *Procne and Itys* dedicated on the Acropolis, and Timotheus' *Leda and the Swan*, closely associated with the final phase of the 'Rich Style' in Athens).[7]

I begin with the *Doryphorus* of Polyclitus (c. 450–430; Figure 7.1) and the Louvre/Munich 'Narcissus' (c. 410–390; Figure 7.2).[8] While they represent different subjects, both pieces are known from multiple Roman copies (54 and 37, respectively); both exhibit formal characteristics that can be dated via independent comparanda in architectural sculpture, vases, and grave reliefs; both are based around a familiar Polyclitan structure; both types were well known in Athens by the beginning of the fourth century, and both belong to the same type: the standing, nude youth.[9]

What strikes us most at the outset are the fundamental differences in the youths' anatomical structure and their consequent poses. On the one hand,

---

[7] In choosing these specific objects as my foci, I have tried to observe a few functional conditions. The first and most obvious is that I have tried to confine my discussions to sculpture for which we have reasonably secure dates. The second is that I have tried to compare sculptures that belong to the same basic type. Finally, I have tried to keep in mind that these three pairs, though stylistically different, also are conceptually similar. This similarity resides in the fact that these sculptures have come to represent (for us) some of the most significant formal developments or possibilities of their respective periods. Now whether or not this type of statement will ever be a 'true' description of the sculpture in question – whether our opinion finds parallels in antiquity and how we can begin to speculate on such a possibility – is one of the oldest and most complex problems in the study of ancient culture (which does not mean that it should be neglected; Jean Rudhardt's famous remark regarding ancient Greek religion – 'La difficulté principale de l'étude des religions me paraît être celle de la compréhension d'autrui' – can apply with equal force to the study of ancient Greek art). For our purposes here, it is sufficient to acknowledge the basic contingency of our statements, to confess that many reasons for stylistic change might be suggested (intended audiences, different media, different patrons, etc.), and to admit that the fact that we find what we are looking for does not mean that we are not looking for the truth.

[8] The *Doryphorus* has often been identified as an Achilles, a Theseus, an athlete, or the embodiment of the *canon*, among many other possibilities (see Beck and Bol 1993, Moon 1995, and now Tanner 2006: 161–70). These speculations, however, have been subordinated to the question of the statue's original appearance and the state of the material evidence ever since Vincenzo Franciosi 2003, 2004 – supported by no less an authority than Petros Themelis 2000: 74–87; 2003: 126–8 – showed that the 'doryphorus' carried a shield in his left hand and therefore may not be the doryphorus at all! The identification of the 'Narcissus' is no less problematic (see Vierneisel-Schlörb 1979: 198–203, with comprehensive bibliography). Hyacinthus, an *ephebe*, or a young athlete have all been proposed, but Narcissus remains the most popular on the basis of his pose and downward glance.

[9] That the pieces were created by the 'Argive' school and thus may not be officially 'Attic' need not excessively trouble us, since we know that Polyclitus and other members of his 'school' (most notably Cresilas and Phradmon) worked in Athens in the late fifth century and that the formal developments he helped pioneer were used in Athens by the late 440s, Argives in Athens: Stewart 1995, Corso 2002. Cresilas: Keesling 2004. Phradmon: Corso 2001, but see J. Morgan 2002. Critique of the 'regional school' model: Jockey 1998; Mattusch 1998; Ridgway 1997: 241–2; and Pollitt 2000.

Figure 7.1: Doryphorus, c. 1.98 m, front. Cast of a Roman copy (Minneapolis) of a
fifth–century bronze (450–430 BC) traditionally attributed to the Argive sculptor Polyclitus.

of course, the *Doryphorus* (Figure 7.1) embodies and engenders a model
(perhaps literally) of *ruthmos* and *summetria*. A conceptual axis drawn from
his tracheal hollow, between his pectorals, to his scrotum forms a gentle
arc, the slight parabola of which flexes slightly to his left; an identical axis
drawn from his scrotum to his left knee counterbalances this and flexes
slightly to his right. With the exception of his head, the formal energy
of the *Doryphorus* is focused frontally and is contained neatly within a
conceptual parallelepiped. This comparatively closed formal structure is
complemented by the firm horizontality of the statue's musculature, which
is divided into heavy, lateral bands. The overall stability of the *Doryphorus*'s
pose is based on an equilibrium provided by the youth's famous chiastic
stance, a stance which both embodies and creates a measured dialectic
between formal opposites: right/left, rest/movement, and straight/curved.[10]
It is for good reason that the ancient sources remind us that Polyclitus
created statues that were 'foursquare' (Pliny, *Natural History* 34.56) and
'suitable for both the battlefield and the gymnasium' (Quintilian 5.12.21).

[10] Stewart 1990: 160–2.

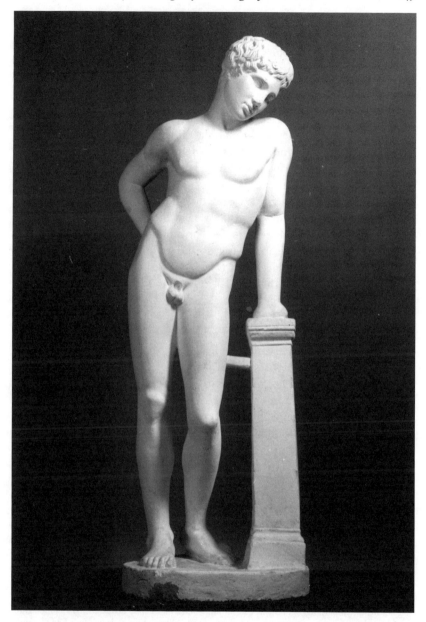

Figure 7.2: 'Narcissus', c. 1.16 m, front. Roman copy of a late fifth or early fourth century bronze (410–390 BC) traditionally attributed to a follower of Polyclitus.

Narcissus, on the other hand, exemplifies and generates a different set of formal concerns (Figure 7.2). While there is no question that the youth is based on a Polyclitan model, a fact that is most clearly evidenced in his legs, it almost seems as if the sculptor of the Narcissus set out deliberately to challenge the stylistic agenda of his famous predecessor. The central axis of the figure is conceived not as a pair of symmetrical arcs but as a subtle S-curve that begins again at the tracheal hollow, bends down through the centre of the torso, and then carries on through the right leg. The contour of the torso is fundamentally curvilinear and serves as the centre for a type of sculptural form that has been described as 'transgressive' or 'artificial' when compared to the *Doryphorus*'s enharmonic unity.[11] The sculptor does not split the torso's vertical structure at the hips, nor does he base his composition around interlocking parabolic axes as is the case with the *Doryphorus*. Rather, the contour of Narcissus' spine and inner left thigh forms a single, tantalising arabesque. Matching this loosening of underlying structure, the sculptor of the Narcissus has replaced the *Doryphorus*'s distinct musculature with a soft, blended anatomy that virtually eliminates Polyclitus' concern with accurate, physiological organisation. Here the *Doryphorus*'s parallel bands of heavy, horizontal muscle in high relief are replaced by an affected sort of figural *sfumato* built up around a limited number of diagonals, most noticeable at his shoulder and hips. Later fourth-century sculptors would build heavily on these stylistic foundations.

In addition to these differences in structure and anatomy, the Narcissus also evidences a more complex sense of movement and three-dimensionality.[12] His right elbow is thrown perpendicularly back into space and breaks the confines of the conceptual rectangle within which the rest of his body stands. In addition, the extension of his left hand, his palm and fingers, is visible only from his proper left, a position from which his profile becomes partially hidden by his shoulder. That *we* must bend slightly to confront Narcissus' face, and that we thereby confuse our own movement with his, enhances this sense of relaxed motion. Our Narcissus

---

[11] Carpenter 1960: 163.

[12] The development of fully three-dimensional sculpture, for example, is one of the best-known concerns of later fourth-century artists. Scopas' Maenad (Stewart 1990: fig. 547, in which three-dimensional viewing is encouraged by formal torsion), Lysippus' Heracles (Stewart 1990: fig. 566, in which three-dimensional viewing is encouraged by narrative action), and the Aphrodite Callipygus (Boardman 1995: fig. 82, in which three-dimensional viewing is encouraged by a combination of formal torsion, narrative action, and visual/sexual titillation) are only the best-known examples within which full, circular appreciation was stressed and expected by fourth-century sculptors and their audience. However, the transitional phase that exists between the relatively static, frontal conception of viewing Greek sculpture in the sixth and middle fifth centuries and the dynamic, three-dimensional conception of viewing that becomes increasingly important in the later fifth and early fourth centuries has never been treated systematically.

was designed to usher the viewer around the sculpture, to acknowledge the unique potential of three-dimensional sculptural objects, and to critique, or destabilise, the primacy of a hitherto privileged frontal position.[13] While there is no doubt that the *Doryphorus* can be circumnavigated and viewed with pleasure, it seems equally clear that this sort of viewing primarily serves to reaffirm the 'foursquare' nature of the *Doryphorus*'s pose. The sculptor of our Narcissus is doing something else.

Indeed, it seems that the sculptor of the Narcissus calls the entire Polyclitan chiastic model into question. One of the first things that we notice about the Narcissus is that his weight and stance display none of the *ruthmos* or *summetria* that made the *Doryphorus* so famous. The weight of Narcissus has been shifted dramatically to his left, the basic chiastic rhythm which sustains the *Doryphorus* has been eschewed, and there is little if any sense of formal symmetry outside that normally present in a human body. The fact that Narcissus places most of his weight against his pedestal seems to dispute the whole idea that a sculpture can support its own weight. It is almost as if the idea of freestanding sculpture that actually stands freely has been acknowledged but then self-consciously rejected in favour of a different goal. If we juxtapose these new formal concerns with some new conceptual and contextual ideas – for instance, if we remember that the two images treat different themes (warrior v. sensual youth) and that the ancient viewer may have been encouraged to move around 'Narcissus' and to observe him voyeuristically as a player in a specific mythologico-theatrical scene within which (his and our) vision and (auto)eroticism are inextricably bound – we could add exponentially to the total impact of these formal and stylistic tricks. The same cannot be said for the *Doryphorus*. In addition to depicting different subjects, the two pieces represent and generate different stylistic interests. The *Doryphorus* is symmetrical, formal, and structured; the Narcissus is curvilinear, erotic, and mannered.

A similar sort of stylistic divergence can be evidenced in relief sculpture associated with Attic cult images. The relief figures from the base of the statue of Nemesis in her temple at Rhamnous (c. 440–420 BC; usually attributed to Agoracritus on the basis of Pausanias (1.33.2)) and a set of relief figures speculatively connected to the base of the statue of Dionysus in his temple at Athens (c. 410–390 BC; attributed to Alcamenes by Pausanias (1.20.3) but often associated with Callimachus in the modern literature) also display important formal variances. Here we see 'Helen' from the base at Rhamnous (Figure 7.3) and 'Maenad 27' possibly from the

---

[13] Culmination of this development: R. Osborne 1998: 226–8.

DAVID BOGGS 2006

Figure 7.3: Helen. Pentelic marble, ca. 440–420 BC, traditionally attributed to the Attic sculptor Agoracritus on the basis of Pausanias (1.33.2). (Remains and reconstruction drawing.)

base in Athens (Figure 7.4).[14] The relief figures on these bases are known from original fragments and multiple copies of neo-Attic reliefs (Dionysus' base, for instance, was the most copied relief in Roman art). Both figures exhibit formal characteristics that can be dated via comparanda in architectural sculpture, vases, and grave reliefs; both scenes from which they come seem to have shown divine 'births' or 'introductions' as was customary for fifth-century cult statue bases; and both were situated inside Attic temples beneath images that remained famous until the Roman period.[15]

While there are some obvious differences in basic pose (frontal 'Polyclitan' v. profile 'Callimachean'), subject-matter (legendary heroine v. bacchante), and dress (peplos v. chiton), what strikes us at the outset stylistically is the difference with which these figures' drapery has been treated. Helen, on one hand, is fully wrapped in a thick, full-length peplos with solid mantle (Figure 7.3). Her drapery is heavy, regular, and strictly architectonic. The fabric on the left side of her peplos is treated as a series of columnar folds. Each fold is carefully separated one from another, and a deep fluting serves as the formal anchor for the piece. In fact, Helen's trailing right leg is the only source of activity that disturbs the metronomic rhythm of these dropping channels. This strict verticality was duplicated by the fall of her mantle, which runs perpendicular to the foot and crown of the statue base, and by the edges of her torso. Helen's drapery communicates little if any sense of motion. It almost appears as if she was conceived as a sculpture of a draped statue, a stylistic decision that is paralleled on other statue bases of Phidias and his circle.[16] This overall effect is enhanced by the relative thickness of the cloth itself and by the division of the torso into two halves by the kolpos of her peplos.

The maenad, on the other hand, represents an exercise in what might be called linear expressionism (Figure 7.4). Her drapery is light, asymmetrical, and fundamentally curvilinear. The flowing folds of the right-hand side of her chiton are treated as a series of concentric arcs which create both a conceptual parenthesis around her torso (when combined with her tympanum) and a prevailing sense of frenzied energy. These curvilinear lines are

---

[14] Base at Rhamnous: Lapatin 1992 and Palagia 2000, both with bibliographies; Kallopolitis 1978 gives good photographs of the sculptural fragments. Base of Dionysus at Athens: Touchette 1995, with a detailed discussion of the problems.

[15] That Touchette's important reconstruction of the Dionysus base is not universally accepted should not bother us, since the presence of similar formal characteristics on the frieze of the Erechtheion (409/8–406/5; *IG* I³ 471; Boulter 1970) seems to ensure that the basic stylistic comparison will be meaningful. Here it is assumed that Touchette's (1995) basic and traditional (Carpenter 1960: 156–7) association of the Maeanads with the Dionysus base is correct; but the matter is contentious.

[16] Palagia 2000.

Figure 7.4: Maenad, c. 1.43 m. Roman copy of a late fifth or early fourth century original (410–390 BC) traditionally attributed to the Attic sculptor Callimachus.

deeply separated from one another, forcing each rhythmic arc to support itself as an autonomous form – the drapery actually creates its own formal reality. This effect is enhanced when we realise that this billow of trailing drapery is actually wider than the maenad's torso; at first glance, it seems as if the cloth itself – rather than the model who wears it – was the focus of the sculptor's most sincere energy. Nowhere is this autonomy of sculptural line more evident than in the heavily stylised omega folds directly above our bacchante's left foot. Here, drapery swirls are blown upward, created, it seems, by tiny puffs of air that match or create the rhythm of her steps.

In addition to these differences in line and motion, the maenad also displays a more complex sense of material transparency. If we start with her breasts and move our eyes down past her lower belly, thighs, and shins, it becomes increasingly clear that the sculptor spent considerable effort ensuring that the body beneath his stylised arabesques was never lost. The sculptor of our bacchante seems just as interested in demonstrating his virtuoso command of a draped female's anatomy as he is in creating a recognisable figure type. The erotically charged female body, in other words, seems to have become the vehicle for a display of ultra-fine sculptural technique.[17] Although some underlying anatomical structure can be seen hidden beneath Helen's peplos, the overall conception of material transparency between the two reliefs is quite different.

One of the most essential contrasts between the two figures is the manner in which the sculptor of the maenad seems to call the entire architectural function of his relief into question. As noted above, the pervasive frontality, stability, and architectonic character displayed in the composition of the Rhamnous base was typical for bases of classical cult statues and constituted a solution to the formal problem created when a cult image was placed over a group of smaller figures. In addition to metaphorically suggesting the earth and sea over which these gods held dominion, the static composition was designed as a fixed, visual foundation for the image above. Helen is columnar and statuesque because she serves as an architectural 'support' for the cult image; the stylistic similarity between Helen and the Erechtheion's caryatids is not a coincidence. But none of this applies to the maenad. Indeed, the sculptor of our maenad seems to be interested in reorientating this sort of structural concern altogether. Rather than provide a solid figural platform upon which a monumental image might be placed, the sculptor of our maenad explodes all sense of measured stability and replaces it with fluid action. If we juxtapose these new formal

---

[17] R. Osborne 1994 and Stewart 1997 give the contexts and problems.

Figure 7.5: Procne and Itys, c. 1.63 m. Pentelic marble, c. 440–420 BC, traditionally
attributed to the Attic sculptor Alcamenes on the basis of Pausanias (1.24.3).

concerns with some new conceptual and contextual ideas, remembering
that the maenad may have been a player in a synaesthetic tableau within
which Dionysiac ritual, eroticism, vision, and music were all inextricably
bound – a tableau in which the god of *enthousiasmos* may have floated above
a writhing band of his followers – we could add exponentially to the impact
of these formal and stylistic ploys.[18] The same cannot be said for Helen. In
addition to depicting different subjects, the two pieces represent and generate different stylistic interests. The sculptor of Helen is concerned with

[18] I am indebted to Andrew Stewart for sharing some of his ideas regarding this statue base with me.

Figure 7.6: Procne and Itys, c. 1.63 m. Pentelic marble, ca. 440–420 BC, traditionally attributed to the Attic sculptor Alcamenes on the basis of Pausanias (1.24.3).

stability, opacity, and functionalism; the sculptor of our maenad appears to be interested in mobility, transparency, and expressionism.

The stylistic differences that we have seen so far converge in our final comparison between *Procne and Itys* (c. 440–420; Figures 7.5–7.6), generally attributed to Alcamenes since it seems to have been dedicated by him on the Acropolis (Pausanias 1.24.3), and *Leda and the Swan* (c. 400–380; Figures 7.7–7.9), speculatively attributed to the Athenian master Timotheus on the basis of its style.[19] Both composition types are known from fifth-century originals (in the Acropolis Museum and in the Boston Museum of Fine

---

[19] That we will compare a fifth-century original with a late Roman copy should not trouble us too much, since the basic stylistic characteristics with which we are concerned manifest themselves in other originals of identical date. The formal characteristics of the copies not only follow the basic scheme of

Figure 7.7: Leda and the Swan, c. 1.32 m, Roman period copy of an early fourth century
original (400–380 BC) speculatively attributed to Timotheus.

the fifth-century Boston statue (Caskey 1925: no. 22; Comstock and Vermeule 1976: no. 37) but can
also be seen in other late fifth- and early fourth-century sculpture from Attica and the Peloponnese.
An early fourth-century statue of Hygieia from Epidaurus (Boardman 1995: fig. 52), for example,
displays identical formal characteristics and has been carefully discussed in connection to the *Leda*
by Levendi (2003: 97–102). Stylistically, both the *Hygieia* and the *Leda* display similar poses, a similar
concern with momentary action, a similar concern with extensive drilling and undercutting, and a
provocative mannerist sensibility when it comes to drapery. Iconographically, both figures exhibit
the same girlish figure, the same slipping peplos that exposes the breast, and the same attribute-type
(animals) placed over their pubic areas. This comparison is important, since it demonstrates that
the stylistic and iconographic characteristics of the Roman copies, in this particular case, accurately
reflect a basic early fourth-century aesthetic.

Figure 7.8: Leda and the Swan, c. 1.32 m, Roman period copy of an early fourth century
original (400–380 BC) speculatively attributed to Timotheus.

Arts, respectively); both exhibit formal characteristics that can be dated via
independent comparanda in architectural sculpture, vases, and grave reliefs;
both belong to the same type and mythological narrative group, and both
show a moment of dramatic climax within their respective stories.[20]

---

[20] *Procne and Itys*: Knell 1978 and Barringer 2005, both with comprehensive bibliographies. *Leda and the Swan*: Ridgway 1981: 67–68; Stewart 1990: 273–4; Bol 1992: 170–3; Yalouris 1992: 70 and nn.

Figure 7.9: Leda and Swan, c. 1.32 m, Roman period copy of an early fourth century
original (400–380 BC) speculatively attributed to Timotheus.

As we might now expect, the two groups are governed by a set of divergent
stylistic concerns. In terms of basic pose, for example, *Procne* (Figures 7.5–
7.6) is relatively closed, frontal, and symmetrical while *Leda* (Figures 7.7–
7.9) is open, multifaceted, and constructed along a series of asymmetrical
diagonals. In terms of basic motion, Procne is comparatively static while
Leda is caught in momentary mid-act. With regards to the handling of

270 and 272; Ridgway 1997: 245–56; Rolley 1999: 206–8; and Levendi 2003: 101–2. Analysis of the
copyist tradition in sculpture and gems: Rieche 1973, Dierichs 1990. Discussion of the theme within
the context of fourth-century Greek sculpture and vases: Lippold 1954. For the fifth-century original
that seems to stand near the beginning of the tradition, see Caskey 1925: no. 22; and Comstock and
Vermeule 1976: no. 37. I am indebted to Ralf von den Hoff for discussing the narrative moments of
each group with me.

drapery, Procne represents a case study in opacity and stability. *Leda*, as Rhys Carpenter eloquently pointed out long ago, displays evidence for a different sort of formal agenda:

The half crouching, nude body is partly exposed and partly draped. The widely spaced folds of her clinging and intermittently transparent chiton have been gathered into high narrow ridges with sharp edges and smooth walls, in a manner wholly impossible to actual cloth. Natural truth has been sacrificed to formal effect in a brilliant-calculated play of light and shadow, carrying ogival and catenary modeling lines over the transparent form and adding sweeping motion lines as a foil for the uncovered body. By these ingenious, concurrent devices an immobile pose has been stimulated into action . . . even the 'anatomic inaccuracies' which have been noted in the bodily proportions may have been intentional transgressions for optical effect.[21]

The most compelling formal contrast between the two pieces, however, is the manner in which the sculptor of the *Leda* uses her impossibly thin drapery as an explicitly theatrical backdrop against which the sculptural action takes place. Leda's drapery is a consciously constructed background against which her body and her action are set for dramatic and aesthetic effect. In other words, the sculptor seems self-consciously to treat his subject as a deliberately 'artistic' re-presentation of the myth within a specifically 'artistic' frame of reference.

The use of self-sustaining drapery as a theatrical background for Attic sculpture seems to have begun c. 445–435 (or slightly earlier) with the Parthenon metopes (most famously, south 27) and culminates in c. 425–421 with the Nike of Paionios (Figure 7.10), whose sweeping mantle both frames her body and provides the windswept scenery through which she descends.[22] *Leda* takes all of this to another level. Indeed, approaching the statue from her left we are actually closed off from the group's narrative action (Figure 7.7). Only with a step to her front (Figure 7.8) is the literal and symbolic epiphany appreciated, and only with a further step to her right (Figure 7.9) is the full complexity of her pose and action revealed. While *Procne and Itys* can certainly be appreciated from multiple points of view, the group remains a predominantly frontal composition and betrays no interest in the self-conscious, dramatic effects like those visible in *Leda*.

What makes this development fascinating is that it suggests that the sculptor of the *Leda* set out to establish Leda's body as an independent

[21] Carpenter 1960: 155–6.
[22] Parthenon metope 27: Stewart 1990: fig. 320. Of course, the impact of the Parthenon's sculptures as stylistic models to be both followed and resisted – on late fifth-century sculptors could never be overstated. See Borbein 2002: 14–15.

Figure 7.10: The Nike of Paionios. Olympia, c. 1.95 m. Pentelic marble, c. 420 BC. The Nike was set up on a triangular pillar over three captured Spartan shields. It was identified by an inscription (*Olympia V*, no. 259) that read: 'The Messenians and the Naupactians dedicated [this] to Olympian Zeus, a tithe from war [spoils]. Paionios of Mende made it and was the victor [in the competition] to make the temple's akroteria.'

object of aesthetico-erotic display – an 'art object' in its own right.[23] And it is not only the mythological story that generates this concern but also the self-conscious visual frame that the artist employs. The effect of the lifting mantle (the erotic epiphany) can be duplicated only by *our* motion

[23] R. Osborne 1994, Stewart 1997.

as viewers moving from right to left. In this manner, the sculptor seems both to acknowledge and to take advantage of the three-dimensional qualities *unique to sculpture*, exploiting them for effect. But there is more. Once the viewer is in position, the same mantle serves to exclude others from the viewer's privileged point of view, thereby producing a new sense of intimacy between object and spectator. The fact that the ultra-fine mantle is itself a miracle of sculptural technique drives home the point. Only by way of literal and metaphorical *virtuosity* is the sculptural epiphany made possible. This kind of language makes little sense when discussing *Procne and Itys*. In addition to depicting different subjects, the two pieces produce and reflect different stylistic values. *Procne* is static, austere, and unaffected; *Leda* is ephemeral, sensual, and theatrical.

There seems little doubt that the end of the fifth century and the beginning of the fourth saw changes in the way that sculpture could be conceived. These formal changes are most clearly manifested in new fascinations with movement, circularity, theatricality, sensuality, transparency, and technical virtuosity. Of course, it is important both to recognise the existence of these ancient stylistic developments and to be mindful of the vocabulary that we have used to characterise and to interpret them. Traditionally, sculptural products of this period that reveal evidence of these new formal concerns have sometimes been described and understood as 'gaudy', 'trivial', 'overemphatic', 'transgressive', 'decorative', or 'irrational', a descriptive terminology that is firmly rooted within modern positivist and historicist models of stylistic development.[24] Here, however, I have tried to portray these changes in a slightly different way: as archaeological evidence for a new kind of sophisticated self-consciousness or, perhaps, a new kind of professionalism within the field of Attic sculpture, the kind of professionalism that might make our interpretative vocabulary (like 'artistic self-consciousness' or 'mannerism' or 'sculptural virtuosity') meaningful within late classical society. My interpretative *ekphraseis*, in other words, suggests that these changes in style are somehow connected to the way in which these sculptors and their work were regarded in late classical culture. And this brings us to our second problem.

AGENCIES

My reading of the stylistic changes in the first section is marked by three interpretative tendencies. The first was that I consistently described the stylistic changes taking place at the end of the fifth century and the

---

[24] E.g. Carpenter 1960: 155–6; Ridgway 1981: 210–13.

beginning of the fourth in Greece and in Athens as sophisticated, self-conscious, or mannerist – a vocabulary that assumes the existence of ancient artistic models that were intentionally subjected to modification, critique, or challenge.[25] The second was that I repeatedly connected aspects of stylistic change to particular technical and compositional problems encountered by sculptors working in the field of sculpture – language that assumes the existence of social actors who were considered, and who considered themselves, to belong to a recognisable class of 'sculptors' in the first place. Finally, the combination of these two trends resulted in my characterisation of these stylistic changes as physical evidence for the development of a new appreciation for a certain kind aesthetic virtuosity within the field of late classical art – an interpretation which assumes the existence of artists or craftsmen self-consciously engaged in the creation of satisfying, pleasing, or (even) beautiful objects that were judged and valued as such by themselves and by their contemporaries. In sum, the way that I have interpreted the stylistic developments above is related to (and maybe based on?) a set of assumptions as to how these sculptors saw both themselves and their work within late classical society.

Now in order for my characterisation of the stylistic changes noted above to be meaningful in late classical Athens, we need to be able to show that the three assumptions noted above correspond with ancient Athenian experience. And to show this, we need to supplement the material evidence discussed above by thinking about how the late classical artists who made these sculptures and generated these stylistic transitions were perceived and treated and understood in *life*.[26] Here, of course, many mysteries remain. How did these artists develop their products, their styles, and their professional identities within the daily contexts of Athenian culture? How, if at all, did these styles and identities affect their earnings, wages, commissions, and careers? What sort of social value or meaning, if any, can we assign to the products of sculptors whose professional identities were associated with the stylistic developments noted above in the first section? And,

---

[25] W. Friedländer 1957 provides the standard view of 'mannerist' thought; Mannack 2001 applies the model to Attic vase-painting with interesting results.

[26] Agency and the historical significance of ancient individuals: Sewell 1992; Dobres and Robb 2000: 8–10; Fowler 2004; Gardner 2004; Hodder and Hutson 2003: 90–105; Johnson 2004. Ancient individuals, and social hierarchies: Wobst 2000; Sassaman 2000; A. Sinclair 2000; Hodder and Hutson 2003: 99–105; Clarke and Blake 1994; Price and Feinman 1995; Clark 2000; Dobres and Robb 2000: 8, 10–11; Joyce 2000; Walker and Lucero 2000; and Duplouy 2006 (which is now fundamental on status and competition in the ancient world). Agency, individuals, and ancient Greek culture: Fowler 2004, C. Thomas 2005, Christ 2006, Duplouy 2006, Farenga 2006, and Tanner 2006: 141–204.

most importantly, was the idea of individual sculptural virtuosity or unique artistic 'mastery' understood and appreciated as such in late fifth- and early fourth-century Athens?[27] In short, if we want to suggest that our characterisation of the stylistic changes in the first section might be 'accurate', then we need to demonstrate that by the beginning of the fourth century an ancient Greek sculptor could have been considered to be (what we would call) a master artist or craftsman by his peers, and we need to demonstrate that this master sculptor's style and technical achievements were valued as such within his community. We cannot meaningfully discuss the notion of ancient stylistic self-consciousness, sophistication, or mannerism without positing the existence of some sort of ancient hierarchy of stylistic value. And we cannot meaningfully discuss the idea of ancient sculptural virtuosity without positing the existence of ancient virtuosi.

I want to address these points via a case study of the early fourth-century Athenian sculptors working on the temple of Asclepius at Epidaurus. The accounts from the temple of Asclepius provide a unique opportunity to discuss the aforementioned problems of style and agency in an epigraphically and archaeologically secure context.

Sometime around 380 BC, the citizens of the small Peloponnesian city of Epidaurus launched a programme of monumentalisation at the nearby healing sanctuary of Asclepius. Whether in response to the Athenian plague or other political factors, Epidaurian Asclepius had acquired an international reputation during the last quarter of the fifth century. This change in status was accompanied by a demand for sumptuous material votives. By the end of the fifth century a massive building programme was under way. In terms of scale, expense, and design, nothing like the Epidaurian building programme had been attempted since Pericles' imperial project in fifth-century Athens.[28] In addition to smaller structures, the programme at Epidaurus included a new temple designed and built by the architect Theodotus (*IG* IV² 102 AI lines 7–9), a chryselephantine cult statue made by the Parian sculptor Thrasymedes (Pausanias 2.27.1–2; *SEG* 15.208; see

---

[27] Of course, the 'signatures' of individual craftsmen seem to point somewhere in this direction already, but this well-known body of evidence (and how to interpret it) is problematic. See Overbeck 1868, Marcadé 1953–7, Seibert 1978, Muller-Dufeu 2002, Tanner 2006: 153–8, and now Keesling: 2007. Recent work on master sculptors: Agoracritos: Despinis 1971; Scopas: Stewart 1977; Euphranor: Palagia 1980; Praxiteles: Corso 1988–91; Damophon: Themelis 1996; Endoius: Keesling 1999; and Cresilas: Keesling 2004. Ridgway 1990: 73–98, and 1997: 237–85 provides the classic critique; see Hurwit 1997 for one response.

[28] Contextual evolution of the sanctuary's development: Wickkiser 2003, Riethmüller 2005. Architectural evolution of the sanctuary's development: Burford 1969; Gruben 2001: 143–53, and Riethmüller 2005, with bibliography.

also *IG* iv² I 198), a flamboyant tholos designed by the Younger Polyclitus of Argos and built by a predominantly Argive workshop (Pausanias 2.27.5; *IG* iv² I 103, l. 15 *et al.*) and an innovative theatre which was also attributed to Polyclitus the Younger in the later tradition (Pausanias 2.27.5).[29]

The project also attracted a number of Athenian sculptors to work on the expensive Pentelic elements of Asclepius' new cult building.[30] *IG* iv² 102 AI–BI, a famous inscription excavated at the site, records the expenses involved in these artists' work and provides a contemporary picture of their various sculptural assignments (Figures 7.15–7.16).[31]

lines 34–35   Timotheus took the contract to make and supply carved reliefs for 900 drachmas; Pythocles was his guarantor.

lines 43–46   Thrasymedes took the contract to construct the ceiling, the cella door and the gates between the columns for 9,800 drachmas; Pythocles, Thepheides, and Hagemōn were his guarantors.

lines 87–88   Hectoridas took the contract to work one-half of the pedimental sculptures for 1,610 drachmas; Philocleidas and Timocleidas were his guarantors.

lines 88–90   Timotheus took the contract for the akroteria over one pediment for 2,240 drachmas; Pythocles and Hagemon were his guarantors.

lines 95–96   Theo– took the contract for the akroteria over one pediment for 2,240 drachmas; Theoxenidas was his guarantor.

---

[29] Theodotus and temple: Burford 1969: 141–4. Thrasymedes and the cult image: Mitsos 1967; Burford 1969: 59–61, 154–5; Krauss 1972; Ridgway 1997: 36; Lapatin 2001: 109–11 (with comprehensive bibliography) and Muller-Dufeu 2002: 537. Polyclitus and the *thumele* and theatre: Burford 1969: 141–5; Seiler 1986; and Kanellopoulos 2006.

[30] Athenian sculptors and Epidaurus: Burford 1969: 155, 202 (table 10); Yalouris 1992; Smith 1993; Lattimore 1997: 257; Ridgway 1997: 41, 366; Feyel 1998; Rolley 1999: 203–8; Levendi 2003: 101–2. Late fifth- and early fourth-century diaspora of Athenian craftsmen: Burford 1969: 203–5; MacDonald 1981, with bibliography. Sculptural and stylistic context of the decorative programme: B. Brown 1973: 5–15. Summary chronological problems and the temple of Asclepius, with detailed comments on style: Yalouris 1992: 82–3. Not all the sculptors were Athenian. The 'Hectoridas', for example, is Peloponnesian. I am indebted to Catherine Keesling for pointing out this fact.

[31] Roux 1961: 84–130 and Burford 1969 give the standard readings of the inscription; Feyel 1998 gives a good overview of the problems. Even so, there is still much left to be done. The contracts for the architectural sculptures – 3,010 drachmas for the pediments, 2,240 drachmas for the akroteria – were paid in Aeginitan drachmas. These rather unusual amounts correspond with the round figures of 4,300 Attic drachmas (for the pediments) and 3,200 Attic drachmas (for the akroteria); see Stewart 1979: 113 n. 31 for the ratios. Burford's line numbers for *IG* iv² I 102A are consistently off by one or two places (e.g. Burford 1969: 213 lines 34–5 = *IG* iv² I 102A lines 36–7). However, since her account remains the translation most easily available in English, her numbers are retained throughout.

Figure 7.11: The east pediment and akroteria of the temple of Asclepius at Epidaurus.

lines 96–97   – took the contract to work the pedimental sculptures in one pediment for 3,010 drachmas; Theoxenidas was his guarantor.

lines 109–110 To Hectoridas for the sculpture in the other pediment, 1,400 drachmas.

These detailed accounts correspond with a well-known set of architectural sculptures from the temple of Asclepius now located in the National Museum in Athens (7.11–7.12).[32] The sculptural fragments show that the temple's east pediment depicted the sack of Troy and that it was made up of about twenty figures (Figure 7.11), including the *xoanon* of the Trojan Athena and a pathetic Priam whose face is a mask of sorrow.[33] As Nikolaos Yalouris has shown, technical details of the east pediment suggest that it was carved in two distinct phases. *IG* IV² 102 BI (lines 87–8 and 109–10) show that two separate payments for two halves of a pediment were made to a sculptor named Hectoridas over a year apart.[34] For this reason the eastern pediment is now commonly assigned to Hectoridas. The western pediment also comprised about twenty figures. This pediment represented the Trojan Amazonomachy (Figure 7.12). The central Amazon (Figures 7.13–7.14) can be identified by her large size, her royal diadem, and the primacy of her position as Penthesilea, the Amazon queen. Her traditional opponent is Achilles, the largest warrior in the gable. Since the workshop of Hectoridas seems to have been engaged elsewhere, the western pediment is now assigned to the unknown sculptor missing from *IG* IV² 102 BI (lines 96–7).[35]

The temple's crowning akroteria, made by the workshops of Theo– (*IG* IV² 102 BI lines 95–6) and Timotheus (*IG* IV² 102 BI lines 88–90)

[32] Yalouris 1992, with comprehensive bibliography.
[33] Priam: Stewart 1990: fig. 459. R. Osborne 1998: 212–13 gives the stylistic context.
[34] Burford 1969: 215; Yalouris 1992: 67–74.
[35] Schlörb 1965 suggested that Timotheus be restored here. Others have proposed Thrasymedes, the sculptor of the cult image (Pollitt 1974: 204–15), Theodotus, the architect of the temple (Marcadé 1986: 172), or even Theodorus, the architect of the early fourth-century tholos at Delphi (Levendi 2003: 101 n. 38). All suggestions are speculative barring the discovery of further evidence.

Figure 7.12: The west pediment and akroteria of the temple of Asclepius at Epidaurus.

Figure 7.13: Penthesilea, front view. The central figure from the western pediment temple
of Asclepius at Epidaurus. Athens, c. 0.90 m, Pentelic marble, c. 380 BC. This figure, and
the pedimental composition to which it belongs may be the work of the sculptor's
workshop whose name is missing from lines 96–7 of *IG* IV² 102A.

Figure 7.14: Penthesilea, rear view. The central figure from the western pediment temple of Asclepius at Epidaurus. Athens, c. 0.90 m, Pentelic marble, c. 380 BC. This figure, and the pedimental composition to which it belongs, may be the work of the sculptor's workshop whose name is missing from lines 96–7 of *IG* IV² 102A.

respectively, showed an abduction scene accompanied by two flanking Nikai on the east and a Nike accompanied by two flanking Nereids on the west.[36] Unlike the pediments, whose figures are often anatomically incorrect, roughly finished, and treated as ultra-high relief, the akroteria are fully articulated and intricately crafted and display the same concern

---

[36] Yalouris 1992. Barringer 1995: 146–7 discusses the iconography.

Figure 7.15: Nike, front view. Nike. An akroterion from the eastern pediment of the temple of Asclepius at Epidaurus, Athens, restored height c. 1.7 m, Pentelic marble, c. 380 BC. This figure may be the work of Timotheus; his contract is recorded on *IG* IV² 102A lines 88–90.

with circularity, theatricality, sensuality, transparency, and technical virtuosity as discussed above in the first section.[37]

A major fragment of a Nike, probably carved by Timotheus, from the northeastern corner of the temple's roof provides important material evidence (Figures 7.15–7.16).[38] The figure was conceived as a dynamic spiral of transparent drapery holding the slender figure of a Nike at its centre (Figure 7.16). Radiating from the proper right side of her torso, the curl of her mantle is characterised by and understood as a series of concentric arabesques. While appropriately impressive from below, as all akroteria were, the dramatic effect of the sculptor's skill is particularly impressive in front of the figure (Figure 7.15). Here the arced edge of the Nike's mantle merges with, or emerges from, the unpinned peplos below her left armpit.

---

[37] Hasty workmanship of the temple's pediments: Yalouris 1992: figs. 8d, 10d–e, 11e, 14d, 18d, 42c, *et al*. Conceptualisation of fifth- and fourth-century pediments as high relief: Croissant and Marcadé 1972: 890 (the temple of Apollo at Delphi); Yalouris 1992: 38 (the temple of Asclepius at Epidaurus); and Touloupa 2002: 40–4 (the temple of Apollo Daphnephorus at Eretria), all with comparanda and references.

[38] Yalouris 1992: 67–74.

Figure 7.16: Nike, bottom view. Nike. An akroterion from the eastern pediment of the temple of Asclepius at Epidaurus, Athens, restored height c. 1.7 m, Pentelic marble, c. 380 BC. This figure may be the work of Timotheus; his contract is recorded on *IG* IV² 102A lines 88–90.

Cupping and emphasising her left breast, this mannerist fold curls up past the torso and then billows outwards in a blossom of windswept drapery let loose by the figure's upraised right arm.[39] Under the Peloponnesian sun, the sense of shadow, energy, and movement created by this dynamic furl of drapery would have been potent. While these supple drapery effects are stunning – made all the more so by the fact that the preserved fragment, like the famous Nike of Paionios at Olympia (Figure 7.10), was carved from a single piece of Pentelic marble – the notion of a solid human figure as the conceptual and physical centre of the composition is never lost. A series of parallel folds that rhythmically duplicate the opening on the right side of the Nike's peplos twist forward around her slender right side and serve to anchor the vortex of drapery on a figural axis. The sculptor's final *tour de force* came in the upper stretches of the mantle, which were slung high between the Nike's outstretched wings. When vividly painted with an array

[39] The sensuality of the specific pose and the connection of Nike to Aphrodite: Gulaki 1981: 89–90; Picón 1993; Leventi 2003: 99.

of brilliant colours, this mantle would have provided a stunning theatrical backdrop for the entire figural composition.[40]

Other ancient testimonia help to invigorate this epigraphical and material evidence and to provide a broader context for the work of the sculptors of Asclepius' temple. Hectoridas, for example, is known to have made another expensive dedication inside the sanctuary of Asclepius (*IG* iv² I 695) while Theo– is often thought to be the architect of the temple (Theodotus), a natural enough assumption.[41] Thrasymedes of Paros also was known in Roman times, and Pausanias (2.27.1–2) provides a detailed discussion of his cult statue at Epidaurus. While these are interesting points, it is worth noting that only the Attic sculptor Timotheus made a significant impact on the later art historical tradition.[42] Pliny included him in a list of famous fourth-century bronze casters (*Natural History* 34.91) and connected him to a statue of Artemis that had been moved to Rome (*Natural History* 36.32), while Pausanias associated him with a statue of Asclepius in Troezen (Pausanius 2.32.4). His best-known associations, however, are with the sculptural programme of the Mausoleum of Halicarnassus (*Natural History* 36.30–31 and Vitruvius 7 *praef.* 12–13) and, much more speculatively, with the famous *Leda and the Swan* group (Figures 7.7–7.9), discussed above in the first section. Indeed, when we juxtapose *Leda* with the eastern akroteria (Figures 7.15–7.16) of the temple of Asclepius, the formal similarities are clear; some sort of connection between the two works seems plausible.[43]

But even if this traditional connection between the akroteria of the temple of Asclepius and a 'Great Master' is acknowledged, it does not help us significantly with our questions about ancient 'artists' and late classical styles

---

[40] Painting of ancient architectural sculpture: Reuterswärd 1960, Tiberios *et al.* 2002, Artal-Isbrand *et al.* 2002, and Brinkmann 2004, with bibliography.

[41] Hectoridas: Muller-Dufeu 2002: 537. The notion that Theo– is Theodotus may be supported by the later tradition, which preserves several examples of architects doing double duty as sculptors. See, for example Scopas (Paus. 8.45–7), Pytheus of Priene (Vitr. 7. *praef.* 12–13; Pliny *Natural History* 36.30–1), Satyrus of Paros (Vitr. 7. *praef.* 12–13; Pliny, *Natural History* 36.30–1), and Polyclitus the Younger (Paus. 6.6.2; 2.27.5). While this idea accords well with the often heterogeneous skills of Greek craftsmen (Burford 1969: 138–45), Yalouris 1992: 68 argues against the restoration.

[42] For this reason, Timotheus is often (Schlörb 1965: 1–5; Yalouris 1992: 70–2; Levendi 2003: 101) given credit for the design of the temple's elaborate sculptural programme. It is sometimes (Yalouris 1992: 185–6; Todisco 1993: 57–8) argued that this understanding of Timotheus' role is confirmed by *IG* iv² 102 AI lines 34–5, which record: 'Timotheus took the contract to work and supply *tupos* for 900 drachmas,' with *tupos* being understood as 'models'. However, as Pollitt 1974: 272–93; Aleshire 1989: 157; Posch 1991; Oliver 2006; and now Palagia 2006b: 263 have shown, *tupos* almost certainly refers to 'reliefs'. These lines probably refer either to a set of metopes over the pronaos or to the relief on the base of Thrasymedes' cult statue.

[43] Yalouris 1992: 67–74; Levendi 2003: 99.

and sculptors. For this, we need to take a closer at the accounts. As noted, *IG* IV² 102 BI lines 87–8, 96–7 and 109–10 make clear that a sculptor whose name is lost to us and Hectoridas each received 3,010 Aeginitan drachmas (4,300 Attic drachmas) for the completion of the temple's two pediments.[44] On the other hand, lines 88–90 and 95–6 show that Theo– and Timotheus each received 2,240 Aeginitan drachmas (3,200 Attic drachmas) for the completion of the temple's two sets of akroteria. The temple's pediments comprised about twenty figures each, while the sets of akroteria were made up of three (west) or four (east) figures. In sum, Hectoridas (for example) was paid 215 Attic drachmas for each of the three-quarters-sized Pentelic statues that he sculpted for the temple's east pediment.[45] Timotheus, on the other hand, was paid 800 Attic drachmas for each of the three-quarters-sized Pentelic statues that he made for the temple's roof.[46]

Why was Timotheus paid four times more than Hectoridas for his sculpture?

Now, since we are concerned with problems of ancient styles and ancient artists, an instinctive response would be to suggest that this epigraphical evidence confirms the existence of a socially based hierarchy (here an economic hierarchy associated with 'skill' or 'technique' or 'status') within which these sculptors operated, and that the 'famous' Timotheus was able to command a higher price for his work because of his position in this hierarchy as a 'master'. For the moment, however, let us resist this intuitive solution. Remember, our evidence for Timotheus' 'fame' is based on Roman sources, and our knowledge of Timotheus' style is confined to his work at Epidaurus and to possible Roman copies of his *Leda and the Swan*, a connection that is speculative.[47] Instead, let our initial response be to look to the material evidence itself.

Is there a fundamental difference between the Pentelic marble used in the pediments and that used for the akroteria which might explain the radical difference in price that exists between the sculptural contracts? Here, the answer is no. The Pentelic marble used for both pediments and akroteria

---

[44] Stewart 1979: 113 n. 31; 1990: 66 provides the monetary ratios; see above, n. 31.

[45] The fact that the amounts paid for the pediments do not divide into round, 'per figure' costs suggests that the pediments were paid for as *compositions*, not as individual pieces. Contrast this with the piece-work on the Erechtheion, *IG* I³ 476.

[46] The price is not high when considered in context. Middle fourth-century sculptors normally made 3,000 drachmas for a single bronze statue – with materials constituting only 300 drachmas of the cost (see *IG* II² 555; Diogenes Laertius [6.35]; Stewart 1979: 109–11). In architectural sculpture, the sculptor Androsthenes, for example, made 5,000 drachmas per Pentelic pedimental figure when he worked on the new temple of Apollo at Delphi (Stewart 1982; 1990: 66). See also n. 49 below.

[47] Schlörb 1965 expands the list of 'known' works significantly.

share identical physical and visual characteristics. Grain size is consistently very fine (c. 0.5–2.5 mm) in both. In terms of luminosity, the sculptures from both architectural zones were observed in diffuse morning light, in noon sunshine, and with a flashlight and magnifying glass. To the naked eye, light refraction at all times was identical. These visual similarities have been confirmed by isotopic analysis.[48] The temple's pedimental sculpture and its akroteria were made of similar high-quality Pentelic stone. It does not seem that the difference in the sculptors' contract wages can be accounted for by a difference in their basic materials.[49]

Another response to the epigraphical evidence might be that the sculptors of the akroteria were responsible for peripheral aspects of their individual projects. Is it possible that Theo–'s or Timotheus' contract included the fashioning of the statue base for their images or maybe the painting of their sculptures? Again, the answer is no in both cases. Bases for akroteria in the classical period were always considered part of their buildings and are almost always carved as one piece with the sima.[50] The two tasks were connected in logistical terms (as opposed to terms of design) only in so far as the temple architect made basic technical and spatial allowances for the installation of roof sculpture. In the case of the temple of Asclepius, this is made clear by *IG* IV² 102 BI lines 97–9, which shows that '– took up the contract for the tiles on the raking cornice of the pediment, the antefixes and the bases for the akroteria for [+]320 drachmas; Atlatidas, Aineas, and Pyrras were his guarantors.' Similar evidence seems to rule out the possibility that subsidiary decoration contributed to Theo–'s and Timotheus' expenses, since *IG* IV² 102 BI lines 99–100 record that 'Eucles took up the contract for the [decoration] of the akroteria for 305 drachmas; Lysion was his guarantor.' Satellite projects cannot explain the added cost of the akroteria. Indeed, even if we (mistakenly) ignore the epigraphical evidence which specifically distinguishes different contracts, it would be extraordinary if the costs involved in setting or painting the akroteria added over 4,800 Attic drachmas to their cost.

[48] I am grateful to Olga Palagia for sharing her research on the use of Pentelic marble at Epidaurus.

[49] Indeed, the actual difference in price for the pediments and akroteria at Epidaurus may be considerably *larger* than it initially appears if the sculptors were responsible for selecting and transporting their own marble, as was sometimes the case (Stewart 1990: 66). If this was so, then the pediments (with forty figures), not the akroteria (with seven figures), should have been significantly more expensive because of the larger number of assistants that would have been needed for carving and the larger amount of raw marble that would have been selected and transported.

[50] The akroteria bases of the Parthenon (Hurwit 1999: fig. 133), the Hephaisteion (W. B. Dinsmoor 1976: 233), the Propylaia (A. N. Dinsmoor 2004: 303–4), and the temple of Athena Nike (Schultz 2001: figs. 3–9) are only the best-known examples.

Another possibility is that the akroteria were gilded.[51] Can the comparatively high cost of the sculptures be explained by the possibility that Theo–'s and Timotheus' sculptures were covered in gold? This solution is the most attractive of our hypotheses based on raw materials.[52] It is also implausible for two reasons. First, as noted, *IG* IV² BI lines 99–100 already record the cost for the final decoration of the akroteria at 305 drachmas. The contract itself shows that peripheral decorative expenses were listed separately and that they were considered to be distinct projects with their own discrete contracts. This is common practice that is attested with absolute certainty elsewhere.[53] In other words, if the temple's akroteria were gilded – which is quite possible, although no traces of gilding were noticed during excavation – then the purchase of the gold and the actual process of gilding the sculpture would have been recorded independently.

Second, even if our hypothetical gilding was (unusually) merged with the contract for the akroteria, it is impossible that the gold leaf required to gild the temple's roof sculpture should have cost over 4,800 drachmas. Leaf gilding did not cost this much. Think of the Athenian goldsmith Adonis from Melite, who earned a grand total of 166 drachmas for the 166 gilding leaves (*petala*) used for the thirty marble rosettes of the ceiling of the Erechtheion's north porch (*IG* I³ 476, lines 291–5).[54] About 5.5 *petala* were

---

[51] Ancient leaf gilding: Kluge and Lehmann-Hartleben 1927: 31–4; Oddy 1985; 1990: 108; 1991. Gilding of ancient marble architectural sculpture: Fengler 1886: 21–33; Paton 1927: 227–31; Reuterswärd 1960; Palagia 1993: 12; Schultz 2001: 2–5; Artal-Isbrand *et al.* 2002; Tiberios *et al.* 2002; St Clair 2004: 174; Higgs 2006: 192; Palagia 2006a: 127; 2006b: 261 (all with bibliographies).

[52] Indeed, the famous gilded Nikai akroteria of the temple of Zeus at Olympia (*Olympia V*, no. 259; Paus. 5.10.4) and gilded Nikai akroteria of the temple of Athena Nike (*IG* II² 1425 lines 103–6 *et al.*; Schultz 2001) would have been known to the Athenian sculptors at Epidauros and could have exerted a strong influence there.

[53] Compare, for example, the procedural stages by which the gilded marble rosettes for the ceiling of the Erechtheion were commissioned and paid for in 408/7 (*IG* I³ 476). First, the model-maker for the rosettes (a sculptor named Neseus) was paid 8 drachmas for his design (*IG* I³ 476 lines 258–66). Second, the goldsmith who made the rosettes' gilding (a craftsman named Adonis) was paid 1 drachma per gilding leaf for his wares (*IG* I³ 476 lines 291–5). Third, the sculptors of the rosettes (a crew of at least nine men, which included the designer Neseus and at least eight other craftsmen) were paid 14 drachmas for carving each rosette (*IG* I³ 476 lines 327–45). And lastly, the master gilder of the rosettes (probably a goldsmith named Sisyphus, see *IG* I³ 476 lines 54–9) was paid an unknown amount for the final gilding of the sculpture (*IG* I³ 476 lines 351–4; Paton 1927: 409). In this case, the accounts (and thus the contracts) for models, gold, sculpture, and gilding were meticulously distinguished to ensure accountability and quality. (*IG* I³ 476 is also important for understanding the processes of production for ancient Greek sculpture generally: Scranton (1969: 33–4, followed by Ridgway 1969: 117, and others), for example, considered the logistical process by which the 'ancient sculptor' worked to be a mystery (his quotation marks). He asks of the Erechtheion frieze: 'Did the designers of the sculptures make a drawing of the frieze, or a model, or simply a verbal description – a *syngraphe*, which, like the architect, he subdivided into individual jobs to be contracted out?' The Erechtheion accounts answer this question in a relatively unambiguous manner.)

[54] Paton 1927: 409. See also n. 53 above.

required for each rosette. Each rosette had a diameter of 22 centimetres. Thus in late fifth-century Athens, it cost about five and a half drachmas fully to gild a circle about 30 centimetres across. The reason for the relatively low cost of gilding (it was cheaper than paper; see *IG* I³ 476 lines 288–91) is that such gilding was purchased in the form of *very* thin leaves not much thicker than c. $\frac{1}{900}$ of a millimetre; hardly any gold was used in their manufacture.[55] When these factors are considered, the addition of hypothetical gold does not seem to account for the akroteria's extraordinary cost. The hypotheses based on raw materials or logistics do not seem to explain the discrepancy between Hectoridas' and Timotheus' wages.

But what happens if we look at style and technique as opposed to logistics or raw materials? Here, a number of interconnected differences between the two sets of sculpture appear. To begin, the akroteria are finished in the round, while the pedimental sculpture is treated as high relief. While the backs of the akroteria seem somewhat cursorily treated (although a fair analysis must take into consideration that they were fully exposed, while the pedimental sculpture was protected by the temple's gable), a comparison between the two architectural zones reveals a marked difference in the manner in which the sculptures were conceived and crafted. The back sides of the pedimental figures are rough, barely finished, and marked with the inevitable dowel holes and struts used to attach them to the tympanum wall. (These characteristics are neither necessary nor inevitable for pedimental sculpture, as the pediments of the Parthenon show.) The rear view of Penthesilea (Figure 7.14), for example, demonstrates how her anatomy collapses when it is out of view. The Amazon's shoulder and arm are flattened out against her side and become simple slabs of marble. Her upper torso, in addition to being unfinished (traces of the point are broadly evident) is marked by the large (c. 1 × 43 cm) socket where a marble strut was used to secure her to the tympanum wall. This utilitarian craftsmanship is evident elsewhere. While the akroteria are also 'frontal', their backs and sides are treated as intricate parts of complex three-dimensional wholes

---

[55] One of our best ancient testimonia to this fact comes from Pliny (*Natural History* 31.19.61), who notes in his discussion of gilding techniques that just 1 ounce of gold could yield as many as 750 micro-thin gilding leaves, each about 10 cm square. Master gilders were prized in the ancient world precisely because they could take very small amounts of gold and stretch it over vast surfaces. Ancient leaf gilding: Kluge and Lehmann-Hartleben 1927: 31–4; Oddy 1985; 1990: 108; 1991. Evidence of leaf gilding on a modest sculptural scale is demonstrated by an early fifth-century statuette of Athena found north of the Erechtheion in 1887 (Stais 1887: cols. 31–4, pl. 4) and by a similar image with a gilded aegis found the same year east of the same building (Studniczka 1887: cols. 133–54, esp. 142–4, pl. 7). A gilt copper wreath found in an early fourth-century tomb at Olynthus (*Olynthus X*, no. 505 pl. xxviii) and two pairs of gilt greaves found in the antechamber of Tomb II and the 'Prince's Tomb' at Vergina (Andronikos 1984: 186, 216) were gilded using similar leaves. See also n. 53 above.

(Figures 7.15–7.16). In terms of basic three-dimensionality, the sculptures in the two architectural zones are different; only the akroteria display evidence of attention to complex circular form.[56]

The interest in mannerist effects and transparent drapery, or lack thereof, constitutes another stylistic and technical distinction between the two sets of sculptures. A comparison of the drapery of Penthesilea (Figure 7.13) and the northeastern akroteria (Figures 7.15–7.16) illustrates the difference. The sculptor of the Penthesilea pulls his drapery over and around the Amazon's figure, both following and emphasising the form beneath. Timotheus, on the other hand, cuts his drapery loose from all practical concerns and treats his marble fabric as pure form that almost seems to exist in its own right and for its own sake. (Indeed, it is almost as if Timotheus' drapery creates its own formal reality.) These differences would have been made more noticeable when the pieces were painted and set in the open air, where the transparent, mannerist arabesques of Timotheus' marble would have created deep pockets of void and shadow, and the billowing mantle of Timotheus' Nike would have served as a theatrical background against which this sophisticated carving took place. The pedimental sculptor's Amazon is representative of straightforward, functional carving. Timotheus' akroterion is a kaleidoscope swirl of form, light and sensuality. Timotheus is doing something different in his work.

The nature and amount of freestanding drapery associated with the akroteria sculpture and the pediments is also worth comparing. Like the Nike of Paionios (Figure 7.10), the eastern lateral akroteria are marked by solid (unpieced) marble elements that extend dramatically away from the central core of the body. The broken marble edges of the left mantle

---

[56] Of course, it could be argued that this difference was 'dictated' by the architectural setting of the sculpture on the temple itself. Even though the Parthenon pediments were fully finished (a fact that problematises arguments based on simple types), in the case of the temple of Asclepius this kind of argument could make sense. And it is precisely here that the complex social interactions between sculptor, patron, and commission become important. If we want to suggest that akroteria were considered (for whatever reason) inherently more complex than pediments (which may or may not be true), then we should probably ask how this knowledge contributed to the choice of sculptor and to what the selected sculptor brought to the table. In Olympia, for example, the Elean officials held a contest for the akroteria of the temple of Zeus, and Paionios won it (*Olympia V*, no. 259, fig. 13). Was the same true for Epidaurus? Was a particular kind of 'master' required or sought for this particular kind of composition? Were only akroteria connected to these sorts of architectural contests? Is this why Timotheus was paid more? Now even if we cannot answer these questions at present, asking them is just as important. More to the point, the possibility that one particular zone of architectural sculpture was considered (for whatever reason) to be more important or more complex than another and that the sculptors of this particular zone were, in fact, paid more certainly seems to merit a discussion within the context of ancient social practice as well as modern typological divisions. And it is precisely this kind of question that could make a complex social history of ancient Greek art significant.

of the northeastern akroterion reveal that the Pentelic marble is less than one millimetre thick at the fracture, and that this thickness was sometimes stretched as far as a *metre* from the core of the piece. Sheila Adam has reminded us that 'while the sculptor was negotiating his chisel around these drapery ridges one false blow would have ruined his work by knocking a hole in the thin wall of marble . . . like filigree, as soon as it was damaged, the whole effect was lost'.[57] A similar fragility of material is not evidenced in the pedimental figures. There, the best-preserved drapery ridges extend no more than 2 millimetres from the figures' central mass. The interest in the physical limits of marble and the boundaries of sculptural technique is confined to the temple's akroteria alone.

The pediments and akroteria of the temple of Asclepius display stylistic differences that can be documented in concrete terms. For example, the styles of Hectoridas and Timotheus are distinct. This difference in style does not correspond with a difference in date – both clearly belonging to the first half of the fourth century. Rather, this difference in style corresponds to a difference in contract wages. Hectoridas was paid 215 Attic drachmas per piece, and produced, as we have seen, a large-scale composition of twenty figures in which he cut technical corners when possible and convenient. Timotheus was paid 800 Attic drachmas per figure and produced a set of sculptures that included at least one marvel of sculptural *technē* – a word that implies craft, art, cunning, and style.[58] In this particular case, exceptional sculptural skill, complexity, and elegance – in other words, some idea of *virtuosity* – seems to have contributed to the determination of a sculptor's pay.

While this evidence might provoke a number of conclusions, the most important for us is that it seems to show that the sculptors at Epidaurus worked within an established social (economic) hierarchy and that their position within this hierarchy was connected to their skills, techniques, and styles. This conclusion is an important step for the justification of our interpretation of the formal transitions offered in the first section of this chapter, an interpretation that was premised upon the existence of master sculptors self-consciously engaged in the creation of satisfying, pleasing, or beautiful objects that were judged and valued as such by their contemporaries. The archaeological and epigraphical evidence from Epidaurus shows that, in some instances at least, this premise is valid. Certain sculptors were considered to be master artists or master craftsmen by their peers and within their communities. And they were paid accordingly. Different styles, the

---

[57] Adam 1966: 94. See also Yalouris 1992: 76–80.   [58] Pollitt 1974: 32–7.

technical skills connected to them, and the sculptors associated with both existed within a hierarchy of value. The best (and maybe even the worst) Greek sculptors – exactly like their ancient peers in the fields of poetry, music, philosophy, rhetoric, and athletics – competed with one another, bragged about the accomplishments, and thereby pushed one another (and themselves) into undiscovered formal and conceptual territory, a territory in which the interpretative vocabulary used in the first section could have made sense.[59] Not every artist could be equally 'well practised in the arts of Athena', as Simonedes once boasted for the sculptor Arcesilas.[60]

The transformations in style that we saw in the first section and the differences between the styles of Hectoridas and Timotheus that we outlined in the second section have little to do with the traditional biologico-evolutionary model of stylistical development currently entrenched in our histories of Greek and Attic art. Rather, these transformations and differences are better understood in terms of culturally situated 'ambition' (*philotimia*), 'competition' (*agōn*), and 'talent' (*idmosunē*) and the culture of struggle that made these words meaningful for individual members of ancient Greek society.[61] If this is true, then the examples of technical and stylistic virtuosity that we discussed in the first section and second section – and the changes in style that we observed – can be partly understood as material evidence for fierce competition between individual artists seeking to elevate themselves within the shifting hierarchies of Greek society by way of individual acts of technical virtuosity – by way of what we might call 'art'. But this conclusion raises yet another problem.

CONTEXTS

The preceding interpretation of the material evidence raises a methodological dilemma. Elizabeth Brumfiel has noted that archaeological analyses based around ancient individuals are particularly vulnerable to distortion and to the projection of contemporary and/or ethnocentric assumptions.[62]

---

[59] For Greek sculptors and social hierarchies generally, see Stewart 1979: 106–11; Lauter 1980; Müller 1988; Hurwit 1997; Schultz 2003. Duplouy 2006 now provides the fundamental model for discussions of ancient competition and the hierarchies that result.

[60] Arcesilas: Diog. Laert. 4.45.

[61] This sort of culture of competition for Greek sculptors (for which there is much Roman evidence, e.g. Pliny, *Natural History* 34.53, 36.17) seems logical enough when placed within the fundamentally *agonistic* character of Greek society (see Onians 1999: 9–104; Neer 2002; Hölscher 2000; Fleischer 2002; and now Duplouy 2006). Such competitions are unambiguously attested to have taken place between potters (e.g. Ath. 12.541a), sculptors (e.g. *Olympia V*, no. 259), architects (e.g. *IG* I³ 64a) and tapestry-designers (e.g. *Ath. Pol.* 49.3).

[62] Brumfiel 2000: 254. See also Bender 1993: 258; Dobres and Robb 2000: 13; Gero 2000.

While the argument advanced above regarding the value of Timotheus' virtuosic style and his expensive akroteria is supported by the archaeological evidence, some would argue that my interpretation is based on an anachronistic social model better suited to, say, *quattrocento* Florence than early fourth-century Greece. (Think of the 200 florins paid to Fra Angelico versus the 84 florins paid to his assistant Benozzo Gozzoli in 1447 by Pope Nicholas V for their work on the chapel of St Peter in Rome.)[63] Indeed, a recent discussion of classical architectural sculpture urges us 'to *remember* that the "discovery" of the artist as a distinct and distinctive personality did not occur until the fifteenth century'.[64]

One response to this legitimate concern would be to re-examine the preceding argument within the social and cultural contexts of late classical ancient Athens. If it could be shown that late fifth- and early fourth-century Athenians saw some artists as recognisable individuals, that they believed that these artists lived and worked within a defined social hierarchy, and that this hierarchy was connected to these artists' skills and styles, then the reading of the material evidence given above could sit on a firmer foundation of contemporary Athenian norms.[65]

Let us consider the late fifth / early fourth-century Athenian painter Pauson (c. 430–380 BC) as a starting point. Although he was not a sculptor, I think that Pauson is an appropriate place to begin because he is an artist who might be considered an 'anonymous craftsman', a nonentity in the field of late fifth-century Athenian painting. Pauson was responsible for no public commissions that we know of, his work never seems to have been copied in the minor arts, and his name – unlike the great painters such as Micon, Zeuxis, or Polygnotus – left almost no trace in later Roman sources. Indeed, in the Roman period, Pauson's artistic personality is known from only one anecdote from (Pseudo-?)Lucian's *Demosthenes, an Encomium* 24:

> They relate about the painter Pauson that he was hired to paint a horse rolling on its back. But instead, he painted the horse galloping with a kicked-up cloud of dirt around it. Now while he was still painting, the man who had hired him interfered and rebuked him for not executing the painting according to instructions. Consequently, Pauson ordered his assistant to exhibit the painting upside down so that the horse seemed to be lying on its back rolling around in the dirt. (Trans. after Loeb)

---

[63] Baxandall 1972: 19–20. Burford (1972: 87–92) shows how a similar workshop structure existed in ancient Greece.
[64] Ridgway 1999: 186 (my italics). See also Ridgway 1997: 242.
[65] Agency and context: Sassaman 2000, A. Sinclair 2000, Wobst 2000, and Hodder and Hutson 2003: 99–105.

Now, for the last half-century, stories like this have come under close scrutiny. And rightfully so. The relationship between patron and painter that Lucian describes does seem, at first glance, more at home in Renaissance Italy than in late fifth-century Athens. And what of Pauson's implied character? Are we to believe that he was free to paint his own subjects, to ridicule his clients? Is this a realistic picture of a late fifth-century Athenian artist? There are many who believe that it is not. However, if late fifth- or early fourth-century evidence could be found to substantiate this Roman view of Pauson as a nonconformist (or even as a bohemian?), then Lucian's story might deserve a second look. More importantly, if traces or stories regarding Pauson's personality and style were preserved in the contemporary record, then his status as unique social actor might become difficult to deny, and the possibility of positing a complex social hierarchy which some Greek artists worked within or, in this particular case, resisted, becomes real.

Pauson gets mentioned in a discussion of the moral character of images by Aristotle (*Politics* 1340a 23–39):

The habit of feeling pleasure or pain at simple representations is not far removed from the same feeling about the real world; for example, if anyone delights in the sight of a statue for its beauty only, it necessarily follows that the sight of the original will also be pleasant to him. The objects of no other sense, like taste or touch, have any resemblance to such moral qualities; but in visible objects there is a little, for there exist figures which are of a moral character, but only to a slight extent, and all do not participate in the feeling about them. Again, these figures and colours are not imitations, but rather indicators of moral habit, indicators which the body gives to states of internal feeling. The connection between [images] and ethics is slight, but since it does exist, young men should be taught to look not at the works of Pauson, but rather at those of Polygnotos and any other painter or sculptor who expresses moral ideas. (Trans. after Loeb)

Here, the visual arts are assumed to be the bearer of ethical values and are categorised, not by way of anachronistic archaeological criteria, but rather by way of known late classical examples – individual artists and their names. The styles and subjects of these artists were understood as the products of particular social actors whose painted, and personal characters are portrayed as diametrical opposites. Polygnotos, of course, expressed 'correct' ideas, while Pauson is somehow 'deviant' and therefore unsuitable for young minds. In fact – and this is a key point – within the context of the *Politics* itself, it seems clear that Aristotle is using these particular artists as a powerful way (literally) to *illustrate* his philosophical point in the most explicit manner possible.[66] That Polygnotos, Pauson, and their different subjects and styles could be used for this sort of argument seems significant.

Other evidence strengthens our impression of Pauson as a unique social actor set within a socially understood hierarchy. In his famous discussion of morality and tragedy in the *Poetics* (c. 350–340 BC; 1448a 1–7) Aristotle points out that:

> Since mimetic artists [*hoi mimoumenoi*] represent people in action, and since the latter should be either elevated or base (for characters almost always align with these two types, as it is through vice and virtue that the characters of all men vary), they can represent people better than our normal level, worse than it, or much the same. It is the same way with painters: the characters of Polygnotos are better than we are, those of Pauson worse and those of Dionysios just like ourselves. Clearly, each kind of mimesis already mentioned will manifest these distinctions, and will differ by representing different objects in the given sense. (Trans. after Loeb)

Here again, the visual arts are assumed to be the vehicles for complex ideas and named artists are characterised as those who via skill and style instil particular values into their work. Art objects and the ideas that they communicated, at least for Aristotle, could be conceptualised as the product of social agents with their own distinct modes of expression. Within the context of the *Politics* itself, it again seems clear that Aristotle is using these particular artists as a way to illustrate his philosophical point in an unambiguous manner. And naturally, our roguish late classical painter Pauson is described as a painter interested in all that is base in human nature.[67]

Now since Aristotle is a philosopher, it might be argued that his view of art and artists stands outside average Athenian experience. This is a valid point. But it also seems a bit limp, since it is precisely this sort of culturally determined relationship that is the object of study for a social history of art in the first place. For it to be meaningful, our social history of Greek art probably should not seek to create generic, 'ideal' viewers for the objects that we study. Rather, the idea would be to acknowledge that different objects would have been experienced differently by different members of Athenian

---

[66] That this passage implies a relationship between an artist and his work that moderns might find fallacious (i.e. that Pauson's character can somehow be discerned in his art) should not trouble us, since the existence of this fallacy in Aristotle simply suggests that he considered the paintings he examined to be the result of intentional action. As such, they were open to moral interpretation like any other deed. Aristotle on human action: Ackrill 1997: 212–30. Theories of agency linked with intentionality: Dobres and Robb 2000: 10; Hodder and Hutson 2003: 101. The intentional fallacy: Ciofi 1978, Wimsatt and Beardsley 1978.

[67] It also suggests that he was embarrassingly popular; I am indebted to Andrew Stewart for discussing his thoughts on Pauson with me.

society and that meaning(s) would have been contingent on an almost infinite number of factors. In this particular example, Aristotle makes sense to us only when certain assumptions about the Athenian intelligentsia and their understanding of the arts are accepted. In this particular case, it seems obvious that Aristotle and his elite audience appreciated the notion of a painter as a specific personality whose work embodied specific ideas. That this idea may not have occurred to slaves, the poor, a metic, or others does not weaken the point. Rather, it suggests that our understanding of Athenian art and culture should be based, in part, around understanding the various cultural intersections that existed between various social hierarchies.

But even if all this seems correct, it still may not fully satisfy. Indeed, it could be argued that Aristotle wrote a generation after Pauson and that his ideas about a painter and his particular personality are no more than a later invention. Fortunately, knowledge of Pauson's antics was not restricted to the fourth-century Athenian intellectual elite. Indeed, the painter's character was widely known to the masses during his own lifetime. This is made clear by several passages from Aristophanes. In *Women at the Thesmophoria* of 411 BC (948–52), for example, Pauson is characterised very meanly, as a compulsive and maybe illegitimate faster, while in the *Plutus* of 388 BC (602), Pauson is considered synonymous with decadent living habits. In the *Acharnians* of 425 BC (854–60), Aristophanes describes Pauson as *pamponeros* (i.e. either 'all depraved' or 'utterly base'), and suggests that Pauson was infamous for ridiculing his clients in public, a characterisation that works quite nicely with what we have already seen in Aristotle and, incidentally, in Lucian.

Now this evidence reveals little about the actual appearance of Pauson's art. What this evidence does reveal, however, is that at least one 'obscure' late classical painter and his paintings were known well enough in his own lifetime to become an emblem for immorality in late fifth-century Athenian society. This does not mean that Lucian's anecdote regarding the rascally Pauson and his rolling horse is true. But it does indicate that Pauson was a recognisable social agent with his own distinct style, subjects, and issues and that he was positioned within a social hierarchy (here an ethical hierarchy) that was perceived as such by his Athenian contemporaries.

Other late classical voices have more to add. Take, for example, Plato's use of Phidias and Polyclitus in the *Protagoras* (c. 380 BC) as Socrates questions Hippocrates about the nature of the sophists:

Suppose, for example, you had decided to summon your namesake Hippocrates of Kos, the Asclepiad, and to pay him a personal fee, and suppose someone asked you – 'Tell me, Hippocrates, in paying a fee to Hippocrates, what do you consider him to be?' How would you answer that? A doctor, I would say. And what would you intend to become? A doctor. And suppose you decided to approach Polyclitus the Argive or Phidias the Athenian and pay them a personal fee, and somebody asked you – 'What is it that you consider Polyclitus or Phidias to be, that you want to pay them this money?' What would your answer be to that? Sculptors (*agalmatopoioi*), I would reply. And what would you intend to become? A sculptor, obviously. (311b–c, trans. after Loeb)

Here Phidias and Polyclitus are characterised as unique social actors that both create and exist within a hierarchy of socially assigned value, in this case a hierarchy of perceived skill or expertise. Plato's dialogue is unintelligible if Polyclitus and Phidias were not considered 'sculptors' with special proficiency in 'sculpture', a point that is reinforced by Plato's language. He specifically calls them *agalmatopoioi* as opposed to, say, *banausoi*. Again, as we have seen before, this particular example is used precisely because Polyclitus and Phidias were so well known within their specific profession and because they were an obvious choice to emphasise a philosophical point.

Even more interesting is Plato's second mention of Polyclitus in the same dialogue. Protagoras concludes his argument regarding ethical instruction:

So now, Socrates, I have shown you by both fable and argument that virtue is teachable and is so deemed by the Athenians, and that it is no wonder that bad sons are sometimes born of good fathers and good sons of bad fathers, since even the sons of Polyclitus, companions of Paralus and Xanthippus here, are not to be compared with their father, and the same is the case in other artists' families. As for these two, it is not fair to make this complaint of them yet; there is still hope in their case, for they are young. (328c, trans. after Loeb)

This is an interesting passage for understanding one early fourth-century Athenian perception of a late fifth-century Greek sculptor. First, we have the sons of Polyclitus, as individual artists, compared to their father and found lacking. Whatever it is that is missing from the sons' work, the passage demands that they and their father be situated within some sort of aesthetico-social scale for it to make sense. (How else could judgement be passed?) Second, we have a possible hint of the social circles within which Polycleitus circulated, since his sons accompany two of Protagoras' students – Paralus and Xanthippus – young aristocrats who could afford to pay Protagoras' expensive fees. (The translation of this phrase as 'companions' is not certain, but it is paralleled elsewhere; see, for example, Herodotus 5.71; in this specific setting, it seems clear that the discussants consider Polyclitus and his sons to be more than manual labourers.) Finally, we have Polyclitus again perceived as an individual whose particular name is being invoked as an obvious example of a specific, socially constructed, *quality* within a socially constructed scale. It is especially significant that this conception of the artist quite naturally extends to 'other artists' families' – a point that would be worth bearing in mind for further discussion of other late fifth-century sculptors and their workshops.

Now again, this reference does not suggest that all (or more than a handful of) sculptors were rich socialites whose famous names immediately inspired awe and admiration. Indeed, we know that this was not the case and that such fame was the exception, not the rule.[68] This reference also does not demonstrate that Pliny's (*Natural History* 34.55) famous remark that Polyclitus was paid 100 talents for a *diadoumenos* is accurate, nor does it give us any insight into Polyclitus' style, other than that it was deeply admired. This passage does show, however, that the notion of the sculptor as a socially placed agent was assumed knowledge for Plato's audience, that they could be considered 'master artists', and that this status was, in this case, directly connected to the quality and apperance of their products, their personal styles.

The same can be said for Phidias. In Plato's *Meno* (c. 380 BC) the philosopher compares the sculptor with Protagoras as a 'master' of his craft who profited handsomely by it: 'Protagoras, for example, earned more money from his art than Phidias, who is so famous for his nobly created works that he made more than ten other sculptors' (91d, trans. after Stewart 1979: 113 n. 34). For the audience of this dialogue, Phidias was admired, rich, and known as an artist who lived within a socially constructed hierarchy, here an economic hierarchy of wealth possibly related to that recognised early in the case of Timotheus. This impression of Phidias was not new to the early fourth century, of course, since the artist was already famous as a sculptor, a point made clear in Aristophanes' *Peace* (421 BC; line 605).

Direct evidence for the ancient perception of a late classical hierarchy of quality in late fifth-century and early fourth-century art is provided by Isocrates' *Antidosis* (354/53 BC):

Although I know that some of the sophists deride my occupation, saying that it has to do with speech-writing for the courts (very much as one might have the effrontery to call Phidias, who made our statue of Athena, a mere coroplast, or say that Zeuxis and Parrhasius practised the same art as plaque-painters), nevertheless I have never deigned to defend myself against their attempts to belittle me, because I considered that their nonsense has no influence whatsoever, and that I had, myself, shown clearly to all that I had elected to speak and write, not on petty disputes,

---

[68] Burford 1972: 28–36; Stewart 1979: 106–11; Lauter 1980; Müller 1988; Hurwit 1997; Schultz 2003.

but on subjects so important and elevated that no one would attempt them except those who studied with me, and their would-be imitators. (2–3, trans. after Loeb).

This unambiguous evidence for the perception of social rank within the population of Athenian artists probably should not be ignored. Indeed such evidence can be widely paralleled.[69] Of course, to these accolades must be added all the usual scorn for lowly craftsmen; that they were 'worthless' (Herodotus 2.167), 'slavish' (Xenophon, *Socratic Memoirs.* 2.8.3–5), and 'bad defenders of the city' (Xenophon, *Economics* 4.2–3). Obviously, both characterisations existed simultaneously, exactly as we would expect from any complex human culture. The simplistic notion of Greek sculpture as 'an anonymous product of an impersonal craft' might be valid in some cases, but it also requires some substantial modification in order to correspond to the nuances of ancient Greek experience.[70]

By the early fourth century, it seems clear that some Athenians could perceive a difference between 'virtuosi' and 'anonymous labourers'. It seems equally clear that the *perception* of these two extreme positions demands the corresponding *existence* of a vast middle ground within which individual workmen, craftsmen, artisans, and artists of various talent and ambition vied for sustenance, wealth, prestige, and glory.[71] It was somewhere in this middle ground that late classical sculptors developed and mediated a new set of self-conscious formal and stylistic concerns, like those discussed in the first section of this chapter. It was somewhere in this middle ground that the sculptors who worked at the temple of Asclepius, discussed in the second section, practised their craft and their art. And it is somewhere in this middle ground that the mind of the ancient Greek sculptor *existed*, transforming complex cultural patterns into new thoughts, new paradigms, new styles, and – ultimately – new sculptural realities.

This discussion of late fifth- and early fourth-century styles, agencies, and contexts raises many questions. Within the context of a book that treats

---

[69] Polygnotus is praised by Plato in both the *Ion* (532e) and the *Gorgias* (448b); he is also mentioned as an artist by Aristotle in the *Metaphysics* (1013b–1014a) and the *Poetics* (1448a, 1450a). Micon's work is discussed as the product of a singular talent by Aristophanes (*Lysistrata* 678–9), while the painter Zeuxis is discussed by Plato twice (*Protagoras* 318b and *Gorgias* 453c) by Xenophon three times (*Economics* 10.1, *Symposium* 4.63, *Socratic Memoirs* 1.4.3) and by Aristotle twice (*Poetics* 1450a, 1461b).

[70] Carpenter 1960: v. (See also Ridgway 1990: 73–98; 1997: 237–85.) Of course, the thousands of 'signatures' of individual craftsmen seem to point somewhere in this direction already, but this well-known body of evidence (and how to interpret it) is problematic. See Overbeck 1868, Marcadé 1953–7, Seibert 1978, Muller-Dufeu 2002, Tanner 2006: 153–8; and now Keesling 2007.

[71] Duplouy 2006 now gives the comprehensive discussion of these social goals in ancient Greek society.

a cultural revolution in Athens, however, there is a final point that might serve us by way of conclusion. In his popular handbook on Greek art, Osborne (1998: 234–5) noted that the third quarter of the fourth century marked 'the invention of the sensational artist' in the modern sense. There is little doubt that this well-known and well-documented conclusion is correct. Indeed, the anecdotes and legends that surrounded the work of Leochares, Lysippus, Scopas, and Praxiteles both in their own lifetimes and beyond represent some of the most spectacular tales of antiquity. But upon what social foundation, if any, was this idea of the sensational artist based? Is it a mere coincidence that, for the first time, Athenian poets and philosophers of the late fifth and early fourth centuries took interest in the contemporary painters and sculptors of their own age? Indeed, it might be argued that Plato's interest in the career of the master sculptor Phidias, for example, reflects a new concern with artists not only as mythological makers of wonders (like Daedalus, for instance) but also as specific social actors who played a role in moving the visual arts in new stylistic and aesthetic directions. And if this was the case, then we should probably seek the social structures responsible for later fourth-century developments within our period of 'cultural revolution'.

CHAPTER 8

The politics of precedence: first 'historians' on first 'thalassocrats'

Elizabeth Irwin

The connection between [Thucydides and Herodotus], so important
and so obvious, has never, I believe, been adequately or systematically
investigated.[1]

Given the enormity of the task, it is hardly surprising that Colin Macleod's
observation remains no less valid today. While a systematic investigation
must lie outside the scope of a single chapter, one can begin to ask just what
is required to investigate adequately the relationship between Herodotus
and Thucydides. In this contribution, I interrogate the criteria customarily
employed in such investigations, providing as a case study the analysis of a
pair of passages whose high degree of intertextuality should pose a challenge
to the way in which we conventionally configure the relationship of these
authors to one another, to their contemporary audiences, to the past, and,
ultimately, to us: Thucydides' and Herodotus' conflict over the status of
Minos as first 'thalassocrat'.

First, however, it is necessary to explain what contribution this chapter
makes to the project of investigating the existence and/or nature of any
cultural revolution in Athens. In a volume dedicated to debating revolution
in Athens between 430 and 380 BC, my contribution is anomalous: not
only will it avoid talking about revolution as such, but Herodotus looms
large despite being held by many to fall barely within our period and of
course hardly an Athenian. The reasons for tolerating these anomalies are
in fact linked. For those investigating the changes and developments –
revolutionary or not – of the late fifth century, Herodotus has proved
useful in constructing 'earlier times' owing to both his content and his
apparent mindset. As such he supplies a convenient foil to Thucydides and

---

[1] Macleod 1983: 157, repeated (and slightly misquoted) by Hornblower 1991–6: II. 30, who surveys
recent scholarship, providing his own useful contribution to future research (pp. 138–45). See also
Raaflaub 2002: 186 n. 117.

his Athens, the starting point from which to plot the achievements of both.[2] Since modern scholarship has imposed this function on his text, it behoves us to be extremely cautious in determining just what kind of co-ordinate – temporal, conceptual, and even ethical – his text actually provides.

Here is where my hesitation to invoke – whether to assert or to deny – the concept of revolution lies.[3] Whether we want to talk about revolutions in history or in historiography, the first step must be the assiduous scrutiny of our texts, particularly with an eye to the reception that they imply in their contemporary audiences and the reception that they were attempting to effect in future readers. The construction of narratives, undertaken prematurely, whether of 'revolution' or more modestly of 'development', threatens to distort the evidence, causing us to view our texts as stages in a trajectory highly suspect in its presumption that our vantage point has an objectivity somehow denied to our subjects. Caution is all the more warranted here in handling the narrative of historiographic revolutions in which objectivity itself is one of the achievements that we plot, often implicitly denying the possibility that grand conclusions based on stylistic and ethical differences in our authors – their choices – are substantiated with little beyond a commitment to the texts' relative chronology. We must take seriously the possibilities that our privileged vantage point is afforded its clarity only through the ravages of reception, and that an alleged objectivity may be little more than a distorting subjectivity arising from our understandable difficulty as outsiders in engaging fully with the context in which our authors wrote and their texts were consumed.

Three points will emerge in the following discussion: first, that whatever else it may have been, objectivity as employed in Thucydides' text is also a rhetorical stance; second, that Thucydides did not discover objectivity as a stance; and third, that there were those among his contemporaries, not least Herodotus, who would not have praised him for the ends to which he claims to employ it in his text. What I hope to contribute with this analysis of first thalassocrats in the first historians is an alternative vantage point from which to begin to assess whether a revolution in the relationship to the past did in fact occur in late fifth-century Athens. To undertake such an assessment, I argue, will require facing our own desire to construct such narratives and

---

[2] Herodotus is the standard against which to measure developments from fields as far flung as religious beliefs to prose style.

[3] I follow R. Osborne 2006 in the critical examination of the scholarly impetus to adduce revolution, though perhaps more cynical about the utility of – and even motivations behind – recourse to grand narratives as such.

to argue for our own firsts.[4] Perhaps Thucydides' real achievement was his success in persuading future audiences that a highly partial account represented a revolution in Greek historiography, and consequently Greek thought.

THE PROBLEM

When it comes to crowning a past figure as the first thalassocrat, Herodotus is frequently observed as 'for once more really critical than Thucydides' in his preference of the historical Polycrates to the mythic Minos.[5] Herodotus urbanely rejects Minos' candidacy:

For Polycrates was the first of the Greeks whom we know to set his mind on being a thalassocrat, apart from Minos from Cnossus, and if indeed there was anyone else before him who ruled the sea; but of the race that we call 'human', Polycrates was the first, and he had great hopes that he would rule Ionia and the islands.[6]

By contrast, although Thucydides foregrounds the difficulties in discovering anything clear about the time before the Persian wars, he nevertheless seems confident enough to endow the Cretan king with historical significance as the first to obtain *kratos* (power) through the acquisition of a navy:

For Minos was the oldest of those we know by tradition (παλαίτατος ὧν ἀκοῇ ἴσμεν) to have obtained a fleet, and he gained mastery (ἐκράτησε) for the most part over the Hellenic Sea and he ruled (ἦρξε) the Cyclades and was the first founder of the majority of them, having driven out (ἐξελάσας) the Carians and established (ἐγκαταστήσας) his sons as their leaders (ἡγεμόνας); and naturally he purged the sea of piracy as far as he was able in order to ensure that greater revenues would reach him (τό τε ληστικόν, ὡς εἰκός, καθῄρει ἐκ τῆς θαλάσσης ἐφ' ὅσον ἐδύνατο, τοῦ τὰς προσόδους μᾶλλον ἰέναι αὐτῷ). (Thucydides 1.4)

Few can ignore that here Herodotus at least *seems* the more critical, but the methods of dealing with that impression are telling. Hornblower gives credit where it is due: 'Incidentally, Herodotus emerges as the more sceptical of the two ("apart from Minos" is dismissive, as is the implication in "human" that Minos is mythical).' 'Incidentally', however, indicates

---

[4] Though generally patronised in ancient authors, *protos heuretes* assertions are hardly avoided in modern scholarship, for a survey of which see R. Osborne 2006. On the concept of the *protos heuretēs* in ancient sources see Kleingünther 1933.

[5] How and Wells 1912: 295, 'for once' endearing with the pleonasm of 'more really'.

[6] Πολυκράτης γάρ ἐστι πρῶτος τῶν ἡμεῖς ἴδμεν Ἑλλήνων ὃς θαλασσοκρατέειν ἐπενοήθη, πάρεξ Μίνω τε τοῦ Κνωσσίου καὶ εἰ δή τις ἄλλος πρότερος τούτου ἦρξε τῆς θαλάσσης· τῆς δέ ἀνθρωπηίης λεγομένης γενεῆς Πολυκράτης πρῶτος, ἐλπίδας πολλὰς ἔχων Ἰωνίης τε καὶ νήσων ἄρξειν (Hdt. 3.122.2).

that the concession will be temporary, and Hornblower ultimately grants Thucydides superiority for his more precise handling of *akoē*.[7] By contrast, those who would begrudge Herodotus *any* critical sophistication over Thucydides are compelled to provide an *apodeixis* of their own critical sophistication in the form of laboured footnotes.[8] More spectacular is the recent transformation of Herodotus' rejection of the mythic Minos into the basis of rendering *Thucydides* the crucial step in the origin of objective Truth in Western thought: Herodotus did not know why he was excluding Minos, while Thucydides aptly demonstrates how one *should* talk about such mythic material.[9]

These responses, however, demonstrate just how threatening our first historians' choice of 'firsts' is to the 'firsts' we have chosen them to be – the 'father of history' in contrast to the first scientific/objective historian. At the heart of our problems with Minos is the very significance for the history of History each of our prose purveyors of the past is to have, and therefore it is not surprising that Herodotus' problem with Minos has had little impact on the foundational stories of History and Historiography that we use these two authors to tell. Indeed, if authorship of these passages were reversed, long footnotes and grand theory would be unnecessary: no one would doubt the direct allusion now only ceded by some.[10] The dismissal of Minos in favour of Polycrates would be taken by all as a manifestation of 'Thucydides' marking out a *spatium historicum* clearly delineated from that of myth. But authorship as it is, Herodotus the critical historian, Thucydides the purveyor of myth, scholarship either notes the phenomenon in passing – 'incidentally', 'here for once' – or manufactures edifices to shore up Thucydides' pre-eminence, a cornerstone of our own 'stories' of the development of Greek – and therefore, Western – historiography.[11]

---

[7] Hornblower 1991–6: II. 125. I return to *akoe* below, p. 200.

[8] See Kallet 1993: 24 n. 11 (and cf. p. 27 n. 21 on Herodotus, Thucydides, and Troy). See also n. 52 below.

[9] Williams 2004: ch. 7, entitled 'What was wrong with Minos?', esp. p. 161: 'The question is to hand, "What excludes Minos?" and if Herodotus were to face it, he would not have an answer.'

[10] For example, see Hornblower's frustration (1991–6: II. 38) at the resistance of some to acknowledging the degree to which Thucydides alludes to Herodotus.

[11] Luraghi's (2000: 233) approach to the proem is more sophisticated: he sees Thucydides as not believing in Minos' historicity, but as taking 'the standpoint of someone who does believe in it' in order to demonstrate that even Minos' sea power was inferior to those of present time. This is right as far as it goes, but there are consequences for Thucydides' rendering Minos a precursor of Athenian naval *archē*, as will be discussed below. On constructing the story of Historiography, see Hornblower 1994: 55.

In this situation some might find Herodotus to blame for the apparent failure of his narrative elsewhere to live up to the critical acumen of 3.122, but the fault may lie nearer to home. When Finley comments, 'Thucydides had old poets, tradition, contemporary evidence and a very powerful and disciplined mind . . . But we, too, cannot write a history of early Greece', he shows precisely what is at stake in our choices[12] in rendering Minos the prototype of thalassocracy, Thucydides emerges rather suspiciously as a prototype of ourselves as modern ancient historians. The relationship could be read – less flatteringly – in reverse: by identifying in Thucydides the 'first' us, we may find ourselves, instead, to be the latest him, all too Thucydidean in our participation in a questionable exercise of compelling the past to furnish us with 'oldests' and 'firsts' in the service of a teleology that culminates in, and congratulates, ourselves as the latest, the last, and – of course – the best.

To investigate the intertextuality adequately, I argue, requires first stepping back from the meanings these texts have acquired in our plottings of conceptual 'firsts' in order to examine instead what these narratives of the past actually were for their audiences. Herodotus and Thucydides wrote in a fifth-century political milieu and addressed politicised audiences. Modern scholarship was certainly not the first to recognise that the past is socially constructed, told for the sake of those in the present; this was clear to Herodotus, Thucydides, and no doubt a majority of their audiences – that is, at least, when it came to looking at someone else's ideological use of it.[13] This recognition necessitates reading the historians' Minos from a late fifth-century perspective, engaging with the texts not as modern ancient historians tracking the generic evolution of history, anxious to establish consensus with our peers, but rather as hostile contemporaries might have done – say, for instance, as an avid supporter of Athenian naval *archē* or a Samian exile in Anaia, or the opposing sides of the faction-ridden Athens of the late fifth century. Or, indeed, as Herodotus' and Thucydides' texts seem to read each other.

'Reading each other': this concept is to be understood first and foremost in a figurative sense as the process whereby our close reading of comparable passages throws light on their distinctive orientations in order to reveal what those differences seem to presuppose of their audiences. It may, however, also be understood in a more literal sense. Quite frankly, there are no definite answers about when either text emerged in the form that has come

---

[12] M. I. Finley 1975: 20. Cf. J. H. Finley 1942: 87.
[13] For an explicit awareness, see, for instance, Hdt. 3.49, 3.2; Thuc. 1.42, 72–5, 123.1, etc.

to occupy our modern editions. As it is, recent scholarship has emphasised the inappropriateness of our model of publication for the circulation of the text of Herodotus; and the same may be said of Thucydides.[14] Oral performance and the possibility of circulation and recirculation of earlier written versions in part and *in toto* of both historians suggest the insufficiency of simple linear models of their relationship.[15] Given, as Hornblower comments, that 'it is even possible that the two men were in a real sense contemporaries and rivals',[16] the relationship of their extant texts is very much open to construction. But at any rate, if the artistry of Thucydides' proem lies not in the total originality of its content, but rather in its stunning epideictic *tour de force* of contemporary intellectual trends – anthropology, ethnography, poetic criticism – then, even, on traditional models of dating and publication, Herodotus could well be seen as responding to Thucydides in so far as he is engaged with the same trends, attitudes, and even *exempla* which informed Thucydides' account.[17]

In what follows my basic premises are these: that it is only by placing to one side (temporarily) our preconceptions of what these authors are doing – our own plotting of historiographical 'firsts' – that we can more fruitfully examine their texts individually; and it is only by such careful examination that a more secure understanding of their relationship may emerge, and with that a better understanding of Herodotus and Thucydides as competing purveyors of the past for contemporary, and ultimately modern, audiences. Only by distancing ourselves from the narratives of precedence we impose on their works can we truly understand what the dispute over thalassocratic precedence meant in and for their historiographical enterprises, and indeed what it ought to mean for our own.

THUCYDIDES' MINOS

Minos in the proem

Thucydides' account of Minos occurs in the first chapters of Thucydides' work, his so-called *Archaeology*. Of course, this title has no basis in Thucydides' text, and consequently in what follows it will be called instead the

---

[14] R. Thomas 1992: 125–6; 1993; 2000: 257–60; 2003; Hornblower 1991–6: II. 26; Raaflaub 2002: 163–4 with n. 46; cf. Bakker 2002: 8–12.

[15] See Hornblower 1991–6: II. 26; Raaflaub 2002: 179, esp. n. 94.

[16] Hornblower 1991–6: II. 123; cf. II. 145 and 1994: 22 n. 41. See also Raaflaub 2002: 186, who endorses this view.

[17] See Luraghi 2000.

proem, for reasons that are both negative and positive.[18] Negative in that the term for us carries with it an entirely different set of associations of 'scientific history': we admire what we see of ourselves in Thucydides' critical self-positioning and therefore reward his efforts by applying to it a title that unacceptably blurs the line between ancient Greek and modern application of this term.[19] Positive, in that what these twenty-three chapters constitute is very much a proem, and as such they have a significant part to play in introducing the *literary* work to follow:[20] as Thucydides' advance team of persuasion, they provide the interpretative framework most conducive to understanding the causes and events of the war;[21] or rather most conducive to rendering his narrative of that war cogent and persuasive. Thucydides' past times are very much the creative projection of his and his audiences' present time. This aspect of the proem is so integral to its design that, once recognised, the conclusion seems inevitable that Thucydides intended to provide a clever implicit demonstration to his more sophisticated audiences of precisely how specious such exercises in reconstructing the past are.[22]

Since the rest of book 1 will show how naval power caused (in the sense of both 'precipitated' and 'made possible') this greatest of wars – and caused this war to be greatest – the antecedents of thalassocracy occupy Thucydides' proem.[23] Among these, Minos occupies a prominent position, appearing twice in this short account, occupying the whole of chapter 4, where he is encountered immediately after such notables (albeit preceding them in antiquity) as the namesake of Greece (Hellen), Homer, and Achilles – and returning in chapter 8.[24] In chapter 4 (quoted above) Thucydides lists

[18] Thucydides' single use of this word (in verb form, 7.69, of Nicias' exhortation) is somewhat disparaging, in the sense of bringing up what is out of date, old-fashioned – as Plato's Hippias suggests, the stuff that goes down well in Sparta (Pl. *Greater Hippias* 285d).

[19] Connor 1984: 22–3 connects Thucydides' *Archaeology* with other contemporary narratives of early man, citing as examples Pl. *Protagoras* 320c–323a and Hippocr. *Ancient Medicine* 3, and referring to Cole 1967: 5 and Norden 1913: 370–4. But this collapses significant distinctions between differing conceptualisations of the past, as Thucydides may also do in merging a heavily mythic narrative with a more abstract developmental one: for instance, *archaeologia* is not the term used of Protagoras' speech (a *muthos*) in Plato, nor is it used in *Ancient Medicine*. The semantic field of *archaeologia* seems to cover specific traditions of the past in the form of genealogies and foundation stories, not theoretical narratives of early human development such as otherwise constituted by the first chapters of Thucydides' proem.

[20] Dion. Hal. *On Thucydides* 20, called it a προοίμιον (on which see Pritchett 1975: 71), and, contrary to modern positive evaluations, said – without explanation – that it would have been best had Thucydides omitted everything from 1.2 to 1.20. On the rhetoric of the proem see Luraghi 2000 and Nicolai 2001.

[21] This is widely recognised: see e.g. Kallet 1993: 21; V. J. Hunter 1982: 45–6; de Romilly 1956: 260–2.

[22] This point need not have any – and in my opinion has little – impact on Thucydides' commitment to the end to which the demonstration is employed. See below.

[23] De Romilly 1956: 247; Kallet 1993: 21.

[24] On the structure of what has been called the *Minoica* see de Romilly 1956: 253.

several achievements of Minos known by tradition (*akoē*): Minos was the oldest of those who obtained a fleet and gained mastery over the Hellenic Sea. He ruled the Cyclades, was in fact the founder (*oikistēs*) of many of them, drove out the Carians and established his sons as *hegemones*. In so doing he rid the sea of piracy as much as he could, 'naturally' (ὡς εἰκός) so that he could ensure his own revenues (*prosodoi*).[25]

In chapter 8, Minos returns and there his actions are rendered a milestone in human progress:

Once Minos had been established as a naval power (καταστάντος δὲ τοῦ Μίνω ναυτικοῦ [cf. Athens of 1.18.2]), travel by sea between peoples improved (for the criminals had been expelled by him from the islands at that very time when he was also colonising them), and those who lived by the sea started to live in greater security, already dedicating themselves all the more so to the acquisition of wealth, and some also put up walls as a consequence of having become wealthier. And in their desire for profit (κερδῶν), the weaker submitted to the slavery of the stronger (οἵ τε ἥσσους ὑπέμενον τὴν τῶν κρεισσόνων δουλείαν), and those more powerful having surplus wealth brought the weaker cities under their control (οἵ τε δυνατώτεροι περιουσίας ἔχοντες προσεποιοῦντο ὑπηκόους τὰς ἐλάσσους πόλεις). And it was more or less under these conditions that the expedition against Troy was later marshalled.

Here Minos functions as template, the first instantiation of the processes of civilisation that for Thucydides culminates inevitably in the circumstances of his day, an exemplar of the process whereby a stronger figure using the sea consolidates a diverse group through his power, establishes hegemony, settles the land over which he rules, and ensures revenues for himself. Yet despite his antiquity, Minos is not actually the first occurrence of this process in the proem: in chapter 3, the first Greek, Hellen himself, has already been described in similar terms – though without mention of revenue – enjoined by those weaker for support, who, as a result, eventually adopt his name: literally, his name prevails over them all (καὶ ἅπασιν ἐκνικῆσαι, 1.3.3).

The analepsis of Minos is significant. Thucydides introduces this theory of development with the quintessential Greek figure, Hellen, and thereby 'hellenises' such progress, anticipating the objections of any who think *archē* is contrary to Greek *nomos*. Once this is established, its recurrence in naval form with Minos is thereby able to transcend the Greek/barbarian dichotomy, not only because according to Thucydides' account his navy pre-dates such distinctions – the collective name *Hellenes* did not yet

---

[25] On ὡς εἰκός in Thucydides as 'naturally', employed to confirm the veracity of a statement on logical grounds, see Westlake 1969. Logic, of course, does not make this conclusion follow so much as contemporary practice does.

exist – but also because the analeptic (sophistic) 'demonstration' of its iterability with Minos renders such growth, even by means of thalassocracy, a universal human, even natural, phenomenon.[26] Thucydides naturalises Minos' innovation, sea power, rendering it not a foreign innovation but rather a variation on a universal theme of growth capable of countering any argument that Athens' thalassocracy is not Greek, but rather an inheritance from a Persia as ethnically and ethically ambivalent as Minos himself.[27] And at any rate, it will be Minos' invention, the navy, that will provide the necessary preconditions for the greatest of past ('pre')Hellenic events, the Trojan War.[28]

That a universalising theory of man underlies this first appearance of Minos gains support by the ethnographical excursus separating Thucydides' two references to Minos (1.5–6). The ethnography shows what is at stake behind the use of Minos: the accepted status of piracy in different times and places reveals an underlying theme of the early part of the proem, namely the legitimacy of piracy. The claim that Minos rid the sea of pirates to ensure his own revenues (1.4) should be conspicuous for its failure to impute any ethical motive for such a policy: Minos acted in his own advantage, not moved by considerations of what is right or just.[29]

Correspondingly, the ethnography of 1.5–6 mobilises two kinds of arguments to create a space to claim the legitimacy of piracy: the discourse of poetic criticism, which invokes the authority of Homer to argue that piracy was a traditional occupation of the Greeks that brought with it no *aischunē* ('shame'); and contemporary ethnography to show that it is still practised by some Greeks today. The *nomoi* both of Greeks of the

---

[26] On the valence of sea power in antiquity see Momigliano 1944. Fifth-century thalassocracy lists have been thought to underlie Thucydides' proem – Myres 1906 and Forrest 1969 – and their creation, no less than their consumption, may well have been the product of a similar ideological agenda, rather than the result of purely academic interest. I agree with Forrest 1969: 95 n. 4, *contra* Myres 1906: 87, that it is unwarranted to deny Herodotus the possibility of access to such lists granted to Thucydides. Such assumptions are based only on Herodotus' comparative failure to be duly impressed by the 'achievement' constituted by thalassocracy, but here, however, he was hardly alone, as the evidence in Momigliano 1944 shows. The background presupposed by 3.125.2 is scarcely distinguishable from Thuc. 1.14.2 and 1.18 (on the Sicilian tyrants).

[27] On the villainy and ethnic liminality of Minos (*Phoenix*, like the Persian fleet) see, for example, Bacchylides 17.29–32 and 53–4 with Barron 1980: 4, and below.

[28] Thuc. 1.8.4 (cf. 1.3.4; 1.9.3); see Kallet 1993: 24.

[29] The same subtext will emerge in 9.3 when Agamemnon's ability to collect his armament is attributed not to *charis*, but to fear: by glossing oath with *charis* Thucydides avoids making the amorality of his claim explicit, namely that such things as oaths are binding only in instances where enforced by fear. (Note the incomplete correlative construction, similarly motivated, of 9.1, οὐ τοσοῦτον τοῖς . . . ὅρκοις κατειλημμένους – as by what?).

past and of Greeks elsewhere in Thucydides' day testify to the relativity of any claim that piracy is immoral, and behind this argument must lie the accusation of Athens' opponents asserting that naval *arche* is nothing more than piracy – Athens as the 'pirate state'.[30]

When Minos returns in chapter 8, he heralds in a more abstract formulation of the process of growth that can be readily mapped on to the contemporary world of the audience through the vocabulary of Athenian *archē* (e.g. ὑπηκόους).[31] Moreover, the passage conveniently disarms such emotive concepts as *douleia* (slavery) by rendering subjection a choice of the weaker, based on their sharing a desire for *kerdē* ('profit') which their weakness would otherwise have left unfulfilled. The manoeuvre anticipates, of course, Athens' assertion of the complicity of the Ionians (1.75.3); and, if the proem's 'scientific' theory of man's development has been successful, readers will be induced to see in this Athenian version a degree of 'objectivity' which no doubt would have appalled many contemporaries.[32]

The proem goes on to present the process once more in the historical period (1.15), where it attains total independence from the mythic paradigms in order to demonstrate as a universal phenomenon the strength that arises from naval power:

So then the Hellenic navies were of such limited quality as described, both those of long ago and those that came later, but nevertheless those who employed them acquired no insignificant strength with them through revenues and in the rule over others (χρημάτων τε προσόδῳ καὶ ἄλλων ἀρχῇ). For through naval operations they subdued the islands, and this was undertaken especially by those for whom their own land was not sufficient.[33]

Ever more abstractly formulated, the process evokes the *telos* of Thucydides' historical narrative, Athens' acquisition of naval *archē*, the newest, last, and greatest thalassocracy, its origin to be narrated in the *Pentekontaetia*,[34] by which time, if the proem has been effective, such a trajectory will be received not as aggressive imperial expansion, but as a dynamic of history,

---

[30] On the arguments, see de Romilly 1956: 253. Cf. [Xen.] *Ath. Pol.* 2.4–5, 13, for an implicit description of naval warfare in terms that suggest piracy, contrasted with the hoplite fighter who conducts war successfully through φιλία and fighting to win (διὰ φιλίας ἰέναι ἢ νικᾶν μαχόμενον). If the *Iliad* should be argued to champion land warfare, even so its ships were suggestively ληστικώτερον (1.10.4).

[31] ὑπήκοος is the language of the *ATL*.   [32] Thuc.1.75.3. Cf. Hdt. 4.142.

[33] On the insufficiency of Athenian land, already established, see 1.2.6.

[34] By then it will have been anticipated by the Athenians' speech of 1.73–8: Thucydides' clinical account of the fifty years, apparently motivated by purely historiographical reasons (1.97.2 – a gap in the literature, factual errors in the work of his colleagues), will support the historical 'truth' of Athens' claims.

an instantiation of the 'natural' growth that comes, and has always come, from naval power. The genius of Thucydides' proem is that it implicitly accepts critics' views that the *aitia* ('blame') for the war lies with Athens' naval *archē*, but through a series of ambitious rhetorical strategies – nothing less than positing a theory of human progress – *archē* is rendered a natural consequence of progress and as such its status as *aitia* is freed from moral censure, no longer 'blame' but now simply the 'reason why'.

Thucydides includes a few choice details to facilitate the link between Minos and Athens. In calling Minos an *oikistēs* of the islanders (1.4), Thucydides recalls Athens' own claims to have colonised Ionia, an event proleptically referred to in 2.6 and repeated in 12.4. Moreover, the digression of 8.1 brings present-day Athens into even closer proximity with Minos: as Minos cleansed the islands of Carian pirates way back when (1.4), Athens of 426 finished up the job by cleansing Delos of the graves of those pirates:

> And no less were the islanders pirates, being both Carians and Phoenicians. For these were the ones who inhabited most of the islands. And this is the proof: for when Delos was purified by the Athenians in this war, and the graves of all those who died in the island were removed, over half were revealed as Carians, recognised by the type of the weapons buried with them and by the manner in which they were buried, which is the same as that used even today.

Further implicit connections are established between the naval supremacy of Minos and Athens. First, revenue: the movement from πρόσοδοι (1.4) to πρόσοδοι χρημάτων (1.15) to χρήματα . . . φέρειν (1.19.2), a circumlocution for *phoros*,[35] facilitates the analogy between Athenian *archē* and the revenues that Minos' naval power guaranteed for itself. Second, succession: in the cases of both Minos and Hellen, Thucydides stresses the establishment of their sons as *hegemones*, a detail that speaks to an audience aware that this greatest of wars is to break out in the second generation of Athenian hegemony. And finally, the appropriation of land: Minos' removal of the *kakourgoi* from the islands and colonisation of them anticipates another Athenian event, and indeed one recorded in Thucydides' text (the second event of the *Pentekontaetia*), Cimon's removal/enslavement of Dolopians from Scyros and its resettlement, an act evoking – according to Plutarch – not Minos, but rather his mythic opponent in its association with the retrieval of the bones of Theseus.[36] It is perhaps not so very surprising that Thucydides forgoes here in the proem any explicit reference to an event falling in the period that he all but excludes entirely from his history; in

---

[35] On the slippage between φόρος and πρόσοδος χρημάτων see 2.97.3; 2.97.5, and Irwin 2007.
[36] See Thuc. 1.98.2; Plut. *Cimon* 8; cf. Paus. 1.17.6.

Table 8.1 *Comparison of Minos and Thucydides' Athens.*

Minos Explicit	Athens Explicit
οἰκιστής of the islands, 1.4 and 1.6.2–.3	Athens as coloniser of Ionia, 1.2.6; 1.12.4
Driving out Carian pirates, 1.4	Removing the bones of the Carian pirates, 1.8.1
Revenue (πρόσοδοι), 1.4	Money (χρήματα . . . φέρειν) 1.19
	Implicit
Sons as *hegemones* (cf. Hellas, 1.3.2), 1.4	2nd generation of the Delian league, *archē*
Remove *kakourgoi* from the islands, 1.8.2	Scyros: Plut. *Cimon* 8 and Thuc. 1.98
οἰκιστής of the islands, 1.4 and 1.6.2–3	Scyros: Thuc. 1.98, ᾤκισαν αὐτοί

this way he may be seen to effect a strategy of allusion through exclusion no less here than in the ominous τὰς νήσους κατεστρέφοντο ('they subjugated the islands') of 15.1. And yet an audience who appreciates the implicit allusion might also appreciate the full extent of what is being omitted in the proem's rationalising treatment of Minos, whether one construes the omission in mythic terms as the sidelining of Theseus, or in historical terms as the sidelining of Cimon, a figure belonging to the events before his war (τὰ . . . πρὸ αὐτῶν, 1.1.3; the parenthetically handled *Pentekontaetia*, 1.97.2). Of course, in the play of myth as history, history as myth, Cimon and Theseus need not emerge as alternatives that are so entirely distinct.[37]

An account that privileges Minos to the exclusion of Theseus may appear surprising, but a brief contextualisation of Thucydides' Minos demonstrates just how strange, significant, and selective Thucydides' choice is. As Thucydides claims, *akoē* may have held Minos as the first master of the sea, but it also held him to be the quintessential villain. While the tragedies are lost to us, Bacchylides 17 seems typical of traditional uses of Minos' myth in the service of justifying Athenian naval *archē*. There the hubris of an orientalised Minos is portrayed: threatening a maiden specified only as Ionian, Minos is thwarted by Theseus, who risks his life to emerge from the conflict with the favour of the sea-gods. The myth provides a 'just so' story about the transfer of naval supremacy from the mythical lawless Minos – *Phoenix* ('Phoenician') like the Persian fleet – to the just Attic hero, the counterpart

---

[37] On the synchronism of Theseus' popularity with Cimon's see Herter 1939: 292; Shefton 1962: 347 n. 74; more generally, see Podlecki 1971; Barron 1980; Tausend 1989; Castriota 1992: 33–62; Hornblower 1991– 6: 1.150; 1.523.

of the historical Delian League Athens.[38] Thucydides implicitly enacts such a transferral from Minos to Athens, but in an untraditional and surprising manner: his hellenised Minos replaces Theseus as prototype of Athens, and here his only failing is not one of hubris, but rather one of scale.[39]

Although unexpected, Thucydides' choice to appropriate Minos as a precedent is not, however, entirely unique. The Platonic *Minos* demonstrates both how unexpected Thucydides' valorisation of Minos is, and the register of discourse to which this choice belongs.[40] The text makes clear (Athenian) popular antipathy to Minos, a figure widely held (λέγεται, 318e1; φήμη κατεσκέδασται, 320d8) to be ἄγριος (fierce), χαλεπός (harsh), and ἄδικος (unjust).[41] And yet, in a manner strikingly analogous to, if also differing from, Thucydides' proem, the early achievement of the Cretan collective, known by *akoē*, is attributed to Minos:[42] according to Socrates, Minos is responsible for the παλαιότατοι νόμοι (earliest laws, 318d2) – those of the Cretans – while for Thucydides Minos is the παλαίτατος to have obtained a fleet (1.4.1). The dialogue stages the same persuasive strategies of Thucydides' *epideixis* as Socrates overcomes his companion's initial aversion to this untraditional evaluation of Minos by drawing on *akoe*, the authority of Homer, and what is εἰκός to persuade his interlocutor of a view that must in fact have been opposite to popular Athenian *akoē*. He argues that the hostile view of Minos is distinctly Athenian and merely a consequence of tragedy – that genre 'most pleasing to the *demos* and most intoxicating to the soul' (δημοτερπέστατόν τε καὶ ψυχαγωγικώτατον) – in which vengeance is taken on an old foe:

And so by stretching Minos on tragedy's rack we take vengeance for those whom he forced us to pay as tribute (ἡμᾶς ἠνάγκασε τοὺς δασμοὺς τελεῖν ἐκείνους). Minos then made that mistake, became an object of hatred to us, and from this, indeed, as you ask, he came into a rather bad reputation (κακοδοξότερος). (321a5–b1)

---

[38] See esp. lines 16–46. For recognition of the political content of this ode, see Barron 1980; Scodel 1984: 137, with bibliography at n. 2; Castriota 1992: 58–62; Mills 1997: 40. The story's ideological function is confirmed by its representation in a painting of the Theseion (Paus. 1.17).

[39] On the *aprosdoketon* in the proem see Luraghi 2000: 229.

[40] For a good recent analysis of the *Minos* see Cobb 1988.

[41] 318d10. Cf. Strabo 10.4.8, who contrasts Ephorus' more positive views on Minos with the *archaioi*, for whom he is τυραννικός τε . . . καὶ βίαιος καὶ δασμολόγος ('tyrannical, violent, and an exactor of tribute').

[42] Socrates' interlocutor's response suggests that linking the known antiquity of Cretan law to Minos is not a necessary or even a welcome association. On the parallel status of the claims made by Thucydides and in the *Minos* see Strabo 10.4.8: ἱστόρηται δ' ὁ Μίνως νομοθέτης γενέσθαι σπουδαῖος θαλαττοκρατῆσαί τε πρῶτος ('History maintains that Minos is an important lawgiver and the first to rule the seas').

As Thucydides' account of Minos (ὡς εἰκός), Socrates' εἰκὼς λόγος consists in a selective rationalising analysis of myth that results in a self-conscious opposition to common views: the two texts point to the Cretan king as a fashionable mythological figure for intellectual appropriation, sophistically construed to be a paradigm of contemporary salience – whether sea power or Dorian law – despite, or rather a consequence of, his being anathema from popular perspectives.

But the *Minos* also fleshes out one important analogy implicit in Thucydides' account of proto-thalassocratic Minos as a proto-Athenian naval power: tribute. When Socrates explains that in tragedy 'we take our vengeance on Minos in exchange for the *dasmoi* he forced us to pay', the companion accepts this explanation for the Athenian hatred of Minos as a likely account,[43] and forgoes his previous hostile view: that is, the exacting of *dasmoi* provides no absolute basis for judging Minos' behaviour as villainous; instead, such an evaluation emerges as specific to Athens, and therefore only relative.

The text's staging of the companion's sudden *volte-face* invites its readers to create their own likely account for just why an Athenian should be prepared to capitulate so easily. Appropriate to the theme of the *Minos*, the answer lies in *nomos*, and one in particular: it is a *nomos* that pertains to late-fifth century Athenian foreign policy and one that even the most relativist of Athenians would claim to be absolute: that involving *kratos* and its material counterpart, tribute.[44] *Dasmos* is the operative term: while it seems that *phoros* was actually coined for purposes of the Delian league, rendering it at least lexically distinct – in Greek – from the *dasmos* required by Persia, the slippage in application of the two words, and the compound *dasmophoros*, allowed for correspondences/analogies to be made between what was otherwise maintained to be two distinct forms of tribute relations, while retaining for *phoros* – at least lexically – a safe distance from its Persian counterpart.[45]

Here in the *Minos* it is used by Socrates to just such an effect: if the companion were to grant the excessive hatred of the tragic stage for Minos as justified on the basis of the tribute he exacted, the door would be open for such responses in Athens' own allies/subjects to be considered legitimate;

---

[43] Δοκεῖς μοι, ὦ Σώκρατες, εἰκότα τὸν λόγον εἰρηκέναι (321b5).

[44] See the Melian dialogue for the baldest statement of the universal *nomos* of empire: Thuc. 5.105.2.

[45] See Thuc. 1.96.2; O. Murray 1966: 150–5; Whitehead 1998: 174–81. *Phoros* could be used of Persian tribute, but *dasmos* is never explicitly used to describe the tribute Athens required of her subjects. The effect of using Minos' *dasmos* to discuss issues relating to Athens' tribute relations with her allies is equivalent to the tragic distancing discussed by Easterling 1997b.

the use of the word *dasmos* politely flags what is at stake for the companion should he insist that the negative evaluation of Minos is not relative and Athenian, but based on certain moral absolutes. But it is unlikely that he would, for underlying the companion's acceptance of this explanation for the Athenians' biased view of Minos is a tacit contradiction in his relativist position: in adopting a relativist position on Minos, he demonstrates that he does subscribe to at least one universal *nomos* – one entirely (but by no means exclusively) Thucydidean – the notion that *archē* is 'natural',[46] and correspondingly so is the hatred induced by it.[47] That the state is natural removes it from moral evaluation; the hatred is meaningless, dictating no moral injunction for the rulers to forgo their hate-inducing behaviour, or for others to stop them. Behind this lies the universal *nomos* at the heart of Thucydides' proem, that tribute relations are natural (ὡς εἰκός), the inevitable consequence of progress and differentiated κράτος, and as such above judgement. And in this respect, on yet another level, the argument of the *Minos* seems to participate in the same intellectual milieu as Thucydides. It is, of course, not the case that the texts are using Minos to the *same* end, but rather that they use Minos *similarly*, even competitively, to different ends. The political views behind these appropriations are in practice vehemently opposed, one using Minos to advocate the supremacy of naval power, the other 'Dorian' law.[48] The politicised rationalisation of myth coupled with the elite valence of Minos as an un*popular* choice places these texts, and the competing positions represented by them, in a shared intellectual climate; the fissure in the ends to which Minos is employed no doubt replicates that which became most visible just before and continuing through the last decade of the fifth century.

So appropriating Minos seems to have been the rage among certain circles, and even a tool in their contests with each other. Here one might wish to consider further Thucydides' appropriation in relation to Athenian naval power. As a historian, is Thucydides to get off scot-free in his choice to stand Minos at the forefront of an account of the origins of thalassocracy? Minos was, after all, no inevitable choice, as Herodotus' preference for Polycrates shows.[49] Certainly, had Thucydides rationalised the Minos myth more fully

---

[46] Thuc. 5.105.2: ἀνθρώπειον τε σαφῶς διὰ παντὸς ὑπὸ φύσεως ἀναγκαίας, οὗ ἂν κρατῇ, ἄρχειν. καὶ ἡμεῖς οὔτε θέντες τὸν νόμον οὔτε κειμένῳ πρῶτοι χρησάμενοι.

[47] Thuc. 2.64.5; 3.39.5. Hatred by one's subjects can even be considered desirable, a sign of strength: Thuc. 5.95. See also the ἀνάγκη of [Xen.] *Ath. Pol.* 1.14.

[48] Compare the Athenian in *Laws* who begins the dialogue by expressing the view of Minos put forward by Socrates in the *Minos* (624a–625a), and later expresses extreme antipathy to a state based on naval warfare (706a–707c) as something bad which the Athenians learned from war with Minos.

[49] See also Pl. *Phaedrus* 229c–230a for ironic dismissal of such rationalising endeavours.

to speak abstractly of Cretan sea power, he would have sacrificed the *frisson* that the unpopular Minos offered an elite readership. Yet the unwillingness to forgo the *aprosdoketon* effect may amount to a more disturbing sacrifice should it prove impossible to divorce entirely this Minos from his embodiment on the tragic stage and, more importantly, from earlier representations like Bacchylides' that stressed his hybris towards Ionians. What kind of precedent does choosing such a precedent set? From a perspective hostile to Athenian *archē* (the elite of Ionia, the Melians, the Peloponnesians, etc.), this particular rationalisation, amounting to an identification with (*not* a moral rehabilitation of) a quintessentially lawless figure, against what is commonly believed (*legomena*) about him, may narrate its own eloquent tale about the deterioration of the ethical status of Athenian *archē*, or at least an abandonment of any perceived need to provide it with an ethical basis. If, according to earlier Delian-league mythology, Athens became leader based on the moral character of her hero and his divine favour against a barbarian villain, a rationalisation figuring Minos as proto-Athenian *archē* could carry implications of the way *archē* has gone – either because mythic *akoē* has 'drifted' in this direction through the allegorising/rationalising trends that are the rage (i.e. Thucydides' proem refracting a trend), or because Thucydides has selectively used *akoe* to suggest as much. It is worth noting Thucydides' hellenisation of his Minos, which may again be read either as a sign of contemporary treatments of Minos or as the efforts of a Thucydides to naturalise this figure for his own agenda. Either way, the possible moral implications of Thucydides' choice ought to cause some unease.

Before modern readers celebrate Thucydides' rationalisation of myth, congratulating the ancients in their struggle to discover the 'truths' that we now of course know, we should question the impetus driving such intellectual trends: Thucydides' contemporaries, no doubt, would not have overlooked more 'rational' and cynical explanations for Thucydides' treatment.[50] Whether Thucydides innovated *in toto* or rather in the particular use to which he put the rationalisation, its presence at the very start of his *History* is marked, albeit difficult to read. For Thucydides' apologists, who see a critic of *archē* behind a text that ostensibly monumentalises the grandeur and tragedy of Athens, the use of Minos as the starting point for what Athens was to become could be read as providing an indication of the darker side of his narrative that only some within his audience will detect;[51] or perhaps, for other readers, those Thucydideans who see *archē*

---

[50] On the fallacies of this view see Most 1999.
[51] These would become fewer the further into the past the fifth century receded and tragedies involving Minos became lost.

as natural, the use of Minos is admirably realist, that is, how an elite – with a sophisticated disdain for questions of morality – may, in contrast to the *polloi*, see *archē*, stripped of any need for moral justifications, simply the product of 'natural' law. Minos' function in this is to demonstrate that how things are now is how they must always have been, and in turn how they will always be κατά τὸ ἀνθρώπινον – a view which of course raises the question of whether this 'realist' view, with its claims to objectivity and universality, does not in fact predetermine the contours of the future, as it is deployed by the present in its use of the past to justify itself.

In short, if Minos was adopted over the decades by (some) Athenian intellectual trends in such a way as to influence *akoē*, the phenomenon would tell its own elegant story about Athens' transformation from leading the Delian league to *archē* and ultimately *turannis*, even if the change should mark not so much a change in the realities of Athenian *archē* as an abandonment of the euphemisms used in the representation of it – at least in some circles. If it was Thucydides who first appropriated Minos in this way (presumably anticipating a willing audience), Minos emerges just as flatteringly ambiguous about Athenian naval *archē* as many of the features of Thucydides' entire *History*: that is, while the possibility exists for reading in this all too Athenian Minos a 'critique' of Athens, most readings will likely (mis?)construe it as praise. But from some perspectives – not least a Herodotean one, as I will argue – constructing a narrative that fosters the potential for such ambiguity, a truly *dissos logos*, could itself be considered immoral.

HERODOTUS ON MINOS

The above discussion would suggest that Herodotus may have been wise to opt for Polycrates as his first thalassocrat, simply 'leaving aside Minos' and the baggage that this figure may have brought with him. Herodotus does not, however, leave aside Minos entirely, and before seeking to understand why Minos is explicitly refused the title of first thalassocrat in 3.122, Minos' first appearance in the *Histories* must be addressed.

Herodotus' Minos: the polyphony of mythic rationalisations

In accord with so much of book 1, Herodotus' Minos turns up in a narrative of ethnic origins, the early history of the Carians, an account that for Kallet rescues Thucydides from historical irrelevance by undermining any alleged critical acumen in Herodotus' dismissal of the mythic

Minos at 3.122.[52] But such a straightforward reading of Herodotus' Minos is unduly naïve. Chapter 171 divides itself easily into three sections, each of which is provocatively intertextual with Thucydides' shaping of Minos into a proto-Athenian thalassocrat and the wider premises underlying his proem.

Persian conquests turn Herodotus' narrative to the Carians, and to Minos' early relationship with them:

Ἅρπαγος δὲ καταστρεψάμενος Ἰωνίην ἐποιέετο στρατηίην ἐπὶ Κᾶρας καὶ Καυνίους καὶ Λυκίους, ἅμα ἀγόμενος καὶ Ἴωνας καὶ Αἰολέας. εἰσὶ δὲ τούτων Κᾶρες μὲν ἀπιγμένοι ἐς τὴν ἤπειρον ἐκ τῶν νήσων. τὸ γὰρ παλαιὸν ἐόντες Μίνω κατήκοοι καὶ καλεόμενοι Λέλεγες εἶχον τὰς νήσους, φόρον μὲν οὐδένα ὑποτελέοντες, ὅσον καὶ ἐγὼ δυνατός εἰμι <ἐπὶ> μακρότατον ἐξικέσθαι ἀκοῇ· οἱ δέ, ὅκως Μίνως δέοιτο, ἐπλήρουν οἱ τὰς νέας. ἅτε δὴ Μίνω τε κατεστραμμένου γῆν πολλὴν καὶ εὐτυχέοντος τῷ πολέμῳ, τὸ Καρικὸν ἦν ἔθνος λογιμώτατον τῶν ἐθνέων ἁπάντων κατὰ τοῦτον ἅμα τὸν χρόνον μακρῷ μάλιστα.

Harpagus followed his conquest of Ionia with campaigns against the Carians, the Caunians, and the Lycians, and he took contingents of both Ionians and Aeolians along with him. Now, the Carians came to the mainland from the Aegean islands. Long ago, when they were subjects of Minos and were called the Leleges, they had inhabited the islands. As far as I have been able to gather from my enquiries, they used not to pay Minos any tribute, but they would man ships for him on demand. So since Minos conquered a great deal of land and was successful in war, the Carians were far and away the most important race at this time.

Here Herodotus drops back into the period of Thucydides' proem, τὸ παλαιόν, and similarly nods to the difficulties of attaining knowledge of this period in language parallel to that of Thucydides' proem: ὅσον καὶ ἐγὼ δυνατός εἰμι <ἐπὶ> μακρότατον ἐξικέσθαι ἀκοῇ corresponds closely to two passages of Thucydides' proem, τὰ γὰρ πρὸ αὐτῶν καὶ τὰ ἔτι παλαίτερα σαφῶς μὲν εὑρεῖν διὰ χρόνου πλῆθος ἀδύνατα ἦν, ἐκ δὲ τεκμηρίων ὧν ἐπὶ μακρότατον σκοποῦντί μοι πιστεῦσαι ξυμβαίνει ('for events before this war and those still earlier are impossible to discover clearly due to the passage of time, but from the signs it was possible for me to trust, examining them to their fullest extent', 1.1.3), and Μίνως γὰρ παλαίτατος ὧν ἀκοῇ ἴσμεν ('Minos was the earliest we know by hearsay', 1.4). The intertextuality involves both the abstract principles and practical

---

[52] See n. 8 above: 'Herodotus is often thought here to be more critical than Thucydides . . . One should note, however, that Herodotus relates Minos' adventures and death elsewhere (1.171.2–3; 1.173.2; 7.169.2; 7.170.1), suggesting that he accepts the basic historicity of Minos'.

difficulties underlying the investigation of τὸ παλαιόν, focusing on the kind of source upon which one must rely for Minos, *akoē*. The parallels, of course, are due in part to a reflex of the 'genre', if we should call it that: the historiographical 'I' investigating, qualifying his results, acknowledging the limitations his sources place on what it is possible to know. It should be noted by those who privilege Thucydides' historiographical skills that there is no qualitative difference in the awareness of these points between the two authors, except in so far as the handling is more nonchalant – less ponderous – in Herodotus.

But 'generic affinity' does not sufficiently describe the relationship between their respective treatments of Minos. Placed together like this, the passages seem not only to read each other, but to do so polemically, vocalising opposing stances in a debate about Minos and his relationship to the Carians. The first contrast is obvious: while Thucydides' *akoē* asserts that Carians were pirates driven out of the islands by Minos, Herodotus' *akoē* asserts that they were islanders who were in fact Minos' *subjects.*[53]

Moreover, while for Thucydides Minos represents the first figure of note in the evolution of naval power, he does not quite realise thalassocracy proper. By contrast, Herodotus seems fully to collapse the distinction of past and present by configuring the Carian relationship to Minos in contemporary terms directly applicable to Athenian *archē*. The only differentiation is not, as in Thucydides, in the limitations on thalassocracy 'natural' to early times, but rather more provocatively in the terms of Minos' hegemony. While the Carians were subjects (κατήκοοι) of Minos, the relationship was not one of tribute (φόρος) but one of manning ships – that is, at least as far as Herodotus could arrive (ἐξικέσθαι) by *akoē* (i.e. using the same sort of source available to Thucydides). Otherwise said, if Herodotus can expect (some of) his audiences to engage in the same strategies implicit in Thucydides' use of Minos, in the *akoe* that he uses Minos' relationship to his subjects corresponds to the original basis of the Delian league, not later Athenian *archē*.[54] And for those induced to entertain the mythic identification of Minos with Athens, Herodotus' final sentence becomes pointed: as Minos (i.e. Athenian *archē*) became successful in war,[55] and generally prospered, the Carians (Ionians) became the most important *ethnos*, a possible

---

[53] On the impossibility of resolving the historians' accounts, see Hornblower 1982: 12, esp. n. 54.
[54] Cf. Thuc. 1.99; the ascription of blame to the allies might suggest the moral anxiety around the changed relationship. There were certainly issues surrounding the use to which the money was put (Plut. *Pericles* 12).
[55] It is worth noting that Thucydides does not mention war in connection with Minos.

Table 8.2 *Thucydides and Herodotus on Minos and the Carians.*

Thucydides	Herodotus
Carians are pirates	Carians are Minos' subjects. No indication of whether or not they are pirates
Islands: driven out of them by Minos	Islands: they inhabited them
Minos' interest in vague πρόσοδοι (*cf.* 1.19)	Not tribute-paying subjects (φόρος), but they man ships for him
Minos' superlative status: παλαίτατος	Superlative status of the ethnos of Minos' subjects: ἔθνος λογιμώτατον . . . μακρῷ
Driven out, by Minos	Driven out, by Dorians and Ionians

reflection of the degree to which Ionianism functioned in the ideology of Athenian *archē*.[56]

A question lingers: are these Carians – here now subjects of Minos – pirates, as they were for Thucydides? Herodotus does not say, leaving a silence for an audience to fill,[57] and depending on how they do so Minos may well be sitting on an empire of piracy. The analogical implications of past for present in this inference may well contribute to explaining the motivation behind Thucydides' long, rhetorically sophisticated, and tendentious excursus on piracy that separates his two references to his Athens-like Minos: Homeric exegesis and ethnography are mobilised to acquit piracy of the charge of *aischunē* ('shamefulness') and thereby pre-empt any critique of naval *archē* that attempts to portray it as such.[58]

Part II of Herodotus' Carian excursus proceeds with an ethnographic digression on their armour:

The Greeks have adopted three practices which were originally Carian discoveries. It was the Carians who originally started tying plumes on to their helmets, they were the first to put designs on to their shields, and they were also the first to fit shields with handles. Previously, no handles had been involved and the universal practice of those who used to wear shields was to manoeuvre them by means of a leather strap which lay around the neck and left shoulder.

Herodotus here seems to reflect a tradition of associating Carians with distinctive types of armour, though as Herodotus is the first author ('of those whom we know') to claim them to be the Carians' *invention*, the claim

---

[56] On Ionianism and Athens see Sakellariou 1990: 137–8; Connor 1993; Hall 1997: 51–6. Herodotus seems to suggest the possibility of associating Ionians with Carians in 1.146, where he says that the early colonists of Ionia from Athens did not bring wives, but married Carian women.

[57] On the significance of such silences see Brock 2004: 171.

[58] Such a charge should be seen as the subtext of the description [Xen.] *Ath. Pol.* 2.5 of the *modus operandi* of a sea power; see n. 30 above (cf. Momigliano 1944).

itself may well be his invention.[59] But regardless of whose invention it was, it remains remarkable that this digression on Carian armour seems likewise to 'talk' to Thucydides' proem. It is, after all, somewhat unexpected that ethnography in general and Carian armour in particular should find themselves in a privileged position in the proem to a history of a contemporary Greek war.

A general point must first be made about how differently each author treats non-Greek *ethnē*, past or present. In the proem (1.6.6), Thucydides asserts what is likely to flatter and persuade his audience easily, namely, that barbarians today are like Greeks of the past:

πολλὰ δ' ἂν καὶ ἄλλα τις ἀποδείξειε τὸ παλαιὸν Ἑλληνικὸν ὁμοιότροπα τῷ νῦν βαρβαρικῷ διαιτώμενον.

There are plenty of other ways in which one could demonstrate (give an *apodeixis*) that the Greeks of the remote past were similar in their practices to barbarians of today.

Occupying a prominent position in his proem, Thucydides' conception of the relationship between Greeks and barbarians is both markedly at odds with the general tenor of Herodotus' *Histories* and in direct conflict with Herodotus' contention that the Carians are responsible for innovations in armour used by Greeks today. Behind Thucydides' and Herodotus' comments lie competing anthropological models.[60] Thucydides' view implies a ranking of cultures on a single scale of evolutionary progress: difference is configured as progress, with Greeks in the lead. In contrast, Herodotus more generally presents different cultures as independent and parallel, comparable in their details but in no way belonging to a single overarching hierarchy of development; and, here specifically, were there a single scale, the Greeks would be trailing, owing their advances in military technology to Carians of the past, one of which responsible for the institution portrayed as the epitome of Greek manhood: the hoplite army. Herodotus' ethnographic excursus poses problems for Thucydides' conception: if someone (τις) should wish to give that *apodeixis* which Thucydides promises, Herodotus has identified an example that one had better not use[61] – although, as we shall see, this is of course what Thucydides implicitly goes on to do.

The difference in the authors' ethnographic premises impacts, however, more directly on the intertextuality of the historians' treatment of Minos.

---

[59] See Snodgrass 1964 generally, and pp. 108–10 on Herodotean invention.
[60] Cf. Bichler 2004: 94–5.
[61] The significance of Herodotus' Carian passage is not to be underestimated: it constitutes one of the very few cross-references that he makes in his work, and not to be forgotten amid the masses of ethnographic excursuses (Hdt. 7.93: ἐν τοῖσι πρώτοισι τῶν λόγων εἴρηται).

Herodotus' excursus on Carian weapons has a rather damaging effect on Thucydides' 'evidence' for the Carian occupation of that island derived from the Delian purification. For Herodotus' account presents the careful reader with a problem in Thucydides' ethnography: if Greek and Carian graves were able to be distinguished – as Thucydides says – by the style of their armour (ἡ σκευὴ τῶν ὅπλων, 1.8.1), they could only have been so on the basis of the contents of Carian graves possessing technologically *more* advanced weaponry than the Greek burials, leading to a conclusion at odds with Thucydides' general assertion regarding barbarian *nomoi* (1.6.6): Greeks of the past had not attained the same level of development as their Carian peers, as any apparent differentiation in their graves would show for those not enamoured of Thucydidean ethnography.

But Thucydides himself might be using this material less than straightforwardly. Since the proem is arguably an *apodeixis* of Thucydides' methodology and stance, his contention deserves careful examination. In chapters 5 and 6 he provides ethnographic *exempla* that lead to the conclusion that πολλὰ καὶ ἄλλα (in emphatic first position) one could provide an *apodeixis* that barbarians of today are like Greeks of the past. The formulation is, however, slippery in two respects. The placement of πολλὰ καὶ ἄλλα lends an ambiguity to the assertion as to whether it will be taken as modifying the verb ἀποδείξειε or the participle διαιτώμενον: can one demonstrate 'in many other respects' a universal claim about the '*homoiotropic*' relationship between early Greek and contemporary barbarian custom, a model of all human development as a single trajectory, or is Thucydides making a more narrow and modest claim about ancient Greeks specific to πολλὰ καὶ ἄλλα in which their living practices were ὁμοιότροπα with present-day barbarians? The rhetoric of the passage may well induce an audience complicit in this ideology to hear the former,[62] when in fact the syntax may be construed as making a more limited claim. But those induced by Thucydides' text into reading the more sweeping claim will be led into contradiction: if present barbarian (Carian) *nomoi* are the same as those of the Greeks of the past, and, at least as Thucydides asserts, present Carian *nomoi* with respect to burial are the same as past Carian *nomoi* (ᾧ νῦν ἔτι θάπτουσιν), then by a kind of transitive postulate, past Carian *nomoi* and past Greek ones should emerge as the same.[63]

---

[62] For this reason commentators provide a lemma ensuring that readers attach the modifier to the participle: Marchant 1905 and Classen 1919: *ad loc.*

[63] The reinterred remains found by Stavropoulos on the neighbouring shore of Rheneia, dating plausibly to this period, have been linked to the Athenian purification; on which see Cook 1955, Long 1958, and Snodgrass 1964. The single enclosure which held the bones led Cook (1955: 268–9) to infer that the Athenians of 426 BC could not be sure whose bones were whose, while the presence of

Of course, Thucydides does not in fact unambiguously claim his statement's universal truth, but his rhetoric invites such a status to follow as an inference refuted only if one thinks quite hard about the example supplied in chapter 8; and of course many will not, for the simple reason that they are committed to Greek superiority and in present-day practice Greek and Carian burial practices are differentiated – Greeks no longer place weapons in their graves, while Carians (or so Thucydides alleges) do.[64] None of this is, however, to say that his arguments do not *persuade*; on the contrary, as with any successful sophistic argument, its cleverness is best demonstrated when the logic of the argument is ultimately revealed as not compelling or – better yet – even flawed.[65] Thucydides may later subtly warn his audience to be wary: his contention in chapter 20 that people are ignorant both of their own history and of the contemporary practices of others could apply likewise to the content of his Delian excursus. If Herodotus could be entertained as responding directly to this sophistic(ated) demonstration, his Carian ethnography would allow less capable souls (whose number will grow as the events become farther away) to cross-examine the *marturion* called forward by Thucydides: if the occupants of the graves could have been differentiated (as Thucydides claims), it would have been on the basis that Carians of the *past* had been, contrary to Thucydides, like Greeks of *today*: a commitment to Greek superiority would have led to a misidentification. But then, of course, differentiation may not have been possible.

Herodotus' excursus on the Carians takes one last turn. In the final section of chapter 171 he tells us, 'Much later, the Dorians and Ionians expelled the Carians from the islands and then they arrived on the mainland.' Viewed from Thucydides' *akoē*, this passage ties up the loose ends left by Herodotus' account by explaining the present-day absence of the

---

Geometric pottery tells strongly in favour of Thucydides' Carians being geometric Greeks. See also Snodgrass 1964: 113, who concludes that on the basis of Thucydides' claims the graves would be indistinguishable. Gomme (1945–81: I. 107) realises the problem, but posits only that Thucydides must have had something else in mind.

[64] On this point see Cook 1955: 268.

[65] This is how I would explain Thucydides' numerical argument in 10.3–5: the argument does not work, and yet it *persuades* because of the authoritative stance he has taken and the feature of human nature he can count on, namely that (the) many will not do the maths – Thucydides' words are to hand (τὰ ἑτοῖμα), and the calculation would amount to the ζήτησις (1.20.3) which the lazy are loath to do; cf. Luraghi 2000: 239–40. Another way in which Thucydides' account may be pulling his less sophisticated audiences' legs is in presenting the Carian customs of burial as continuing unchanged for over 800 years (noted by Cook 1955: 269, but he sees Thucydides as 'believing' this, which I am inclined to doubt). The dubious evidence provided by material culture is of course the subject of the ensuing chapters of the proem, and seems a contemporary concern, even represented in tragedy: see, for instance, Eur. *Cyclops* 9.

Carians in the islands, since his Minos is not responsible for their expulsion. The need to reconcile accounts is uncannily apposite here: at this very point Herodotus chooses to raise the issue of sources. Here he cites the Cretans as having been his authority: 'With respect to the Carians this indeed is what the Cretans say happened.' The citation of a source can have contrary effects on readers: the authority it represents can evoke a sense of truth, or equally undermine the claim's truth status by reminding an audience of the inherent bias of all accounts. And indeed Herodotus will add that 'the Carians themselves disagree'. It is a simple reminder and one based on what we honour as essential to good historiographical method: that one needs to be aware of whose tradition is being used – Cretan or Carian – when constructing the story of Minos and his relation to the Carians. This qualification of his *logos* by named sources should, however, cast a critical light on Thucydides' version: given Herodotus' choice to fracture his *akoē* at this point, what happens to the evocation of an unqualified *akoē* employed by Thucydides as the basis of his knowledge of Minos (1.4)? Whose *akoē* was he using, and who is the community circumscribed by the 'we' who 'know (ἴσμεν)'? This is precisely the question that Herodotus' account of Minos insists we ask.

Here we would do well to compare Herodotean and Thucydidean *akoai*, and to begin to challenge the role *akoē* has had in reinforcing the traditional narrative of Thucydidean progress in relation to Herodotus. Hornblower's conclusion in comparing Thucydides 1.4 and Herodotus 3.122 is instructive:

> *Perhaps* the point is to stress *more precisely* than Herodotus had done the legitimacy of using 'hearsay' evidence when dealing with such ancient events. In any case 'hearsay' should, I am suggesting, be seen as part of an argument with Herodotus, not as a direct statement about Thucydides' own route of access to the tradition. This, then, is an example of a passage, the proper eludication of which is impossible without reference to Herodotus, although its meaning is perfectly clear; Thucydides expected his readers to recall or turn up the relevant bit of Herodotus.[66]

No doubt Hornblower is correct to infer that an argument about the status of *akoē* must lie behind this intertextuality, but if a relevant bit of Herodotus ought to be recalled to elucidate Thucydides' use of *akoē*, it is 1.171, and there, on the subject of *akoē*, Herodotus is *more precise* than Thucydides: in distinguishing between ἀκοαί – Cretan and Carian – he makes apparent the problem inherent in drawing on *akoē* as a basis for knowledge: just whose? And yet our own narratives plotting the history of historiography have run rampant, obscuring what could have been apparent from the most basic

---

[66] Hornblower 1991 6: II. 125, my italics.

philological method. Despite the nature of his work, Herodotus refers to *akoē* far less than Thucydides (6 times and 12 times, respectively), always (unlike Thucydides) with reservation if not also with strong scepticism,[67] and *never* as the basis of knowledge: in contrast to Thucydides, Herodotus *never* qualifies ἴδμεν with *akoē*.[68] Thucydides' formulation ἀκοῇ ἴσμεν is quite simply *not* Herodotean.

Once *akoē* has been fractured, what then does Carian *akoē* suggest that Carians 'know' about themselves? The answer is something uncannily evocative of what Athenians believe to be true about *themselves*. Herodotus writes:

They don't agree with the Cretans, but think they are indigenous mainlanders (νομίζουσι αὐτοὶ ἑωυτοὺς εἶναι αὐτόχθονας ἠπειρώτας) and have always had the name they have now. For proof, they point to (ἀποδείκνῦσι) the antiquity of the sanctuary of Carian Zeus at Mylasa. Mysians and Lydians are allowed to use this too, on the grounds that they are related to the Carians, because in Carian legend Lydus and Mysus were the brothers of Car. So Mysians and Lydians can use the sanctuary, but no other non-Carians can, even if they speak the same language as the Carians.

Autochthony is famously dear to the Athenians – one of the first things alluded to by Thucydides in his proem[69] – while the strange practices of the temple of Zeus at Mylasa that exclude those without mythic familial relations (even should they speak the same language) smack strongly of those regarding the exclusion of Dorians from the temple of Athena on the Acropolis, which Herodotus will so famously narrate in the story of Cleomenes at 5.72.[70] One might ask whether the mention of Ionians and

---

[67] Hdt. 2.29.1; 2.123.1; 2.148.6; and esp. 4.16.1 and 4.16.2: in terms of *akoē*, the company Minos keeps, books 2 and 4, is telling. Note the collocation in 2.123 with γράφω, as if to underscore that writing will not make *akoē* anything more than what it is. And yet Thucydides is rarely (at least overtly) critical: unlike Herodotus, he seems to use *akoē* for reports (his or others') that will go unchallenged by their audiences, for good or ill; at other times, he suggests that with the correct critical skills, *akoē* may become more than it is, a possibility that Herodotus seems to reject. The recent discussion of Luraghi 2006 is flawed by reliance on academic *akoē* rather than giving attention to Herodotus' use of the term.

[68] Compared with Thucydides' ἀκοῇ ἴσμεν (1.4.1; 7.87.5) Herodotus' ἐξικέσθαι ἀκοῇ (1.171; 4.16.2) provides a nice warning: where one arrives using *akoē* ought to be kept distinct from what is known. See also Shimron 1973: 48, who notes that the phrase πρῶτος τῶν ἡμεῖς ἴδμεν in Herodotus is restricted to events lying between Croesus' time and Herodotus' own.

[69] A mainstay of Thucydides' story of early times: Thuc. 1.2.5. On Athenian autochthony see Hornblower 1991–6: I. 12–13 with bibliography.

[70] Hdt. 5.72: 'Go back, Lacedaemonian stranger, and do not enter the precinct, since it is not lawful that Dorians should pass in here.' For a gratuitous Athenian–Carian connection (unverifiable, yet included), see Isagoras of 5.66.5 (cf. Plut. *Morals* 860e) and 5.88.1, where Herodotus makes a point of specifying that the style of clothing Athens adopted was not Ionian but Carian. A full survey of how Herodotus treats Carians, certainly relevant, is outside the scope of this discussion.

Dorians immediately heading this final section of the excursus was not over-determined, functioning to place in an audience's mind Greek ethnic distinctions analogously based on (constructions of) mythic ancestry at the expense of shared language.[71]

The intertextuality of the historians' appropriations of Minos is rich: if Thucydides' *akoē* constructs a Minos who is a prototype of Athens, Herodotus' account of early times first suggests a Minos ruling Carians as Athenians did Ionians in early Delian-league practice, only to introduce a contrary version in which Athens is ultimately reflected among the Carians, raising the question of just which mainland these 'Carians' reached after their expulsion, Ionia or Attica, and indeed whether their name has always been, as they say, the same. Thucydides uses analogy to render the Athenians of his day the Minos of the past, eliding any reference to their mythological subjection to Minos; Herodotus, in contrast, uses analogy precisely to focus on that subjection, to render Athenians Ionians, an analogy that strikes at the heart of a deep ambiguity about whether Athenians were, despite fifth-century ideology to the contrary, really originally Ionians (Carians). Returning to the beginning of the Minos excursus, it becomes clear that Herodotus has prepared us for the instability of signifier and signified: in 1.171.2, these Carians were originally called Leleges, the two names evoking the same people at different times; in the *logos* to follow, 'Carians' look at first like Ionians, then later like Athenians, one name evoking apparently two different peoples at different times, yet perhaps one group that came to settle Attica.[72]

But were/are those 'Carians' pirates? That is something Herodotus' text is as non-committal about as Thucydides' text is about the general moral status of piracy in his own day.

Leaving aside Minos

Having interrogated Herodotus' account of Minos, we can now turn finally to his being left aside in favour of Polycrates at 3.122. The tone of this passage (quoted above) must again be stressed: not only are πάρεξ Μίνωος and the

---

[71] On this subject, Herodotus' history generates irony when his Athenians of 8.144.2 stress common language as a basis of unity.

[72] I say apparently different because if first impressions are corrected and the Carians are seen to evoke instead the same people, Herodotus' Cretan *akoe* suggests a different and, for the Athenians, less flattering rationalisation of the Minos myth than that of Thucydides: the famous *dasmos* paid to Minos was none other than Athens' naval subjection to Crete; see Whitehead 1998: 175, who cites among other testimony Isoc. 10.27; Pl. *Laws* 706c; Arist. fr. 485. On the change in the Carians' name, see again 7.93, where Herodotus' back reference to this section again alludes to this.

implication in 'human' dismissive, but Herodotus does further injury to any model that privileges the Cretan king by granting the possibility that some nameless τις might possibly have a claim to priority – Minos has no more privileged status simply for being able to be named; and indeed, naval *archē* itself is not presented as *all that.*

Herodotus' grounds for excluding Minos, as not belonging to the ἀνθρ-ωπηίη γενεή, has become a cornerstone of discussions of the development of Greek historiography: Herodotus is seen as (or denied to be) asserting here the laudable distinction between a *spatium mythicum* and *spatium historicum.* The consequences of framing the passage solely in these terms are damaging: by maintaining that the myth/history distinction is the only one Herodotus is concerned to make by ἀνθρωπηίη γενεή, his position with respect to 'myth' becomes understood as inconsistent across the *Histories.*[73] Since this passage seems to get it 'right' by the standards of our historiography while others do not, it occupies at best a privileged but flukish status within reams of otherwise sub-critical historiography or – as Thucydides might label it – *logoi* more pleasing than true. Others grant it not even that.[74]

The distinction must have something to do with Minos' belonging to the generation, γενεή, in which gods were still personally involved with humans, a distinction traditional in archaic hexameter poetry.[75] And yet the addition of the qualification λεγομένη adds something to the formulation, self-consciously presenting the constructedness of the classification: λεγομένη can simultaneously mean what is traditionally said (λέγεται), that is, this archaic idea of a 'temps des dieux et temps des hommes',[76] or what is being said by Herodotus' more sophisticated contemporaries, a distinction their intellectual circles make about the status of myth. Either way, the dismissal of Minos in this context represents a hostile response to the trend lying behind Thucydides' appropriation of Minos:[77] a strong

---

[73] See Shimron 1973 and Raaflaub 2002: 159 with n. 36 for a reminder of Herodotus' attention to such delineations of time.

[74] See e.g. Kallet 1993: 24 n. 11, and n. 52 above.

[75] See Most 1997: 112–13, who argues that epic usage renders the heroic age (to which Minos would belong) and iron age as two *geneai* in a shared *genos*. It remains possible that poetic criticism and linguistic theory of the fifth century likewise came to the same conclusion and are responsible for Herodotus' emphasis.

[76] Vidal-Naquet 1960. For a recent critical approach to this view (which I admit I do not fully appreciate), see Williams 2002: 158–60.

[77] The treatment of gods and heroes as equivalent to men in moral argumentation is characteristic of sophistic arguments, employed to challenge conventional views: see Ar. *Clouds* and Eur. *Hippolytus* 438–81; interestingly, Socrates' extended speech in [Pl.] *Minos* 318e6–320d7 wreaks havoc on these distinctions, rendering the godlike Minos almost a god (at the same time as making him a paradigm for men in the present), and, in turn, Zeus a sophist.

reassertion of categories in the face of such agenda-ridden collapsing of the boundaries – 'this is what is said, and here it will be maintained'.[78] Herodotus emerges, as elsewhere, sophisticatedly reasserting conventional beliefs. But an examination of what is at stake in this qualification will show it to be far from conventional for its own sake: the assertion is ethical.

With λεγομένη readers may be invited to consider what is 'meant' (λεγομένη) by ἀνθρωπηΐη, an invitation scholars have in essence accepted when they discuss whether his phrase denotes the *spatium historicum*. Yet no one has considered the expression in Herodotean terms and the Herodotean connotations of the adjective 'human' (ἀνθρωπηΐος). The adjective is programmatic in the *Histories*, used to denote the conditions that prevailed upon all men, the vicissitudes of human fortune: 'Therefore knowing that human good fortune (τὴν ἀνθρωπηΐην . . . εὐδαιμονίην) never remains in the same place, I will remember both alike' (1.5). When Herodotus here places Minos outside this race, he is putting him outside the experiences common to every reader of Herodotus' text, subject to the fluctuations of life, for whom good fortune cannot remain constant. This is exactly what the life of Herodotus' *protos*, Polycrates, well demonstrates at this moment in book 3 (3.120–5). Excluded from such reckonings by his status, Minos can appear meaningfully in no shared comparative framework with those who come after, whether Polycrates or any of the thalassocrats to follow, even if they should succeed where Polycrates failed and exert *archē* over all the islands.

Again if Herodotus is used to read Thucydides' use of Minos as a prototype of Athenian naval *archē*, what emerges is a warning about the inappropriateness of the comparison: even if Minos were to be all that *akoe* holds him to be, he can never be πρῶτος or παλαίτατος in a comparative framework that includes the present: what applies to him does not apply to those who follow, precisely because he is, unlike them, not subject in the same way to τὸ ἀνθρωπήιον.[79] In a sense, though, here it is Herodotus' turn to be disingenuous; for, in fact, when we encounter Minos a last time in the *Histories* (7.170), he does certainly go the way that many rulers belonging to the ἀνθρωπηΐη γενεή go. The Cretan thalassocrat dies a violent death – in Sicily – to which I return in the Conclusion.

---

[78] This would not be far from Herodotus' approach to such motivated uses of myth as he parodies in his own proem: he provides his audience the opportunity to laugh at the bias of the Persian *logioi* who use the Trojan War to justify their hostility against the Greeks, exposing his audience to exactly the same laughter should and when they use the same mythic material to argue the opposite case.

[79] For the Athenians' patronising use of this term, suggesting their own elevation above what it represents, see 8.144.

Preferring Polycrates

Amid modern preoccupation with whether Herodotus' dismissal of Minos represents fluke or milestone in the history of Greek thought, the significance of Herodotus' first choice – Polycrates – for both historians has been neglected. Herodotus' mention of Polycrates is no passing one: his narrative of book 3 lingers over the Samian tyrant, explicitly drawing his audience's attention to the length of his digression: ἐμήκυνα δὲ περὶ Σαμίων μᾶλ-λον . . . μᾶλλόν τι περὶ Σαμίων ἐμήκυνα ('I have gone on about Samian affairs for some length . . . for rather long I have gone on about the Samian affairs', 3.60). Yet this Samian digression is not especially long, and the reasons justifying its length – the three unparalleled engineering feats: a temple, a mole, and a tunnel – are not entirely straightforward, given the significance the excursus on Polycratean Samos will have for the wider themes and narrative of book 3,[80] and indeed for the *Histories* themselves as expressed in his proem: Polycrates will be the first Greek to demonstrate the changeability of human fortune, and Samos the first big Greek city to become small (1.5). As this significance warrants, the digression is, however, *rather* long, and is virtually monumental compared to Thucydides' cursory treatment of Polycrates among the early thalassocracies of his proem: while Herodotus dismisses Minos in two words and a generalising clause, dedicating instead some twenty-six chapters to Polycrates in the first instance, and five later (3.120–5), Thucydides by contrast spends only one sentence on Polycrates, and instead commits a tenth of his narrative of early naval power to a reconstruction of Minos that he admits is hardly σαφῶς. The question is raised, how should one account for the wide disparity in the texts' handling of Polycrates?

Thucydides' treatment is easy to explain: as Herodotus' Polycrates fits the overarching theme of his proem; so too does Thucydides' Polycrates comply with his proem's demonstration of the relative insignificance of the achievements of Greeks living after Troy but before Athenian naval supremacy.[81] Connected to Minos and Athens by the Delian theme at 13.6, Thucydides' one-line treatment renders Polycrates the least significant of the three: 'Polycrates, the tyrant of Samos and having strong naval resources, both made other islands subject to him and having taken Rheneia he

---

[80] See Immerwahr 1957. The story of Polycrates with that of Periander included therein interacts meaningfully with the themes of the Cambyses story: like the Persian king, one Greek tyrant kills his brother and harms his subjects, while the other's rule, like Cambyses', founders on the issue of succession.

[81] It should be noted that Thucydides' casual dismissal of the significance of historical thalassocracies prior to introducing Athens (καὶ εἴ τινες ἄλλοι, 14.3) is highly intertextual with Herodotus' dismissal of any thalassocracy prior to Minos (εἰ δή τις ἄλλος πρότερος τούτου).

dedicated it to Delian Apollo.' His is among those most powerful, but still primitive (14.1), navies by which 'nevertheless (ὁμῶς)' early figures 'acquired not the least strength (ἰσχὺν . . . οὐκ ἐλαχίστην)', strength attained and measured by the Athenian standard, revenue and *archē* (χρημάτων τε προσόδῳ καὶ ἄλλων ἀρχῇ) (15.1). But the concession is quickly qualified at 17: these navies, belonging as they did to tyrants, acted to increase only their own households (ἐς τὸ τὸν ἴδιον οἶκον αὔξειν) – not the *polis* – and 'no achievement worthy of mention (*axiologon*) was accomplished by them, unless perhaps by individuals against their own neighbours'. Fitting with the aim of the proem, the heavily qualified account expertly dismisses early rivals to Athens' greatness: even if, like Athens, Polycrates did gain mastery over other islands, it was not for his city's benefit and, even if in some cases he ruled the same islands as those ruled by Athens, the feat was less impressive given that they were his neighbours. All efforts are taken to make Athens' thalassocracy unprecedented. The single other mention of Samos in the proem can be seen to serve subtly the same end: 'The Corinthian shipwright Ameinocles apparently built four triremes also for the Samians; and it was well on 300 years before the end of the war narrated here that he came to the Samians' (13.3). An apparently neutral statement of fact savoured by modern ancient historians carries with it further connotations: whereas Samos had triremes for a full 300 years, within just a few years of becoming *nautikoi* Athens repulsed the Persians (1.18.2) and stepped into *archē*, 'late' (ὀψέ, 1.14.3).[82]

The understated, yet persistent, dismissal of Polycratean Samos as a prece-dent for Athens' naval achievement contrasts with the treatment of Poly-crates later in Thucydides (3.104), where their similarity in their purifica-tions of Delos, muted in the proem, is instead highlighted. Athens' removal of the graves on Delos to nearby Rheneia allows a gratuitous connection with Polycrates, who paid analogous honour to Delos: 'For Rheneia is so close to Delos that Polycrates, the tyrant of the Samians, for some time a naval power, while he ruled over other islands also seized Rheneia and ded-icated it to Delian Apollo, binding it with a chain to Delos'.[83] To the core sentence repeated from the proem, Thucydides adds the ritual detail of the chain, and concerning his relationship to the islands, he replaces ὑπηκόους

---

[82] Likewise in this passage the citation of the first naval battle as between Corcyra and Corinth is by no means given for antiquarian interest: it pre-empts any negative evaluations of Athens taking sides with (or even encouraging) a colony against her mother city ('they've been at it for 300 years'), the act which is going to be for this narrative the showcased cause of the war; see Hornblower 1991–6: I. 45.

[83] Πολυκράτης ὁ Σαμίων τύραννος ἰσχύσας τινὰ χρόνον ναυτικῷ καὶ τῶν τε ἄλλων νήσων ἄρξας καὶ τὴν Ῥήνειαν ἑλὼν ἀνέθηκε τῷ Ἀπόλλωνι τῷ Δηλίῳ ἁλύσει δήσας πρὸς τὴν Δῆλον.

ἐποιήσατο with the crucial concept of *archē* (ἄρξας) and acknowledges its duration (τινὰ χρόνον). The possibility of recognising Samos as a worthy *historical* precedent for Athens is now allowed, no doubt because here it will not detract – as it would in the proem – from the scale and dimensions of Thucydides' war.[84] But there is another reason for elaboration here: a Delian connection that acknowledges Polycrates as a historical precedent for Athens has a specific function in (a narrative of) 426 BC, where it was (is) *sumpherōn* to stress that Athens was certainly not the first to make the Ionians ὑπήκοοι.[85]

Indeed, what Thucydides' excursus on Minos specifically and his proem generally obscure is precisely what Herodotus' treatment of Polycrates foregrounds: that Samos could be considered the Athens of the sixth century. Herodotus' epilogue to his death is magnificent:

> But as soon as he arrived in Magnesia Polycrates died a horrible death (διεφθάρη κακῶς) in a way that was worthy neither of him nor of his aims (οὔτε ἑωυτοῦ ἀξίως οὔτε τῶν ἑωυτοῦ φρονημάτων); for apart from the tyrants of Syracuse no other one of the Greek tyrants is worthy to be compared with Polycrates when it comes to magnificence (μεγαλοπρεπείην συμβληθῆναι). (Herodotus 3.125.2)

Such is the fitting coda to a figure introduced with such promise (3.39):

> Immediately in just a short time the affairs of Polycrates grew and he was on everyone's lips throughout Ionia and the rest of Greece. For wherever he directed his campaigns, everything yielded to him easily. And he obtained 100 penteconters and 1000 archers.[86]

As in the case of the Athens of Thucydides' proem, in a short time and straight away Polycrates' affairs begin to grow; like Minos and his Carians in Herodotus, he becomes talked about all over Ionia and Greece and is extremely fortunate in war; and like historical Athens it began with his

---

[84] This will not be the only time that Thucydides is selective in revealing the strength of Samos: see the late assessment of the danger of the Samian Revolt, Thuc. 8.76.

[85] Indeed, that Polycrates purifies Delos after having had naval power 'for some time' (ἰσχύσας τινὰ χρόνον replacing ἰσχύων of 1.13.6) strengthens the analogy with Athens of 426 BC. The event was likely to have political and religious significance, a response to the unrest of the allies and to the plague no doubt popularly explained as divine anger (*pace* Thucydides), the perceived need for the Athenians to perform anew her relationship to her Delian-league allies: see Hornblower 1991–6: 1. 516–25.

[86] ἐν χρόνῳ δὲ ὀλίγῳ αὐτίκα τοῦ Πολυκράτεος τὰ πρήγματα ηὔξετο καὶ ἦν βεβωμένα ἀνά τε τὴν Ἰωνίην καὶ τὴν ἄλλην Ἑλλάδα· ὅκου γὰρ ἰθύσειε στρατεύεσθαι, πάντα οἱ ἐχώρεε εὐτυχέως. ἔκτητο δὲ πεντηκοντέρους τε ἑκατὸν καὶ χιλίους τοξότας. The phrase ὅκου (ὅκη) ἰθύσειε στρατεύεσθαι is marked: it was used of Cyrus' belief before he falls before the Massagetae (1.204.2); cf. Xerxes in 7.8 b.2. Cf. Thuc. 1.70 for the phenomenon being not distinctly Persian but also Greek, and universal, and indeed evocative of Athens.

obtaining ships.[87] And here it must be recognised that Herodotus' treatment is more in line with other ancient sources (including Thucydides 3.104) which reflect the strength and splendour of archaic Samos, immortalised in the phrase *Polycrateia erga*, the works of a figure deemed 'not king of Samos alone, but even of the entire Hellenic sea'.[88]

Again, Herodotus *explicitly* draws attention to the length of his Samian excursus, justifying it by appealing to their superlative *erga*. Indeed, for Herodotus, Polycratean Samos continues to vie, at least culturally, with fifth-century Athens: its temple is νηὸς μέγιστος πάντων νηῶν τῶν ἡμεῖς ἴδμεν ('the biggest of all temples we know'). Its application largely denied to the period before his war, the Thucydidean *axiologon* ('worthy of recounting', e.g. 1.1.1, 1.14.2, 1.17)[89] is used only a *single* time by Herodotus in the whole of the *Histories* in a passage denying Greeks anything *axiologon* except this very temple of the Samians and that of the Ephesians.[90] How would Athenian audiences enticed by Thucydidean (Periclean) visions of what their archaeological remains will tell later people (1.10.2–3) hear the implications for the future in Herodotus' claim that Samos' archaic temple is still superlative even in their own time?

Provocations aside, despite *megaloprepeiē* and ambitious *phronemata*, Herodotus' Polycrates is nevertheless no less subject to the vicissitudes characteristic of the *anthropeiē geneē*. The comparative frame he is put in by the assertion that he is *protos* cannot but raise questions about what might await those later to whom he is implicitly compared,[91] particularly if they count on their *anthropeiē eudaimoniē* remaining constant and are easily enticed (and deceived) by *chremata*.[92] Athenians of the present, if Thucydides' proem is any indicator of their mindset, would do well to heed the implicit warning – that is, if it is not already too late.[93]

---

[87] For the similarity of Samos and Athens compare *FGrHist* 539 F 2 with [Xen.] *Ath. Pol.* 2.7–8 and the fragment of Hermippus (63) quoted in Athen. 27e–28a.

[88] Arist. *Politics* 1313b24; Anac. 491 *PMG* = Himer. *Orations* 29.22. See also Athen. 540c–541a for the wealth and luxurious living of Polycratean Samos.

[89] See also 4.48; 5.74 (2×); 6.60; 4.23; 3.109; 2.10.

[90] Hdt. 2.148.2.

[91] On the function of counting in Herodotus, see J. G. W. Henderson 2007.

[92] Polycrates comes to his end (Hdt. 3.123–4), deceived with a ruse similar to the one used by the Egestans on the Athenians (Thuc. 6.46.1); see Kallet 2001: 71–6. It may, however, be a veiled allusion to this recent event: Smart 1977: 252.

[93] The issue of dating will be discussed briefly below, but see Smart 1977: 251–2, who points out that early nineteenth-century scholarship placed Herodotus in the last decade of the fifth century or later. Raaflaub's (2002: 186 n. 114) view on dating should be seen for what it is, a predetermined notion of what the text was in its final instantiation: 'See also Moles 1996: 276 about why his (and my) view of Herodotus' purpose makes it difficult to date the *Histories* later than 415 or 414.'

CONCLUSION: THE DEATH OF A PRECEDENT

In 7.170, Herodotus tells his third and final story about Minos, his violent death in Sicily: 'For it is said that when Minos arrived in Sicania, which is now called Sicily, in search of Daedalus (κατὰ ζήτησιν Δαιδάλου), he died a violent death (βιαίῳ θανάτῳ).' It is a story of overwhelming detail, telling first of Minos' disaster in Sicily, his *biaios thanatos*, and then of the failure of the Cretans whose attempts to avenge his death ultimately result in a disaster for them deemed by Herodotus superlatively to be the φόνος Ἑλληνικὸς μέγιστος οὗτος δὴ ἐγένετο πάντων τῶν ἡμεῖς ἴδμεν ('The greatest Hellenic slaughter of all those we know'). Again, it is a story whose very presence in his *logos* Herodotus has chosen to highlight: 'But these affairs involving the people of Rhegium and the Tarentum have arisen as an addition to my *logos* (ἀλλὰ τὰ μὲν κατὰ Ῥηγίνους τε καὶ Ταραντίνους τοῦ λόγου μοι παρενθήκη γέγονε).' One might be forgiven for thinking that this is just another Herodotean digression, but it is rather an exceptional one to which he singularly applies the term *parenthekē*: its status as an addition is to be noticed.[94]

In an intellectual climate where Minos has been made the mythological double of Athens, Herodotus' *parenthekē* may lead to some worrying inferences. Thucydides describes the disaster of his modern-day Minos in Sicily in nearly identical terms:

ξυνέβη τε ἔργον τοῦτο [Ἑλληνικόν] τῶν κατὰ τὸν πόλεμον τόνδε μέγιστον γενέσθαι, δοκεῖν δ᾽ ἔμοιγε καὶ ὧν ἀκοῇ Ἑλληνικῶν ἴσμεν.

This was the greatest [Hellenic] deed of those in this war, or, in my opinion at least, even of Hellenic events that we know by *akoe*. (7.87.5–6)

The intertextuality is manifest, but is it allusion? And if so, how is the direction to be construed? These questions obviously cannot be pursued to the extent they deserve here. I, for one, find it exceedingly difficult to accept that Herodotus' *parenthekē* could have been written prior to the Athenian disaster in Sicily,[95] and likewise find it implausible that Thucydides would risk describing his momentous event,[96] the one that he constructs as

---

[94] This is the single instance in the *Histories* where Herodotus applies this word to his narrative; otherwise it is used in 1.186.1; 7.5.3; 6.19.1.

[95] As Smart 1977: 252 also did, some thirty years ago, who notes that apart from Sophocles' undated *Kamikoi*, Herodotus is the first author to tell of Minos' death in Sicily. Sophocles and Herodotus, so often on the same page, may both be responding to the intellectual trend represented by Thucydides of identifying Athens with Minos.

[96] 'They were beaten at all points and altogether; all that they suffered was great; they were destroyed, as the saying is, with a total destruction, their fleet, their army – everything was destroyed, and few out of many returned home. Such were the events in Sicily.'

justifying the claims of his proem, in terms that would evoke this apparently throwaway event in Herodotus' *Histories* had he had Herodotus' *parenthekē* to read. *If* the relationship between the two texts should be construed as one of allusion, it must be that Herodotus is alluding to Thucydides, and again the allusion would carry a polemic tone consistent with that demonstrated to prevail throughout Herodotus' treatment of Minos' thalassocracy.[97] Questions are raised. Just what did happen when 'Minos' made a *zetesis* in Sicily, that is, when Athens' naval *archē* made a *zetesis* into bringing Sicily under her control? And given that Thucydides uses the term *zetesis* in relation to his own work, one may also wonder whether his *History* should be understood specifically as a presentation of his *zetesis* into the cause of the Sicilian disaster.[98] A full excursus on the terms and characters of Herodotus' *parenthekē* cannot be undertaken here; it is complex. But this *parenthekē* on Minos is highly suggestive: if Thucydides' narrative of the rise and fall of Athenian naval *archē*, with Minos tied to its mast, is read (and may have been originally presented) as a *zetesis* into why the Sicilian expedition failed, one may ask what should be considered to have been its finds. According to Thucydides' text – or at least its surface – the disaster of Sicily seems not to have been the inevitable consequence of Periclean policy, a policy that had the West well on the agenda, even precipitating war with the Peloponnesians to ally with Corcyra; it cannot have been, since Pericles (apparently) advised the Athenians not to expand during the war, and clearly the Peloponnesian War, being – according to Thucydides, at least – a *single* war,[99] was not over when Sicily was undertaken; therefore Sicily was a venture not doomed from its (Periclean) conception, but rather doomed by its execution, and therefore its failure detracts not at all

---

[97] Some have made a case for Thucydides' use of *panolethria* alluding to Herodotus' use of the term at 2.120.5: see Strasburger 1958; Marinatos and Rawlings 1978; Hornblower 1991–6: II. 29, 145. A much more coherent narrative emerges, however, when the allusion is read in the opposite direction. Herodotus insists, stressing the view as his own (not that of the Egyptians – καὶ ταῦτα μὲν τῇ ἐμοὶ δοκέει εἴρηται), that the *panolethrie* of Troy demonstrates a universal truth that 'great crimes receive great punishments from the gods' (ὡς τῶν μεγάλων ἀδικημάτων μεγάλαι εἰσὶ καὶ αἱ τιμωρίαι παρὰ τῶν θεῶν 2. 120.5). Hardly alluding specifically to this passage, Thucydides' τὸ λεγόμενον ill fits the uniqueness that Herodotus claims for his interpretation, pointing sooner to a generic saying, probably about the famous and total destruction of Troy. On this reading, Herodotus would then take this λεγόμενον, *panolethrie*, as a *kledon*, spoken about Troy, but, as he narrates it, as yet unfulfilled for the Greeks in requital for the atrocity of Menelaus in Egypt. An attentive audience is left to consider when and what that punishment was / is / will be, creating an effect similar to the anticipation left by the anger of Talthybius (7.133, 137) where the fate of the Spartan heralds raises the question of what lies as divine vengeance in Athens' future: given its claimed provenance (i.e. Ethiopia, Thuc. 2.48) and temporal proximity to the 'vengeance' taken on the Spartan heralds, the plague would be a fair guess.

[98] That ζήτησις seems to be a buzz-word connected to Sicily is suggested by Eur. *Cyclops* 14 (cf. 17)

[99] B. S. Strauss 1997; see also P. Green 2004: 87.

from Athens' glorious (imperial) past, a past that may be (with the help of this text?) resurrected in her future. Needless to say, the *zetesis* of others may have resulted in rather different conclusions, and provided a more fundamental – moral – *aition* for its failure.

Is such a disrespectful view of the achievement represented by Thucydides' historical *zetesis* warranted? I close with a Thucydidean paradox that we as modern ancient historians must not take lightly. Thucydides complains that 'for the many (τοῖς πολλοῖς) an investigation (ζήτησις) of the truth is laborious and they turn to whatever is at hand (τὰ ἑτοῖμα)' (1.20.3), and yet, he closes his prologue by commenting on how considerately he has written up the efforts of his own *zetesis*: 'I set forth first the causes and the differences so that no one may ever have to investigate (ζητῆσαι) what the origin was from which a war of such magnitude for the Greeks came to exist' (1.23.5).[100] I would ask, does reading his *zetesis* count as our own *zetesis*, or in our accepting Thucydides' account too implicitly has he rendered us like the many turning to τὰ ἑτοῖμα? We owe it to the Milesians, and other Thucydidean silences, to think hard about this question.[101]

I hope to have demonstrated the significance – historical, political, and ethical – that the intertextuality of Thucydides and Herodotus on the role of 'Minos' should be given in constructing narratives of precedence, and how an appreciation of this intertextuality contributes to our understanding of both historians, of the audiences for whom they competed to provide a 'meaningful' representation of the past, and even ultimately of the relationship of their texts to each other. A soft reading of their intertextuality recognises each text as representing the choices that were available to each historian to make and what those choices presuppose of their audiences; a harder reading reveals something about the politics of constructing the past in the late fifth century; and the hardest reading will raise questions about the dating of our texts, the possibility of intentional allusion between authors, and the direction in which that allusion should be seen to have occurred. The answer to the last question may prove surprising.

If we apply Thucydides' own cynical realism to his work, his relentless dedication to what is εἰκός, it emerges as very likely that Thucydides provided a version of the past that many Athenians of his present could be happy with, and one that they could be happy imagining the future

---

[100] 1.20.3: οὕτως ἀταλαίπωρος τοῖς πολλοῖς ἡ ζήτησις τῆς ἀληθείας, καὶ ἐπὶ τὰ ἑτοῖμα μᾶλλον τρέπονται. 1.23.5: τὰς αἰτίας προύγραψα πρῶτον καὶ τὰς διαφοράς, τοῦ μή τινα ζητῆσαί ποτε ἐξ ὅτου τοσοῦτος πόλεμος τοῖς Ἕλλησι κατέστη.

[101] On Miletus see [Xen.] *Ath. Pol.* 3.11 (cf. *SEG* 37.4). For more sceptical treatments of Thucydides' claim to objectivity, see Badian 1993: ch. 4 and more recently P. Green 2004: ch. 4.

receiving as a *ktema es aiei*. If Thucydides did capitalise on the efficacy of a rhetorical stance that we as modern historians and philosophers have come to recognise and valorise, seeing ourselves in Thucydides no less than his audiences saw themselves in the excursus on Minos that his text offered, that does not necessitate our also congratulating him for the use to which he put it. Those of us who are citizens of modern democracies mutating before our eyes into unabashedly expansionist empires should be worried about the kind of precedent for ourselves that we have been establishing in Thucydides, about the degree to which Thucydides' account has not often been recognised for what it is, and how hard it is for the timeless warnings of a Herodotus even to be heard as such, let alone heeded.

CHAPTER 9

The form of Plato's Republic

Alex Long

One of the many innovations an Athenian would have witnessed in the early fourth century was the arrival of a new vehicle for reflection and inquiry: the Socratic dialogue. A major catalyst for this development was of course the historical Socrates himself, although it is uncertain to what extent Socratic authors viewed their output as faithful records of Socrates' own behaviour and theory.[1] But even though Socrates' life and death were of decisive importance for the emergence of this new genre, we may still wonder whether a share of the responsibility lies in less contingent factors, and in the present context we may ask whether the phenomenon was part of a broader 'cultural revolution'. Should we seek more general cultural or social factors (such as those explored elsewhere in this volume) to explain the entry of Socratic dialogues into the literary and philosophical arenas?

In this chapter I approach the question not through a survey of Socratic literature but through the study of one celebrated Socratic dialogue, Plato's *Republic*. I have chosen *one* dialogue, not only because of limitations of space, but also out of a conviction that the contribution of dialogue form and thus the rationale for dialogue form are best appreciated through the study of *individual* dialogues;[2] I hope that my findings will provide some support for my conviction. And I have chosen *this* dialogue on the grounds that many scholars agree that it is in the *Republic* that Plato most clearly distances himself from his Socratic heritage, openly challenging Socrates' psychology, his conception of virtue, and his particular brand of dialectic.[3]

My thanks to M. M. McCabe, Robin Osborne, Malcolm Schofield, David Sedley, and James Warren for their comments on various drafts of this chapter, and to the participants at the 'Anatomy of Cultural Revolution' conference, where one such draft was presented.

[1] On which see Kahn 1996: ch. 1.   [2] Compare Kraut 1988: 178.
[3] See Sesonske 1961: 31; Nussbaum 1980: 86–8; Reeve 1988: xii and ch. 1; Schofield 1993: 184; Beversluis 2000: 379–83. But, for a recent challenge to this view of the *Republic*, see Rowe 2006: 10–12. The

The *Republic* thus seems an especially promising place to find a motive for dialogue form independent of the historical Socrates.

My argument is largely negative. There is a growing consensus about the philosophical rationale (or at least *a* fundamental philosophical rationale) for Plato's use of dialogue form, in the *Republic* and elsewhere, and a historicist might cite this rationale to connect the development of the new genre with its social and political context. It is widely agreed that Plato's commitment to dialogue form reflects a view of philosophy as interpersonal dialogue, or as essentially involving interpersonal dialogue; on this account, Plato continued to write dialogues because, throughout his life, he thought such dialogue essential to philosophy.[4] When Plato and, perhaps, other Socratics employed dialogue form, they did so because they saw dialogue with others as the *only* context for the kinds of inquiry and discussion in which they were engaged. For convenience I will call this interpretation an 'essentialist' approach to the dialogue form. Such an account offers our historicist a foothold, for he may well suggest that this view of dialogue should be seen in the light of the abundance of fora for debate and discussion in contemporary Athens.[5] A citizen of democratic Athens enjoyed exceptional opportunities to participate in political dialogue, and to witness (and indeed participate in) dramatic dialogue, and, our historicist would argue, this may explain the importance ascribed to dialogue by Socrates and his heir(s). Indeed, it has been argued that Plato's *Republic* itself acknowledges a connection between philosophical dialogue and contemporary democratic dialogue; Socrates claims that anyone who wished to establish a city, as they are now doing, would have to go to a *democracy* to choose a constitution (557d), and this has been taken to signal the importance of democratic institutions for dialogues such as that of the *Republic*.[6]

In what follows I will show some difficulties for this sort of account, though my target will be more the consensus about philosophical rationale than my imaginary historicist. I will argue that while the *Republic* grants that interpersonal dialogue is of fundamental importance for the success of its own inquiry, it does not depict such dialogue as essential to philosophy, but

---

choice of dialogue form for the *Republic* is particularly remarkable, given that Plato's work was written against a tradition of πολιτεία literature which had not taken this form (on which see Menn 2005).

[4] See e.g. R. Robinson 1953: 77; Rowe 1993: 4; Rutherford 1995: 9; Gonzalez 1998: 274; Gill 2002: 150; Morgan 2002: 177.

[5] Compare the account of 'tragedy's moment' in Goldhill 1986: ch. 3.

[6] See Monoson 2000: 167–9 and Roochnik 2003: 79.

sets out a problem for – and briefly suggests an alternative to – philosophical conversations with others. I begin with my own positive account of the *Republic*'s use of literary form, describing a contribution of the characters and their dialogue to argument and doctrine, and aiming to show that the particular content of this text is indispensable for an adequate philosophical account of its use of dialogue form. The second section of this paper then challenges the 'essentialist' account of the Platonic dialogue sketched above. I conclude with some brief reflections on what a historicist could salvage from my account.

I

The Socratic dialogue allows for the depiction of *character* in a way that alternative forms such as the treatise do not,[7] and so, given the extent to which moral and psychological reflections on character dominate the argument of the *Republic*, it would be no surprise if they proved to dominate the dramatic and dialectical context of that argument as well. In this section I set out a significant and sustained aspect of Plato's use of character in the *Republic*, illustrating a way in which he took advantage of the distinctive possibilities of this genre and so offering a rationale for his use of dialogue form in this work.[8] The central books of the *Republic* are exceptionally emphatic about the range and variety of the philosopher's intellectual interests. I will argue that Plato uses characterisation to develop this conception of the philosopher, and suggest that our text dramatises a tension between the philosopher's desire for learning and the demands of carrying through a set project. As we explore this tension we will also get a sense of the importance of interpersonal conversation for Socrates' enterprise in the *Republic*.

When Socrates describes philosophers in book 5, the first characteristic ascribed to them is hunger for *all* branches of learning. He notes that anyone who loves something delights in it as a whole (474c8–10), illustrating this point with brief discussions of amorous types and those who love wine and honour (474d–475b). The philosopher, he concludes, desires all wisdom (475b8–9), and pursues it 'insatiably':

τὸν δὲ δὴ εὐχερῶς ἐθέλοντα παντὸς μαθήματος γεύεσθαι καὶ ἀσμένως ἐπὶ τὸ μανθάνειν ἰόντα καὶ ἀπλήστως ἔχοντα, τοῦτον δ᾽ ἐν δίκῃ φήσομεν φιλόσοφον.

---

[7] See Nehamas 1998: 35 and Blondell 2002: 54.

[8] I do not present the following discussion of character as an *exhaustive* account of the contribution of dramatic context to the argument of the *Republic*. For example, I provide no interpretation of the setting of the dialogue in Cephalus' house, but see Griffith and Ferrari 2000: xi–xiii.

But the person who is undemanding and willing to sample every sort of study, and who attacks learning eagerly and is insatiable, him we shall justly call a philosopher.[9]

Now the sort of learning sought by philosophers is restricted during the following discussion of the lovers of sights and sounds (475e–480a). There philosophers are distinguished from devotees of the Dionysia and students of petty crafts. In a later passage Socrates is consequently more specific about the learning philosophers love, restricting it to 'the study that reveals to them something of that being which is always and is not made to wander by generation and destruction' (485a10–b3). But Socrates then reaffirms that the philosopher will nonetheless desire to learn *everything* of that kind (485b5–8).

The desire for understanding is of course central to Plato's conception of the philosopher.[10] But this insistence on the *range* of the philosopher's intellectual interests is unique to the *Republic*. The philosopher's wish to sample such a range will be of use to Plato when he prescribes a long and varied programme of study for the future rulers of Callipolis, his ideal city. But the drama of the *Republic* suggests that indulging this almost omnivorous desire can jeopardise the success of an inquiry.

Socrates exemplifies the philosopher's desire;[11] from his arrival in Cephalus' house he is eager to learn. His response to Cephalus' genial welcome is to state that he enjoys talking to the very old because he feels he has something to *learn* from them (328d8–e4). He proceeds to quiz Cephalus about old age (328e4–7).[12] When Socrates describes his reaction to Cephalus' reply at 329d8–e1 he tells us that he admires the old man's answer, wishes him to keep talking, and so stirs him to say more. In this passage Socrates' narration of the conversation invites the reader to get beneath the philosopher's skin and see what is making him behave in the way he does.[13] And at least here he seems intent on learning everything

---

[9] 475c6–8. All translations from the Greek are my own; unless specified otherwise, all references are to Slings' edition of the *Republic* (Slings 2003). Compare the discussion of desires in 437b9–439b. For similar descriptions of the philosophical nature see 376b9–10, 485b5–8, and 581b6–c5. The eroticism of the philosopher's desire is emphasised in 490a–b.

[10] Compare the contrast between the philosophical and the wise in *Lysis* 218a, *Symposium* 204a–b, and *Phaedrus* 278d.

[11] Compare Socrates' specifically *erotic* expertise in *Symposium* 177d7–e3 and 193e4–5, *Phaedrus* 227c3–5, 257a7–8 and 266b3–5. See Roochnik 1987 and Rowe 1998: 136.

[12] Beversluis complains that in the exchange with Socrates 'the unsuspecting Cephalus has been pounced on quite unfairly' (2000: 198). Pounced on he is, but as a prospective source of information, I suggest, rather than as a prospective stooge for refutation.

[13] See Rutherford 2002: 250. I do not mean to suggest that this is the only purpose Socrates' narration serves: the narration of his reaction to Thrasymachus at 336d–e, for example, seems to me more a part of Plato's characterisation of Thrasymachus than of Socrates.

he can from Cephalus, rather than goading a complacent interlocutor to reflection and self-scrutiny, for he states that he wishes Cephalus to keep speaking because of *admiration* for his reply.[14]

We might compare, albeit with more reservations about his sincerity, Socrates' insistence during the vagaries of his conversation with Thrasymachus that they are conducting an *inquiry*,[15] and his assurance that he regards his quarry, justice, as more precious than gold (336e4–9). Socrates also presents himself, at least, as eager to learn from others when Thrasymachus proposes to show him a superior account of justice: Socrates proposes to learn (337d3–5), is ostensibly willing to pay for Thrasymachus' teaching (337d6–8), and invites Thrasymachus to teach them all (338a1–3). Thrasymachus complains that Socrates' wisdom is to learn from others and not thank them, to which Socrates agrees that he learns from others but claims that he pays them back to the best of his ability (338b1–7) by giving praise 'enthusiastically' (338b8). Of course, the way in which he learns will prove to be anything but passive and we may suspect with Thrasymachus (337a) that his praise of this particular putative teacher as 'clever' (337a2) is disingenuous, but I see no indication in the text for reading *everything* Socrates says here as insincere or for doubting that he is genuinely hungry to learn from others.[16]

It might seem that Socrates' desire to learn from his interlocutors, if genuine, could only be a virtue. So when the reflections on justice have apparently failed at the end of book 1, we might hold Thrasymachus' recalcitrance responsible.[17] But Socrates squarely blames *himself* rather than Thrasymachus (354b). And I think he is right. Socrates is represented (and represents himself) as a voracious seeker of knowledge. At 347d–e Thrasymachus has posed Socrates a number of theses with which he could engage: an account (and, perhaps, a definition) of justice as the advantage of the stronger, and also the claim that the life of an unjust person is better than a life of justice. Socrates chooses to tackle the latter first, merely on the grounds that it seems 'a much bigger' issue (347e2–3). By his own lights, it is the former, the nature of justice, that should be settled first.[18] But such is his intellectual appetite that he cannot resist what seems to be a more

---

[14] Irony? But the statement of admiration is not of course addressed to Cephalus, or indeed to any other interlocutor to whom Socrates could be speaking in a teasing or ironic manner. And surely Socrates would welcome Cephalus' suggestion that a person's character is more important than his age in determining his happiness (329d).

[15] 348b3; 349a5–6; 350e11–351a2; 352d2–7.

[16] On Socrates' insincerity at 337a see Nehamas 1998: 57–8.

[17] For Thrasymachus' intractability and lack of commitment see e. g. 351c5, 351d6; 352b4–5; 354a10–11.

[18] See Barney 2006: 58.

substantial, meaty question. I suggest then that it is Socrates' hunger for learning, here surprisingly unfettered by his usual procedure, that lets him down.

This is precisely the way Socrates himself invites us to read his failure at the end of the first book (354b1–c1). He compares himself to 'gluttons' who snatch at whatever they are offered before they have finished off their previous course. That is analogous, he claims, to the way in which he has set aside the question of the nature of justice to carry out inquiries about its merits. 'I could not hold myself back from going over from that topic to this one,' he says (354b8–9). So the depiction of Socrates in book 1 suggests that the philosopher's yearning for understanding needs to be tempered and checked by proper method.[19]

The philosophical hunger for learning remains with Socrates in the later books of the *Republic*. In these books Plato evidently wishes to improve on book 1 and give Socrates a more convincing reply to Thrasymachus. And so he faces a problem. For Socrates can hardly instantly transform himself into a different dialectician. How, then, can the dialogue acquire the requisite method and rigour? The solution would seem to lie in the contributions of Socrates' friends. Despite Thrasymachus' hostility or indifference, we have frequently been reminded in book 1 that there are several other people present in Cephalus' house who remain thoroughly absorbed in and committed to the inquiry (336b, 338a, 344d). It is their intervention that keeps the inquiry going: as far as Socrates was concerned, the conversation could have ended after book 1 (357a).[20]

Glaucon, dissatisfied as he is with the conversation of book 1, does not merely ask Socrates to produce some better arguments at the beginning of *Republic* book 2. He sets him a specific project. Glaucon begins by distinguishing three ways in which something might be good (357b–d). He then asks Socrates to choose the way in which justice is good (357d4), to which Socrates replies that he believes justice to be good both for itself and for its products (358a1–3). It is thus established what sort of good Socrates thinks justice is and therefore precisely what position he has to defend. For Glaucon states that Socrates' view that justice is good in *itself* is particularly controversial (358a4–6). And so he tells Socrates that he wants to hear both

---

[19] Scholars have, however, suggested that Socrates fails in *Republic* book 1 precisely because he adheres to a chosen method, the 'elenchus'. See particularly Reeve 1988: 21–2; Blondell 2000: 135–36; 2002: 184–6, 190, 222. But Socrates himself blames the sequence of his arguments and not their negative or personal character.

[20] Roochnik rightly emphasises the importance of Glaucon for 'the forward momentum of the *Republic*' (2003: 56).

what justice and injustice are and 'what power either has in itself in the soul' (358b4–6).[21] Socrates does not, then, stumble upon the correct approach by himself; the agenda is set for him by Glaucon, who says that he will show Socrates the *way* in which he wants him to praise justice and criticise injustice (358d5–7). In 358b he has specified that Socrates should settle the nature of justice and injustice and the effect they have in themselves in the *soul*.[22] He thus recommends the procedure through which the *Republic* will eventually succeed in answering the questions posed in book 1.

Glaucon's challenge is completed by Adeimantus, who feels that the most important points have yet to be made (362d1–5). Adeimantus repeats Glaucon's prescription that Socrates should say what justice and injustice are in themselves and within the *soul* (366d7–367a1), asking Socrates to show what justice and injustice do in themselves to their practitioners (367b1–6; 367d1–3; 367e1–4). He thus ensures that Socrates' praise will not be merely of the *appearance* of justice (367b–c).

The brothers' intervention also shows that Socrates is not the only one smitten with learning. Glaucon speaks of his 'desire' to hear about justice and injustice (358b4–5), and during his speech Socrates praises the vigour of his challenge (361d4–6). When Socrates protests that he may not be capable of the task they have set him, Glaucon and the others beg him to help justice and not to abandon the argument (368c). And when Socrates begins his inquiry he slips quite naturally into dialogue with Glaucon and Adeimantus (368d–e). In what follows, then, we will see the philosophical hunger for knowledge driving an inquiry, as in book 1, but from book 2 the inquiry will be a collaborative enterprise and will have to meet the demands of a set project. No more will Socrates be allowed simply to stray from the task in hand to more weighty philosophical questions. From book 2, as we will see, before undertaking fresh lines of inquiry Socrates often checks that he has the approval of his interlocutors, who closely monitor his inquiry, asking him in several passages to amend or justify his proposals.[23]

But the dialogue from book 2 cannot be so uniformly characterised. The desire for learning shared by Socrates and the sons of Ariston remains a potential threat to the demands of answering Glaucon's challenge, and yet this desire is also necessary, given the scale and complexity of their task. Recall that the philosophical hunger is for a wide range of learning. The

---

[21] See also 358d2–4.

[22] Just and unjust souls have already featured in the arguments of the first book (353d–354a), and Glaucon may have this passage in mind. But there Socrates argued that the soul's functions or business (ἔργα) will be performed poorly by an unjust soul and well by a just soul, whereas Glaucon's request is for an account of the nature and value of justice and injustice in the soul itself.

[23] See 372c–e; 419a; 422a; 449c; 457d–e; 487b–d; 519d.

brothers set Socrates a specific but ambitious task in book 2, yet such is their appetite for learning that their conversation is frequently stretched to tackle studies in greater length and in greater detail than even this project would demand.

The tension between Socrates' assignment and the philosophical craving for knowledge emerges gradually during the course of the dialogue. The study of politics is introduced as of only instrumental interest, a task to assist their inquiry about the justice and injustice of an individual (368d–369b). And the direction of the inquiry is carefully supervised at the beginning of their discussion. Socrates scrupulously checks with his interlocutors before undertaking his political inquiry (369a1, 369b4–5). He later defends his decision (after Glaucon's complaint) to discuss a 'fevered' city on the grounds that it may help them see the origin of justice and injustice in cities (372e4–6). When he mentions the education of the guards, he begins by asking the brothers if they think that such a discussion will assist their inquiry into justice and injustice (376c9–d2). Adeimantus replies that it will indeed further their ethical inquiry. But, with this point agreed, their task now demands capacious intellectual appetites: Socrates insists that the inquiry into education must be thoroughly pursued, even if it proves rather long (376d6–7), and that they should behave as if they were 'at leisure' (376d9–10).[24] And yet these appetites need to be restrained, and it is Socrates who now seems to have taken this to heart. Adeimantus suggests that they set out the stories that will be told to the young in their state, and Socrates must remind him that they should not embark on such a discussion, as they are not poets but founders of a city at the moment (378e–379a).

But as the political discussion proceeds it starts to take on an appeal and impetus of its own. In book 3 Socrates discusses the ways in which stories are told to the young and asks whether poets are to narrate as imitators in their city. Adeimantus suspects that he is considering whether comedy and tragedy are to be admitted to their state, but Socrates suggests that more than this may be at stake (394d). Whereas in book 2 Socrates checks that the reasoning he is following will help to answer the brothers' challenge, here it seems he neither knows nor cares where the inquiry will take them:

οὐ γὰρ δὴ ἔγωγέ πω οἶδα. ἀλλ᾽ ὅπῃ ἂν ὁ λόγος ὥσπερ πνεῦμα φέρῃ, ταύτῃ ἰτέον.

For I myself do not know yet, but let us go wherever the discussion, like a wind, may take us.[25]

---

[24] Compare 374e11–12.   [25] 394d7–9.

Adeimantus approves (394d10). When this discussion of speeches and stories comes to an end, Socrates notes not that they have pursued enough
study of the subject to further their inquiry about an individual's justice and
injustice, but that they have 'completely concluded' this subject (παντελῶς
διαπεπεράνθαι, 398b7).[26]

This is not to say that their appetite for discovery is fully indulged. When
at the beginning of book 4 Adeimantus interrupts and asks Socrates how
he would answer an objection that the guards would not be happy in their
regime (419a), Socrates' reply takes us back to the challenge Adeimantus
himself helped to pose. They set out, he reminds Adeimantus, to establish a
state with an eye to the greatest happiness of the city as a whole so that they
could find justice and injustice and pass judgement on them both (420b–c).
And the question of the happiness of the city's guards is hardly irrelevant to
an inquiry into the effect of justice on one's happiness. Nonetheless, at least
within the drama of the *Republic*, the subject is broached not because of such
considerations but because Adeimantus is taking an increasing interest in
the political study in its own right. The political venture is again signalled as
being undertaken for its own sake at 422a, where Adeimantus asks Socrates
how the city's poverty could fail to prevent it from fighting wars successfully.
Here Adeimantus' concern is explicitly about their city's practicability and
survival, rather than its exemplification of moral qualities.[27]

But it is in book 5 that this phenomenon is most striking.[28] There Pole-
marchus and Adeimantus intervene to prevent Socrates omitting what they
see as a significant part of the argument, the communism of women and
children (449a–c). And Adeimantus states that what concerns them is not
a flaw in Socrates' reply to the ethical challenge posed in book 2, but a
problem of *political* philosophy:

μέγα γάρ τι οἰόμεθα φέρειν καὶ ὅλον εἰς πολιτείαν ὀρθῶς ἢ μὴ ὀρθῶς γιγνό-
μενον.

For we think it is of great, indeed universal importance for a constitution whether
this is arranged properly or not.[29]

---

[26] Compare 403c4–6.
[27] *Pace* Annas, who claims that in 412b–427d Plato 'is concerned with the ideal state only in the sense
of the *ideally just state*, and does not dwell on any of its features except in so far as these are relevant
for establishing its justice' (1981; 101, emphasis original). See Schofield 1993: 183. Annas has argued
at greater length more recently that in the *Republic* the role of the ideal city is to provide a model for
understanding an ideal person – and a model for *internal* emulation (1999; see particularly pp. 80–1).
Contrast Annas' ethical reading of the *Republic* with the Straussian fixation on the politics of the
work; Bloom suggests that the *Republic* is devoted to setting out 'the relationship of the philosopher
to the political community' (1968: 307).
[28] See Murphy 1951: 76.   [29] 449d4–6.

At this point even Socrates seems to grow weary. He tells his interlocutors that they have stirred up a vast 'swarm' of arguments which he foresaw and avoided (450a–b), and protests that the company came to hear discussions of a moderate length (450b). But his interlocutors will have none of this. Glaucon replies that the measure of such discussions is an entire life and insists that Socrates must not flag in his exposition (450b–c). Soon afterwards Socrates must be told not to hesitate to expound his views (450d3), and Glaucon has to tell him twice more to speak on (451b3–4, b7).

In this passage we have a reversal of book 1. There Socrates was avid to hear and scrutinise other people's views, to the extent that he left Thrasymachus alienated and resentful. But now Thrasymachus joins in the request to hear Socrates' exposition (450a), and it is Socrates who is subjected to strong pressure from the assembled company to give an account. The reversal is further marked by the way in which Thrasymachus now uses in his rejoinder one of Socrates' images from book 1. In his earlier discussion with Thrasymachus Socrates contrasts their ethical inquiry with a search for gold, claiming that justice is a more valuable quarry (336e). Now in book 5 Thrasymachus throws this comparison back in Socrates' face:

χρυσοχοήσοντας οἴει τούσδε νῦν ἐνθάδε ἀφῖχθαι, ἀλλ' οὐ λόγων ἀκουσομέ-νους;

Do you think these men have come here now to smelt for gold, rather than to listen to arguments?[30]

This reversal indicates that the philosophical hunger with which Socrates has been characterised is no mere idiosyncrasy. By having his interlocutors take on the role Socrates plays and even the images he uses in book 1, Plato emphasises that the hunger for learning is not just a Socratic quirk but a trait *all* philosophers share. And this will of course be crucial to Socrates' response to a later challenge; it is thanks to the characteristics of philosophers that Socrates' city can be shown to be a possibility.

This later challenge, Glaucon's insistence that Socrates address the possibility of their city (471c), will incite an additional wealth of metaphysical and epistemological discussion. Again, Socrates is initially hesitant and Glaucon tells Socrates to speak on and not to waste time (472b2). At this point Plato shows how far their desire for conquering new philosophical terrains has taken them from their original task. Socrates observes that it was an inquiry into justice and injustice that has brought them there (472b), to which Glaucon retorts, 'So what?' (472b6). 'Nothing,' Socrates

---

[30] 450b4 5.

replies (472b7), and proceeds to explain that they were originally interested in an ideally just individual as a paradigm or model (472c), rather than in showing the possibility of making such models real (472d). And their good city, too, was created as a model (472d–e). For these purposes, then, their discussion is none the worse if it cannot show the possibility of such a state (472e). But, Socrates adds, a different inquiry is now to be attempted for Glaucon's sake (472e). Plato thus signals that a new project is being instigated, one different from the task of answering Glaucon's challenge that was initially followed so faithfully.[31]

Socrates' discussion of the practicability of their city takes him to the end of book 7. He then returns to the comparison of just and unjust lives, and in book 9 he answers the brothers' challenge with a triumphant and seemingly conclusive flourish.[32] The very existence of *Republic* book 10 has therefore, quite naturally, met with some surprise.[33] Socrates does not justify the continuation of the conversation after the end of book 9 by showing that the brothers' challenge has yet to be fully answered. So here again, I suggest, we have the philosophical appetite taking the bit between its teeth. But here at last it can be given its head. With the challenge of book 2 decisively countered, Socrates now proceeds in book 10 to reopen the question of poetry, conducting a fresh discussion of imitation on a broader psychological and metaphysical canvas.[34] He charges on to prove the immortality of the soul (608c–611a) and to set out the rewards of virtue, a topic the brothers originally asked him not to discuss (612bff.). Socrates can now set aside the constraints placed on his inquiry in book 2 and fully indulge his craving to venture into new philosophical territory.[35]

---

[31] Socrates states at 484a5–b2 that they are 'going to see how a just life differs from an unjust one'. This might be thought to indicate that their inquiry in book 6 is still instrumental to answering Glaucon's challenge. The account of the philosopher will be used in book 9 to enrich the comparison of lives, and this passage shows that Socrates believes that a full reply to the challenge of book 2 has not been made. But Socrates need not be read here as viewing their *current* task as constructing such a reply; the reference could of course be to the project of books 8 and 9.

[32] See particularly 580b–c.

[33] See Annas 1981: 335. Annas calls book ten 'an odd-man-out in the book', complaining for example that in its discussion of forms 'book 10 injects, as an afterthought, confusion and conflict over what looked like a relatively clear point' (pp. 227, 232). Subsequently she suggests a later date of composition for the tenth book (p. 335).

[34] L. Strauss, noting the incongruity of Socrates' return to the question of mimesis after the discussion of justice is apparently over, suggests that poetry is discussed again because it bears on the question of justice after all. He observes that Socrates has stated that poets praise tyrants and receive honour from them (568a–d) and he concludes that 'the poets therefore foster injustice' (1964: 133). But it is not as advocates specifically of *injustice* that poets are criticised in book 10.

[35] This may, I conjecture, be one of the reasons why the *Republic* has to end with a narrated *myth*. With Socrates' philosophical appetite unfettered, it is only by shifting to a different sort of discourse from inquiry that the dialogue could ever come to an end. I do not deny that some of the material in book

So in both the first and the last book of the *Republic* Socrates' philosophical appetite is off the leash, unencumbered by the demands of fulfilling a set project.[36] But whereas in book 10 Socrates continues to make discoveries, in book 1 Socrates and his interlocutors are left dissatisfied with or disaffected by his arguments. It is thanks to the prescriptions of Glaucon and Adeimantus that Socrates' inquiry is successful from book 2, and thanks to the psychological and metaphysical insights gained during the course of this inquiry that he is able to continue making discoveries in book 10. Although in the *Republic* the hunger for knowledge remains the central characteristic of the philosopher, we are nonetheless shown not only the need for this appetite, but also the need for this appetite to be disciplined, if the philosopher is to attain the understanding for which she longs.[37]

II

Let us now turn to the importance of dialogue with others for Socrates and, more generally, for the philosopher in the *Republic*. It is, I have argued, thanks to the interventions of his interlocutors that Socrates constructs a successful account of justice and provides abundant additional material to defend and develop his suggestions.[38] This may be suggested implicitly by the intriguing précis of a discussion similar to that of the *Republic* at the

---

10 addresses challenges posed by Glaucon and Adeimantus in book 2. In the earlier book Glaucon outlines arguments that suggest that the unjust man is dearer to the gods than the just (362c), and Adeimantus notes that it is claimed that the gods make life difficult for the virtuous (364b–d) and discusses the fate of the souls of the just and unjust after death (363c–d; 364e–365a; 366a–b). These points receive answers in book 10, where it is agreed that a just person will be dearer to the gods (612e) and Socrates discusses the ways in which justice and injustice affect the disembodied soul's journey. So Plato clearly wished to raise and rebut these further points. But, at least on the level of drama, the discussion does not continue because the brothers are dissatisfied with Socrates' response. Note that Glaucon himself is said to be astonished when Socrates begins to discuss the immortality of the soul (608d4–5).

36 Burnyeat has already noted 'ring composition' in the *Republic*, but between books 2 and 10 (1999: 288). Kahn has argued that 'Book 1 is the formal counterpart to Book 10' inasmuch as 'both are autonomous units, detachable from the rest of the work and almost exactly the same in length' (1993: 136).

37 With the dramatic illustration of the philosopher's desire for knowledge in the *Republic*, compare *Theaetetus* 172c–d and 187d–e, where digressions are said to illustrate the philosopher's leisure for intellectual pursuits. For Socrates' own philosophical desire see *Theaetetus* 169b–c and 183d.

38 Clay has already noted that it is only because of the interventions of Socrates' interlocutors that some of the most celebrated discussions of the *Republic* take place (1988: 22–3). But Clay takes the way in which Socrates' assertions in the *Republic* are revised and questioned by his interlocutors to show that *no* such discussion could be declared closed. For example, he claims that 'Plato has, in the closure of Book 1 and the opening of Book 2, suggested that any claim for the closure of such a discussion must be illusory'. He also cites 419a and 449b, declaring that 'these challenges within the *Republic* should shake our confidence in the closure of any Socratic argument in the *Republic*' (1988: 22, 23). But if Plato expected and invited criticism from his readers, that does not make the claims

beginning of Plato's *Timaeus*. There Socrates narrates that 'yesterday' he discussed the constitution and citizens of the best polity, in which each citizen was assigned a single pursuit, with the task of guarding the city entrusted to women and men who are nurtured in music and gymnastics and denied private property; proposals for the civic administration of marriages and procreation are then summarised (*Timaeus* 17c–19a). But despite the palpable similarities between this regime and Callipolis, much of the conversation of the *Republic* is omitted from Socrates' summary. In the *Timaeus* Socrates promises to retell only 'the main point' (κεφάλαιον, 17c2; 19a8) of the previous day's discussion, but surely some mention of the defence of justice, the partition of the soul, epistemology, and metaphysics would feature in a summary of the *Republic*'s κεφάλαιον.[39] And Timaeus' statement that 'that is just what was said' (αὐτὰ ταῦτ' ἦν τὰ λεχθέντα, 19b1) suggests that nothing of substance has been overlooked in Socrates' synopsis.[40]

The absentees have been noted and the inference rightly drawn that the reference is not simply to the meeting portrayed in the *Republic*.[41] But another discrepancy has not, I think, received sufficient attention.[42] Whereas Socrates emphasises in the *Republic* that his project is a collaborative venture, the political discussion summarised in the *Timaeus* would seem to have taken the form of a Socratic *monologue*. Timaeus says that yesterday they were 'entertained' by Socrates (17b2–3). Far from disputing this

---

of Socrates and the brothers less 'important' than this invitation to criticise (*contra* Clay 1988: 22). And some of Clay's examples of revisions within the *Republic* are questionable. He claims that the central books question 'the initial optimism' about the possibility of Callipolis becoming real (1988: 29). But where is such simple 'optimism' to be found? Clay seems to see it in the way Socrates calls Glaucon, Adeimantus, and himself the 'founders' of Callipolis and 'thus anticipates the role of the Cretan, Kleinias, in the *Laws*, who was to be the *oikistēs* of the new Knossian colony of Magnesia'. But what in *Republic* books 2–4 suggests that the three interlocutors are 'founders' in this literal sense? And, as Clay himself notes (p. 29), Socrates refers to his political project as a 'dream' before the central books (443b). It seems better to me to speak of the attention of the *Republic* shifting in book 5; as Socrates himself observes (472d–e), the practicalities of making Callipolis real were simply not at issue in the early books. For further discussion of Plato's commitment to Socrates' claims in the *Republic* see Rowe 2006: 8–10.

39 Owen, emphasising the continuity between this summary and the *Republic*, notes that in the *Timaeus* Socrates promises only the κεφάλαια and that Socrates then quotes from passages of the *Republic* (1965: 330). Owen is unimpressed by the omissions, noting that 'Plato . . . calls the central books [sc. of the *Republic*] a digression' in *Republic* 543c5 (p. 330). But nowhere is the defence of justice dismissed in such terms in the *Republic*.

40 See Cornford 1937: 4.

41 See Cornford 1937: 4–5; P. Friedländer 1958–69: III. 356–7; Gill 1977: 287 n. 6. As scholars have noted, further evidence in favour of distinguishing this conversation from that of the *Republic* is the setting of the former immediately before a Panathenaic festival (21a2), whereas the *Republic* is set directly after the festival of Bendis.

42 But see P. Friedländer 1958–69: III. 357 n. 5.

description of the previous day's political undertaking, Socrates describes it as 'accounts spoken by me' about the constitution which seemed best 'to me' (17c1–3). He later narrates that he was asked by Timaeus, Critias, and Hermocrates to produce a political exegesis and that he granted them this favour (20b1–2).[43] The very use made of the feast motif also suggests that Socrates' discourse took the form of a monologue; whereas in a dialogue both parties make contributions throughout, in the *Timaeus* it is agreed that the assembled philosophers should take turns to provide intellectual cuisine for the others' enjoyment (17b2–4; 20b7–c3; 21a1–2; 26e7–27b8).

The absence of many of the *Republic*'s topics from the outline in the *Timaeus* is not, I suggest, unrelated to the fact that Socrates' exposition took the form of a monologue. Here we may have confirmation that some of the most famous material in the *Republic* is broached only because of the intrusion and criticism of Socrates' collaborators. If Socrates alone had provided intellectual fare for Cephalus' guests, the discussion of the *Republic* would have been significantly impaired.

So both the *Republic* and also, perhaps, the opening of the *Timaeus* suggest that dialogue with others is necessary for the success and richness of Socrates' inquiries in our text. But this is not to claim that any philosopher or any philosophical inquiry would be so dependent. And it would be unfortunate if the *Republic* were to make this stronger claim. For the text depicts Socrates not only enjoying successful and collaborative conversation with Plato's brothers, but failing to develop a proper exchange with Thrasymachus.[44] If a philosopher needs candid exchange to make any headway, what is he to do when faced with Thrasymachus and those who, like him, refuse to see a conversation through when the argument seems to run against their convictions or tell against their credibility? Indeed, the end of book 1 could be read as setting out a *problem* not merely for Socrates' intellectual appetite, but for his conversational mode of philosophising itself.

But the *Republic* also offers two solutions to this problem. The first has already been acknowledged, and is quite in keeping with the essentialist

---

[43] For descriptions of Socrates' discourse as a monologue see also *Timaeus* 20b6–7; 25e2–3; 26c7–8; 26d2. Friedländer asserts that these passages suggest that on the day before that of the *Timaeus* 'Socrates reported . . . a conversation' (1958–69: III. 357 n. 5). But there is no suggestion that Socrates' exposition took the form of a narrated dialogue.

Socrates also describes the constitution as being proposed by 'us'; see *Timaeus* 17c7; 17d2; 18a5; 18c1; 18c8; 18d8; 19a1; 19b4; 19c2. But this is not sufficiently telling to outweigh the evidence that the political discussion was a monologue. Compare *Phaedrus* 265a6, where Socrates asserts that '*we* said that love is a sort of madness': here the reference is to Socrates' own speeches rather than to dialogue between him and Phaedrus.

[44] See II. 1/ above.

reading of dialogue form: simply trade in Thrasymachus for more sympathetic and tractable interlocutors.[45] Glaucon and Adeimantus take his place and, as noted above, their contributions not only facilitate but often trigger Socrates' discoveries. We might compare this replacement with the open preference, in later dialogues, for pliable interlocutors.[46] But philosophical inquiry now seems to call for an interlocutor of a certain moral and intellectual stamp, one who is willing to take part in a (possibly extensive) intellectual search and capable of providing relevant and appropriate challenges. Of course, in the *Republic* Socrates is able to call on Adeimantus and Glaucon, but what if no suitable partner is available? Here Plato gives a second, more radical solution; the philosopher must still proceed by testing accounts and asking questions, but this sort of exchange can be conducted with *himself*.

This solution is sketched very lightly within the *Republic*. In his account of the dialectician, the expert in questions and answers (534d–e), Socrates notes that someone understands a subject only if he can give an account of it 'to *himself* and to someone else' (534b4–6). So it would seem that in dialectic one can offer an account to *oneself* as well as to others for scrutiny and testing.[47] And thus there is the possibility of internalising the sort of criticism and scrutiny provided for Socrates by Glaucon and Adeimantus. Socrates also gives an example of how this internal dialogue might get started. He notes that when we are faced with contradictory appearances we are provoked to ask ourselves questions to resolve the confusion, describing the soul as 'stirring up thought in itself' (524e–525a). So Plato may believe not only that this sort of internal dialectic could be cultivated, but also that it is the natural and inevitable response to perplexity.

Later dialogues will revisit the option of self-interrogation. In both the *Theaetetus* (189e–190a) and *Sophist* (263e–264a), thinking is famously described as internal dialogue.[48] And, at least in the *Theaetetus*, Plato notes the difficulties posed by an interlocutor's refusal to practise dialectic, and so, as in the *Republic*, *internal* dialectic offers a solution to a problem broached elsewhere. The first part of the *Theaetetus* tackles Protagoras' relativism and Heraclitus' theory of flux in the *absence* of a committed Protagorean

---

[45] See Scott 1999. [46] See *Sophist* 217d and *Parmenides* 137b–c.
[47] See Dixsaut 1997: 6; Sedley 2003: 2.
[48] Brinkmann suggests that the thinking envisaged here must be deficient, as it is said to lead to 'opinion' (*Sophist* 264a): 'the soul engaged in monological discourse with itself is particularly vulnerable to error or deception precisely because its διάνοια is said typically to issue in opinion' (1997: 32). But the Stranger's talk of 'opinion' here is of no significance for our assessment of inner dialogue; references to 'opinion' are inevitable, as his project here is to explain how διάνοια, δόξα, and φαντασία can be false and true (263d6–8).

or Heraclitean interlocutor. This is no accident, for it is suggested that neither party would get involved in dialectic. Were Protagoras' relativism true, Socrates says, the attempt to criticise one another's opinions and the practice of dialectic would be merely a waste of time, as everyone's opinions would be correct (161e–162a). As for the Heracliteans, it is claimed that they never offer a firm account or remain engaged in conversation (179e–180c), so comprehensive is their opposition to stability. The *Theaetetus* thus offers fresh reasons to suppose that dialogue with some parties is impossible; there are not only those who, like Thrasymachus, lack the moral qualities required of a co-operative interlocutor, but others who have a doctrinal or partisan aversion to dialectic itself. So it is natural to suppose that Plato sees *internal* dialogue as a solution to this difficulty.

Why then is Socrates so reliant on interpersonal dialogue in the *Republic*? Despite Socrates' many discoveries, it is clear from several famous passages that there are more substantive truths and techniques which Socrates and his interlocutors have yet to master. In book 4 Socrates voices an opinion that they will never obtain a grasp 'precisely' (ἀκριβῶς) of the tripartition of the soul from the methods they are currently employing, mentioning a 'longer and fuller road' to the same subject (435c–d; cf. 504a–d). He and Glaucon agree that they will be satisfied 'at present' to discuss the subject in a manner worthy of what they have already said (435d). Nowhere in the *Republic* is this longer road undertaken.

When Glaucon asks for a detailed discussion of dialectic Socrates replies that his interlocutor will 'no longer be able to follow him' (533a1). But it would seem that Socrates himself is uncertain of these matters, for he refuses to affirm the truth of the impression he has of dialectic (533a2–5). It is *eagerness*, not knowledge, which he has to the full (533a2). So Socrates' dependence on the interventions of his interlocutors may reflect his lack of full dialectical expertise.[49]

And note that during the course of the *Republic* Socrates himself gives *both* sides of the exchange in some thoroughly dialectical passages, where (as often) the text recognises and confronts the objections other people will make to its proposals.[50] Now it might be thought that interpersonal dialogue is needed to do justice to the way in which this work is repeatedly represented as being in dialogue with Socrates' (and Plato's) contemporaries.

---

[49] See also Socrates' suggestion that he does not have knowledge of the Good (506c2–3) and may not be able to outline its nature (506d5–7), and the hesitancy of his alignment of the ascent from the Cave with the ascent of the soul to what is intelligible: 'I suppose god knows', he says, 'if this is true' (517b6–7).

[50] Compare e.g. 452b–c; 452e–453a; 473e–474a; 487c–d; 499d–500a; 500d–e; 501c–502a; 606e–607a; 607b.

Such a reading would seem to be confirmed in 453a7–9, where Socrates proposes that he and Glaucon conduct a discussion between themselves on behalf of people hostile to their suggestions so that *both* parties can have their say. But what follows suggests that *interpersonal* dialogue is not essential after all to such engagement. Socrates starts to argue on behalf of their opponents (453b1), with Glaucon answering their objections. But Glaucon proves unable to answer these objections (453c5–7), and so it falls to Socrates himself to reply to them (453eff.). Far from suggesting that interpersonal dialogue is required to engage with imagined objectors, the *Republic* shows Socrates both posing the objections and rebutting them himself.[51] It would seem, then, that interpersonal dialogue is inessential for a philosopher in possession of the requisite expertise, and on occasion for Socrates himself.

III

It is tempting to assume that the use of a certain genre will reflect a corresponding outlook, and that such a literary commitment will mirror a doctrinal commitment; in the case of Plato and other Socratics, it is tempting to view their commitment to dialogue form as expressing a thorough commitment to dialogue with others. We have seen, however, that both the philosopher and the historicist of my introduction should resist these temptations, or at least should not assume that there is a direct avenue from an author's choice of form to his beliefs. In the *Republic* we have a text written in dialogue form and illustrating distinctive merits of dialogue with others, yet also showing awareness that such dialogue can prove impossible and lightly airing internal debate as an alternative. From this our historicist should draw two lessons. The first is simply that the most celebrated Socratic dialogue has a more equivocal view of dialogue with others than he might have expected; if there was a 'cultural revolution' in Athens, it (and Plato's own reflections on it) gave rise not only to enthusiasm about dialogue, but also to anxiety about the possible failure of dialogue.

The second is that if he is to set out the rationale for dialogue form (and then the cultural reasons for that rationale) he must tackle the content and

---

[51] Compare the response to an imaginary lover of sights and sounds who objects to their claim that he has only opinion, not knowledge (476d–e). Glaucon is asked to answer on behalf of this opponent (476e7–8). But we have been left in no doubt that Glaucon's own sympathies are with Socrates (474a–b; 475e6–7), and Glaucon accedes suspiciously quickly on behalf of this aesthete to Socrates' argument that knowledge and opinion have different objects (477b). It is *Socrates* who breaks off his line of reasoning (477b11–13) and produces a more rigorous discussion of δυνάμεις to defend this thesis. Again, it is not thanks to the *interpersonal* nature of the dialogue that the objection is properly answered.

exchange of an individual dialogue, or at least of dialogues individually. For it has proved necessary to examine both the conversation of the *Republic* and the claims put forward in that conversation to appreciate the text's nuanced view of dialogue's promise and frailty, as well as its dramatic exploration of the philosophical character. It is difficult to see how we could have grasped this view if we had offered merely general reflections on dialogue form and were unaided by the detail of an individual text.

There is one aspect of my study which my historicist could certainly exploit. In my first section I argued that Socrates' dialogue with his inter-locutors dramatises the philosopher's desire for understanding and the importance of method for its satisfaction. Plato's preoccupation with the philosopher's desire stems in large part from his political concerns: his proposal that philosophers should rule cities is buttressed quite explicitly by claims that philosophers will have a certain nature and certain virtues because of their love for learning.[52] Philosophical rule makes the ideally just city possible, and so the claim that our projected rulers will have this character is central to the political argument of the *Republic*. If Plato finds his solution in the selection and formation of a certain sort of character, this may be related to the trend in late fifth-century Athens to ascribe responsibility for political upheavals to outstanding individuals and their personal qualities.[53] If such individuals had done Athens harm, they could yet make Plato's city possible if equipped with an overpowering desire for understanding. But this desire needs to be disciplined if their intellectual progress (and so their rule) is not to go amiss, as we can see both from Socrates' educational prescriptions and from his own conversation with Thrasymachus and the two brothers.

But, once again, here our focus is on the specific agenda and content of the *Republic*. So these programmatic remarks suggest that the historicist, no less than the philosopher, is on better ground when engaging with an individual text. In conclusion, then, I suggest a move away from synoptic accounts of Plato's (or other authors') reasons for writing dialogues, philosophical as well as historicist. It is better to select a dialogue and discover how *it* gains from being a dialogue.

---

[52] See e.g. 485b–87a (note that the basis for these claims is the philosopher's love of all learning: 485a10–b9), and the philosopher's reluctance to rule at 520e–521b.

[53] See particularly the study of Alcibiades in Gribble 1999, and note Gribble's remarks about Plato's discussion of the philosophical nature (pp. 23, 219–20).

CHAPTER 10

Aristophanes' Assembly Women *and Plato, Republic* book 5

Robert Tordoff

This chapter re-examines the old question of the relationship between Aristophanes' *Assembly Women* and certain passages in the fifth book of Plato's *Republic* with the aim of throwing light on how political comedy, such as that of Aristophanes, is read by Plato and the Socrates of his *Republic*. But it will quickly become apparent that this is a two-way street; the results of this study also reflect on the way that Aristophanes' self-fashioning as an 'intellectual critic' presents a challenge both to the boundaries of Plato's philosophical territory and to our understanding of comedy as a genre in late fifth- and early fourth-century Athens.[1] When Aristophanes starts talking about a revolution, Plato's response, as we shall find, has anticipated by nearly twenty-four centuries many of the problems of modern criticism of comedy in his concern over what is serious and what is merely comic in the work of a poet like Aristophanes.[2]

The precise nature of the relationship between *Assembly Women* and *Republic* book 5 has been the subject of much discussion. There are clear parallels between the two texts, but whether one has influenced the other is hotly disputed, and if influence is admitted, both its direction and its degree are open to contest. The passages in which there are correspondences between the two works are, for the most part, well known and have been frequently cited.[3] In brief, the aspects of a revolutionary constitution shared between *Assembly Women* and *Republic* book 5 are the political role of women and the systems of communal organization of property, food, and

---

[1] The question of the relationship between *Assembly Women* and *Republic* book 5 is notoriously problematic. For a particularly succinct and lucid discussion see Schofield 1999: 34, cf. 51. The term 'intellectual critic' is borrowed from Ober 1998. My understanding of Aristophanes' *Assembly Women* is much influenced by Ober's analysis of the play (pp. 122–55).

[2] It will be immediately apparent that the framework of serious/comic within which this argument is situated owes a huge debt to the discussion of Silk 2000: 301–49.

[3] The passages which are frequently paralleled are listed and discussed by Adam 1902: 345–55; Halliwell 1993: 224; Sommerstein 1998: 14–15; Ussher 1973: xvi. See, further, David 1984: 20–9; Ober 1998: 154–5; Rothwell 1990: 9–10. My account owes a great deal to (but also seeks to extend) the work of Nightingale 1995: 172–92.

sex. *Republic* book 5 differs most markedly in the important respect that it envisages military service for women, which *Assembly Women* does not mention.

Clearly the direction of influence in this relationship depends on the dates of composition of these works. It is all but universally held that *Republic* book 5 is later than *Assembly Women*,[4] but in general scholars have been unwilling to countenance the suggestion that Plato derived material for his *magnum opus* from a piece of comic theatre by Aristophanes.[5] Thus a problem persists with explaining the relationship between these texts.[6] The two answers that have been suggested are that either Aristophanes was satirising ideas Plato would later write up in the *Republic* but were already circulating in some draft form, whether written or oral, or that both Aristophanes and Plato drew on a lost common source which provided them with the basis for their experimental political systems.[7] The standard objections to these theories of the relationship between *Republic* book 5 and *Assembly Women* are that satirising an obscure work of political philosophy would not be funny for the vast majority of the audience, whether that work is held to be the *Republic* itself in some inchoate form, or the lost common source for both the *Republic* and the *Assembly Women*; and that, since, according to Aristotle (*Politics* 1266a31–36; 1274b9–10), Plato was unique in suggesting a constitution that included communism

---

[4] Dates for *Republic* as early as 387 BC have been canvassed but most scholars favour the late 370s. See Fuks 1977: 51; Ussher 1973: xvii n. 1. The argument that Plato had already formulated the ideas that Aristophanes then parodied in *Assembly Women* has been restated recently by Thesleff 1989: 11–14. It has been suggested that the play has an esoteric stratum containing references to Plato and other Socratics (Thesleff 1989: 11 n. 38) and the Pythagoreans (Demand 1982). For the purposes of the present argument (that the Socrates of the *Republic* exhibits particular concern for a type of intellectualising comedy exemplified by Aristophanes' *Assembly Women*), these questions can remain open. It is worth remarking, however, that if Aristophanes is engaging humorously with Plato's early political thought it would seem to strengthen rather than to diminish the case for a Platonic response in *Republic*. The date of *Assembly Women* (for discussion see Ussher 1973: xx–xxv) is also controversial. Fortunately, for the purposes of this discussion, it is only the relative dating of the two works that is at issue.

[5] Dettenhofer 1999: 98 remarks that 'die Vermutung daß Aristophanes Platons Ideen zugrundelegte, *scheint* sich auf dem ersten Blick aufzudrängen' (my emphasis), but argues that Aristophanes merely presents a male–female role-reversal rather than 'Gleichwertigkeit der Geschlechter'. The suspicion arises in turn that what really informs this view is the implicit assumption (widespread in modern scholarship) that the relationship between philosophy and comedy could only ever be unidirectional. Cf. Ussher's remarks, 1973: xvii with n. 4, and xx. As this chapter seeks to show, this tells us more about our own hypostatisation of genres than it does about fourth-century Athens and Plato's struggle to define his philosophical project as *the* sole authoritative political discourse in the city.

[6] A splendid exception to the general trend is Nightingale 1995: 172–92, who has argued persuasively that Plato both draws on and reacts against Aristophanic comic material. A few scholars have argued that Plato did draw on Aristophanes on the grounds that *Republic* itself offers a satirical presentation of its themes; see e.g. A. D. Bloom 1968; Saxonhouse 1978.

[7] See Dawson 1992: 37–40; Schofield 1999: 34, cf. 51.

of property, sex, and parenthood, there cannot have been a lost common source.[8]

If we accept the near consensus of modern scholarship that *Assembly Women* pre-dates *Republic* book 5, then the possibility of Aristophanes' influence on *Republic* must remain open. The standard objections to the next move – averring that Aristophanes did influence the ideas of *Republic* book 5 – are that Plato's Socrates makes no explicit mention of *Assembly Women* or, for that matter, of Aristophanes, while the particularly controversial theme in *Republic* book 5 of women's military training is not to be found in Aristophanes' drama. To the charge that Socrates does not mention Aristophanes or *Assembly Women* by name, but at most by veiled allusion, we can reply that Socrates elsewhere has a habit of making oblique references to Aristophanes and being chary of using his name, and that from Plato's point of view, by the time he was completing *Republic*, Aristophanes was already dead and there was little to gain by having Socrates name him and immortalise the author of the comic mockery against which he was concerned to guard.[9] Concerning the objection that there are no women soldiers in *Assembly Women*, it is sufficient to suggest that various plays, including Theopompus' *Stratiotides*, may have had a collective impact and that *Assembly Women* was simply the most outspoken among these.[10] Plato, it is our contention, was concerned to defend the radical political proposals that Socrates makes in *Republic* book 5 against a particular type of humiliating mockery that derives from the comic stage, of which Aristophanes stood as an obvious standard-bearer.

It is a bold move to assert that Plato must have known the *Assembly Women*, but, as we shall find, the close parallels between the two texts and other references to the theatre make it clear that Plato is thinking of the

---

[8] See Dawson 1992: 39. This passage is also frequently cited to argue that Aristotle shows that *Assembly Women* was not understood as a piece of political theory: see recently Dettenhofer 1999: 99, 'diese Aussage kann nur bedeuten, daß Praxagoras Programm . . . nicht als ein neuartiger Verfassungsentwurf verstanden wurde'. This line of reasoning is not particularly persuasive. It rests on the unfounded assumption that Aristotle must have remembered *Assembly Women* in making his remarks, but, even if this had been the case, it would only show that Aristotle did not consider the play to be an outline of a political constitution. Plato, as we shall find, is not concerned about how a philosopher understands the play, but about how ordinary Athenian citizens *might* think about this sort of comedy.

[9] In *Apology* 18c–d Socrates refers merely to 'a comic poet', and Aristophanes is actually named as the author of *Clouds* only at 19c. In *Symposium*, Socrates refers to Aristophanes by echoing his words; the comic poet notices but Plato denies him a reply (205d9–10; 212c4–6). See also *Republic* 529b; *Menexenus* 235c. By the time of the production of *Assembly Women*, Socrates is already dead, and the time of the dramatic date of *Republic*, generally agreed to be about 410 BC, is many years before *Assembly Women*. Curiously, the relevance of this aspect of the dramatic realism of the *Republic* to the argument against the relationship between the two works appears to have entirely escaped comment.

[10] On the place of *Stratiotides* in this context, see Sommerstein 1998: 9–10.

problems that comic drama presents to his construction of the ideal city, and this makes it very likely that he did remember Aristophanes when he composed *Republic* book 5.[11] Given the nature of the evidence pertaining to this issue, it is impossible to come to a firm conclusion, and scholars have long had to be content with weighing up the weaker and stronger arguments on either side. This chapter takes it as axiomatic that, given the relative dates of the two texts, there are no incontrovertible grounds for excluding Aristophanes' influence on Plato and that the possibility of a relationship between these two texts requires a full and detailed exploration.[12]

Our next question is this: why would Plato be concerned about the ridicule of the comic poets, and what is it about *Assembly Women* that makes it a problem for a writer of political philosophy? The first part of that question hardly needs an answer when the reader recollects Socrates' insinuation in *Apology* that the jurors might have formed their impressions of him with the assistance of a certain comic poet.[13] The second part of the question takes us into a much wider debate about what sort of a political discourse comedy is in the Athens of the fifth and fourth centuries BC. We have to consider the context of Attic comedy in the early fourth century, in which *Assembly Women* belongs, and examine what sort of a play *Assembly Women* is.

Aristophanes' late plays, *Assembly Women* and *Wealth,* exhibit clear differences when compared to his plays of the fifth century:[14] the role of the chorus in the fourth-century comedies is significantly different;[15] the relationship between comedy and politics appears to have shifted, particularly in the reduction of *ad hominem* attacks;[16] the parabasis has largely disappeared;[17] the ever-elusive voice of the author has receded still further;[18] and

---

[11] This assertion is made by Adam 1902: 354. For the view that *Assembly Women* is only minimally relevant to *Republic* book 5, see Halliwell 1993: 225. Sommerstein 1998: 13–17 attributes to the play a much greater degree of influence on Plato. See, further, David 1984: 20–9.

[12] Cf. Dettenhofer 1999: 99: 'die voneinander unabhängige Entstehung beider Texte [gilt] als erwiesen'. While it is true that no ancient source connects the two works (p. 99 n. 21), absence of evidence is not evidence of absence and the refusal to allow any relationship between the two is, as I shall demonstrate, overly prescriptive, dependent on an anachronistic view of the impermeability of generic boundaries, and of doubtful value for understanding the intellectual climate post 404 BC in which texts like *Republic* were written.

[13] I hope to discuss elsewhere the reasons why a straightforward causal link between Aristophanes' *Clouds* and Socrates' conviction is problematic in view of the evidence of *Apology*.

[14] On the changes in Attic comedy in general, see Arnott 1972; Sutton 1990. Reckford 1987: 344 and Rothwell 1990: 24 present the case for classifying *Assembly Women* as Old Comedy.

[15] See Dobrov 1995; R. L. Hunter 1979; Maidment 1935; Rothwell 1992; Slater 1995.

[16] See Dillon 1987, esp. 155, 170, 174–6.

[17] See, however, Hubbard 1991: 246–51 on the 'parabatic passages' in *Assembly Women*. Slater 1995: 40 n. 32 discusses a possible parabasis dating to c. 345 BC.

[18] See Dobrov 1995b: esp. 95.

Aristophanes' relationship with tragedy seems to be different.[19] All these qualitative differences, so clearly observed by comparing *Assembly Women* or *Wealth* with a play like *Frogs*, have led scholars of Athenian comedy since the Hellenistic period to wonder whether the two late plays should be grouped with the political invective of Cratinus and Eupolis as Old Comedy, or whether they really belong in a different category. Since they are not like the New Comedy of Menander, the label 'Middle Comedy' was at some stage invented for them. All generic attributions are necessarily strategic, and we should exercise due caution by examining the concerns that motivated the creation of the term 'Middle Comedy', before we decide whether it should be accepted as a description of Aristophanes' late plays.

The problem of Middle Comedy is one whose origins reach right back to the fourth century BC. Aristotle certainly recognises a distinction between older and more modern comedy but he makes no mention of a transitional period that can be thought of as 'Middle Comedy'.[20] It is likely that the tripartite division of comedy into Old, Middle, and New is the work of the Alexandrian scholars.[21] Aristotle has, however, had significant influence in this area even if he did not invent the idea of 'Middle Comedy', since, as two recent articles by Heinz-Gunther Nesselrath (2000) and Keith Sidwell (2000) show with exemplary clarity, Aristotle's history of Attic comedy describes a development of the form which is explicitly (and indeed principally) shaped by political influences. In this respect Aristotle has been followed by many later scholars.[22]

An alternative perspective is offered by the earliest histories of Attic comedy, which attest a sharp divergence of views as to how comedy developed from the old, political, Aristophanic kind to the new, less overtly political Menandrian comedy.[23] This tradition sees the development of the genre as 'a phenomenon of general culture (not of politics)'.[24] As Eric Csapo has argued, there are good reasons for thinking that no strongly linear development of comedy, on the Aristotelian model, ever actually occurred. Rather, different kinds of comedy existed in Athens alongside each other.[25]

---

[19] Dobrov 2001: 17 observes that one striking feature of *Assembly Women* is the absence of a model from tragedy: the play 'is remarkable for realizing its metatheatrical utopia *without* an underlying tragic framework'.

[20] Arist. *Nicomachean Ethics* 1128a22–4; cf. *Poetics* 1451b11–15.

[21] Nesselrath 2000: 238; cf. Nesselrath 1990: 172–87, esp. 186. Nesselrath credits Aristophanes of Byzantium with the tripartite division of comedy.

[22] See Sidwell 2000.   [23] On the politics of Menandrian theatre, see Lape 2004.

[24] Nesselrath 2000: 237. Cf. Nesselrath 1990: 45–51, 174–5.

[25] Csapo 2000. Cf. J. J. Henderson 1995: 181; Sidwell 2000: 255–6.

The term 'Middle Comedy' is, then, a heavily loaded generic label which purports to characterise a period of comedy according to a particular view of political history and its alleged influence on comedy. Perhaps unsurprisingly, then, as views of Athens' fourth-century economic and political situation have changed, so have views of Middle Comedy. Middle Comedy's beginnings have traditionally been set against a background of decline in democratic Athens, supported by a history of Athenian social and economic deterioration in the first half of the fourth century BC. Comedy and the chorus, so the argument ran, went into a sharp decline in the fourth century as the natural corollary of an economic slump, political quietism and apathy, and the rise of a more introspective and private society. Recently the view of fourth-century economic history that underpinned the decline of comedy has been challenged by a number of scholars, and the resultant revisionism in the study of the history of fourth-century Athens no longer sees the defeat in the Peloponnesian War as an irreversible blight on Athens' prosperity.[26]

Meanwhile, historians of the Athenian theatre have demonstrated that the institution of the *choregia* continued to function without any known interruption through the fourth century, at least until the period of Macedonian hegemony and the rule of Demetrius of Phaleron.[27] There is also evidence for the continued vitality of the chorus in fourth-century Athens.[28] When we look for an account of why comedy moved towards the Menandrian form of 'social comedy' and its narrative and dramatic concern with realism, the decline of the *choregia* is no longer accepted as a factor.

Recent scholarship has detected various other trends in the role of the comic chorus of the fourth century, and argued for their particular influence on the development of comedy from Aristophanes to Menander. Considering the reasons for the rise of Menander's realism, Niall Slater (1995: 45) has argued that these traits of Menandrian theatre were due to the internationalisation of Athenian comedy, which succeeded because comic poets created 'a standardized and portable product'. An easily exportable comic play exhibited certain features which, Slater argues, account for the changes between Old Comedy and New Comedy. An international audience had less interest in Athenian politics (p. 32); metatheatrical references to comic competition were obsolete beyond the Athenian festivals, and therefore

---

[26] For a review of the scholarship, see Rothwell 1992. See further Burke 1992; David 1984; French 1991; Isager and Hansen 1975; Strauss 1986.

[27] See Rothwell 1992.

[28] On the evidence for the chorus in the fourth century, see R. L. Hunter 1979; Maidment 1935; and especially Rothwell 1992, whose conclusions are accepted by Wilson 2000: 267, with n. 16.

dropped out of currency (p. 33); plays were written which would *allow for* choral lyrics but did not require them, facilitating performance in a variety of contexts and with a range of resources to hand (pp. 39–41). The result of this decline in topical material, metatheatrical poetic rivalry, and the choral role (though not the presence of the chorus, at least in Athens) was the rise of a comedy which embraced realist conventions in plot and the maintaining of dramatic illusion in performance.[29]

There are, then, two interrelated problems in the modern debate over what generic attribution to apply to *Assembly Women* and *Wealth*. There is the question of whether we should use the term 'Middle Comedy' and refer to a period, or whether we should think more in terms of a sub-genre. Secondly, there is the question of how far the periodisation of comedy is determined by political change. Rather than see Middle Comedy as a period in which comedy sloughed off its more exuberant and vocal political role and began to change its appearance towards the politer social realism of Menander, the growing consensus is that a certain *type* of less vociferous and extravagant comic drama, which had long been around, became fashionable and dominated the Attic stage for the middle years of the fourth century. In other words, what we see is not a periodic development of a monolithic entity called Attic Comedy, but a period characterised by the popularity of a certain style of comic theatre.

Increasingly, scholarly discussion of the history of Attic comedy is moving towards the view that the generic distinctions between the highly political Old Comedy and the social New Comedy of Menander can no longer credibly be used to characterise epochs of the linear development of comic style. Comedy staging politicians and other high-profile public figures continued into and even beyond the fourth century,[30] while mythological burlesque was extremely popular between 420 and 400 BC,[31] and stylistic features of Middle Comedy are also found in the fifth century.[32] The concept of a period of Middle Comedy, squeezed at both ends, suffers particularly heavily. Even Heinz-Gunther Nesselrath, one of the most significant defenders of periodisation, in a highly detailed study of fourth-century comedy, sets the dates defining Middle Comedy, as a period, very narrowly, to 380–350 BC.[33] Even if we accept Nesselrath's schema, Aristophanes' last extant plays (and *Assembly Women* in particular) fall comfortably outside that period and belong to the last twelve or thirteen years of Old Comedy.

---

[29] See Arist. *Poetics*. 1451a36–b15, with Webster 1970: 114–16.
[30] This is demonstrated by Webster 1970: 10–56. C. P. Jones 1993 shows that comedy of the political kind continued even in imperial times.
[31] Webster 1970: 85.   [32] Rosen 1995.   [33] Nesselrath 1990: 331–45, esp. 334.

It may be wisest, given the state of the evidence, to avoid postulating a linear historical development of comedy and particular historical moments when sudden changes in form and style occurred, and to think more in terms of 'a gradual shift in audience sympathy from a political to an ethical style of drama'.[34] Such an approach has the advantage of allowing a period to be characterised by the dominance of a certain style of comedy, but without the mechanical rigidity of the Aristotelian developmental model.[35]

But, despite this, we should not neglect the importance of the evolutionary history of comedy in shaping the canon as we know it. It has recently been suggested that Aristophanes' plays survived the canonical selections of Greek literature made in Alexandria precisely because Aristophanes' career can be used to document the Aristotelian-influenced view of a change from Old to Middle to New Comedy.[36] In that case, the reason plays such as *Acharnians* and *Knights* survive is partly that Aristophanes went on to write *Assembly Women* and *Wealth*. Perhaps we should respond by according these late works a little more attention than they have traditionally received.

What sort of theatre do *Assembly Women* and *Wealth* represent? They stand in an uneasy relationship both to Aristophanes' earlier work, with which they are usually contrasted unfavourably,[37] and to the New Comedy of Menander. Wrestling with the problem of the disappearance of choral songs from *Wealth*,[38] Kenneth Dover wondered whether to search for the key to this change in the fashion of the times or in Aristophanes himself, by this time very much on the threshold of old age. In a footnote Dover muses that 'the possibility that Aristophanes had had a stroke cannot be absolutely excluded; but then one would have expected him to go on trying to write the kind of play he was used to, rather than write a new kind'.[39]

In many ways Aristophanes did continue to write the kind of play to which he was accustomed: *Assembly Women* and *Wealth* are comic dramas predicated upon the iniquities of Athenian society and politics, in which respect they are not so different from *Frogs*, or from *Lysistrata*, or for that matter from *Knights* and *Acharnians*. Yet they are also a new kind of comedy in view of their particularly sharp focus on the social and economic

---

[34] Csapo 2000: 133.   [35] See the criticisms of Csapo 2000: 123–5.

[36] Sidwell 2000. Cf. Nesselrath 2000: 240: 'The Alexandrian view of Aristophanes as the focal point of Old Comedy and the promising germ of New may – in the process of selection of dramatic texts that took place in later antiquity and condemned all other such texts to oblivion – have given Aristophanes' plays one decisive advantage over those of his rivals.'

[37] For a collection of deprecatory views of *Assembly Women*, see David 1984: 1 n. 1.

[38] See Dover 1972: 195; Handley 1953.

[39] Dover 1972: 195 n. 7. The year of Aristophanes' birth is not known, but it is generally thought to be no more than a few years either side of 450 BC.

problems of Athens and the dramatisation of innovative constitutional reform and the complete social upheaval of the city, which are not present in the earlier extant plays. As the foregoing discussion has urged, the fact that Aristophanes' late works do not exhibit such an abundance of political material in the form of *ad hominem* vituperation and explicitly critical, or even hortatory, political comment, should not immediately lead us to suppose that Aristophanes' interest in and commitment to political discourse has declined; the change may be more in terms of style and approach.[40] The poet has not lost his voice. Rather, he has made a decision to adopt a different register of political discourse.

Aristophanes' *Assembly Women* is undoubtedly a political play; it is about Athens and how the city might be reorganised for the collective good of her citizens. In this way, to whatever period or sub-generic category we assign it, *Assembly Women* positions itself differently from the surviving plays of the fifth century in its interest in a complete social and economic restructuring of the polis rather than an immediate solution to Athens' current woes. Where plays such as *Acharnians*, *Knights*, *Lysistrata*, and *Frogs* pursue an individualist escape from or a topical remedy for the city's contemporary troubles, the two late plays are characterised by their distinctively *systematic* approach to righting Athens' wrongs (whether through the imposition of an entirely new constitution, in *Assembly Women*, or the complete redistribution of economic resources, in *Wealth*). It is this strategy of subjecting a systematic treatment of Athenian political organisation to comic ridicule that, as we shall see, particularly attracted Plato's attention. Before presenting our reasons for advancing this argument, we turn first to a brief review of the action of the *Assembly Women* and the presentation of its major themes.

The women of Athens, under the leadership of Praxagora, attend and deceive the assembly and install themselves in control of the city. Praxagora institutes communism of property and sex. With the women in power and the city reformed, Aristophanes stages the reactions of Praxagora's husband Blepyrus and various other men to this feminine *coup d'état*. Not everyone is prepared to endorse communism of property, and one particular 'Dissident' plots to have his share of the communal feast without making over his goods

---

[40] Sommerstein 1984 argues that Aristophanes in the late plays is passionately concerned with poverty and inequality in Athenian society, suggesting that the change in Aristophanes' political stance to greater social concern was caused by his own impoverishment after Athens' defeat in the Peloponnesian War. I hesitate to endorse such a biographical interpretation of *Assembly Women* and *Wealth*, preferring to see the change as part of a wider intellectual movement which produced among many other works Plato's political philosophy, but it is important not to do away with the possibility of political engagement.

and chattels to the city.[41] The scene that follows is the notorious 'rape of Epigenes' by three old women,[42] after which the play ends somewhat abruptly with Blepyrus summoned to dinner and the audience told they can all join in the feast too, if they go home. Thus the play that dramatises the amalgamation of Athens into a single *oikos* and the shattering of some of the most important divisions of Athenian society makes its joyous finale available to its audience only if they accept the *status quo* by returning each to his own private life.

There is one central problem in this drama that provides the impetus for the plot: the city stands in desperate need of reform. Somebody has to do something to 'save the city'. Wondering why his wife has disappeared and what happened at the assembly, Blepyrus turns to his friend Chremes.

ΒΛΕΠΥΡΟΣ
ἀτὰρ τί τὸ πρᾶγμ' ἦν, ὅτι τοσοῦτον χρῆμ' ὄχλου
οὕτως ἐν ὥρᾳ ξυνελέγη;
ΧΡΕΜΗΣ
                    τί δ' ἄλλο γ' ἢ
ἔδοξε τοῖς πρυτάνεσι περὶ σωτηρίας
γνώμας καθεῖναι τῆς πόλεως;

BLEPYROS: But why did such a hell of a crowd gather so early?
CHREMES: Because the *prutaneis* decided to hold a debate about saving the city, why else? *Assembly Women* 394–7[43]

Saving the city is a preoccupation for Aristophanic comedy most memorably in the *Frogs*, but looking back some twenty years to *Acharnians* and *Knights* it may be observed that the question of saving the city is firmly part of a larger debate about the extent to which comedy has a role in Athenian politics.[44] The claim that Aristophanes' comic plays offer benefits to the

---

[41] There is no textual authority for naming this character the 'Dissident'. Some critics call him the 'Sceptic', others the 'Selfish Citizen'. The manuscripts refer to ANHP B. We should note that such titles are loaded in respect to reading *Assembly Women* as, for example, political/theoretical or social/moral comedy. For the view that this character is a typical sophist, see Rothwell 1990: 62; cf. Ober 1998: 147.

[42] Epigenes is also a conventional name for the character otherwise referred to as the 'Young Man'. On his name, see Taaffe 1993: 124 n. 39.

[43] The text of Aristophanes is the Oxford Classical Texts edition of Hall and Geldart. All translations of Greek are my own unless otherwise specified.

[44] This is what I refer to as 'the Aristophanic question', which I hope to discuss in much greater detail in another place. For an acute and concise summary of the major issues in scholarship on Aristophanes, see Fisher 1993a: esp. 31. For discussion of σωτηρία in Aristophanes see Frey 1948. For the significance in Greek culture of the salvation of the city provided by those inhabitants of the city who are constitutively outside the citizen body (in case of *Assembly Women* by a woman, Praxagora), see Kearns 1990.

city is made repeatedly in the 420s BC; it is prominent in the *Frogs*; and it is made with renewed emphasis in the *Assembly Women*.[45]

The precise nature of Aristophanic comedy's engagement with politics has been much discussed, with reference to a series of questions which all devolve upon the issue of how far comic drama produced, and was intended to produce, concrete political effects. Among the items of discussion are the question of the extent to which Aristophanes' *Clouds* was responsible for the trial and execution of Socrates in 399 BC; whether naming certain names in comedy was ever restricted by decree of the assembly; the extent to which Aristophanes' *Frogs* was responsible for the return of the exiled oligarchs; and whether Cleon did or did not prosecute Aristophanes for his production of *Babylonians* in 426 BC.

The sheer scale and difficulty of these problems mean that none of them can be adequately discussed here, let alone all three, but we shall refer briefly to one of them as an illustration of certain constitutive difficulties with reading Aristophanes. The problem of Cleon's attempted prosecution of Aristophanes is notorious in studies of both Attic comedy and Athenian law.[46] Without underestimating the complexity of the intricate knot of issues at stake here, I would like to offer a few brief observations. The factual question of whether Cleon actually did attempt to prosecute Aristophanes, or whether it is a comic fiction, is and will remain, without the appearance of fresh evidence, unanswerable.[47] Therefore, while we cannot simply consign the trial to humorous invention, we also cannot escape the possibility that Aristophanes' references to the prosecution are all part of the joke and, consequently, we cannot say on those grounds with any certainty that Old Comedy had a political voice to which politicians like Cleon might respond with litigation or the threat of it.

The only position that it is possible to adopt on this question which is not, in view of our evidence, ultimately an act of faith, is to say that Aristophanes *represents* his comedy as politically important.[48] That would

---

[45] E.g. *Knights* 149; *Peace* 695; *Frogs* 1436; *Assembly Women* 394ff.; 401. Aristophanic references to σωτηρία are collected and discussed by Frey 1948.

[46] An immense bibliography on this subject could be cited. For an overview of the major lines of argument see Mann 2002: 105–7. For discussion of the 'history' of Aristophanes' feud with Cleon, see Carawan 1990; Storey 1995: 7–11.

[47] The theory that in *Acharnians* Aristophanes refers to a fictional prosecution staged in the *Babylonians* was suggested by Lübke in 1883; see Carawan 1990: 146. The most powerful proponent of this argument in recent scholarship is Rosen 1988: esp. 63–4. S. D. Olson 2002: xxx, although he inclines to the view that the prosecution is historical, observes that the balance of the evidence is such that it is impossible to decide.

[48] On Aristophanes' self-fashioning, see Goldhill 1991: 167–222. Rosen and Marks 1999 offer an interesting analysis of Aristophanes' fictional autobiography by comparison with 'gangsta rap'. For a very

remain the case whichever way the question of Cleon's prosecution might be resolved by the appearance of new and conclusive evidence. But even if the evidence emerged that Cleon had attempted to prosecute Aristophanes over the production of the *Babylonians*, it would not satisfactorily prove that Comedy was an integral part of the Athenian democratic political process, from which the Athenians expected political guidance and advice, a view that has gained the status of an orthodoxy in recent years.[49] All that it would demonstrate is that in the particular circumstances of 426 BC Cleon and his supporters decided that Aristophanes' comic ridicule had gone far enough for it to be *taken seriously*. I place particular weight on the phrase 'taken seriously', because it illustrates very clearly a key problem of interpreting comic texts: their seriousness is always partly (but also necessarily and importantly) constructed in their reception – it is not simply immanent in the text.[50]

Even if Cleon *took it seriously* in 426 BC, it does not necessarily follow that comedy always had this effect and that there is a direct and necessary causal link between the parabasis of *Frogs* and the recall of the exiled oligarchs, or between *Clouds* and the prosecution and conviction of Socrates. What it shows is that there are certain situations in which it is advantageous to laugh something off as just a joke and other situations in which revenge and litigation may seem the more attractive option. The calculation will always be a delicate one. A large part of the difficulty with interpreting comedy politically is its inherent potential for multiple interpretations.[51] Aristophanes frequently asserts the political importance and usefulness of his comedy, but he also bemoans the lack of its influence on the Athenians.[52]

When Praxagora confidently informs us that she will offer advice on saving the city, we should recognise that we are playing a game that has been going on throughout Aristophanes' career, as the poet explores the role of comedy in Athenian politics, claiming that his comedy has a political didactic element that makes it good comedy that deserves to win the prize.[53]

---

different view of this issue, which has been extremely influential and understands comedy as an established political institution, see J. J. Henderson 1990.

[49] See e. g. J. J. Henderson 1990, 1998.

[50] Excellent though it is at uncovering the semantic slippage in 'seriousness' and despite its appreciation of audience heterogeneity (2000: 309 n. 26), Silk's account only finesses this problem.

[51] For an excellent discussion, see Cottom 1989: esp. 1–40.

[52] *Clouds* 518–94; *Wasps* 1015–59.

[53] I would go so far as to suggest that the idea of comedy *representing* itself as a serious political voice, making a claim for its social function, as a means to winning the prize is already an established *topos* in the 420s. Cratinus (fr. 52 KA) assimilates political advice and comic victory with the words νικῶ μέν ὁ τῇδε πόλει λέγων τὸ λῷστον.

Towards the end of the *Assembly Women* the leader of the chorus turns to the judges and gives them the following piece of advice:

τοῖς σοφοῖς μέν τῶν σοφῶν μεμνημένοις κρίνειν ἐμέ,
τοῖς γελῶσι δ' ἡδέως διὰ τὸν γέλων κρίνειν ἐμέ·
σχεδὸν ἅπαντας οὖν κελεύω δηλαδὴ κρίνειν ἐμέ

Intellectuals, remember the intellectualising and vote for me;
Those of you here for a laugh, remember the laughs and vote for me;
In fact I'm asking pretty much everyone to vote for me! *Assembly Women* 1155–8

These lines go right to the heart of the problem with the seriousness of comic texts. Is *Assembly Women* a serious attempt at political philosophy or is it just a joke? It may turn out to be a bit of both, depending on how seriously you take it, or whom you ask. For example, Suzanne Saïd argues that we have to take the play seriously because its presentation of the concepts of communism and gynaecocracy simply must demand a serious response.[54] Whether that reason is found to be compelling or not, many readers of this play have taken it to be a thought-experiment in political philosophy, to belong to a tradition of Greek utopian theorising, or otherwise to exemplify a particular strain of political polemic,[55] while others have urged that this is comedy, that it is all a joke, and that we should not be taking it all so seriously. For example, Ussher (1969: 30) declares: 'It is mistaken to cast Aristophanes κωμῳδοποιός as political theorist or thinker . . . Aristophanes is playing for the laughs. This is a simple truth.'[56] The polarisation of views here demonstrates precisely our point: some critics construct seriousness and see the play as political theory; others do not.

Traditionally the criticism of *Assembly Women* has favoured a dark, ironic interpretation of the play.[57] Much has been written in this vein on the role of the so-called 'Dissident citizen', on the imagery of death and the

---

[54] 'Il faut . . . prendre au sérieux *l'Assemblée des femmes* précisément parce qu'elle met en scène la gynécocratie et le communisme et rejoint l'ethnographie et la philosophie.' Saïd 1979: 33.

[55] See, in particular, Ober 1998: 122–55 for *Assembly Women* as political philosophy. Bichler 1995, who offers a general survey of utopianism in Old Comedy (pp. 85–109), discusses the place of Aristophanes' play, which he calls 'sein großter Beitrag zur Geschichtes des utopischen Denkens' (p. 103), in the tradition of Greek utopian thought (pp. 105–8), but his view of *Assembly Women* is so strongly influenced by the tradition of reading the play ironically that ultimately he sees it as no more than '[eine] lustige Demontage des großen utopischen Wunschtraums von der Güter- und Frauengemeinschaft' (p. 107). Dettenhofer 1999 finds Aristophanes ridiculing Spartan social practices and therefore implicitly against a pro-Laconian shift in Athenian policy, and supportive of Thrasybulus and the rejection of the peace negotiations with Sparta in the winter of 392/391.

[56] Cf. MacDowell 1995: 306–9, 320–3, esp. 323; Slater 1997. Saïd 1979: 59 remarks extremely aptly: 'comme si le sens ne pouvait se manifester qu'aux dépens du comique et surtout en son absence'.

[57] For a review of interpretations of the *Assembly Women*, see Sommerstein 1984: 315–16. On the importance of irony in Aristophanes' late works, see Flashar 1975.

failure of male potency in the play, and on the question of whether the banquet promised at the end of the play will or will not materialise.[58] The question of irony in *Assembly Women* is inseparable from the political interpretation of the play: generally speaking, those scholars who accentuate the darker, threatening elements of the play see it, for that very reason, as a sharp critique of economic and social communism, or the excesses of democratic rule, or both.[59] On the other hand, those critics who wish to play up the comic pleasure of the *Assembly Women* and who explain its more problematic moments as comic fun tend to see the play as either a celebration of comic license and holiday spirit or simply as less political than other readers like to think it.[60]

By way of illustration I propose to discuss very briefly the relationship between the two key scenes in this dispute over irony in *Assembly Women*. These are the scene with the 'Dissident', who refuses to part with his property but still wants to partake of the feast, and the scene of the rape of the young man, Epigenes. A crucial but highly problematic link between these scenes lies in the possibility that the 'Dissident' who refused to hand over his property to the state and Epigenes, the victim of the three old women, are in fact one and the same.[61] If Epigenes is also the citizen who refuses to participate in Praxagora's communism of property, then the moral impact of the scene is significantly different from that which most critics have assumed and been horrified by. If Epigenes is seen as being justly rewarded for his earlier refusal to give his goods to the city and for his unearned share of the common feast, then the scene is less shocking and, therefore, less of an indictment of Praxagora's communist system.[62]

Even if the 'Dissident' and Epigenes were to be identified as the same man, the scene would still retain its capacity for producing disgust and revulsion in some readers, since most have taken the incidents involving the 'Dissident' and Epigenes as very different sorts of illustration of very

[58] On the role of the 'Dissident' see Slater 2002: 222–3, who suggests that he may be 'Epigenes' of the next scene. For death motifs and sexual imagery in the play, see Saïd 1979: 60; Slater 1989; 2002: 226; Zeitlin 1999: esp. 179, 187. On the banquet see Roos 1951; Sommerstein 1984: 322; and for further references see Slater 2002: 229.

[59] See Bowie 1993: 265–6; Ober 1998: 122–55; Saïd 1979: esp. 34; Saxonhouse 1992: esp. 18; Taaffe 1993: 103–33.

[60] See esp. McGlew 2002: 191–211; Slater 2002: 207–34. Sommerstein 1984: 315–19 argues against reading the play as an ironic attack on communism, preferring to see Aristophanes' political sympathies as lying with the poor.

[61] Critics frequently remark that we do not find out what scheme the 'Dissident' uses to cheat the system, but few have made this connection. See Slater 2002: 221, 223. Slater attributes this suggestion to S. Douglas Olson, but I have been unable to find its place of publication.

[62] On the unpleasant characterisation of Epigenes, see Sommerstein 1984: 319. For the criticism of communism that this scene is taken to indicate, see Saïd 1979: 33–69; Saxonhouse 1992: 19.

different failures in Praxagora's scheme. Helene Foley remarks that 'the scene with the three hags is considerably more horrifying in its tone and consequences than the scene where Chremylus argues with his neighbour over contributing his goods to the common pool'.[63] As Niall Slater (2002: 229) observes, the problem is that whereas the 'Dissident' scene throws the ability of economic communism to function into doubt, the Epigenes scene seems to question whether sexual communism is a good idea, since there is apparently little doubt that it will work. While the 'Dissident' scene is interpreted in merely functional terms, the 'rape of Epigenes' has tended to provoke a strongly moral reaction. Froma Zeitlin calls it 'a low-point of degradation . . . yield[ing] only chaos and violence'.[64] As the three old women who demand Epigenes' favours carry him away to what he anticipates as a living death, many critics have found an excess of comic grotesquery amounting to horror rather than laughter. Yet what the girl suggests the audience is about to see in the competition between her and the first old woman is τερπνόν τι καὶ κωμῳδικόν, something delightful and comic (*Assembly Women* 889).

Which is it, then? Is this scene a repugnant demonstration of the failure of sexual communism and a damning indictment of political innovation, or is it merely a 'randy, boisterous, grotesque triumph of comic energy', as Matthew Dillon and David Konstan describe it (1981: 382)? The answer to that is, of course, that it depends how seriously you decide to take it, which the sharp division of views in the modern scholarship on the play neatly illustrates.

A handful of critics have suggested that one well-known Athenian did take *Assembly Women* seriously, or that at least he took the threat of some of its ridicule seriously. This is of course Plato. Plato, this chapter argues, did take *Assembly Women* seriously, and the starting point for the anxiety about comedy that Plato evinces in *Republic* book 5 is precisely its potential to appear both to be a vehicle of serious discussion and at the same time to be just playing for laughs. Plato found *Assembly Women* a problem on more

---

[63] Foley 1982: 20. This allows critics to maintain a positive attitude to the idea of a redistribution of wealth along communist lines, e.g. Sommerstein 1984: 322, while condemning the fate of 'Epigenes'. Along similar lines, the dispute over the identity of the δεσπότης at the end of the play, for which see S. D. Olson 1987, 1991, partly turns on the argument that Chremes is more deserving of comic triumph than Blepyrus because we have seen him make over all his goods to the city.

[64] Zeitlin 1999: 175. Cf. Saïd 1979: 34. A different view is held by McGlew 2002: 205, who comments: '"Let the old women have the young lad", Aristophanes and his audience seem to say with a casual shrug.' Halliwell 2002 tries to circumvent the problem by arguing that the scene presents the women as prostitutes rather than as citizens and is therefore less shocking than it has appeared to many of its critics. See also the remarks of J. J. Henderson 1987: 118–19 and González Terriza 1996, who shows very compellingly how fantasy, fear, and laughter coalesce in this scene.

than one level. He saw a much more important application of the ideas presented in the play than for provoking derision, and he was acutely aware of the grave risks involved in falling foul of comic mockery. In much the same way, however, that the problem of Aristophanes' brush with Cleon does not answer once and for all the question of the nature of comedy's political voice, so the suggestion that Plato took *Assembly Women* seriously does not mean that fourth-century comedy has become a polis institution for philosophical discussion.[65] All that the suggestion commits itself to is the view that when Plato considered *Assembly Women* he decided that it was in some measure a threat because it presented innovative political ideas in a way that opened them to ridicule, compromising the sober evaluation of the theoretical political system envisaged in the *Republic*; and, more worryingly, he saw a comic drama that could be taken to be an authoritative discussion of political theory.

Andrea Nightingale has set forth a fascinating analysis of Plato's response to Aristophanes' *Assembly Women* in her book *Genres in Dialogue*. In her words Plato 'is arguably more indebted to comedy than to any other literary genre' and he 'clearly took the ideas [of *Assembly Women*] much more seriously than Aristophanes did' (1995: 172, 177 n. 16). The crucial point arises again here: seriousness is constructed rather than immanent, and Plato in the *Republic* is cautiously constructing a serious treatment of the comic material of Aristophanes' *Assembly Women*. Nightingale cites various passages from *Republic* book 5 to prove her point, though in my view she does not go far enough in examining just how closely and carefully Plato makes his text engage with Aristophanes and comic theatre.

The discursive structure of this section of the *Republic* works to anticipate ridicule and to create a philosophical context in which it is disarmed. The theme of the problem of ridicule is established before we reach the discussion of the role of women in the city:

ἐν γὰρ φρονίμοις τε καὶ φίλοις περὶ τῶν μεγίστων τε καὶ φίλων τἀληθῆ εἰδότα λέγειν ἀσφαλὲς καὶ θαρραλέον. ἀπιστοῦντα δὲ καὶ ζητοῦντα ἅμα τοὺς λόγους ποιεῖσθαι, ὃ δὴ ἐγὼ δρῶ, φοβερόν τε καὶ σφαλερόν, οὔ τι γέλωτα ὀφλεῖν· παιδικὸν γὰρ τοῦτό γε· ἀλλὰ μὴ σφαλεὶς τῆς ἀληθείας οὐ μόνον αὐτὸς ἀλλὰ καὶ τοὺς φίλους ξυνεπισπασάμενος κείσομαι περὶ ἃ ἥκιστα δεῖ σφάλλεσθαι.

For there is safety and confidence in speaking the truth with knowledge about the greatest and most intimate concerns to those who are wise and close to us. But to speak when one is in doubt and searching while he speaks, which I am doing, is a

---

[65] On the fourth-century comic portrayal of philosophers and philosophy, see Arnott 1972: 70–1; R. L. Hunter 1983: 229.

fearful and hazardous task – not for fear of being laughed at, for that is childish – but in case I miss the truth and, stumbling, drag down my friends in matters where it is particularly important not to. *Republic* 450d10–451a4[66]

This topic, Plato tells us, is about things which are particularly important; there must be no mistakes (περὶ ἃ ἥκιστα δεῖ σφάλλεσθαι). There is a danger of incurring ridicule, but fear of that is childish. From the passages that follow we might wonder to what 'childish fears' even the philosopher can succumb, when faced with the public humiliation of comic mockery. As Nightingale has argued, Plato's strategy in this part of the *Republic* works very specifically to combat ridicule from a particular quarter. The following passage characterises the source of the problem:

τάχα δὲ οὕτως ἂν ὀρθῶς ἔχοι, μετὰ ἀνδρεῖον δρᾶμα παντελῶς διαπερανθὲν τὸ γυναικεῖον αὖ περαίνειν.

Perhaps this is the right way, after the male drama is finished, to go through the female one. *Republic* 451c1–3

Plato has finished the section about men's training and political participation and now he moves on to the section about women, but why the reference to 'drama'? Plato seems to be steering us towards the anticipation that it is the stage that is going to present the problem of ridicule of innovative political thought. Nightingale does not cite or discuss this passage, which is a pity, since it would reinforce her argument that Plato is thinking about the stage and is keen to defend himself against the threat of ridicule in a comic play.[67] When Socrates eventually proposes that women should partake in gymnastic training, the issue of mockery comes to the fore and the discussion of the ridiculous proceeds in the following manner:

ἴσως δή, εἶπον, παρὰ τὸ ἔθος γελοῖα ἂν φαίνοιτο πολλὰ περὶ τὰ νῦν λεγόμενα, εἰ πράξεται ᾗ λέγεται.

Perhaps, then, much of what we have said would look ridiculous by comparison with the present custom, if it were done according to our discussion. *Republic* 452a7–8

There is a danger that the serious proposals that Socrates is advancing will appear ridiculous, but only to those who lack sense:

μάταιος ὃς γελοῖον ἄλλο τι ἡγεῖται ἢ τὸ κακόν, καὶ ὁ γελωτοποιεῖν ἐπιχειρῶν πρὸς ἄλλην τινὰ ὄψιν ἀποβλέπων ὡς γελοίου ἢ τὴν τοῦ ἄφρονός τε καὶ κακοῦ, καὶ καλοῦ αὖ σπουδάζει πρὸς ἄλλον τινὰ σκοπὸν στησάμενος ἢ τὸν τοῦ

---

[66] The text of *Republic* is the Oxford Classical Texts edition of Burnet.
[67] This passage is, however, remarked on by Sommerstein 1998: 16 n. 73.

ἀγαθοῦ . . . καὶ δοτέον ἀμφισβήτησιν εἴτε τις φιλοπαίσμων εἴτε σπουδαστικὸς
ἐθέλει ἀμφισβητῆσαι.

For whoever considers anything ridiculous except what is bad is a fool, as is anyone who plays for laughs by looking to any other standard of the ridiculous than foolishness or baseness, and anyone who is eager to establish any other benchmark of the beautiful than the good . . . and we must open the discussion to debate seriously or as a joke. *Republic* 452d6–e6

With those last words, Plato's discussion of comic mockery here touches on the central problem of interpreting comedy: how seriously is it to be taken? But this is not an isolated instance: the problem informs the whole discussion of this section of the *Republic*.

ὁ δὲ γελῶν ἀνὴρ ἐπὶ γυμναῖς γυναιξί, τοῦ βελτίστου ἕνεκα γυμναζομέναις,
ἀτελῆ τοῦ γελοίου σοφίας δρέπων καρπόν, οὐδὲν οἶδεν, ὡς ἔοικεν, ἐφ᾽ ᾧ γελᾷ
οὐδ᾽ ὅτι πράττει. κάλλιστα γὰρ δὴ τοῦτο καὶ λέγεται καὶ λελέξεται, ὅτι τὸ
μὲν ὠφέλιμον καλόν, τὸ δὲ βλαβερὸν αἰσχρόν.

The man who makes a mockery of naked women exercising because it is best that they do 'plucks the unripe fruit of laughter's cleverness' and has no idea, it seems, what he is laughing at or how he is behaving. For the most beautiful thing that is said and that ever will be said is this, that the helpful is beautiful, and the harmful shameful. *Republic* 457b1–5

What looks comic in this particular case, Plato argues, needs to be taken seriously for the purposes of his philosophical project. When Socrates remarks that a man who culls the unripe fruit of laughter's cleverness (or 'the wisdom of laughter') does not possess understanding or knowledge, Plato emphasises that some people might mistake the comic for philosophical thought. The point becomes sharper when we look at the source of the quotation about 'plucking the unripe fruit of cleverness'. The author of this comment is Pindar and he is said to have directed it at 'natural philosophers'.[68] Plato has then taken Pindar's 'unripe fruit of cleverness' and inserted 'laughter' (*to geloion*) into a text that mocks thinkers, turning the quotation against those who mock philosophy. Pindar's text has been remodelled as a comic text, with the comic interposing itself into the sphere of σοφία. Plato's adaptation of Pindar could hardly point more clearly towards the problem of the sort of intellectualising comic poetry that Aristophanes has put on stage: it looks like philosophy. This is further illustrated in the following passage, which draws explicit attention to the contested ground between philosophy and drama:

---

[68] Pindar, fr. 209 (Maehler). τοὺς φυσιολογοῦντας ἔφη Πίνδαρος ἀτελῆ σοφίας καρπὸν δρέπειν.

καὶ ὁ Γλαύκων ἔφη· πολλοὶ ἄρα καὶ ἄτοποι ἔσονταί σοι τοιοῦτοι· οἵ τε γὰρ φιλοθεάμονες πάντες ἔμοιγε δοκοῦσι τῷ καταμανθάνειν χαίροντες τοιοῦτοι εἶναι, οἵ τε φιλήκοοι ἀτοπώτατοί τινές εἰσιν ὡς γ' ἐν φιλοσόφοις τιθέναι, οἳ πρὸς μὲν λόγους καὶ τοιαύτην διατριβὴν ἑκόντες οὐκ ἂν ἐθέλοιεν ἐλθεῖν, ὥσπερ δὲ ἀπομεμισθωκότες τὰ ὦτα ἐπακοῦσαι πάντων χορῶν περιθέουσι τοῖς Διονυσίοις, οὔτε τῶν κατὰ πόλεις οὔτε τῶν κατὰ κώμας ἀπολειπόμενοι. τούτους οὖν πάντας καὶ ἄλλους τοιούτων τινῶν μαθητικοὺς καὶ τοὺς τῶν τεχνυδρίων φιλοσόφους φήσομεν; οὐδαμῶς, εἶπον, ἀλλ' ὁμοίους μὲν φιλοσόφοις.

And Glaucon said, 'You will be giving the name of philosopher to many strange people, for all those who love being spectators seem to be what they are by delighting in learning something. And those who always love listening to something new are a strange lot to be counted philosophers. They wouldn't want to come to a debate or any such activity, but as though they hired out their ears to every chorus in the country they run around all the festivals of Dionysus, not missing a single one, neither in the cities nor in the villages. Are we going to call all these, and others of the same sort, and all the practitioners of minor arts philosophers?' 'By no means,' Socrates said; 'but they are *like* philosophers.' *Republic* 475d1–e2

There are people, we are told, who go running around all the festivals of Dionysus who are not philosophers; no, says Socrates, but they are *like* philosophers. Again, this passage does not receive any attention in Nightingale's study, but it supports very strongly the view that a certain type of (comic) drama and philosophy are not easily distinguished and that they are contesting the same territory. Plato's aim, then, is to make sure that it is quite clear that philosophy is a strictly different activity from the intellectualism of comic drama:

ἢ οὐ μνημονεύομεν, ὅτι φωνάς τε καὶ χρόας καλὰς καὶ τὰ τοιαῦτ' ἔφαμεν τούτους φιλεῖν τε καὶ θεᾶσθαι, αὐτὸ δὲ τὸ καλὸν οὐδ' ἀνέχεσθαι ὥς τι ὄν; μεμνήμεθα. μὴ οὖν τι πλημμελήσομεν φιλοδόξους καλοῦντες αὐτοὺς μᾶλλον ἢ φιλοσόφους, καὶ ἆρα ἡμῖν σφόδρα χαλεπανοῦσιν ἂν οὕτω λέγωμεν; οὔκ, ἄν γέ μοι πείθωνται, ἔφη· τῷ γὰρ ἀληθεῖ χαλεπαίνειν οὐ θέμις. τοὺς αὐτὸ ἄρα ἕκαστον τὸ ὂν ἀσπαζομένους φιλοσόφους ἀλλ' οὐ φιλοδόξους κλητέον; παντάπασι μὲν οὖν.

'Do we not recall that we said those [who are fond of opinion as opposed to knowledge] loved and hung upon voices and beautiful colours and such like, but could not bear the beautiful itself as something real?' 'We do.' 'Then shall we offend them if we call then philodoxists rather than philosophers, and will they be very angry if we say this?' 'Not if they are persuaded by me', he said, 'for it is not lawful to be angered at truth.' 'Then those who welcome the real in each and every kind should be called philosophers, not philodoxists?' 'By all means.' *Republic* 480a1–13

It is not difficult to see Plato characterising Aristophanes as a 'philodoxist' and therefore definitely not a philosopher. The focus in this passage on voices and beautiful colours and use of the verb *theasthai* are all again suggestive of drama and spectacle and are, therefore, particularly suitable for Plato's engagement with Aristophanes and comedy. The cumulative effect of all these passages gives the distinct impression that, as Plato systematically constructs philosophy as an authoritative intellectual practice and systematically excludes rival types of intellectual discourse, drama, and in particular a drama like *Assembly Women*, is very much in his sights. In summary, there are two important points here. First, the evidence of *Republic* book 5 shows marked Platonic anxiety about the sort of intellectualising comedy that Aristophanes' *Assembly Women* represents. Secondly, that anxiety points very clearly to an Aristophanic strategy of presenting comic poetry as more than just a few laughs, but as an important and authoritative political and philosophical voice.

There are, as we have seen, good reasons for Plato to avoid immortalising Aristophanes' inappropriate laughter in *Republic*.[69] But how seriously does Plato take the intellectual side of Aristophanes' comedy? That question seems to require two answers, depending upon what aspect of comedy Plato is responding to. Plato certainly takes seriously the power of comic ridicule, which is deleterious in regard to truly innovative political thought, mocking the very idea of the place that women would have among the guardians. On another level, Plato clearly thinks that the ideas that Aristophanes has held up to ridicule can be turned to a more important purpose in the creation of Callipolis and, in yet a further sense, he takes seriously the threat that the intellectualism of a comedy of the stamp of *Assembly Women* presents to philosophy by seeming to be philosophical. But does Plato take Aristophanes seriously as a thinker? Allan Bloom (1968: 380–2) thought that Plato took Aristophanes very seriously indeed:

> Book V is preposterous, and Socrates expects it to be ridiculed. It provokes both laughter and rage in its contempt for convention and nature . . . As such it can only be understood as Socrates' response to his most dangerous accuser, Aristophanes, and his contest with him. In the *Ecclesiazusae* Aristophanes had attacked the public in the name of the private . . . Socrates suggests that, if philosophy rules, the political can triumph over the private life. If he is right, he can show that Aristophanes did not understand the city because he did not understand philosophy.

Bloom's understanding of the *Republic* as a satire of the political ideas of a dangerous rival, Aristophanes, has found only limited support. Arlene Saxonhouse, who is sympathetic to this view of the *Republic*, aptly sums up the problem with the question: 'If it is funny in Aristophanes, why

---

[69] See above, p. 244.

isn't it funny in Plato?' (1978: 891). Saxonhouse's question is a particularly interesting way of framing the problem here because implicit in it is the neat syllogism: Aristophanes is funny; the same material occurs in Aristophanes and in Plato; therefore the same material must be funny in Plato as well as in Aristophanes. The problem with this reasoning is that it reduces comedy to mere humour, allowing no space for a poet like Aristophanes to appeal to the significance of his work in any other terms, and it refuses to acknowledge the ways in which its audiences and readers may or may not decide to take something seriously, as we have seen Plato doing. 'If it is funny in Aristophanes, why isn't it funny in Plato?' misses the point that seriousness is not merely immanent in a text, fails to see Plato's carefully orchestrated attempt to reinforce the plan of Callipolis against comic defamation, and is blind to Aristophanes' self-positioning as an authoritative, intellectual voice in the competitive arena of the Athenian dramatic festivals.

CONCLUSION

In *Assembly Women* Aristophanes had started talking about a revolution in the public context of an Athenian dramatic performance. Plato seems to see two problems with this comic presentation of what looks remarkably like political philosophy. First, it may cause many of its audience to find the radical ideas it presents simply laughable – it is inimical to serious, sober, reflective discussion (452a–e; 457a). Secondly, and perhaps more worryingly, the comic treatment of important political concepts may be taken by some to offer a serious and important critique of an issue, in which case Athenians might think they have extracted from comedy the answers that Plato claims only philosophy can provide (475d–e). In either case, whether the audience is taking comedy seriously or seeing it as all a joke, comedy's engagement with politics is detrimental to the ideas that are advanced in *Republic* book 5 – both intellectual satire and uncomprehending ridicule are a problem for the philosopher.

As we have seen, Aristotle bears witness that Plato was unique in devising a political system of communism of property, sex, and parenting. Where Aristotle disqualified, omitted, or was simply ignorant of Aristophanes as a political thinker, Plato took him more seriously, and he took seriously the risk that others would see a comic poet as a political philosopher, as an authoritative, intellectual voice in the city. Does this, then, demonstrate that

Aristophanes was one of the 'constituent intellectuals of the demos'?[70] The answer to that is, I think, no, but Plato was concerned that Aristophanes' intellectual self-fashioning in the vast public context of a dramatic festival could be taken to be an important contribution to political thought (and, indeed, one that could be set in opposition to the ideas canvassed in the *Republic*) by Athenians who found more in comedy than just the laughs. Modern scholarship on Aristophanes' *Assembly Women*, which continues to debate whether the play is a serious exercise in political theorising or just a comic drama, is a compelling demonstration that Plato was right.

[70] The phrase is taken from J. J. Henderson 1990: 272.

CHAPTER II

Greek tragedy 430–380 BC

Edith Hall

PROBLEMS

The fifty-year period under scrutiny in this book poses a challenge to the theatre historian whose focus is Greek tragedy. Its inauguration is approximately marked by the first production of Euripides' *Medea* (431 BC), after which only eight surviving tragedies can be dated with certainty (this means dating their premières at Athens, not the time of their conception or composition, which may have taken place years previously): Euripides' *Hippolytus* (428), *Trojan Women* (415), *Helen* (412), *Orestes* (408), and posthumous *Iphigenia in Aulis* and *Bacchae* (405); Sophocles' *Philoctetes* (409) and posthumous *Oedipus at Colonus* (401). Much of the chronology of tragic performances is so speculative as to create a misleading sense that unknown waters have been charted. No other surviving play can be precisely assigned to any particular year, during the entire period 430–380, although some speculative dates are more plausible than others (for example, Euripides' *Phoenissae* must belong to the period 411–409, and *Hecuba* has a *terminus ante* of 423).[1] A few definite dates have also been preserved for the productions of important lost or fragmentary plays (for example, we know that Euripides' *Andromeda* was performed alongside *Helen* in 412).[2] It remains, however, an unpalatable truth that from this period alone we are missing several hundred new tragedies and dozens of their accompanying satyr dramas. Moreover, not all plays were similarly significant in terms of either theatrical or cultural history: many important surviving plays which almost

The research that underlies this article has been generously supported by the AHRC grant to the Archive of Performance of Greek and Roman Drama. The argument benefited greatly from contributions made at the July 2004 conference in Cambridge, especially from the comments of Paul Cartledge, Armand D'Angour, Pat Easterling, Simon Goldhill, Josh Ober, Robin Osborne, and Richard Seaford. It would have been difficult for me to pursue the topic in the first place without help from Eric Csapo.

[1] For *Phoenissae*, see the hypothesis by the scholar Aristophanes plus Scholia on *Frogs* 53. *Hecuba* must have premièred before *Clouds* (i.e. by 423 BC).
[2] For an overview of Euripidean chronology, see Collard 1981: 2.

certainly came from this era (e.g. Sophocles' *Electra* and Euripides' *Heracles*) are impossible to date; several of the plays that made the biggest impact at the time are missing, among them Euripides' scandalous *Aeolus* (performed prior to *Clouds*), which featured sibling incest, and *Auge*, which involved childbirth in a temple.[3]

Another obstacle is aesthetic prejudice. Until a path-breaking article by Easterling (1993), scholars almost universally bought into Aristophanes' myth, as elaborated in *Frogs* (405 BC), that tragedy had declined swiftly and terminally after Euripides and Sophocles had died, shortly before the end of the Peloponnesian War.[4] Some scholars claim that they can hear in fragments a distinction between the words composed by fifth-century 'poets' and fourth-century 'versifiers'.[5] But how do we define things like real 'poetry' as opposed to versification, or what we might today call 'tone' and 'feel'? Nobody has superseded the conclusion reached more than a decade ago by Easterling, that for the implicitly derogatory terms conventionally used to describe fourth-century tragedy (sensationalism, triviality, and affectation), we could substitute 'elegance, sophistication, refinement, clarity, naturalism, polish, and professionalism – a new kind of cosmopolitan sensibility deeply influenced by, and interacting with, the classical repertoire' (p. 569).

It is also important to be aware not only how long fifty years can be in theatre history, but how certain key constituents in drama can *at the same time* remain virtually unchanged; in Marxist terms, this would mean recognising theatrical art's 'relative autonomy' in relation to shifts in its sociopolitical and economic contexts, even while recognising the inevitability of that relationship.[6] There is something different about the tone of John Osborne's *Look Back in Anger*, which premièred on 8 May 1956, and the tone of contemporary plays, fifty years later, even though proscenium stages, social realism, naturalistic acting, and quotidian domestic settings are still (despite the encroachments of multicultural, physical, and ritual theatre) very much part of the theatrical scene today; they are exemplified, for example, in Arnold Wesker's *Groupie* (2001). It was as recently as 2003 that Arthur Miller's *Finishing the Picture* received its première, although its author was born in 1915 and wrote his first play in 1936, before even the Second World War. Yet a fundamental 'cultural revolution' – that in the West

---

[3] On the impact made by these two, see further E. Hall 2006: ch. 3.

[4] See Easterling 1993, and (as a statement of the conventional view she was challenging) Kuch 1993.

[5] See e.g. the language used in the apparatus criticus of a papyrus fragment of a tragedy which might date from our period (*TGrF* F 665).

[6] The idea, proposed by Engels, was first elaborated by Althusser 1971.

in the late 1960s – fell between the dates of both *Look Back in Anger* and Wesker's latest play, and also between the earliest and most recent of Arthur Miller's dramas.[7] The diction, ethos, and atmosphere of drama composed before and after the 1960s watershed are everywhere slightly altered, and yet pinpointing precise examples is difficult.

EVIDENCE

One of the few scholars to have attempted to define the aesthetic sensibility of the earlier fourth century is T. B. L. Webster. He identified as a particular feature of the period a phenomenon in which 'artists and writers often look for contrasts in their material, contrasts such as god and man, reality and appearance, heroic and everyday life, and either express these directly or sometimes imply them by emphasising one term of the contrast' (1956: 5). Certainly, fourth-century vase-painting increasingly uses binary conceptual contrasts, and allocates different physical levels to divine and to human characters in drama. An example of an image mediating another distinction – between the roles actors and *choreutai* assumed in drama and their own, 'real' identities – is offered by what is probably the sole substantial piece of evidence for a tragic performance in the period 400–380, namely, the Pronomos vase.[8] This is an elaborate celebration of the performance of a tetralogy, probably written by the figure on the vase named Demetrius, who holds a script (unless he is the chorus-trainer or *choregos*). The vase dates from the late fifth or early fourth century; it is named after Pronomos the aulete, prominent in the scene. The vase-painting might have been related to an actual painting of the cast on a *pinax*, commissioned and erected alongside victory tripods in the sanctuary of Dionysus Eleuthereus.[9] The figures representing actors in the roles of Heracles, Pappasilenos, and probably Laomedon all hold masks, revealing their real faces; eleven of the twelve *choreutai* do the same. Just one has donned his mask and practises a satyric dance step. Nine of the chorus members are labelled with their own personal names, along with the musicians and Demetrius.

Controversy surrounds the identity of one figure within the divine ambience, seated on the couch beside Dionysus, Ariadne, and Himerus. This female figure, holding a female mask, is I believe a personification of the theatrical medium in which all the actors and *choreutai* had just been

---

[7] On the 1960s as 'cultural revolution', see Marwick 1998.

[8] *ARV* 1336, 1. Naples, Museo Archeologico Nazionale, inv. 81673 (H 3240). The vase-painting is reproduced in e.g. Bieber 1961, and Easterling and Hall 2002: fig. 6.

[9] See Arist. *Politics* 1341a34–6. Csapo and Slater 1995: 69–70.

performing, i.e. *Tragoidia*; she is here Tragedy relaxing during the satyr play, *Tragoidia paizousa* as she was sometimes called.[10] She is an example of another turn-of-the-century cultural phenomenon identified by Webster (1956: 7), the development of an intellectual shorthand of personifications, whether ornamental, persuasive like Virtue and Vice in Xenophon's allegory of the Choice of Heracles[11] and Isocrates' personified Philosophia in his *Panegyric*, or explanatory like Aristotle's personification of Tragedy maturing and reaching her *telos*.[12] She represents an advance in the visual conception of Tragedy from the 430s, when personifications of literary genres – or at least, anthropomorphic figures bearing the names of categories of performance – began to make regular appearances on Attic red-figure vases.[13] If you had asked an Athenian citizen in 430 what he thought Tragedy looked like, he would undoubtedly have said that she was a maenad – an attendant of Dionysus, a member of the *thiasos*, a companion of satyrs and their children. The earliest surviving image labelled *Tragoidia* was painted by a member of Polygnotus' workshop soon after 440 BC. Here *Tragoidia*, a satyr child called *Komos*, and Ariadne attend a seated Dionysus; *Tragoidia* holds a *thursos* and a baby hare. She seems to link Dionysus and Ariadne with theatre, an institution which had an important if indefinable impact on the fifth-century visual depiction of the *thiasos*.[14] Yet this *Tragoidia* is no personification in any modern (or even fourth-century or Hellenistic) sense of that term. Moreover, all the other fifth-century vases on which *Tragoidia* certainly appears imagine her as a maenad, pursued by satyrs:[15] it is only at the time of the Pronomos vase that there are other possible examples of Tragedy defined *explicitly* in relation to the drama competitions.[16]

When it comes to the *nature* of early fourth-century tragic drama, however, it becomes difficult to pinpoint specific illustrative examples. I suspect that even the earliest fourth-century tragedies were already more *self-consciously* 'poetic' in the way Xanthakis-Karamanos (1980) has argued was a characteristic of the more substantially documented tragedy of the later fourth century; it is also likely that the iambic sections were already moving

---

[10] Demetr. *On Style* 169. I argue this in detail in E. Hall 2007.

[11] Xen. *Symposium* 2.1.21–34.

[12] Arist. *Poetics*: 4.1449a9–15. On the evolution of personification during the whole period, see now Stafford 2000.

[13] See Fränkel 1912; Froning 1971; Couelle 1991.   [14] See Schöne 1987: 190.

[15] She is pursued by a satyr on the neck of a volute-krater from Gela, c. 430 BC, in New York (MMA 1924.97.25), and lies asleep and naked, approached by a priapic satyr named Cissus on a late fifth-century red-figured vase in the Ashmolean Museum, Oxford (G 284). For images and a discussion see Kossatz-Deissmann 1997 and E. Hall 2007.

[16] She is probably depicted as a winged Nike attending a victory tripod on a fragmentary late fifth-century pelike in Barcelona (Arch. Mus. 33).

nearer to what in rhetoric, where styles were beginning to be taxonomi-
cally discriminated, would have been regarded as a polished and elaborate
style that drew attention to itself. But the problem in *proving* this type
of intuition is what makes the date of the tragedy *Rhesus* important. This
argument is notoriously circular: the play *Rhesus* gets dated to the fourth
century by the application of aesthetic criteria derived from studying the
literary and dramatic qualities of (what else but) the play *Rhesus*.[17]

The tragedy has come down in the manuscripts of Euripides, who almost
certainly wrote a play of that title: but its lack of interest in women, slightly
clunking rhetoric, and undoubted philosophical naïvety do not 'feel' Euripidean. Several other factors suggest not only that it is by someone other than
the author of *Medea* and *Orestes*, but that it dates from the fourth century:[18] a
Muse sings lyrics from the *mechanē*, something unprecedented by a divinity
in extant fifth-century tragedy. She is also, arguably, a *self-consciously literary*
choice of *dramatos prosopon* that belongs later than the fifth century. She
perhaps signifies a generic relation of the play with the *Iliad* that is unlike
anything we know about fifth-century tragedy's self-reflexive moments, and
belongs in an era when *tragoidoi* and *rhapsodes* were beginning to compete
for honours and status on the festival circuit. These arguments exist quite
apart from the characterisation of Rhesus as a *miles gloriosus*, a close relation
of the martial *alazōn* of New Comedy.

But there is no date for *Rhesus*, and it is impossible to be sure that it is not
a fifth-century work; nearly a thousand tragedies written before 400 have
disappeared, creating a chasm in our knowledge that compromises our ability to be certain about what type of tragic poetry any one of the many active
playwrights of that era might have written.[19] The desire to date the play
to between 400 and 380 stems from the absence of any other tragic text –
even a fragment – that can be proved to belong to those years. Almost
all the great fourth-century tragedians come into play slightly later, in the
next generation. Aeschylus' great-grandson Astydamas won his first victory in 372, Theodectes his in 368; Aphareus put on his first production
in 369/8.[20] Some of the plays by these authors, such as Theodectes'
Lynceus, were important enough to be discussed in detail in Aristotle's
Poetics (1455b29). All three were pupils of Isocrates, and therefore likely
to have been interested not only in effective rhetoric but also in refined

---

[17] William Ritchie's spirited attempt (1964) to defend the Euripidean authorship of the play (by arguing
that its less impressive features were a result of its having been written fairly early in his career) is
respected as a work of scholarship, but not widely believed.
[18] See E. Hall 1999b: xxv–xxviii and further bibliography at xlviii.
[19] Knox 1979: 8.   [20] *IG* II² 2325.

composition;[21] yet these refined composers remain just too late for us. It would have been satisfying to be able connect Chaeremon's admired *Achilles Thersitoktonos* with *Rhesus*, because they share a setting against Trojan War camp life. But Chaeremon belongs to the middle of the fourth century, when there was also a revived interest in staging *Iliad*-related themes, for example in Astydamas' famous *Hector*.

THEATREGOERS

It remains, however, inevitable that the experience of a spectator of a tragedy in 380 was qualitatively different from that of a spectator in 430. The differences may have been manifested in detail, tenor, and small degree rather than in wholesale change, but dealing in nuances may be what anatomising cultural change requires. One way of ridding ourselves of the artificial thresholds that have obscured the importance of the decades 400 to 380 would be to imagine ourselves into the subjective consciousness of Athenian citizens who had witnessed the development of the theatre during the entire half-century in question.

We can even give our hypothetical theatregoers names; Euegetes of Pallene really was *choregos* for Antiochis in the boys' dithyramb in 387/6, when he must have been over forty years of age; he will probably have known Iasus of Collytus, a *choregos* for the men's dithyramb for Aigeis in the same year.[22] Iasus was a sculptor who worked on the Erechtheion between 408 and 406, where he was paid the not inconsiderable sum of 80 drachmas for carving two figures, namely a 'woman with a female child leaning against her'.[23] It is therefore possible that both men were born between 450 and 440, survived both plague and death in battle, and by 380 had witnessed the development of tragedy in Athens over our entire period. Both had experience in choral performance and the festival competitions; both must have had contacts in circles interested in *mousike*. Neither was a controversial figure or prominent in politics. Iasus may have had local experience of deme theatre, since his intramural deme of Collytus, adjacent to the theatre of Dionysus, had incorporated drama into its festivals by about 370 BC (and possibly decades earlier.)[24] As a sculptor he would have understood the techniques of visual

---

[21] Webster 1956: 67.

[22] *IG* II² 2318.204–5, 206–7. I am extremely grateful to Professor P. J. Rhodes for his assistance in identifying suitable individuals.

[23] *IG*i³ 478.178. For a discussion of the relative sums paid to the different types of workmen on the Erechtheion, see Randall 1953.

[24] Aesch. *Against Timarchus* 157; Csapo: forthcoming. Is it too fanciful to recall here that in Aristotle's version of the story, Collytus was the deme from which Phye, a tall Thracian flower-seller, was chosen

as well as musical art, material as well as performance culture. It is possible that these men, like any two randomly selected individuals, would have reacted in radically different ways to changes in tragedy over this period. As a visual artist, Iasus, for example, might have been excited by the refinement of artistic sensibility, and have enjoyed experiments and innovation; Euegetes, the sponsor of choral performances by the young, might have had a more conservative streak, and have feared the erosion of the traditional education of young men through disciplined training in choral *mousikē*.

Indeed, one of the few certain qualitative differences between tragedies performed in 430 and those even two decades later concerned the type of music the audiences would have heard. Iasus and Euegetes will certainly have noticed a difference between the music in 380 and the choruses which they will themselves have performed as children.[25] Although by the middle of the fifth century dithyrambs were occasionally written without strophic responsion,[26] Iasus and Euegetes will have been brought up on songs with refrains where each strophe sounded rhythmically like its partner, and performers and audience alike always knew what position had been arrived at in the overall metrical scheme. But by the late 420s, astrophic songs were inserted into tragedies.[27] By the time of Euripides' late plays (above all *Orestes*), when he had come under the influence of the avant-garde citharodic composer Timotheus, he was writing asymmetrical, rhythmically 'freeform' songs of technical arduousness which demanded specialist singing actors: astrophic song challenges the performer's memory and expressivity, which explains why in tragedy it is usually associated with soloists rather than choruses.[28]

Astrophic monodies are usually sung by self-absorbed women at moments of emotion or interiority, or by traumatised barbarians.[29] They involve much repetition of individual words,[30] and the distinctive feature of 'melism', where one syllable is extended over more than one note; in the parody of recent Euripidean lyric in *Frogs* (1309–64), Aristophanes had certainly identified its key idiosyncrasies.[31] The New Music really did sound new; its practitioners were lambasted by traditionalists. Even the physical production of the voice was different. The actors had to use a much

---

by Peisistratus to stand in his chariot and act the role of Athena (*Ath. Pol.* 14.1)? Herodotus says her deme was, rather, Paiania (1.60.1).

[25] Even before the dramatic choruses are taken into account, a thousand citizens will have taken part each year in the dithyrambic choruses at the Athenian Dionysia. See West 1992: 17; E. Hall 2002b: 5–6.

[26] Arist. *Rhetoric* 3.1409b.   [27] See e.g. Eur. *Hecuba* 1056–106.

[28] [Arist.] *Problems* 10.15. E. Hall 2002b: 13–24.   [29] Damen 1990: 134–5; E. Hall 1999a: 118–20.

[30] *Iphigenia in Aulis* 1289–90.   [31] See Csapo 1999–2000; 2003: 71–8.

more relaxed sound; Timotheus distinguished his own beguiling vocal tim-
bre from the out-of-date singers who 'mauled' their songs, straining and
yelling with the far-ringing voices of heralds.[32]

Beyond the advent of the New Music, it is, however, difficult to identify
any 'revolutionary' qualitative changes in the tragedies of Sophocles and
Euripides after 430. But there was certainly an expansion in the total amount
of tragic theatre performed. Any septuagenarians at the Dionysia of 380 BC
would have had the correct impression that there had been a boom in
tragedy. Eric Csapo has recently accumulated so much evidence for deme
theatre in the late fifth century that our understanding of how tragedy was
consumed by the population of Attica must be revised. The Lenaea and
City Dionysia premières may have been intended for audiences of Athenian
allies and citizen males, but it is difficult to be so sure about the gender
and social status of deme audiences. And there is evidence, almost certainly
from the fifth century, for the performance of songs by Euripides in the
deme of Anagyrous;[33] both Aristophanes and Sophocles seem to have been
involved with productions at the rural Dionysia at Eleusis.[34] Other demes
which may have hosted fifth-century festival productions of tragedy include
Thoricus and Icarion, and, by the early fourth century, Rhamnus, Salamis,
and Piraeus; an inscription of the early fourth century, found near the deme
of Halai Aixonides, commemorates the performances of plays directed by
dramatic poets including Cratinus and Sophocles.[35]

   This epigraphic evidence corresponds with the literary evidence in Plato,
who says that some enthusiasts went round all the different Dionysia, and
avoided missing a single production;[36] in response, deme festival managers
tried to capitalise on theatre fever by ensuring that the different deme
shows did not coincide. Tragedy was also beginning to shake itself free
of the competitive performances at the festivals of Dionysus; by the late

---

[32] *PMG* 791.218–20.
[33] *IG* I³ 969; Stephanis 1988: no. 164; previously dated to the late fifth or the fourth century, this
    inscription is placed by Csapo: forthcoming in the 430s.
[34] An inscription on a column base dedicated by two *synchoregoi*, found at Eleusis (*IG* I³ 970), suggests
    in conjunction with the Dionysia victor list that Aristophanes and Sophocles were involved with a
    production at the rural Dionysia at Eleusis between 425 and 406 BC; see Csapo and Slater 1995: 129
    on *IG* I² 3090, and especially Csapo: forthcoming.
[35] *IG* II² 3091; I am very grateful to Eric Csapo for allowing me to see his Nellie Wallace lecture 3
    (forthcoming), to which I owe many of these references.
[36] Pl. *Republic* 5.475d.

420s tragic excerpts could be performed at the symposium, or even in the
lawcourts.[37] By 380 there were centres of theatrical activity elsewhere in
mainland Greece – at Corinth, the Isthmus, Eretria, and Phigaleia. Despite
its popularity in the Attic demes, tragedy had always been regarded as
less locally Athenian than comedy, since there was no tribal element in the
organisation of tragic competitions, at least beyond the selection of judges.[38]
And tragic plays had long been put on abroad if the local statesmen could
afford to commission one of the big Athenian playwrights to do a play
for them. Aeschylus had a relationship with the Sicilian tyrants, and his
plays were performed for Hieron of Syracuse – *Persians* with its Athenian
interest as well as *Women of Etna*.[39] Euripides occasionally wrote plays to
be performed away from Athens, such as his *Andromache* (probably written
for performance in honour of the King of the Molossians), even before he
and Agathon struck up with Archelaus of Macedon after the death of the
less culturally aspirant Perdiccas II (in 413 BC).[40]

There is also early fourth-century evidence for travelling actors who
could set up their stages in market-places, especially in Megale Hellas.[41]
Far more people could have access to theatrical productions: reactionary
males began to deplore the fact that women, children, and slaves by now
all had their opinions on tragedy, and were influenced by it.[42] The western
Greeks certainly adored vases with scenes related to Euripidean theatre;
this strongly implies that plays were being produced regularly, not only
around Heracleia in southern Italy by the end of the fifth century, but at
Taranto, Metapontum, and Catane.[43] The provenance of actors later in
the fourth century shows that this craze encouraged young western Greek
men to aspire to acting careers. And after 413 BC there was something newly
vigorous about the attempt of the Macedonian monarchy, which had strong
links with the god Dionysus, to attract major tragedians including Euripides
and Agathon northwards, where their plays were performed at Dion.[44]

THEORY

The export of tragedy coincided with its increasing theorisation. One sign
of this is the different relationships within which tragedy began to be
configured. Her natural next of kin was satyr drama, with which she was
invariably connected in the fifth-century imagination, but it may have been

---

[37] *Clouds* 1371–2; *Wasps* 579–80.   [38] R. Osborne (1993) 33.   [39] *Life of Aeschylus* 18.
[40] On *Andromache* see E. Hall 1989: 180–1 and nn. 70, 74; more generally, see Taplin 1999.
[41] See Taplin 1999: 38.   [42] Pl. *Laws* 7.817b–c.
[43] Taplin 1993: 19; Csapo: forthcoming.   [44] See Revermann 1999–2000; Maloney 2003.

becoming less obvious already by 380 that satyr plays belonged at the ends of groups of three tragedies; by mid-century this order of performance was abandoned at the Athenian Dionysia, and in its place a new order was introduced whereby a single satyr play was performed separately at the opening of the competitions.[45] Tragedy's relationship with comedy had always been close (although families never produced both tragic and comic poets),[46] but it was the fashion for comic parody of tragedy, probably not inaugurated until well into the Peloponnesian War, that started audiences thinking about the generic differences between the two, by creating humour out of the bathetic puncturing of elevated effects.[47] And it was comedy, apparently, that first encouraged the theatregoers to think diachronically about the evolution of tragedy from the earlier fifth century (i.e. from long before 430), and to contrast the registers adopted by Aeschylus and Euripides respectively. The appearance of Muse of Euripides in his *Frogs* (1305–8), a slattern with a talent for playing the castanets and fellatio, must have incarnated the difference between tragedy in the 450s and (Euripidean) tragedy by 405, which was felt to be sexy, downsized, more demotic, and above all more *approachable*.[48]

There is evidence from comedy in the first part of the fourth century that it continued to develop popular ideas about the formal distinctions between the two genres – for example, how they engineered plot closure.[49] But it was the collision of material from different genres in the Platonic dialogue that precipitated the development of ancient categories of genre in general.[50] And it was with *epic* that in educated circles, by 380, tragedy was perhaps most likely to be discussed – both were solemn types of festival performance designed to make people feel awe, fear, and vicarious grief.[51] Analysing tragedy and epic, and comparing the two, will have become easier once it became possible to purchase texts: even though Aristophanes was certainly exaggerating in his *Frogs* when he said that all the ordinary Athenians could now get access to books (52–4; 1105–18), books had by Plato's day become relatively easy (if expensive) to acquire, and were collected by cultured Athenians.[52]

---

[45] See the excellent discussion of Easterling 1997c: 214–16.   [46] Sutton 1987.

[47] Silk 1993.   [48] See E. Hall 2000: 409–10.

[49] See the famous fragment of the comedy *Poetry* by Antiphanes, in which it is complained that tragedians bring in a god in the machine when they have run out of ideas about how to wind up the plot (fr. 189 K-A).

[50] Nightingale 1995, Most 2000, P. Murray 2002.

[51] See e.g. Pl. *Republic* 10.598d 7–8; 607a 2–3, and the unnamed critics of tragedy whom Aristotle is answering in *Poetics* 25.

[52] Pl. *Apology* 26 d–e.

Such men would probably also have been aware that Plato himself had been developing his argument that all art which represents something – a painting or a sculpture just as much as a dramatic or epic poem – is somehow dangerous, on the ground that painters, and sculptors (like Iasus), as well as poets, do not have the opportunity and time to acquire complete knowledge of all the phenomena and dimensions of existence that they aspire to portray. It may even have been popularly understood that Plato was arguing that it was in the theatre, where men dressed as women and imitated undignified individuals, as well as encouraging spectators to weep and give vent to unmanly emotions, that depictions of things are both at their most false and at their most psychologically dangerous.[53] For the early fourth century was certainly an exciting time for the *discussion* of tragedy: it may even have been in the 380s that Plato began working on his *Phaedrus*, in which he addressed not only the emotional function but also the structure of the tragic genre. Indeed, this dialogue shows that the possibility had been raised that someone might claim he could teach the art of tragedy by virtue merely of his ability to compose speeches calculated to raise pity or fear or any other emotion; this possibility could then be dismissed with the rejoinder that tragic poets would despise anyone who thought that tragedy did not require fitting those speeches together so as to blend with one another and form a coherent whole (268c).

REPERTOIRE

Plato cites the three fifth-century tragedians in a way that demonstrates that they were all live cultural presences, and his dislike of tragedy seems focused on Euripides. But I suspect that audiences felt that Sophocles was, in his austere way, just as experimental; *Philoctetes* (409) is arguably the most avant-garde ancient tragedy, intellectually if not theatrically. Its minimalist setting is a polis-free desert island; there are no women, kin relationships, or deaths. Its *peripeteia* uniquely takes place entirely within an individual psyche (that of Neoptolemus). It was certainly unusual for Sophocles to prove that such a morally contemptible person as this play's Odysseus could have some of the right answers to ethical questions (ends can justify means), and full understanding of the play requires knowledge of Protagorean political theory.[54] But the poet explicitly associated with

---

[53] For an elegant summary of the issues involved in Plato's case against mimetic art, and especially the relationship of Homeric epic to the case as a whole, see P. Murray 1996: esp. 19–24.

[54] It is revealing that *Philoctetes* was chosen to accompany, in a double bill, the English première of Samuel Beckett's existential *Play* at the Old Vic in 1964. See Worth 2004: 274 and n. 15.

innovation was undoubtedly Euripides, whose popularity throughout the entire half-century in question seems to have increased with every production. The première of his *Orestes*, put on in 408 (a year before Iasus was hired to work on the Erechtheion), was perhaps the most talked-about theatrical event of the time – it was hilariously funny, nobody knew how the plot would turn out, and it worked incomparably well in performance.[55] It broke the dramatic illusion in iconoclastic and decidedly comic ways, for example at the point when Electra addressed the audience in the second person plural as 'you' in the absence of anybody else on stage, as if she were an Aristophanic protagonist (128).

In the last period of his career Euripides seems to have had access to a particularly brilliant *tragoidos* who could cope with both coloratura melody and high tessitura at the same time; accordingly, in *Orestes* he gave him a role in which he not only sang an aria in the role of Electra, but had to impersonate a barbarian eunuch who sang an elaborate high-pitched astrophic aria instead of a standard messenger speech. This may at first have seemed like one of Euripides' archaising complimentary responses to the exotic barbarians in Aeschylus, but the music was far too modern and Timothean for that impression to last long.[56] But best of all, the tension in the theatre was so great that the leading actor, Hegelochus, fluffed a line, saying that a polecat rather than calm had emerged from the storm, and instantly brought the house down (279); amazingly, the production seems to have reoriented itself, and the play promptly became perhaps the most popular tragedy in antiquity (other candidates were *Telephus* and *Medea*).[57]

It is worth thinking further about *Orestes*, since it demonstrates one technical feature which is relevant to the quest for an aesthetic – if not a cultural – revolution. In some of the spoken parts of this comedy, the metre edged closely towards sounding like the rapid resolved iambics which Euripides' audience were more used to hearing in comedy. Iambics were already the metre which most often occurred spontaneously in ancient Greek speech, which made them sound natural, according to Aristotle.[58] Resolved iambics simulated ordinary speech, which often had successive short syllables, even more closely than iambic trimeters already did. One of the few certainties about the changes over time in Euripidean drama is

[55] Evidence for all three of these critical reactions is to be found in the ancient hypothesis which says that the drama is one of the most successful on the stage, has a plot which occurs in no other author, and has a conclusion 'more of the comic type' (*to drama komikoteran echei tēn katastrophēn*).
[56] See E. Hall 2002b: 10 and n. 26.
[57] See Ar. *Frogs* 303 with Scholia *ad loc.*; Sannyrion fr. 8 and Strattis fr. 1.2–3 K-A.
[58] *Poetics* 1449a26; *Rhetoric* 3.1408b 33–5.

that his several *securely dateable* plays consistently increase the number of resolved iambic feet.[59] Although this certainly does not mean that we can use metrical resolution to provide dates for undated plays, since any particular individual play might for aesthetic reasons be written in a particular metrical tone, a broad overall pattern is apparent. If Iasus and Euegetes saw the première of Euripides' *Medea* as teenagers in 431 BC, they may not have noticed that only about 6 per cent of the iambic lines displayed resolution. It is unlikely that they were counting. Yet they will almost certainly have had a general apprehension that there was something freer and easier about the spoken rhythms of Euripides' plays by the time of *Orestes* (408 BC), in which the proportion of resolved long feet had skyrocketed to 40 per cent.[60] This accords with the model that sees greater naturalism of both acting styles and diction as a characteristic of the evolution of Greek tragedy, along with the greater complexity of the overlap between the tone and manner of comedy and tragedy.[61] The same went for the level of colloquialisms in *Orestes*, which was significantly higher than in any surviving tragedy witnessed before.[62]

There must have been many fans of Euripides who continued to insist, like Dionysus at the beginning of *Frogs*, that there could never again be a tragic dramatist to touch his brilliance, and that all those who succeeded him, including the briefly voguish Iophon, were insignificant chatterboxes in comparison. But most of these Euripides-lovers probably enjoyed the exciting plays of intrigue and pathos which seem to have been on offer in the theatre in the early fourth century, as well as the revivals of Euripides performed by ever more virtuoso actors. The best new plays probably included those by Antiphon the playwright (not to be confused with Antiphon the oligarch and/or Antiphon the sophist), who subsequently went to the court of the aspiring tragedian Dionysius, Tyrant of Syracuse, and was sentenced to a particularly unpleasant death for insouciance.[63] References in fourth-century authors suggest that Antiphon's *Jason* was popular, but his *Meleager* broke completely new ground in psychological subtlety; at any rate, it is for a delicate ethical point about interpersonal relationships that it is remembered by Aristotle. The play included a scene in which Plexippus reproached Meleager for failing to pick up a hint about what was expected of him, even though the hint was dropped by someone he was supposed to care about.[64]

---

[59] It was Zielinski (1925) who first noticed that Euripides' dated plays displayed an increasing proportion of resolved iambics.

[60] See the table in Ceadel 1941.   [61] Valakas 2002, Csapo 2002.

[62] Stevens 1976: 64–5.   [63] Arist. *Rhetoric* 2.6. 1385a9.

[64] 55 Antiphon F 1b *TgrF* = Arist. *Rhetoric* 2.2.19–20, 1379b13.

Aristotle implies that a good man should be able to intuit what a friend wants, and that only an insensitive man would expect the friend to ask for it directly. It is difficult to think of a fifth-century tragedy where psychological insensitivity to hints was a central issue!

Perhaps the most famous of Antiphon's psychological tragedies was, however, his *Andromache*. This demonstrated ethical delicacy by creating an episode in which Andromache tried to save Astyanax by having him adopted.[65] The fourth-century audience was used to seeing Andromache lament over Astyanax in both Euripides and his imitators,[66] but what they admired about Antiphon's play was the innovative subtlety of his characterisation of her maternal altruism. The play took care to discriminate her motivation in sending Astyanax away to be brought up by an adoptive mother: she was seen to be putting his needs above hers, indeed accepting that if it would save his life he must never know his mother's true identity.[67]

This fashion can be seen as an extension of the interest Euripides had already shown in the inner life of the nuclear family, especially the plight of young women thrown on their own resources. His *Ion* may have felt innovative at its première because it feels so *private*, so internal to an individual *oikos*. Regardless of the importance of Ion's ancestry to the Athenian myth of autochthony, of which much has recently been made, the dramatic narrative focuses on one married couple and their sexual histories: it is not any great war or international conflict that has caused the problem.[68] The occasion for the action is a domestic outing to a cult centre, anticipating the visit in Menander's *Old Cantankerous* of the entourage accompanying Sostratus' mother to the shrine of Pan on Mount Parnes. Every single mortal cast member is part of Creusa's household (even the partisan messenger), except the Pythian priestess who has played a crucial role in the family as Ion's adoptive mother. Creusa's astrophic monody achieves greater interiority, in its evocation of the 'recovered memory' of a teenager's trauma, than anything expressed even by victimised tragic heroines before: it is evidence of a newly intimate dramatic subjectivity. The private family life in that play, indeed, with its collusive ending and sexual secrets, on the

---

[65] Antiphon's play may have been one source for Ennius' influential republican Roman tragedy *Andromacha*.

[66] See e.g. *TgrF* adesp. fr. 644, an Oxford papyrus first edited by Lobel 1936.

[67] Arist. *Eudemean Ethics* 7.4.9, 1239a = *TgrF* 55 Antiphon F 1; see also the development of the same thought at *Nicomachean Ethics* 9.9.1159a 27, where the diction seems to be inspired by poetry (*dokei de en tōi philein mallon ē en tōi phileisthai einai* (sc. *hē philia*)). The example Aristotle provides is once again the selfless mother who hands over her children to others and does not expect to be loved back.

[68] For *Ion* as a public charter myth, see above all Loraux 1993.

extant evidence is a new departure, and one whose repercussions by 380 may already have begun to affect comedy as well as tragedy: raped maidens and foundlings were already creeping into the more light-hearted genre.

If either of our theatregoers was a high-minded old patriot, he might indeed have complained that tragedy was less political than it once was, that its focus had shifted from the glorification of the heroic mythical past (especially that which reflected well on Athens and democratic values) to the private life of traumatised maidens and mothers. He might well feel that contemporary tragedians were inclined to make their characters speak more rhetorically than politically, as Aristotle was by mid century to say that tragedians now (*hoi nun*) write speeches *rhetorikōs* rather than *politikōs*.[69] Yet the scraps of later fourth-century and Hellenistic tragedy themselves do not imply that political affairs were of less interest to tragedians – indeed, there seems to have been a revival of interest in the history play.[70] Tragedy did not become any less to do with the government of the polis, but it did become less Athenocentric in the sense that there are few signs of the type of play designed to elaborate specifically Athenian mythical history, or the aetiology of exclusively Athenian cults and civic institutions.[71] The sub-species of Athenian tragedy such as *Suppliant Women* and *Erechtheus* seems to disappear, and in his *Poetics* Aristotle (a non-Athenian) does not specify Theseus as one of his ideal tragic heroes, alongside the Argive Orestes and Thyestes, the Theban Oedipus, the Calydonian Alcmaeon, and the Tegean Telephus.[72]

Presumably, during the process by which tragedy metastasised over the entire Greek-speaking world, it became inappropriate for its content to be so explicitly designed to glorify Athens, create aetiologies for Attic cults, or validate Athens' right to govern other city-states (as *Eumenides* did, and *Heraclidae* and arguably Sophocles' *Oedipus at Colonus*). But there is no evidence that tragedy became less 'political' in a broader sense of the term; generally defined models of acceptable behaviour in leaders were universally dramatisable (except, perhaps, in Syracuse!), and could be made suitable for viewing in any city with almost any kind of constitution. Greeks will probably have agreed on what makes a good leader, almost regardless of the nature of their polity. Plato's Athenian in *Laws* regarded tragedy as an

---

[69] *Poetics* 1450b7; see also *Rhetoric* 1403b31–5. See Xanthakis-Karamanos 1979.

[70] See e.g. *TGrF* adesp. 685 (a papyrus fragment lamenting a Persian king), Theodectes' *Mausolus*, and the unidentified history play portrayed on the fourth-century 'Dareios vase' (Naples 3523); see also E. Hall 1996a: 8–9 with fig. 1. If I were to break – just once – my self-imposed ban on citing *Rhesus* in evidence, it would be to point out that its chorus is one of the stroppiest and most democratically inclined in Greek tragedy (see e.g. 10, 132).

[71] On which see e.g. J. Hall 1997: 100–3.   [72] *Poetics* 1453a17–22. E. Hall 1996b: 299–300.

effective form of political communication; he says that tragedians are rivals and competitors (*antitechnoi te kai antagonistai*) in presenting alternative and by no means equally proper representations of the polis; he therefore urges that tragedies should be scrutinised before they are granted permission to be performed (7.817b–c).

REVIVALS AND SPIN-OFFS

Perhaps the most important landmark in the history of tragedy between 430 and 380 was the institution in 387/386, during the archonship of Theodotus, of the revival of old tragedies at the Athenian Dionysia as a regular part of the festival programme.[73] There had been revivals of Aeschylus in Athens before, for example in 425 BC,[74] and a plausible case can be made that it was the energetic sons of famous playwrights who ensured that their works were re-performed, especially Aeschylus' son Euphorion, Sophocles' son Iophon, and Euripides' son Euripides;[75] indeed, the year before the actual revivals were instituted as a permanent feature, Sophocles the younger won the competition with his production. But Aeschylus was apparently not neglected in the fourth century, either: Plato quotes his *Niobe*, *Semele*, and *Award of Arms*, and the evidence of vase-painting suggests the revival of at least eight further Aeschylean plays.[76]

Pressure to introduce the revivals may also have come from the public, and more particularly from actors, who must have relished the opportunity to break free from contemporary playwrights. They could now build up a repertoire of famous roles contained in the old plays; newly independent from festivals which staged competitions in the productions of new works, they could tour with these celebrated roles to distant places if the pay was good enough. Cleandrus, the tragic actor who won the prize in the year that the annual revivals were added to the festival programme,[77] had been sighted in Leucas, which was on the route to Italy, as early as a few years after the Decelean War of 413 BC.[78] The impact of such actors on the texts of the plays must not be under-estimated. Revivals at this time, decades before the Lycurgan recension of tragedy, must often have presented an adapted version of the original play, beefed up by and for the star performer.[79] There is explicit evidence for the actor Theodorus demanding that the character he was playing as protagonist be given the prologue, on the ground that

[73] *IG* II² 2318.201–3.   [74] Ar. *Acharnians* 10.   [75] See Sutton 1987.
[76] Pl. *Republic.* 379e, 381d, 383b; Webster 1956: 31.   [77] *IG* II² 2318.199–200.
[78] [Dem.] *Against Euboulides* 13 (delivered c. 345 BC); see Csapo: forthcoming.
[79] Page 1934: 18; Dihle 1981.

audiences always sympathise most with the first voice that they hear;[80] in practice this must have meant that new and additional prologues needed to be created hastily and prefixed to favourites in the repertoire. This sort of thespian input explains why, for example, *Iphigenia in Aulis* has two prologues, a more drastic intervention in the text than the standard 'actor's interpolation' in the form of the addition of an extra simile, or a rhetorical question, to a monologue later in the play.

Another result of the institution of the revivals was new playwrights' practice of writing plays on themes which had been made familiar in established masterpieces. Thus in 363 the actor Androsthenes became the first named individual to play the role of Medea, as well as the role of Phaethon, in two new plays by Theodorides which must have borne a strong relationship to Euripides' two popular plays with the same titles.[81] There were certainly some scenes in plays which closely reworked Euripides' masterpieces without exactly copying.[82] One of the few tragic fragments of any length that *could* come from a play first performed between 400 and 380 is preserved on a papyrus (*TgrF adesp.* F 665 = PSI 1303), and shows that it covered the same story as Euripides' *Phoenician Women* (itself a text that shows a high degree of adaptation and editing in the interests of re-performance[83]). In the scene from which the fragment derives, Eteocles and Polynices confront one another in the presence of Jocasta, just as they do in Euripides' *Phoenissae* (446–637).[84]

But the author of the derivative version has made efforts to make the relationship between Jocasta and her sons more intense and perhaps more believable. With maternal authority she demands that they both hand over their swords, and she retains them throughout the argument. She also makes Polynices promise to abide by her decision, as if the future of the Theban dynasty would be decided by a hothead's promise to his mother. The fratricides plunge into a brawl in snappy, vituperative stichomythia, a more informal way to open their debate scene than the symbouleutic orations with which the equivalent dialogue commences in the Euripidean *Phoenician Women*. The later play also deploys new vocabulary in order to enliven the language, for example the term *merizein to diadema*, 'to share the tiara' (fr. adesp. 665.14 *TgrF*), in the sense of 'to split up the Theban

---

[80] Arist. *Poetics* 7.1336b27–31.   [81] Stephanis 1988: no. 182.

[82] For the process, see e.g. the Hellenistic hypothesis to Aeschylus' *Persians*, a play reported to have been modelled on (*parapepoiesthai*) the *Phoenissae* of Phrynichus. Although the term can have pejorative connotations, it usually means 'to alter slightly' (Paus. 5.10.1) or 'to copy with alterations' (Ath. *Deipnosophistai* 12.513a).

[83] See Mastronarde 1994: 39–49.

[84] There is an English translation in Page's edition, 1942: 172–81.

kingdom'. The author could have been a contemporary of Xenophon, who refers to the Persian king's tiara as *to diadema* in his *Cyropaedia* (e.g. 8.3.13), a work usually dated to c. 380 BC.

Theatregoers in the 380s will also have been struck by the degree to which the comic poets had come to depend on the plays of the tragedians. There were ever more theatrical burlesques of the type of story the tragedians told (a sub-genre of humorous theatre that Plato the comic poet, following Cratinus, had developed), in addition to extended and detailed parodies of particular tragedies, in the tradition of Aristophanes' assault on Euripides' *Aeolus* in *Aeolosicon*. But since it is possible to date the earliest plays of the prolific comic dramatist Eubulus to as early as the 370s,[85] by 380 rumours may have been circulating about a precocious youth who knew Euripides virtually off by heart, and could make people laugh at his travesties of Euripides: certainly as an adult he wrote burlesques of such popular tragedies as *Ion*, *Auge*, and *Antiope*. Although Euripides could write grim tragedy until the very end of his life, if that is when he composed *Iphigenia in Aulis* and *Bacchae* (first performed 405 BC), in the late fifth century it may already have been felt that it was increasingly difficult to distinguish the rightful parameters of tragedy from those of comedy; *Helen* (412) is arguably more a comedy than a tragicomedy. It is aimed more consistently at producing laughter than has generally been appreciated. It was also at about that time that Agathon wrote an experimental tragedy, *Antheus*, in which all the characters were invented figures, like those in comedy, rather than the conventional tragic cast of figures familiar from myth.[86]

ACTORS

When Iasus and Euegetes were young, the great actors were men like Andron, a prizewinner at the Dionysia.[87] The superb Tlepolemos, Sophocles' favourite actor for several years,[88] may have been the first person to realise some of the most famous roles in world theatre. Oeagrus was a moving Niobe and a favourite of the type of citizen represented by Aristophanes' Philocleon.[89] These actors could squeeze huge emotion just from their posture, or silence, or the contrast between their controlled speech and their laments. But the professionalisation of acting and the emergence of superstars began during the first ten years of the war with Sparta, after which the protagonists' roles became increasingly dominant. It was during

---

[85] R. L. Hunter 1983: 7–10.   [86] Arist. *Poetics* 1451b 19–21.   [87] *IG* ii[2] 2325.
[88] *Clouds* 1266.   [89] *Wasps* 579–80.

that period that an actor's prize was added to the proceedings at the Lenaea.[90] The poetry delivered by these actors also became subtly more intricate and decorative, in a way that Iasus may have felt found a parallel in similar developments in sculpture: the elaborate detail on the reliefs of Nikai on the Acropolis Temple of Athena Nike (c. 420 BC) has reminded several scholars of the increasingly virtuosic and expressive roles sought out by the best actors of the time.[91] The flowing drapery, so fluid it almost looks as though it is wet and adhering here and there to the skin beneath, is indeed reminiscent of the delicate, repetitive, but asymmetrical, free-flowing lyric diction in the New Music. Sculpture and dramatic poetry, as well as its delivery, became simultaneously more dynamic and realistic while evincing a more luxuriant and self-conscious sense of being artistic and theatrical. These trends are manifested in the fluid drapery on the Erechthion caryatids as much as the lyrics of the Euripidean Electra and her chorus.[92]

Such elaboration is also evident in many iambic fragments of the fourth-century tragedians, especially in messenger narratives, favourites of virtuoso star actors.[93] An illuminating example is what happens to the familiar comparison of a female figure with a statue or a painting, an *agalma* or a *graphē*, in Euripides. Most of these are simple similes expressed in no more than two iambic lines; the most elaborate, in Euripides' *Helen*, entails the heroine saying, 'I wish that I could wash off my beautiful appearance, like paint off a beautiful statue, and replace it with an ugly one' (262–3).[94] But such analogies, typically, by the mid fourth century, were being elaborated in much more extended figures. In Chaeremon's *Oineus* an actor had to sustain over seventeen lines an ecphrasis which described an entire maenadic scene in which several figures in succession are compared with figures in a painting.[95]

---

[90] Probably in around 432, but at any rate by 423 BC. The precise date depends on reconciling the evidence from several inscriptions, for a discussion of which see Csapo and Slater 1995: 227–8.

[91] See Pollitt 1972: 111–35, with Valakas 2002: 84.

[92] On the innovative diction of *Electra* see especially Csapo 2003: 71–8.

[93] See J. R. Green 1999: 53–4; Easterling 2002: 38.

[94] See Zeitlin 1994; E. Hall 2006: ch. 4.

[95] 'One was lying in the pale moonlight, her shoulder strap relaxed to disclose her breast; another girl's left flank was loosened to view as she danced; naked to the sight of the sky, she looked like a living picture (*zosan graphen ephaine*), while the colour of her skin, white to the eyes, gave off a radiance which contrasted with the effect of the dark shadows . . . and the crocus imprinted on the woven texture of their robes was a sun-like image of shadow (*skias eidolon*).' See also 71 Chaeremon fr. 1, from his *Alphesiboia*, a complicated comparison with a waxwork. These figures anticipate the Hellenistic taste for intricate ecphraseis, on which see Manakidou 1993.

The most important actor during our theatregoers' lifetimes was probably Nicostratus. He and Callipides were virtually synonymous with the genre and were perceived as having brought tragedy to its acme.[96] Nicostratus was still winning at the Dionysia in 399 BC, and he won the Lenaea at least thrice.[97] What spectators remembered was the way he could reduce them to tears simply by a particular trick with tetrameters when he recited them to the accompaniment of the *aulos*,[98] and above all his superb delivery of messenger speeches.[99] Some theatregoers by 380, especially in the revivals of old favourites, may have felt that some of the new actors were becoming a little *too* obsessed with their own delivery at the expense of the content of their speeches; there were certainly grumbles by the time Aristotle wrote his *Rhetoric* that the actors had actually become more important than the poets, just as the rhetors with flashy delivery styles were more likely to win political debates than those with the commanding arguments.[100]

If Euegetes was conservative in taste, he would have disliked Callipides, Nicostratus' contemporary. Although he was the most lively and emotive of tragic actors, Callipides' innovative style went to extremes. He was outstandingly popular at Athens, winning at the Lenaea no fewer than five times, and he was remembered for his acting in Callistratus' *Amphilochus* and *Ixion*.[101] He made a particular impact in the evergreen role of Euripides' Telephus, who himself had to impersonate, in the course of the play, a hero temporarily hired as a lower-class porter. Callipides was an exceptional mimic, and enjoyed imitating the gestures of all social types, including the movements of 'low-grade' women.[102] Such an acting style lent itself to comic comment, and it is little surprise that Aristophanes made a comic actor impersonate Callipides' histrionic excesses in his *Women Pitching Tents* (fr. 490 K-A), while Strattis named a whole comedy *Callipides*. Yet Callipides was only doing what many in the tragic audience wanted. The same mimic element could be seen in the voice many tragic actors used, in their quest to effect exact pitch and rhythm.[103] Even the auletes who accompanied the choruses were beginning to move in ways that imitated the subject about which their chorus was singing.[104] Actors risked derision if they clung to the old-fashioned exaggerated type of vocal delivery, which aimed at volume and depth (the derisive term used was *barustonos*), rather than subtle affective modulation.[105]

---

[96] Phld. *Rhetoric* 1.197.   [97] *IG* II² 2318.164; 2325.253.   [98] Xen. *Symposium* 6.3.
[99] Zen. 1.42.   [100] Arist. *Rhetoric* 3.1403b 24–30.   [101] *IG* II² 2325.253; 2319.82–3.
[102] *Poetics* 1461b26–1462a14, with Csapo 2002.   [103] Pl. *Republic* 3.397a–c; Csapo 2002: 138.
[104] Arist. *Poetics* 1461b30–2.
[105] See Page 1934: 16 (in reference to Aeschines and Simulus). On the cultural importance of the actor's voice in the fourth century, see above all Easterling 1999: 157–62.

It cannot have been long after 380 that the man who subsequently became probably the most famous actor of all antiquity began his illustrious career. Theodorus of Athens, incomparable in the roles of Sophoclean and Euripidean heroines, was already wealthy enough by 362 to make a large contribution to the rebuilding of the temple of Apollo at Delphi.[106] Later in his professional life he seems to have visited the island of Thasos, for a remarkable choregic monument in the Thasian sanctuary of Dionysus celebrates his performance in the tragic role of a blind old man. The role is represented on a mask originally held by a statue allegorically representing Tragedy. She stood on a semicircular arc behind a Doric portico, alongside Dionysus, Comedy, and two others. Beneath the statues were the accompanying inscriptions: 'Tragedy, Theodorus acted; Comedy, Philemon acted; Dithyramb, Ariston of Miletus played the aulos; Nycterinus, Batalus played the aulos.'[107] From the perspective of this volume the significant feature is the conceptualisation of Tragedy as a statuesque and dignified female, identified with a famous actor and a melancholy role. In 430 BC *Tragoidia* had still been conceived as a cheerful maenad, the companion of boisterous satyrs. Here she has not only divorced herself from the wild thiasos, left Athens, and metamorphosed into a stately matron, but is inseparable from the man who performed her. Tragedy has come to be identified less with the poet than with the actor who could carry his masks to every polis that could accommodate his performance.[108]

CULTURAL REVOLUTION?

During the period 430–380 BC, tragic theatre was undeniably a growth industry, and the content of plays was subject to innovation, modification, and an increase in finely tuned nuances in poetic effect and sensibility. Whether this picture justifies the use of the term 'revolution' must, however, be open to question. It is self-evident that the journey undertaken by tragic drama over the half-century under examination does not support the term 'cultural revolution' in the sense of its original usage; this appears to have been an English rendering of part of the Chinese label given to the consciously engineered ideological campaign of 1966–76, the Great Proletarian Cultural Revolution, which arose out of Mao Zedong's

---

[106] *IG* II² 2325.262; *IG* II² 2325.31. See Stephanis 1988: no. 1157. On Theodorus in Euripides see Plut. *Pelopidas* 29.4–6; Aelian *Miscellany* 14.40; Lada-Richards 2002: 414–15; E. Hall 2002a: 421–3. For his Sophoclean roles, see Plut. *Symposium* 9.2.737b; Dem. 19.246.

[107] See Devambez 1941, Salviat 1979, Grandjean and Salviat 2000: 92–4 with figs. 45–8.

[108] E. Hall 2007.

Socialist Education Movement (1962–5). Nor does the evidence for the changes in tragic drama validate the use of the term 'cultural revolution' as it swiftly came to be deployed in the late 1960s, in reference to the shifts in Western taste and ideology inaugurated in those years, above all massive secularisation.[109] But the term 'cultural revolution' is now in common use to describe, retrospectively, many instances of change – the religious impact of Christianity on the Roman Empire, the socio-economic impact of the invention of the printing press, or the political impact of Fascism on art and literature.[110] None of these phenomena provides, however, a useful equivalent to the changes in the nature or consumption of tragic drama in the period 430–380 BC.

Yet the most familiar contemporary use of the term 'cultural revolution' alludes to the impact of the internet,[111] which, although stemming (like printing) from a technological breakthrough, almost instantly produced wholesale changes in political practices, personal relationships, the construction of identity, civic self-sufficiency, education, sport, recreation, entertainment, and the conduct of business and commerce. It is the single most important factor in the globalisation (and massive personal fortunes) of celebrities, as of pressure groups, ideas, beliefs, information, reference tools, news agencies, markets, commodities, and access to them. That is, it is the single most important factor in the emergence of a cultural and commercial *koinē* expressed in the (American) English language, but which can appeal across numerous and diverse types of society and political constitution in the subsistence economies of the Third World as much as the advanced capitalism of the First. Indeed, some of the features that characterise this most recent of phenomena to be described as a 'cultural revolution' make it an unexpectedly illuminating comparand when it comes to what happened to tragedy between 430 and 380 BC: namely, the emergence of wealthy star professionals, rapid expansion of access to theatre, both locally in Attica in deme theatres and across the social spectrum, internationalisation, commodification of an internationally recognised repertoire of 'classic' favourites, and emergence of a 'product' that could appeal in a great variety of venues in inherently different types of political culture, provided that the audiences could speak Greek. Indeed, it is possible to argue that it was

---

[109] On the 'cultural revolution' of the 1960s, see Marwick 1998; on secularisation at that time, C. G. Brown 2001; on the arts, E. Hall 2004.

[110] For Christianity as 'cultural revolution' at Rome, see Kreis 2001. For Gutenberg's press, see e.g. J. M. Bloom 1999; for Fascism, see B. C. Anderson 2000.

[111] See e.g. Batelle 1996, Waldera 2001.

theatre that determined the importance of the Attic dialect to the emergent
Hellenistic Greek *koinē*.

If the term 'cultural revolution' is understood in its most recent application, therefore, perhaps the citizens of ancient Aegean and southern Italy
did perceive the changes in their public world of entertainment as such, in
so far as these changes shared some features with what people today may
feel is happening to global culture since the arrival of the internet. Being
able to download Ridley Scott's *Gladiator* (2000) in a peasant community
in Uzbekistan may not, ultimately, feel so dissimilar from welcoming a star
Athenian *tragoidos* performing *Antigone* in a remote rural deme or on a
makeshift stage erected in a marketplace in the uplands of Megale Hellas
in 380 BC. The technologies by which movies are transmitted around the
world have altered beyond recognition over the last fifty years, above all in
the invention of the video recorder, long before the internet. Films which
used to be watched solely in First World cinemas have now become part of
a cultural *koinē* and commodity on a global scale.

Yet *Gladiator*, despite the invention of digital special effects, fundamentally differs little from Stanley Kubrick's *Spartacus*, made four decades previously in 1960 (just before the modern West's own first 'cultural revolution'
during the 'Swinging Sixties'). *Gladiator*, just like *Spartacus*, is a fundamentally realist action-packed linear narrative recounting the deeds of a moral
hero-cum-gladiator fighting tyranny at Rome; it features a decadent ruler,
a heterosexual love relationship, a revenge theme, and a sad but uplift-
ing ending. Similarly, the plays watched by ancient Greeks in 430 and in
380 BC, despite some technological developments in scenery design and
stage machinery,[112] were almost identical if subjected to *any* formal crite-
rion of theatrical analysis. They offer an excellent example of the capacity
of artistic forms to lag behind economic and political developments – of
the 'relative autonomy' of art in relation to its material and social infras-
tructure. Tragedies were still verse dramas in predominantly Attic Greek
about families in the mythical past, which aimed at arousing pity and
fear, and were designed (at least for their premières) to be performed by
three masked actors, a masked chorus, and an aulos-player, all gorgeously
attired. Even if their local focus on Attic cults had diminished, their religion and metaphysics were fundamentally unaltered. They continued to use

---

[112] There has been insufficient space in this chapter for a survey of possible developments in stage
technology during this period (that this was a lively area of innovation is suggested by e.g.
the apparent allusion to the revolving *periaktoi*, or devices displaying alternative background
scene paintings, in Pl. *Republic* 7.518c). For the controversies surrounding the crane, see
Mastronarde 1990.

conventional elements (e.g. prologue, debate scene, and messenger speech in iambics; choral lyric; theophany). By 380 BC, the venues, audiences, and cosmopolitan outlook that tragedy embodied, if they had not been revolutionised, had certainly been subject to drastic change; but the form and content of tragedy, as well as the sensibility it expressed, had altered only in small degrees.

CHAPTER 12

The sound of mousikē: reflections on aural change in ancient Greece

Armand D'Angour

The musical developments that took place in Greece in the late fifth century BC have been characterised, in both ancient and modern times, as 'revolutionary'. The evidence for specific technical developments associated with the progressive musical practices of the period includes some tenuous indications of a new approach to sung music. Euripides in particular may have championed a new musical style which involved the wholesale divorce of melody from the natural pitch contours of Greek speech.[1] Such a change would have been felt as peculiarly disturbing, in that it created an aural disjunction between the inherent and arguably the most fitting (*prepon*) melic interpretation of a poetic passage and its actual performance. But musical innovation of any kind could be justified by appeal to the age-old presumption that novelty in music (or, more accurately, in *mousikē*) was something to be striven for and applauded. While an explicitly positive attitude towards the new is unusual in Greek culture generally, it was apparently sanctioned in the case of *mousikē*: 'Praise old wine, but the bouquet of songs that are new,' Pindar gnomically remarks (*Olympian Odes* 9.53). Such favourable attitudes could be, and were, bolstered by the Homeric verses put into the mouth of Telemachus in the first book of the Odyssey (1.351–2): τὴν γὰρ ἀοιδὴν μᾶλλον ἐπικλείουσ' ἄνθρωποι | ἥ τις ἀκουόντεσσι νεωτάτη ἀμφιπέληται – 'people most applaud the song that comes around most new to those listening'.[2]

While various elements, social and technical, may be identified as contributing to the sense of revolutionary change in music, one of the more intractable problems faced by scholars is to try to identify how the *sound* of ancient music might have changed in practice. A clearer appreciation of the aural dimension of ancient musical experience might help us understand better the criticisms of conservative commentators such as Plato and

[1] Ways in which such a characterisation might be substantiated are proposed in D'Angour 2006.
[2] The verses are cited by a scholiast in relation to Pindar's dictum at *Olympian Odes* 9.63.

Aristoxenus, in practical and musicological terms as well as from sociological and psychological perspectives.[3] The Homeric verses cited above are clearly intended to refer to the narrative content of epic singing (*aoidē*) rather than, or at least in conjunction with, its melodic form. But when Plato introduces these verses into a discussion of the so-called New Music (which he will first have encountered in his youth), he does so in a slightly variant version.[4] The Platonic text replaces *akouontessi* (listeners) with *aeidontessi* (singers), so that the novelty of the music is refocused from the perspective of the composer or performer rather than from that of the audience. This change of perspective has important consequences, given that the kind of musical innovation entertained by a specialist and practitioner may involve considerations crucially different from what comes across as novel to a listener. On the whole, in Plato's view, the audience should be content with a limited kind of musical innovation – 'a new song rather than a new kind (*tropos*) of sung music'.[5] But simply changing the lyrics, as it were, was far from sufficient for the creative practitioners of the age, who sought to extend the bounds of their *technē* to such a degree that, in Plato's view, they perverted the essential nature of *mousikē* in a dangerous and socially subversive fashion: 'styles of music are never altered without the drastic consequences for the regulation of society'.[6]

THE SOUND OF CHANGE

How, then, did such musical change and innovation actually impinge on the aural experience of audiences and listeners in ancient Greece? Such a question invites broader reflections on how the changing sound of music, and indeed other familiar elements of the 'sound world' (including the spoken word), are felt to be an integral element of cultural change. The aural dimension of life is a characteristic component of any particular age and time; a complex matrix of auditory elements, of which music is a particular and perhaps a salient ingredient, may seem to define an era. 'Music' nowadays tends to encompass both formal traditions of musical composition and performance comprising roughly five centuries of Western classical music, as well as recent popular manifestations such as the multiple varieties of jazz, pop, and world music. In the case of classical music, there

---

[3] Csapo 2004 gives a brilliant survey of the social and political dimensions of the New Music, to which this discussion is indebted.
[4] Pl. *Republic* 424bc.   [5] Pl. *Republic* 424bc; cf. *Laws* 665c.
[6] This view is attributed to the musician-sophist Damon of Oa, evidence for whose career is reconsidered by Wallace 2004.

exists a generally accepted periodisation of musical styles – Renaissance, Baroque, classical, Romantic, expressionist etc. – which may be mapped on to similar historical expressions in the visual arts. Such categories reflect at some level changes (not necessarily simultaneous) in the institutions and practices of the societies in which such music is composed and performed.[7] Thus, for example, the orderly architecture of J. S. Bach's great church music seems to harmonise with the kinds of religious and architectural orders that characterise the era in which he composed, while the *Sturm und Drang* of late Beethoven tallies with the political upheavals and revolutionary turmoil of the early nineteenth century. The lyrical expressiveness of Romantic music is apt for an age noted for its espousal of sentimentality and self-expression. The atonal experiments of the second Viennese School (Schoenberg, Webern, *et al.*) seem to herald an emerging age of *Angst* and alienation, while the jagged chords of Stravinsky's *Rite of Spring* evoke a sense of the barbarism and relentless mechanisation of the early twentieth century.

In the case of all the above, composers and highly trained performers have pushed forward the boundaries of the traditional domain of musical style and compositional technique. The new styles of music, despite often striking the listening public at first as unnatural and rebarbative, soon enter the ears and minds of a new generation, and help to define for them and for succeeding generations a new aural *Zeitgeist*, an auditory spirit of the age. The way such auditory developments reflect and interact with technical progress, as well as with changing social structures and mores, is an immensely complex topic with widespread philosophical and historical ramifications. To take one example, one may think of the rapid evolution in the course of the so-called 'democratic' twentieth century of the vast new musical stream of popular and populist musical styles, in parallel with – but soon far outstripping in terms of demographic appeal – the continuing performance and composition of classical music. The different strands of popular music have developed their own compositional and performance conventions, drawing on elements from the classical tradition of Western music and combining them with new elements from the worlds of folk entertainment, popular dance, and, in the case of jazz and blues, Afro-American slave song. This very description is reminiscent of Aristophanes'

---

7 Modern historians often detect a time-lag between artistic movements e.g. classicism, Romanticism, and social change, with artistic developments usually seen (in retrospect) as precursors to socio-political change. A similar case might be made for ancient music, but our sources are insufficiently detailed as regards chronology. The career of Timotheus, viewed as the peak of the New Music, coincided with, rather than preceded, the Peloponnesian War; but as I argue in D'Angour 2006, the seeds of musical 'revolution' were sown by the theorists and performers of preceding generations.

(humorously exaggerated) characterisation of Euripidean lyrics as a *mélange* of genres, low and high: 'This fellow gathers his honey promiscuously, from whores' songs, Meletus' drinking-songs, Carian pipings, dirges and dance-tunes.'[8] Each successive stage of musical development can come to encapsulate the spirit of an age or decade – though increasingly these succeeding periods seem to be measured in years rather than decades. In the English-speaking world, for instance, one may tick off the decades of the twentieth century with reference to twenties dance-hall music, thirties jazz, forties crooners, fifties rock'n'roll, and then of course, the advent *à la* Larkin of 'sexual intercourse . . . in 1963, between the end of the Chatterley ban and the Beatles' first LP'. Each of these types of music could be (and probably has been) incorporated into the soundtrack of a period drama or historical film to evoke unmistakeably a sense of the particular age in question.

CONTEXTS OF LISTENING

A further, intrinsic, feature of this evolution in the modern age is the way mass media and new technologies of communication have served to disseminate musical and aural experiences to new and increasingly vast global audiences, while allowing for an increasing diversification of styles and tastes. This is evident in another example of the kind of auditory phenomenon that seems to define an age and an ethos, that of the accent of spoken English. The clipped tones of BBC newsreaders broadcasting on the radio, or rather the 'wireless', in the 1940s and '50s, are instantly recognisable, and familiar enough to call forth potentially nostalgic memories in the older generation or alternatively to constitute amusing caricatures for younger listeners. The introduction of broadcasters with regional accents was still a matter of contention in the 1970s, since when widely different vernaculars (including pseudo-transatlantic accents and so-called 'estuary' English) have become common across the proliferating audiovisual media networks.[9] The debate over BBC English pronunciation largely related to the shifting class structures and the status associations of accent in British society. It is an interesting reflection on the way auditory phenomena can help to define an era that one might be able to identify the date of a radio

---

[8] Ar. *Frogs* 1301–3; on the mixing of genres cf. Pl. *Laws* 700d.
[9] 'Estuary English' is a term originally coined by linguist David Rosewarne in 1984 to describe popular forms and accents of English spoken around the river Thames and its estuary, subsequently defined as 'a mixture of non-regional and local south-eastern English pronunciation and intonation' (Rosewarne 1994).

news broadcast as much from the accents and tones of the newsreader as from what he or she says.

A related consideration is the development of new contexts and arenas for the presentation and communication of spoken and sung words, and for the reception of auditory phenomena in general – undifferentiated 'noise' as well as sound. Until the nineteenth century, for instance, there were few public buildings specifically dedicated to regular mass entertainment other than a few popular theatres. Opera houses and concert halls were the preserve of an elite, whereas in the twentieth century such venues, in addition to cinemas, discotheques, pop stadia and other auditoria, emerged as arenas for new kinds of public entertainment. More significantly, the growing world of sound has been increasingly diffused via radio, television, the internet, and the MP3 player into the private space of the home. Indeed, one of the features of modern auditory experience is its sheer ubiquity, the barrage of sound to which people are constantly exposed, whether in the form of piped background music that accompanies the mundane activities of daily life, or in the selected soundtracks made available as a result of the historically unprecedented access to broadcast and recorded sound on a wide variety of media. So when one thinks of the ways an era or decade might assume a particular character through *what* is heard, one must also consider *how* and in what context the heard material is communicated and performed, and the media whereby it is disseminated to listeners.

These contextual aspects have often served to indicate various specific functions fulfilled by music, song, and speech; whether they are, for instance, essentially religious in nature, or ceremonial, or celebratory, or whether intended to entertain, to instruct, or to inform. Innovation of one sort can seem to arise when there is deliberate or unconscious blurring of such functional boundaries. In the seventeenth century, for instance, the *sonata da chiesa*, a musical structure associated with church liturgy, was extended to become the basis of the familiar sonata form used in secular instrumental and symphonic music. Conversely, the rich polyphony of secular instrumental music was appropriated by composers such as Palestrina for use in religious contexts – a practice that at the time attracted the Church's disapproval on the grounds that this so-called *musica nova* was aimed at inducing earthly pleasure and unsuitable to a context of worship.[10] In the early twenty-first century, the latest pop tunes are digitally processed for downloading on to listeners' iPods, and lucratively repackaged as the ubiquitous ringtones of mobile phones.

[10] See e.g. Fellerer 1953.

THE MUSIC OF WORDS

In the ancient Greek world, sung music was an integral part of the lives of many Greeks in both public and private contexts, in festal, religious, and sympotic occasions. But what idea can we form of the 'sound world' that would have pervaded Greek life at different periods, or of the way that aural dimension may have altered over the course of a century or even a decade? The investigation of musical experience invites diverse avenues of study. One could, for instance, explore the development of musical instruments, and the changing use and composition of choruses; one might consider the growth of new venues for public communication and entertainment, such as the construction of the Odeion at Athens and of theatres around the Greek world; one might try to assess the impact of the introduction of foreign cult ceremonies and practices into Greece, featuring the kind of ecstatic Asiatic music which could be grafted on to the worship of Dionysus. One could broaden the investigation into the area of noise, by asking how new kinds of building and construction such as that of temples and theatres, or methods of transport such as ships and racing-chariots, or advances in mining, manufacture, and metalwork, contributed new elements of auditory experience – on the lines of the study of 'pandemonium', a term that has been used to characterise the unprecedentedly high level of noise experienced by the beneficiaries and victims of the machine age.[11] Here I will only try to pinpoint some particular aspects of cultural change in this respect. My focus will be on the evidence available for the music of dithyrambs and dramatic performances in Athens, whence we may perhaps glean an indication of how the aural reception of these genres changed or shifted in the course of the fifth century.

There is a case for suggesting that the auditory dimension in the ancient Greek world would have been an even more defining element of cultural experience, and therefore of a sense of cultural change, than it is in the modern world. This is not just because of the much-studied question of the predominance of oral communication and performance over the written word. It is also because *mousikē* in archaic and classical times was, as Havelock famously emphasised, much more intertwined with words and with discursive meaning than 'music' tends to be for us, and because it overwhelmingly represented collective rather than private experience.[12] Moreover, there was some kind of continuum, at least until the mid fifth

[11] Jennings 1985. Noise and bustle are graphically evoked by Plutarch's description of the Periclean building programme (*Pericles* 12.6).
[12] Havelock 1963; Ford 2003: 16–17 reasserts the former's important insight.

century, of the rhythmic and melodic structures employed in public events such as dithyrambic performances in the theatre, and those used in more informal settings such as symposia. To hear music invariably meant to hear words in rhythm accompanied by melody. If we are to credit the lengthy philosophical debates about *ēthos*, the nature of the melody and in particular its mode or *harmonia* seemed to retain, even in the absence of words, something of the character of the words to which it was set, or to which it might be most fittingly applied.[13] Equally, because the words of spoken Greek themselves had a natural music in their pitch inflections, the difference between, say, Homeric *aoidē* and rhapsodic recitation may not have been as great as is sometimes assumed; less great, for instance, than the difference between a song and a declamation would be today.[14] The grammarian Diomedes, long after the fifth century, advised those who wished to read ancient dramatic lyric to try to do so musically (*emmelōs*) even if, he said, they did not know the correct melody.[15] This surely implies that a native reader of Greek drama would, even in his time, have had some natural sense about how to melodise the words. This melodisation would most easily have been related to pitch accents, in the same way that rhythm could be directly related to syllabic length.

In Aristophanes' *Clouds* (1353ff.), when Strepsiades asks his son Pheidippides to sing a named *epinikion* by Simonides, 'How the ram was shorn', the implicit assumption is that as a well-educated young man he will at least be competent, even if reluctant, to pick up his lyre and sing a familiar piece of music to an identifiable or appropriate melody. The likelihood that this would be a recognisable tune with a fixed sequence of notes is very remote. There would have been no notated text to preserve something like a musical score which Pheidippides might follow, or from which he would have learned the music.[16] His familiarity with the song would have arisen from hearing it repeatedly sung on such occasions by others, and from having learned at home or school the musical techniques to allow him to re-perform it in a recognisable version, rather than as any kind of replica of what Simonides himself would have composed and sung. These musical techniques, I have previously argued, would most likely have involved the application of the correct mode and appropriate genera to the verses

---

[13] W. D. Anderson 1966.

[14] Some unusual accents preserved by Alexandrian scholars were conventionally used in rhapsodic recitations, and may have been fossilised indications of musical pitch: see West 1981: 114.

[15] Diom. Gram. ap. Dion. Thrax 6.2.8–11 Uhlig; E. Hall 1999a: 98.

[16] There is no evidence for the development of musical notation until the fourth century, and even then the ability to read it would have been confined to a small group of experts; Aristoxenus (2.39–41) is dismissive of its usefulness.

of poetry, making any subsequent rendition at least partly improvisational within these bounds.[17]

It may be helpful to suggest a parallel with traditions of Koranic recitation in the Muslim world. An Islamic reciter (*qâri*'), if asked to recite a passage of the Koran on different occasions, will aim to do so in a correct way each time, but each recitation will be different. Reciters work within a set of rules for the cantillation of the verses of the Koran, rather than singing them to a fixed tune.[18] Some such flexibility seems inevitable in the context of the oral transmission of music. We could perhaps compare Strepsiades' request to asking someone who has learned the piano to play and sing a well-known theme tune or popular song. It might be expected that such a rendering would more or less reproduce the rhythm and shape of the tune, and one would certainly hope that the basic key structure and melody would be recognisable even if the harmonies were sketchy. But it is instructive to note where this parallel breaks down: a conscientious modern performer would be trying as far as possible to retrieve the precise form of a remembered original, whereas the notion of such musical precision is out of place in a world of oral song-transmission. Melodic replication could be no more expected than verbatim precision in the citation of an ancient poetic text – a flexibility instantiated by the variant Platonic quotation of the Homeric verses cited above.

EURIPIDES V. AESCHYLUS

Pheidippides' objection to Strepsiades is not that the poetry of Simonides is old-fashioned, but that singing to the lyre is *passé* (*archaion*); 'like an old woman shelling barley', he retorts disdainfully (1358). The image this conjures up is the repetitive manual action that would accompany the singing (in either context), but it also suggests that the sound of the music itself would be felt to be simple and repetitive – the sort of chanting that one would expect to accompany a repetitive action of any kind. On similar lines, in Aristophanes' *Frogs* (1297) Aeschylean lyrics are compared in their monotony to *himoniostrophou melē*, 'rope-winders' songs' (i.e. work songs with a repetitive refrain). Instead of singing a respectable Aeschylean lyric, Pheidippides chooses to declaim an ethically dubious *rhēsis* from Euripides, a choice that might be compared to someone turning down a request

[17] D'Angour 2006: 278–80.
[18] Al Faruqi 1987: 7: 'Qur'ânic recitation is a solo vocal genre of improvisatory, free-rhythmed style. Each recitation is a unique event since no qâri' seeks to imitate or repeat an earlier recitation of his own or any other reciter.'

for a Schubert *Lied* in favour of a rap song by Eminem. While we should probably imagine a *rhēsis* to be rendered in a more musically heightened fashion than ordinary speech, it may be significant that Pheidippides does not choose a Euripidean lyric passage to sing. What we know about Euripidean lyric melodies suggests that they would have been sung to the kind of music that could not lend itself to easy repetition by an educated amateur trained in the traditional style of *mousikē*. The story of the Athenian prisoners in Syracuse in 413 BC who were able to save their lives by singing some of the latest lyrics by Euripides implies that a few would have been sufficiently highly trained, presumably as choreuts rather than as professional musicians, to offer more than passable renditions of such complex and difficult arias.[19] Their competence might have had something to do with increased opportunities to hear the music of drama, in deme theatres and non-Athenian performance venues; recent explorations have emphasised the existence of a professional drama circuit for actors in the fifth century and the rapid growth of theatre venues around the Greek world.[20]

Aristophanes' wholesale parody of the new musical style, as represented by dithyrambists such as Cinesias and Timotheus, encompasses the astrophic lyrics attributed by the character of Aeschylus to Euripides, notoriously including the extension of a single syllable over several notes in *heieieieilissō*.[21] By contrast, Aeschylus is characterised by his antagonist as κακὸν | μελοποιὸν ὄντα καὶ ποιοῦντα ταῦτ' ἀεί – 'a third-rate melodist who uses the same music over and over again'.[22] In so far as instrumental embellishments within the lyrics are attributed to Aeschylus, they are confined to the monotonous *tophlattothrat* of the strumming of the lyre. Even allowing for a large dose of comic parody, it seems a reasonable inference that the distinctions drawn in this way between the styles of the earlier dramatist and the later point to the different and complex effects employed in the music of Euripidean drama. Aristophanes can represent the experience of the latter to his audience in terms similar to those he uses about the kind of effects used in the music of the professional dithyrambists. In an enlightening analysis of the Aristophanic parody of Aeschylean lyric, J. Danielewicz has demonstrated that not only are the Aeschylean verses chosen for parody by 'Euripides' identical to each other in metre, but by and large they also correspond in terms of the pitch accent of the words, suggesting that they will have been sung to what was recognisably an identical melody.[23] The verses cited all end with a so-called enoplian colon (short-short-long-short-short-long-short-short-long-long),

---

[19] Plut. *Nicias* 29.2.3. [20] Csapo 2004: 208 nn. 5 and 6. [21] Ar. *Frogs* 1314, 1348.
[22] Ar. *Frogs* 1249–50. [23] Danielewicz 1990.

to which we may conveniently compare the rhythm of the opening phrase of Mozart's Symphony no. 40. But whereas Mozart gives us an answering phrase of different melodic shape, and indeed goes on to develop the theme with masterly variety, the clear impression we are given is that the Aeschylean verses would simply have employed the repetition of a single identical melodic phrase time and again.

We may also note that the enoplian colon also provides a standard ending to the dactylic hexameter, following the opening hemiepes (long-short-short-long-short-short-long). So it is possible that the sense of monotony would be reinforced by the rhythmical associations with the epic hexameter verses recited by rhapsodes; a late fragment of melody set to hexameter verses shows that an identical melodic form could be employed from verse to verse.[24] If so, they would have imparted a characteristically monotonous feel to citharody, for which we may perhaps find a modern equivalent in the droning incantations of the Serbian *guslari* recorded by Milman Parry.[25] Perhaps, indeed, this gives us a flavour of how Aeschylean lyrics may have sounded besides those of Euripides; a late source tells us that Euripides was known for 'extending the use of modes and genera and employing a far greater variety of notes than his predecessors'.[26] Testimonia point to a close personal and professional association between Euripides and the revolutionary 'New Musician' Timotheus of Miletus. The fragments of Timotheus' nomes and dithyrambs exhibit an unprecedented rhythmical irregularity and complexity, which doubtless would have been accompanied by an equally irregular melodic structure. Timotheus notoriously boasts about the *kainotēs* of his songs, and by increasing the number of the lyre's strings from seven to eleven he could lay claim to having extended the instrument's tonal and modal range.[27]

MODULATIONS IN DITHYRAMB AND DRAMA

The dithyramb in particular was the focus of much of the furore surrounding the reception of the New Music in the latter half of the fifth century.[28] The novelty of the music in the period is regularly associated with specific technical aspects of music in the genre, such as the use of modulation between modes, *metabolē*.[29] It is as if this latter innovation violated some

---

[24] West 1992: 287–8.   [25] Lord 2000: includes a recording.   [26] [Psell.] *On Tragedy* 5.
[27] Pherec. K-A fr. 155; Paus. 3.12.9–10.   [28] Csapo 2004: 212ff.
[29] The word for 'modulation', *metabolē* may itself have contributed to the reasons why conservative critics found the music so disturbing, since it seemed in some very literal way to indicate change or 'revolution'. Csapo 2004: 229–30 shows how the New Music's terminology mirrored its claims to innovation and heterogeneity.

unwritten convention that a song should stick to a single, correct, mode from beginning to end: Aristotle recounts how the musician Philoxenus started off his dithyramb *Mysians* in the Dorian mode, but was 'naturally drawn back to the Phrygian as being the suitable mode for his composition' (*Politics* 1342b8–12). The implication that music should preserve a kind of proto-Aristotelian 'unity of *harmonia*' suggests a rough comparison to the notion that the tonic should serve as the consistent home key in Western sonata form. To *metabolē* one might add *anabolē*, the unaccompanied instrumental passages that increasingly became a feature of dithyrambs (and their solo counterparts, *nomoi*) and gave professional soloists an opportunity to show off their instrumental and vocal virtuosity.[30] This kind of display may have seemed to many out of place in what had originally been a solemn choral genre, and was still regularly performed as such at the Dionysiac festivals by massed circular choruses of men and boys in the tribally organised competitive events.[31]

In *Birds*, Aristophanes depicts the Athenian dithyrambist Cinesias flaunting the bizarre musico-poetic innovations of his *anabolai*: 'I soar heavenwards on wings of gossamer, flying from one melody to the next . . . intrepid in mind and body, ever seeking the new!' (1372–5). The kind of musical complexity to which this testifies would be far better suited to performance by professional musicians, either on their own or in small professional troupes, than to traditional amateur choruses. In addition there appears to have been a mixing of categories in the late fifth century, which has led to uncertainty about the classification of such pieces as Timotheus' *Persians*. Could it have been intended as a dithyramb for competitive performance by a large circular chorus, or was it a *nomos* intended for the professional soloist and composer to perform? Of course, it may have been both, perhaps featuring solo episodes interchanging with choral refrains, rather as we might imagine the original amoebean genre described by Archilochus when he says: 'I know how to lead off the lovely song of Lord Dionysus, the dithyramb, when my wits are blitzed with wine.'[32] Indeed, such performances may have borne a marked similarity to the interchange we might imagine took place between chorus and coryphaeus in performances of drama. Scholars have emphasised the dramatic possibilities of dithyrambs such as Timotheus' stormy *Nauplios*, *Skylla*, and *Semele's*

---

[30] Particularly on the aulos: Csapo 2004: 216–21.

[31] On the changing form of the dithyramb from archaic times to the fifth century see D'Angour 1997.

[32] Archil. 120W. These lines themselves seem to represent the 'leading off' of a song, perhaps a dithyramb (Callimachus fr. 544 Pf. appears to refer to this fragment as a 'prelude', *phroimion*). The metre, trochaic tetrameter catalectic, may have particular Dionysiac associations: it occurs at a juncture of high intensity in Euripides' *Bacchae* (604–41).

Birthpangs;[33] Melanippides' *Marsyas* may have exploited both lyre and aulos in its realisation.[34] If these dithyrambic *nomoi* were, as has been suggested, equivalent to light operettas, then it seems likely that musical influences ran both ways – from dithyramb to drama and back again.

CONCLUSIONS

What emerges from these considerations is that late fifth-century audiences, at least in Athens, experienced in venues such as theatre and Odeion a richer and fuller sound world than did earlier generations. It is likely that traditional elite techniques and practices of music-making were becoming unfamiliar to the more socially diverse audiences (perhaps including slaves, freedmen, and foreigners) who found more to enjoy in modern styles of music. Such listeners were prone to be enthusiastic recipients of, rather than participants in, highly specialised musical performances and exciting instrumental experiences such as the gyrational performances of an aulete such as Pronomus of Thebes.[35] They would not have been in a position to reperform such music with any competence in informal situations, unlike those of former generations who might readily have performed a Simonidean ode in the symposium.

The upper classes hankered after the old styles and fashions of music-making. Specifically, Aristoxenus laments the way the subtle enharmonic *genera* of the earliest music such as the auletic *nomoi* of Olympus had given way to the less demanding diatonicism of his day – the result, as he disdainfully suggests, of musicians seeking to make music more palatable to the masses.[36] We might in the same way contrast the rich chromatic direction of late Romantic music with the simpler diatonic structures of twentieth-century pop. Aristophanes more than once mentions the 'sweetness' of Phrynichus' music, and Plato speaks of the perfection exuded by a simple paean by Tynnichus which transcends its old-fashioned style.[37] Plato was particularly disapproving of the idea of purely instrumental music, considering the sound of unaccompanied aulos or lyre to be no more edifying than the grunting or neighing of animals.[38] But this was clearly an aspect of the auditory experience of his times, an experience which extended to a far broader audience than the unaccompanied lyre- and aulos-playing that had already made their mark in competitive festival events of the early sixth century.[39]

[33] Csapo 2004: 213–14.   [34] Boardman 1956: 19.   [35] Paus. 9.12.5–6.
[36] Aristox. *Harmony* 1.123.   [37] Ar. *Wasps* 220; *Birds* 748f.; Pl. *Ion* 534d.
[38] Pl. *Laws* 669e–670a.   [39] Paus. 10.7.7.

The overall picture, then, is that the musical experience of Greeks, particularly that of Athenians, shifted in various directions between the sixth century and the fourth. Classical *mousikē*, the basis of traditional elite education in music, became a more specialised and professional pursuit. As it was presented to increasingly larger and more democratically constituted audiences, it adopted complex new forms while losing some of its more subtle harmonic characteristics. Musical innovations in drama and dithyramb interacted to create richer instrumental, melodic, and rhythmical techniques which left earlier music sounding at best sweetly nostalgic, and at worst monotonous and repetitive. In Athens, these aural developments related both to the increasingly democratic nature of participation in musical and dramatic events over the course of the fifth century, and to the establishment of new performance venues that reflected that democratisation.[40] The regular and intensive feedback of competitive events performed in front of huge audiences will have sharpened the ears of audiences and professionals alike, and whetted their appetites for novelty and excitement. But these qualities were felt to have superseded traditional qualities of subtlety, simplicity, and decorum; and much of the auditory excitement will have been contributed by non-Athenian musical practices, whether introduced by performers from other *poleis*, or even from non-Greek spheres of influence in the north and the east to which the developing *archē* of Athens eagerly exposed itself.

The increasingly rapid changes of musical styles prompt an interesting analogy with the modern musical scene. What happens when the pace of change, and the replacement of one style by a new one, increase at a rate at which it no longer seems possible to keep up with all the latest expressions of popular musical fashion? Rap, hiphop, house, grunge, R&B . . . or Phrynis, Melanippides, Cinesias, Timotheus, Philoxenus? One reaction is that, amid the revolutions of fashion, listeners are increasingly drawn to the stability of the classics, with all the qualities of enduring value and formal and aesthetic excellence associated with that term.[41] In the fourth century, an awareness of classicality manifests itself in explicit terms, as represented by such initiatives as regular and official attempts to preserve and re-perform written and musical texts of outstanding quality.[42] A sense of momentous developments in the sound of *mousikē* may perhaps be considered a key factor in the emerging consciousness of the value of the classical.

---

[40] Plato (*Laws* 701a–b) coins the term *theatrokratia*, rule of the theatre mob.
[41] Porter 2005b: 39 f.   [42] See D'Angour 2005.

References

Ackrill, J. (1997) *Essays on Plato and Aristotle*. Oxford.

Adam, J. (1902) *The Republic of Plato with Critical Notes, Commentary and Appendices*, I. Cambridge.

Adam, S. (1966) *The Technique of Greek Sculpture*. London.

Al Faruqi, L. I. (1987) 'The cantillation of the Qur'an', *Asian Music* 19: 1–25.

Aleshire, S. B. (1989) *The Athenian Asklepion: The People, Their Dedications and the Inventories*. Amsterdam.

Allen, R. E., ed. (1965) *Studies in Plato's Metaphysics*. London.

Alscher, L. (1956) *Griechische Plastik*, III: *Nachklassik und Vorhellenismus*. Berlin.

  (1957) *Griechische Plastik*, IV: *Hellenismus*. Berlin.

Althusser, L. (1971) 'Ideology and ideological state apparatuses: notes towards an investigation', in *Lenin and Philosophy and Other Essays*, tr. B. Brewster: 127–86. London.

Anderson, B. C. (2000) 'The cultural revolution of fascism', review of George L. Mosse, *The Fascist Revolution: Toward a General Theory of Fascism*, *First Things* 103 (May): 59–62.

Anderson, J. K. (1963) 'The statue of Chabrias', *AJA* 67: 411–13.

Anderson, W. D. (1966) *Ethos and Education in Greek Music*. Cambridge, Mass.

Andronikos, M. (1984) *Vergina: The Royal Tombs and the Ancient City*. Athens.

Annas, J. (1981) *An Introduction to Plato's Republic*. Oxford.

  (1999) *Platonic Ethics, Old and New*. Ithaca.

Annas, J., and Rowe, C., eds. (2002) *New Perspectives on Plato, Modern and Ancient*. Cambridge, Mass.

Arena, R. (1989) *Iscrizioni Greche Arcaiche di Sicilia e Magna Grecia: Iscrizioni di Megara Iblea e Selinunte*. Milan.

Arnott, W. G. (1972) 'From Aristophanes to Menander', *G&R* 19: 65–80.

Artal-Isbrand, P., Becker, L., and Wypyski, M. T. (2002) 'Remains of gilding and ground layers on a Roman marble statue of Hygeia', in Lazzarini 2002: 240–9.

Asheri, D. (1988) *Erodoto, le storie, Libro I: La Lidia e la Persia*. Milan.

  (1990) *Erodoto, le storie, Libro III: La Persia*. Milan.

Aston, T., and Philpin, C., eds. (1985) *The Brenner Debate: Agrarian Class Structure and Economic Development in Pre-industrial Europe*. Cambridge.

Aupert, P., and Jordan, D. R. (1981) 'Magical inscriptions on talc tablets from Amathous', *AJA* 85: 184.

Badian, E. (1993) *From Plataea to Potidaea: Studies in the History and Historiography of the Pentecontaetia.* Baltimore and London.

Bagnall, R. (2002) 'The effects of plague: model and evidence', *JRA* 15: 114–20.

Bakker, E. J., de Jong, I. J. F., and van Wees, H., eds. (2002) *Brill's Companion to Herodotus.* Leiden, Boston, and Cologne.

Barnard, M. (2001) *Approaches to Understanding Visual Culture.* New York.

Barney, R. (2006) 'Socrates' refutation of Thrasymachus', in Santas 2006: 44–62.

Barringer, J. (1995) *Divine Escorts: Nereids in Archaic and Classical Greek Art.* Ann Arbor.

Barringer, J., and Hurwit, J., eds. (2005) *Periklean Athens and Its Legacy: Problems and Perspectives.* Austin, Tex.

Barron, J. (1980) 'Bakchylides, Theseus and a woolly cloak', *BICS* 27: 1–8.

Batelle, J. (1996) 'Reading the Net: a cultural, not technological, revolution', *SCDzine* 17.2, <www.scd.ucar.edu/zine/96/summer/articles/2.netrev.html>.

Baxandall, M. (1972) *Painting and Experience in Fifteenth-Century Italy.* Oxford.

Bek, H., and Bol, P. C., eds. (1993) *Polykletforschungen.* Berlin.

Bender, B. (1993) 'Cognitive archaeology and cultural materialism', *CAJ* 3: 257–60.

Benediktson, D. (2000) *Literature and the Visual Arts in Greece and Rome.* Norman, Okla.

Beversluis, J. (2000) *Cross-Examining Socrates: A Defense of the Interlocutors in Plato's Early Dialogues.* Cambridge.

Bichler, R. (1995) *Von der Insel der Seligen zu Platons Staat: Geschichte der antiken Utopie.* Vienna.

(2004) 'Herodotus' ethnography: examples and principles', in Karageorghis and Taifacos 2004: 91–112.

Bieber, M. (1961) *The History of the Greek and Roman Theater*, 2nd edn. Princeton.

Blanshard, A. J. L. (1999) 'Rhetoric, Identity and Ideology in the Athenian Lawcourt'. PhD dissertation, University of Cambridge.

Blondell, R. (2000) 'Letting Plato speak for himself: character and method in the *Republic*', in Press 2000: 127–46.

(2002) *The Play of Character in Plato's Dialogues.* Cambridge.

Bloom, A. D. (1968) *The Republic of Plato: Translated with Notes and an Interpretative Essay* (2nd edn 1991). New York.

Bloom, J. M. (1999) 'Revolution by the ream: a history of paper', *ARAMCO World Magazine* 50.3 (May/June): 26–39.

Boardman, J. (1956) 'Some Attic fragments: pot, plaque, and dithyramb', *JHS* 76: 18–25.

(1978) *Greek Sculpture: The Archaic Period. A Handbook.* London.

(1985) *Greek Sculpture: The Classical Period. A Handbook.* London.

(1995) *Greek Sculpture: The Late Classical Period and the Sculpture in Colonies and Overseas.* London.

Boedeker, D., and Raaflaub, K. A., eds. (1998) *Democracy, Empire and the Arts in Fifth-Century Athens.* Cambridge, Mass.

Boegehold, A. L. (1967) 'Philokleon's court', *Hesperia* 36: 111–20.

Boegehold, A. L., *et al.* (1995) *Agora* XXVIII: *The Lawcourts at Athens: Sites, Buildings, Equipment, Procedure, and Testimonia.* Princeton.

Bol, P. C. (1992) *Forschungen zur Villa Albani: Katalog der antiken Bildwerke*, III. Berlin.

Bol, P. C., ed. (2004) *Geschichte der antiken Bildhauerkunst*, II. Mainz.

Bommelaer, J.-F. (1981) *Lysandre de Sparte: Histoire et traditions.* Athens.

Bonner, R. J. (1905) *Evidence in Athenian Courts.* Chicago.

Borbein, A. H. (1973) 'Die griechische Statue des 4. Jhs. v. Chr', *JdI* 88: 43–212.

(1995) 'Die bildende Kunst Athens im 5. und 4. Jahrhundert v. Chr.', in *Die athenische Demokratie im 4. Jahrhundert v. Chr.*, ed. W. Eder: 429–67. Stuttgart.

(2002) 'Klassische Kunst', in *Die griechische Klassik: Idee oder Wirklichkeit*, ed. P.-K. Schuster and W. Jacob: 9–25. Mainz.

Borg, B. (2002) *Der Logos des Mythos: Allegorien und Personifikationen in der frühen griechischen Kunst.* Munich.

Boulter, P. (1970) 'The frieze of the Erechtheion', *AntP* 10: 7–28.

Bowie, A. M. (1993) *Aristophanes: Myth, Ritual and Comedy.* Cambridge.

Bradford, J. (1957) *Ancient Landscapes: Studies in Field Archaeology.* London.

Brenner, R. (1976) 'Agrarian class structure and economic development in pre-industrial Europe', *P&P*: 30–75.

Brinkmann, K. (1997) 'Commentary on Dixsaut', *Proceedings of the Boston Area Colloquium in Ancient Philosophy* 13: 28–33.

Brinkmann, V., and Wünsche, R. (2004) *Bunte Götter: Die Farbigkeit antiker Skulptur. Eine Ausstellung der Staatlichen Antikensammlungen und Glyptothek München in Zusammenarbeit mit der Ny Carlsberg Glyptotek Kopenhagen und den Vatikanischen Museen, Rom, 15 Juni bis zum 5 Sept. 2004.* Munich.

Britnell, R. (1996) *The Commercialisation of English Society, 1000–1500.* Manchester.

Brock, R. (2004) 'Political imagery in Herodotus', in Karageorghis and Taifacos 2004: 169–79.

Brommer, F. (1942) 'Herakles und die Hesperiden auf Vasenbildern', *JdI* 57: 105–23.

Brouskari, M. (1999) *To thorakio tou naou tis Athinas Nikis* (= *ArchEph* Suppl. 137). Athens.

Brown, B. (1973) *Anticlassicism in Greek Sculpture of the Fourth Century* BC. New York.

Brown, C. G. (2001) *The Death of Christian Britain.* London and New York.

Brugnone, A. (1976) 'Defixiones inedite da Selinunte', in *Studi di Storia Antica Offerti dagli Allievi a Eugenio Manni*: 67–90. Rome.

Brumfiel, E. (2000) 'On the archaeology of choice: agency studies as a research stratagem', in Dobres and Robb 2000: 249–56.

Bruneau, P. (1975) 'Situation méthodologique de l'art antique', *AntCl* 44: 425–87.

Brunt, P. A. (1988) *The Fall of the Roman Republic and Related Essays.* Oxford.

Bruun, C. (2003) 'The Antonine plague in Rome and Ostia', *JRA* 16: 426–34.

Buckler, J. (1972) 'A second look at the monument of Chabrias', *Hesperia* 41: 466–74.

Burford, A. (1969) *The Greek Temple Builders at Epidauros*. Toronto.

(1972) *Craftsmen in Greek and Roman Society*. London.

Burke, E. (1992) 'The economy of Athens in the classical era: some adjustments to the primitivist model', *TAPA* 122: 199–226.

Burn, L. (1987) *The Meidias Painter*. Oxford.

(1989) 'The art of the state in late fifth-century Athens', in *Images of Authority: Papers Presented to Joyce Reynolds* (= *PCPS* Suppl. 16), ed. M. M. Mackenzie and C. Roueché: 62–81. Cambridge.

Burnett, A. P., and Edmondson, C. N. (1961) 'The Chabrias monument in the Athenian Agora', *Hesperia* 30: 74–91.

Burnyeat, M. F. (1999) 'Culture and society in Plato's *Republic*', *The Tanner Lectures in Human Values* 20: 215–324.

Buschor, E. (1947) *Bildnisstufen*. Munich.

(1971) *Das hellenistische Bildnis*, 2nd edn. Munich.

Camp, J. M. (1986) *The Athenian Agora: Excavations in the Heart of Classical Athens*. London.

Camp, J. M., and Kroll, J. H. (2001) 'The Agora Mint and Athenian bronze coinage', *Hesperia* 70: 127–62.

Carawan, E. (1990) 'The five talents Cleon coughed up', *CQ* 40: 137–47.

Cargill, J. (1994) *Athenian Settlements of the Fourth Century* BC . Leiden.

Carpenter, R. (1929) *The Sculpture of the Nike Temple Parapet*. Cambridge, Mass.

(1960) *Greek Sculpture: A Critical Review*. Chicago.

Carter, L. B. (1986) *The Quiet Athenian*. Oxford.

Cartledge, P. A. (1985) 'Rebels and *sambos* in classical Greece: a comparative view', in Cartledge and Harvey 1985: 16–46.

(1987) 'Review of Carter (1986)', *Hermathena* 142: 60–4.

(1990) 'Fowl play: a curious lawsuit in classical Athens (Antiphon XVI, frr. 57–9 Thalheim)', in *Nomos: Essays in Athenian Law, Politics and Society*, ed. P. A. Cartledge, P. Millett, and S. Todd: 41–61. Cambridge.

(2001) 'The effects of the Peloponnesian (Athenian) War on Athenian and Spartan societies', in *War and Democracy: A Comparative Study of the Korean War and the Peloponnesian War*, ed. D. McCann and B. S. Strauss: 104–23. Armonk, New York.

Cartledge, P. A., and Harvey, F. D., eds. (1985) *Crux: Essays Presented to G. E. M. de Ste Croix on his 75th Birthday*. Exeter.

Caskey, L. (1925) *Catalogue of Greek and Roman Sculpture*. Boston, Mass.

Castriota, D. (1992) *Myth, Ethos and Actuality*. Madison.

Ceadel, E. B. (1941) 'Resolved feet in the trimeters of Euripides', *CQ* 35: 66–89.

Chaniotis, A. (1992) 'Watching a lawsuit: a new curse tablet from south Russia', *GRBS* 33: 69–73.

Christ, M. R. (1990) 'Liturgy avoidance and *antidosis* in classical Athens', *TAPA* 120: 147–69.

(1998) *The Litigious Athenian*. Baltimore and London.

(2006) *The Bad Citizen in Classical Athens*. Cambridge.

Christidis, A. Ph., Dakaris, S., and Vokotopoulou, J. (1999) 'Magic in the oracular tablets from Dodona', in Jordan *et al.* 1999: 67–72.

Ciofi, F. (1978) 'Intention and interpretation in criticisim', in Margolis 1978: 307–24.

Clairmont, C. W. (1983) *Patrios Nomos: Public Burial in Athens during the Fifth and Fourth Centuries* BC. *The Archaeological, Epigraphic-Literary and Historical Evidence* (= *BAR International Series* 161). Oxford.

Clark, J. (2000) 'Towards a better explanation of hereditary inequality: a critical assessment of natural and historic human agents', in Dobres and Robb 2000: 92–112.

Clark, J., and Blake, M. (1994) 'The power of prestige: competitive generosity and the emergence of rank societies in lowland mesoamerica', in *Factional Competition and Political Development in the New World*, ed. E. Brumfiel and J. Fox: 17–30. Cambridge.

Classen, J. (1919) *Thucydides*, I, 5th edn. Berlin.

Clay, D. (1988) 'Reading the *Republic*', in Griswold 1988: 19–33.

Cobb, W. S. (1988) 'Plato's *Minos*', *Ancient Philosophy* 8: 187–208.

Cohen, E. (1992) *Athenian Economy and Society: A Banking Perspective*. Princeton.

Cole, T. (1967) *Democritus and the Sources of Greek Anthropology*. Chapel Hill.

Collard, C. (1981) *Euripides* (= *G&R New Surveys* 14). Oxford.

Comstock, M., and Vermeule, C. (1976) *Sculpture in Stone: The Greek, Roman and Etruscan Collections of the Museum of Fine Arts, Boston*. Boston, Mass.

Connor, W. R. (1984) *Thucydides*. Princeton.

(1993) 'The Ionian era of Athenian civic identity', *PAPS* 137: 194–206.

Cook, R. (1955) 'Thucydides as archaeologist', *BSA* 50: 266–70.

Cornford, F. M. (1932) *Before and After Socrates*. Cambridge.

(1937) *Plato's Cosmology*. London.

Corso, A. (1988–91) *Prassitele: fonti epigrafiche e letterarie. Vita e opere*. 3 vols. Rome.

(2001) 'Phradmon: the itinerary of a classical Greek sculptor from the style of Polycleitus to the Rich Style', *NumAntCl* 30: 53–71.

(2002) 'The Argive masters at Athens from Pericles to Thrasybulus', *NumAntCl* 31: 91–112.

Cortazar, J. (1977) 'Continuidad de los Parques', in *Final del juego*. Madrid.

Cosmopoulos, M., ed. (2004) *The Parthenon and Its Sculptures*. Cambridge.

Costabile, F. (2000) 'Defixiones dal *Kerameikos* di Atene, II: maledizioni processuali', *Minima Epigraphica et Papyrologica* 4: 17–122.

Cottom, D. (1989) *Text and Culture: The Politics of Interpretation*. Minneapolis.

Couëlle, C. (1991) 'Les noms de la gloire et du plaisir: étude et fonctionnement des personages inscrits dans la céramique attique de la fin du Vème siècle av. J.-C.' PhD dissertation, Montpellier.

Coulter, G. (2005) *Expressions of Agency in Ancient Greek*. Cambridge.

Cox, C. A. (1998) *Household Interests: Property, Marriage Strategies, and Family Dynamics in Ancient Athens*. Princeton.

Croissant, F., and Marcadé, J. (1972) 'Sculptures des frontons de temple du IVᵉ siècle', *BCH* 96: 887–95.

Csapo, E. (1999–2000) 'Later Euripidean music', in *Euripides and Tragic Theatre in the Late Fifth Century* (= *Illinois Classical Studies* 24–5), ed. M. Cropp, K. Lee, and D. Sansone: 399–436. Champaign.

(2000) 'From Aristophanes to Menander? Genre transformation in Greek comedy', in Depew and Obbink 2000: 115–33.

(2002) 'Kallipides on the floor-sweepings: the limits of realism in classical acting and performance styles', in Easterling and Hall 2002: 127–47.

(2003) 'The dolphins of Dionysus', in *Poetry, Theory, Praxis: The Social Life of Myth, Word and Image in Ancient Greece*, ed. E. Csapo and M. Miller: 69–98. Oxford.

(2004) 'The politics of the New Music', in Murray and Wilson 2004: 207–48.

(forthcoming) 'Show biz: economic conditions contributing to the rise of the acting profession in the fifth and fourth centuries BC'.

Csapo, E., and Slater, W. J. (1995) *The Context of Ancient Drama*. Ann Arbor.

Curbera, J. (1999) 'Defixiones', in *Sicilia epigraphica: Atti del convegno di studi Erice, 15–18 Ottobre 1998* (= *Annali della Scuola Normale Superiore di Pisa* 4.1): 159–86. Pisa.

Currie, B. (2005) *Pindar and the Cult of Heroes*. Oxford.

Damen, M. (1990) 'Electra's monody and the role of the chorus in Euripides' *Orestes* 960–1012', *TAPA* 120: 133–45.

Damsgaard-Madsen, A. (1988) 'Attic funeral inscriptions: their use as historical sources and some preliminary results', in *Studies in Ancient History and Numismatics Presented to Rudi Thomsen*, ed. A. Damsgaard-Madsen, E. Christiansen, and E. Hallager: 55–68. Aarhus.

D'Angour, A. J. (1997) 'How the dithyramb got its shape', *CQ* 47 (1997) 331–51.

(2005) 'Intimations of the classical in early Greek *mousikê*', in Porter 2005a: 89–105.

(2006) 'The New Music – so what's new?', in Goldhill and Osborne 2006: 264–83.

Danielewicz, J. (1990) 'Il *nomos* nella parodia di Aristofane (*Ran.* 1264 sgg.)', *AION* 12: 131–42.

David, E. (1984) *Aristophanes and Athenian Society of the Early Fourth Century BC*. Leiden.

Davies, J. K. (1971) *Athenian Propertied Families, 600–300 BC*. Oxford.

(1978/93) *Democracy and Classical Greece*. London.

(1981) *Wealth and the Power of Wealth in Classical Athens*. New York.

(1995) 'The fourth-century crisis: what crisis?', in *Die athenische Demokratie im 4. Jahrhundert v. Chr.*, ed. W. Eder: 29–39. Stuttgart.

Dawson, D. (1992) *Cities of the Gods*. Oxford.

de Grummond, N., and Ridgway, B. S., eds. (2000) *From Pergamon to Sperlonga: Sculpture and Context*. Berkeley.

de Jong, I. (2002) 'Homer', in *Narrators, Narratees, and Narratives in Ancient Greek Literature: Studies in Ancient Greek Narrative*, 1, ed. I. de Jong, R. Nünlist, and A. Bowie: 13–24. Leiden.

de Romilly, J. (1956) *Histoire et raison chez Thucydide*. Paris.

de Ste Croix, G. E. M. (1981) *The Class Struggle in the Ancient Greek World*. London.

Demand, N. (1982) 'Plato, Aristophanes, and the speeches of Pythagoras', *GRBS* 23: 179–84.

Depew, M., and Obbink, D., eds. (2000) *Matrices of Genre: Authors, Canons, Society*. Cambridge, Mass., and London.

Despinis, G. (1971) *Sumboli sti meleti tou ergou tou Agorakritou*. Athens.

Detienne, M. (2000) *Comparer l'incomparable*. Paris.

Dettenhofer, M. H. (1999) 'Praxagoras Programm: eine politische Deutung von Aristophanes' *Ekklesiazusai* als Beitrag zur inneren Geschichte Athens im 4. Jahrhundert v. Chr.', *Klio* 81: 95–111.

Devambez, P. (1941) 'Sculptures d'un monument chorégique à Thasos', *Monuments Piot* (= *Monuments et mémoires publiés par l'Académie des inscriptions et belles-lettres*) 38: 93–116.

Develin, R. (1989) *Athenian Officials, 684–321 BC*. Cambridge.

Dickie, M. W. (2000) 'Who practised love-magic in classical antiquity and in the late Roman world?', *CQ* 50: 563–83.

Diehl, E. (1964) *Die Hydria: Formgeschichte und Verwendung im Kult des Altertums*. Mainz.

Dierichs, A. (1990) 'Leda-Schwan-Gruppen in der Glyptik und ihre monumentalen Vorbilder', *Boreas* 13: 37–50.

Dihle, A. (1981) *Die Prolog der Bacchen und die antike Überlieferung des Euripides-Textes*. Heidelberg.

Dillon, M. (1987) 'Topicality in Aristophanes' *Plutus*', *CA* 6: 155–83.

Dinsmoor, W. B., and Dinsmoor, W. B., Jr (2004) *The Propylaia to the Athenian Akropolis: The Classical Building*. Oxford.

Dinsmoor, W. B. (1923) 'The inscriptions of Athena Nike', *AJA* 27: 318–21.
  (1976) 'The roof of the Hephaisteion', *AJA* 80: 223–46.

Dixsaut, M. (1997) 'What is it Plato calls "thinking"?', *Proceedings of the Boston Area Colloquium in Ancient Philosophy* 13: 1–27.

Dobres, M.-A., and Robb, J. E., eds. (2000) *Agency in Archaeology*. London and New York.

Dobrov, G. (1995a) *Beyond Aristophanes: Transition and Diversity in Greek Comedy*. Atlanta.
  (1995b) 'The poet's voice in the evolution of dramatic dialogism', in Dobrov 1995a: 47–97.
  (2001) *Figures of Play: Greek Drama and Metafictional Poetics*. New York.

Dodds, E. R. (1951) *The Greeks and the Irrational*. Berkeley.

Douglas, M., and Wildavsky, A. (1982) *Risk and Culture*. London.

Dover, K. J. (1968) *Lysias and the Corpus Lysiacum*. Berkeley.
  (1972) *Aristophanic Comedy*. Berkeley.
  (1988) 'The freedom of the intellectual in Greek society', in *The Greeks and Their Legacy*: 135–58. Oxford.

Dow, S. (1935) 'Greek inscriptions: nos. 37–38', *Hesperia* 4: 71–91.

Dubois, L. (1989) *Inscriptions grecques dialectales de Sicile*. Rome.

Duhn, F. von (1887) 'La necropoli di Suessula', *RhM* 2: 263–94.

Duncan-Jones, R. (1996) 'The impact of the Antonine plague', *JRA* 9: 108–36.

Duplouy, A. (2006) *Le prestige des élites: recherches sur les modes de reconnaissance sociale en Grèce entre les Xe et Ve siècles avant J.-C.* Paris.

Easterling, P. (1993) 'The end of an era? Tragedy in the early fourth century', in Sommerstein *et al.* 1993: 559–69.

    ed. (1997a) *The Cambridge Companion to Greek Tragedy.* Cambridge.

    (1997b) 'Constructing the heroic', in Pelling 1997: 21–37.

    (1997c) 'From repertoire to canon', in Easterling 1997a: 211–27.

    (1999) 'Actors and voices: reading between the lines in Aeschines and Demosthenes', in Goldhill and Osborne 1999: 154–66.

    (2002) 'Actor as icon', in Easterling and Hall 2002: 327–41.

Easterling, P. E., and Hall, E., eds. (2002) *Greek and Roman Actors.* Cambridge.

Elsner, J. (2003) 'Style', in Nelson and Shiff 2003: 98–109.

Faraone, C. (1985) 'Aeschylus' ὕμνος δέσμιος (*Eum.* 306) and Attic judicial curse tablets', *JHS* 105: 150–4.

    (1991) 'The agonistic context of early Greek binding spells', in Faraone and Obbink 1991: 3–32.

    (1993) 'Molten wax, spilt wine and mutilated animals: sympathetic magic in Near Eastern and early Greek oath ceremonies', *JHS* 113: 60–80.

    (1996) 'Taking the "Nestor's Cup Inscription" seriously: erotic magic and conditional curses in the earliest inscribed hexameters', *C A* 15.1: 77–112.

Faraone, C., and Obbink, D., eds. (1991) *Magika Hiera: Ancient Greek Magic and Religion.* Oxford.

Farenga, V. (2006) *Citizen and Self in the Greek City State.* Cambridge and New York.

Farrar, C. (1988) *The Origins of Democratic Thinking.* Cambridge.

Fellerer, K. G. (1953) 'Church music and the Council of Trent', *Musical Quarterly* 39: 576–94.

Fengler, L. (1886) *Dorische Polychromie.* Berlin.

Feyel, C. (1998) 'La structure d'un groupe socio-économique: les artisans dans les grands sanctuaires grecs du IVe siècle', *TOPOI* 8: 561–79.

Figueira, T. J. (1991) *Athens and Aegina in the Age of Imperial Colonization.* Baltimore.

Fine, J. V. A. (1951) *Horoi: Studies in Mortgage, Real Security, and Land Tenure in Ancient Athens* [= *Hesperia* Suppl. 9]. Princeton.

Finley, Jr, J. H. (1942) *Thucydides.* Cambridge, Mass.

    (1966) *Four Stages of Greek Thought.* Stanford.

Finley, M. I. (1973) *The Ancient Economy.* London. (Updated edn with foreword by I. Morris, Berkeley, 1999).

    (1975) *The Use and Abuse of History.* London.

Fisher, N. R. E. (1988) 'Greek associations, symposia and clubs', in *Civilizations of the Ancient Mediterranean*, II: *Greece and Rome*, ed. M. Grant and R. Kitzinger: 1167–97. New York.

    (1993a) 'Multiple personalities and Dionysiac festivals: Dicaeopolis in Aristophanes' *Acharnians*', *G&R* 40: 31–47.

    (1993b) *Slavery in Classical Greece.* Bristol.

Flashar, H. (1975) 'Zur Eigenart des aristophanischen Spätwerkes', *Aristophanes und die alte Komödie,* ed. H. J. Newiger: 405–34. Darmstadt.

Fleischer, R. (2002) 'Die Amazonen und das Asyl des Artemisions von Ephesos', *JdI* 117: 185–216.

Flensen-Jensen, P., Nielsen, T. H., and Rubinstein, L., eds. (2000) *Polis and Politics; Studies in Ancient Greek History Presented to Mogens Herman Hansen on His Sixtieth Birthday, August 20, 2000.* Copenhagen.

Foley, H. P. (1982) 'The "female intruder" reconsidered: women in Aristophanes' *Lysistrata* and *Ecclesiazusae*', *CP* 77: 1–21.

Ford, A. (2003) 'From letters to literature: reading the "song culture" of classical Greece', in Yunis 2003: 15–37.

Forrest, W. G. (1969) 'Two chronographic notes', *CQ* 19: 95–110.

Förtsch, R. (1997) 'Die Nichtdarstellung des Spektakulären: griechische Bildkunst und griechisches Drama im 5. und frühen 4. Jh. v. Chr.', *Hephaistos* 15: 47–68.

Fowler, C. (2004) *The Archaeology of Personhood: An Anthropological Approach.* London and New York.

Fowler, R. L. (1996) 'Herodotus and his contemporaries', *JHS* 116: 62–87.

(2003) 'Herodotus and Athens', in *Herodotus and His World*, ed. P. Derow and R. Parker: 305–18. Oxford.

Foxhall, L. (1992) 'The control of the Attic landscape', in Wells 1992: 155–9.

(1993) 'Farming and fighting in ancient Greece', in *War and Society in the Greek World*, ed. J. Rich and G. Shipley: 134–45. London.

(1996) 'The law and the lady: woman and legal proceedings in classical Athens', in Foxhall and Lewis 1996: 133–54.

(2002) 'Access to resources in classical Greece: the egalitarianism of the polis in practice', in *Money, Labour and Land: Approaches to the Economies of Ancient Greece*, ed. P. A. Cartledge, E. E. Cohen, and L. Foxhall: 209–20. London.

Foxhall, L., and Lewis, A. D. E. (1996) *Greek Law in its Political Setting: Justification and Justice.* Oxford.

Franciosi, V. (2003) *Il 'Doriforo' di Policleto.* Naples.

(2004) 'O doryphoros tis Pompias', *CORPUS* 56: 18–23.

Fränkel, C. (1912) 'Satyr – und Bakchennamen auf Vasenbildern.' PhD dissertation, Bonn.

French, A. (1991) 'Economic conditions in fourth-century Athens', *G&R* 38: 24–40.

(1993) 'A note on the size of the Athenian armed forces in 431 BC', *Ancient History Bulletin* 7: 43–8.

Frey, V. (1948) 'Zur Komödie des Aristophanes', *MH* 5: 168–77.

Friedländer, P. (1958–69) *Plato,* 3 vols. London.

Friedländer, W. (1957) *Mannerism and Anti-Mannerism in Italian Painting.* New York.

Froning, H. (1971) *Dithyrambos und Vasenmalerei in Athen.* Würzburg.

Fuks, A. (1977) 'Plato and the social question: the problem of poverty and riches in the *Republic*', *Ancient Society* 8: 49–83.

Gàbrici, E. (1927) 'Il santuario della Malophoros a Selinunte', *MonAnt* 32: 67–90.

Gabrielsen, V. (1987) 'The *antidosis* procedure in classical Athens', *C&M* 38: 7–38.
 (1994) *Financing the Athenian Fleet.* Baltimore and London.
 (2002) 'Socio-economic classes and ancient Greek warfare', in *Ancient History Matters: Studies Presented to Jens Erik Skydsgaard on His Seventieth Birthday* [= *ARID* Suppl. 30], ed. K. Ascani, V. Gabrielsen, K. Kvist, and A. H. Rasmussen: 203–20. Rome.
Gadbery, L. M. (1992) 'The sanctuary of the Twelve Gods in the Athenian Agora: a revised view', *Hesperia* 61: 447–89.
Gager, J. G. (1992) *Curse Tablets and Binding Spells from the Ancient World.* Oxford.
Gallant, T. (1991) *Risk and Survival in Ancient Greece: Reconstructing the Rural Domestic Economy.* Cambridge.
 (2001) *Modern Greece.* London.
Gardner, A. ed. (2004a) *Agency Uncovered: Archaeological Perspectives on Social Agency, Power and Being Human.* London.
 (2004b) 'Introduction: social agency, power and being human', in Gardner 2004a: 1–18.
Garlan, Y. (1988) *Slavery in Ancient Greece.* Ithaca.
Garner, R. (1987) *Law and Society in Classical Athens.* London.
Garnsey, P. (1988) *Famine and Food Supply in the Graeco-Roman World: Responses to Risk and Crisis.* Cambridge.
Gauthier, P. (1985) *Les cités grecques et leurs bienfaiteurs (IVe–Ier siècle avant J.-C.): contribution à l'histoire des institutions* [= *BCH* Suppl. 12]. Athens.
Genette, G. (1980) *Narrative Discourse.* New York.
Gero, J. (2000) 'Troubled travels in agency and feminism', in Dobres and Robb 2000: 34–9.
Gill, C. (1977) 'The genre of the Atlantis story', *CP* 72: 287–304.
 (2002) 'Dialectic and the dialogue form', in Annas and Rowe 2002: 145–71.
Giuliani, L. (2002) 'Bilder für Hörer und Bilder für Leser', in *Die griechische Klassik, Idee oder Wirklichkeit: eine Ausstellung der Antikesammlung Berlin im Martin-Gropius Bau, 1. März bis zum 1. Juni 2002:* 338–43. Berlin.
 (2003) *Bild und Mythos: Geschichte der Bilderzählung in der griechischen Kunst.* Munich.
Goette, H. R., ed. (2002) *Ancient Roads in Greece: Proceedings of a Symposium Organized by the Cultural Association Aigeas (Athens) and the German Archaeological Institute (Athens) with the Support of the German School at Athens, November 23, 1998.* Hamburg.
Golden, M. (1992) 'The uses of cross-cultural comparison in ancient social history', *EMC/CV* 11: 309–31.
 (2000) 'A decade of demography: recent trends in the study of Greek and Roman populations', in Flensted-Jensen *et al.* 2000: 23–40.
Goldhill, S. (1986) *Reading Greek Tragedy.* Cambridge.
 (1991) *The Poet's Voice: Essays on Poetics and Greek Literature.* Cambridge.
 (1994) 'Representing democracy: women at the Great Dionysia', in Osborne and Hornblower 1994: 351–68.
 (1999) 'Performance notes', in Goldhill and Osborne 1999: 1–29.

Goldhill, S., and Osborne R., eds. (1999) *Performance Culture and Athenian Democracy*. Cambridge.

eds. (2006) *Rethinking Revolutions through Ancient Greece*. Cambridge.

Gomme, A. W. (1933) *The Population of Athens in the Fifth and Fourth Centuries* BC. Oxford.

(1954) *The Greek Attitude to Poetry and History*. Berkeley.

Gomme, A. W., Andrewes, A., and Dover, K. J. (1945–81) *A Historical Commentary on Thucydides*, 5 vols. Oxford.

Gonzalez, F. J. (1998) *Dialectic and Dialogue: Plato's Practice of Philosophical Inquiry*. Evanston.

González Terriza, A. A. (1996) 'Los rostros de la Empusa: monstruos, heteras, niñeras y brujas: aportación a una nueva lectura de Aristófanes "Ec." 877–1111', *CFC* 6: 261–300.

Gordon, R. (1999a) 'Imagining Greek and Roman magic', in *Witchcraft and Magic in Europe*, II: *Ancient Greece and Rome*, ed. B. Ankarloo and S. Clark: 159–276. London.

(1999b) 'What's in a list?', in Jordan *et al.* 1999: 239–78.

Graf, F. (1994) *La magie dans l'antiquité gréco-romaine*. Paris.

(1997) *Magic in the Ancient World*. London.

(2000) 'Der Mysterienprozess', in *Grosse Prozesse in antiken Athen*, ed. L. Burckhardt and J. von Ungern: 114–27. Munich.

Grandjean, Y., and Salviat, F. (2000) *Guide de Thasos*, 2nd edn. Athens.

Green, J. R. (1999) 'Tragedy and the spectacle of the mind: messenger speeches, actors, narrative, and audience imagination in fourth-century BCE vase-painting', in *The Art of Ancient Spectacle*, ed. B. Bergmann and C. Kondoleon: 37–63. New Haven and London.

Green, P. (2004) *From Ikaria to the Stars: Classical Mythification, Ancient and Modern*. Austin.

Greenberg, J. (2003) 'Plagued by doubt: reconsidering the impact of a mortality crisis in the second c. AD', *JRA* 16: 409–25.

Greenwood, E., and Irwin, E., eds. (2007) *Reading Herodotus: The Logoi of Book 5*. Cambridge.

Gribble, D. (1999) *Alcibiades and Athens: A Study in Literary Presentation*. Oxford.

Griffith, M., trans., and Ferrari, G. R. F., ed. (2000) *Plato, The Republic*. Cambridge.

Griswold, C. L., ed. (1988) *Platonic Writings, Platonic Readings*. New York.

Grmek, M. (1988) *Diseases in the Ancient Greek World*. Baltimore.

Gruben, G. (2001) *Griechische Tempel und Heiligtümer*. Munich.

Gulaki, A. (1981) 'Klassische und klassizistische Nikedarstellungen'. PhD dissertation, Bonn.

Hahland, W. (1930) *Vasen um Meidias*. Berlin.

Hall, E. (1989) *Inventing the Barbarian: Greek Self-Definition through Tragedy*. Oxford.

(1996a) 'Is there a polis in Aristotle's *Poetics*?', in *Tragedy and the Tragic*, ed. M. Silk: 295–309. Oxford.

ed. and trans. (1996b) *Aeschylus' Persians*. Warminster.

(1997) 'The sociology of Athenian tragedy', in Easterling 1997a: 93–126.

(1999a) 'Actor's song in tragedy', in Goldhill and Osborne 1999: 96–124.

(1999b) 'Introduction' and 'Select bibliography', in *Euripides' Bacchae and Other Plays*, trans. J. Morwood: ix–xlviii. Oxford.

(2000) 'Female figures and meta-poetry in Old Comedy', in *The Rivals of Aristophanes*, ed. D. Harvey and J. Wilkins: 407–18. Exeter.

(2002a) 'The ancient actor's presence since the Renaissance', in Easterling and Hall 2002: 419–34.

(2002b) 'The singing actors of antiquity', in Easterling and Hall: 2002 3–38.

(2004) 'Why Greek tragedy in the late twentieth century?', in Hall *et al.* 2004: 1–46.

(2006) *The Theatrical Cast of Athens: Interactions between Ancient Greek Drama and Society*. Oxford.

(2007) 'Tragedy personified', in *Visualising the Tragic*, ed. C. Kraus, S. Goldhill, H. Foley and J. Elsner (2007): 221–56. Oxford.

Hall, E., Macintosh, F., and Wrigley, A., eds. (2004) *Dionysus Since 69: Greek Tragedy at the Dawn of the Third Millennium*. Oxford.

Hall, J. (1997) *Ethnic Identity in Greek Antiquity*. Cambridge.

Halliwell, S. (1993) *Plato, Republic V*. Warminster.

(2002) 'Aristophanic sex: the erotics of shamelessness', in *The Night of Reason: Erotic Experience and Sexual Ethics in Ancient Greece and Rome*, ed. M. C. Nussbaum and J. Sihvola: 120–42. Chicago.

Handley, E. W. (1953) 'COROU in the *Plutus*', *CQ* 3: 55–61.

Hansen, M. H. (1978/1983) '*Nomos* and *psephisma* in fourth-century Athens', *GRBS* 19: 315–30. (Reprinted with addenda in Hansen 1983: 161–77.)

(1981) 'The number of Athenian hoplites in 431 BC', *SymbOslo* 56: 19–32.

(1982) 'Demographic reflections on the number of Athenian citizens 451–309 BC', *AJAH* 7: 172–89.

(1983) *The Athenian Ecclesia, I: A Collection of Articles, 1976–83*. Copenhagen.

(1985) *Demography and Democracy: The Number of Athenian Citizens in the Fourth Century BC*. Herning.

(1988) *Three Studies in Athenian Demography*. Copenhagen.

(1989a) *The Athenian Ecclesia, II: A Collection of Articles, 1983–89*. Copenhagen.

(1989b) 'Political activity and the organisation of Attica in the fourth century BC', in Hansen 1989a: 73–91.

(1989c) 'Review of R. K. Sinclair, *Democracy and Participation in Classical Athens*', *CR* 39: 69–76.

(1989d) '*Rhetores* and *strategoi* in fourth-century Athens', in Hansen 1989a: 25–72.

(1992) 'Review article: a magisterial inventory of Athenian officials (Develin, *Athenian Officials*)', *CP* 87: 51–61.

ed. (1993) *The Ancient Greek City-State*. Copenhagen.

(1999) *The Athenian Democracy in the Age of Demosthenes: Structure, Principles, and Ideology*, 2nd edn. Bristol.

Hansen, M. H., *et al.* (1990) 'The demography of the Attic demes: the evidence of sepulchral inscriptions', *Analecta Romana Instituti Danici* 18: 25–44.

Hanson, V. (1981) *Warfare and Agriculture in Ancient Greece*. Pisa.

(1992) 'Thucydides and the desertion of Attic slaves during the Decelean War', *CA* 11: 210–28.

(1999) *Warfare and Agriculture in Classical Greece*. Berkeley.

Harding, P. (1988) 'Athenian defensive strategy in the fourth century', *Phoenix* 42: 61–71.

Harrison, E. B. (1988) 'Style phases in Greek sculpture from 450–370 BC', in *XIIè Congrès International d'Archéologie Classique, Résumé des Communications February 16–17 1986*: 99–105. Athens.

(1996) 'Pheidias', in *Personal Styles in Greek Sculpture* [*YCS* 30], ed. O. Palagia and J. J. Pollitt: 16–65. Cambridge.

(2005) 'Athena at Pallene and in the Agora of Athens', in Barringer and Hurwit 2005: 119–31.

Hartswick, K. (1983) 'The Athena Lemnia reconsidered', *AJA* 87: 335–46.

Harvey, D., and Wilkins, J., eds. (2000) *The Rivals of Aristophanes*. London.

Hatcher, J., and Bailey, M. (2001) *Modelling the Middle Ages: The History and Theory of England's Economic Development*. Oxford.

Havelock, E. A. (1963) *Preface to Plato*. Cambridge, Mass.

Hedrick, C. (1999) 'Democracy and the Athenian epigraphical habit', *Hesperia* 68: 387–425.

Henderson, J. G. W. (2007) '"The fourth Dorian invasion" and "the Ionian Revolt" (Herodotus 5.76–126)', in Greenwood and Irwin 2007: 289–310.

Henderson, J. J. (1987) 'The older women in Attic comedy', *TAPA* 117: 105–29.

(1990) 'The demos and the comic competition', in Winkler and Zeitlin 1990: 271–313.

(1995) 'Beyond Aristophanes', in Dobrov 1995a: 175–83.

(1998) 'Attic Old Comedy, frank speech, and democracy', in Boedeker and Raaflaub 1998: 255–73.

Henige, D. (1998) *Numbers from Nowhere: The American Indian Contact Population Debate*. Norman, Okla.

Herter, H. (1939) 'Theseus der Athener', *RhM* 78: 289–326.

Higgs, P. (2006) 'Late classical Asia Minor: dynasts and their tombs', in Palagia 2006b: 163–207.

Himmelmann, N. (1967) *Erzählung und Figur in der archaischen Kunst*. Wiesbaden.

Hintzen-Bohlen, B. (1997) *Die Kulturpolitik des Eubulos und des Lykurg*. Berlin.

Hodder, I., ed. (1987) *Archaeology as Long-Term History*. Cambridge.

(2000) 'Agency and individuals in long term processes', in Dobres and Robb 2000: 21–33.

Hodder, I., and Hudson S. (2003) *Reading the Past: Current Approaches to Interpretation in Archaeology*. Cambridge.

Hoff, R. von den (2007) 'Naturalism and classicism: the style and perception of early Hellenistic portraits', in Schultz and von den Hoff (2007).

Hölscher, T. (2002) *The Languages of Images in Roman Art*. Cambridge.

(2000) 'Die Amazonen von Ephesos: Ein Monument zur Selbstbehauptung', in ΑΓΑΘΟΣ ΔΑΙΜѠΝ, *mythes et cultes: études d'iconographie en l'honneur de Lilly Kahil* (= *BCH* Suppl. 38), ed. P. Linant de Bellefonds: 205–28. Paris and Athens.

Hopkins, K., and Burton, G. (1983) 'Political succession in the Late Republic (249–50 BC)', in *Death and Renewal: Sociological Studies in Roman History*, II, ed. K. Hopkins: 31–119. Cambridge.

Hopkins, M. K. (1966) 'On the probable age structure of the Roman population', *Population Studies* 20: 245–64.

Hornblower, S. (1982) *Mausolus*. Oxford.

(1987) *Thucydides*. London.

(1991–6) *A Commentary on Thucydides*, 2 vols. Oxford.

(1992) 'The religious dimension to the Peloponnesian War', *HSCP* 94: 169–97. ed. (1994) *Greek Historiography*. Oxford.

(2000) 'The *Old Oligarch* (Pseudo-Xenophon's *Athenaion Politeia*) and Thucydides: a fourth-century date for the *Old Oligarch*?', in Flensted-Jensen 2000: 363–84.

(2004) *The Greek World, 479–323 BC*. London.

Houser, A. (1951) *The Social History of Art*. London.

How, W. W., and Wells, J. (1912) *A Commentary on Herodotus*, 2 vols. Oxford.

Hubbard, T. K. (1991) *The Mask of Comedy: Aristophanes and the Intertextual Parabasis*. Ithaca.

Humphreys, S. C. (1985) 'Lycurgus of Butadae: an Athenian aristocrat', in *The Craft of the Ancient Historian*, ed. J. W. Eadie and J. Ober: 199–252. London. [Reprinted with afterword in S. C. Humphreys, *The Strangeness of Gods: Historical Perspectives on the Interpretation of Athenian Religion*: 77–129. Oxford.]

(1993) 'Public and private interests in classical Athens', in *The Family, Women and Death*: 22–31. Ann Arbor.

Hunt, P. (1998) *Slaves, Warfare and Ideology in the Greek Historians*. Cambridge.

Hunter, R. L. (1979) 'The comic chorus in the fourth century', *ZPE* 36: 23–38.

(1983) *Eubulus, the Fragments*. Cambridge.

Hunter, V. J. (1982) *Past and Process in Herodotus and Thucydides*. Princeton.

(1994) *Policing Athens: Social Control in the Attic Lawsuits, 420–320 BC*. Princeton.

Hurwit, J. M. (1997) 'The death of the sculptor', *AJA* 101: 587–91.

(1999) *The Athenian Acropolis: History, Mythology, and Archaeology from the Neolithic Era to the Present*. Cambridge.

Immerwahr, H. R. (1957) 'The Samian stories of Herodotus', *CJ* 57: 312–22.

(1990) Attic Script: A Survey. Oxford.

Irwin, E. (2007) '"5.1–2 and 3–10: What's in a name?" and exploring the comparable: onomastics, ethnography and *kratos*', in Greenwood and Irwin 2007: 41–87.

Isager, S., and Hansen, M. H. (1975) *Aspects of Athenian Society in the Fourth Century BC*. Odense.

Jacquemin, J. (1999) *Offrandes monumentales à Delphes*. Athens.

Jahn, M. (2003) *Narratology: A Guide to the Theory of Narrative*. <www.unikoeln.de\~ameo2/pppn.html> (28 July 2003). Cologne.

Jameson, M., Jordan, D. R., and Kotansky, D. (1993) *A Lex Sacra from Selinous* (= *GRBS* Suppl. 11). Durham, NC.

Janko, R. (1997) 'The physicist as hierophant: Aristophanes, Socrates and the authorship of the Derveni papyrus', *ZPE* 118: 61–94.

   (2001) 'The Derveni papyrus (Diagoras of Melos, *apopyrgizontes logoï*?): a new translation', *CP* 96: 1–32.

   (2006) 'Socrates the freethinker', in *A Companion to Socrates*, ed. S. Ahbel-Rappe and R. Kamtekar: 48–62. Oxford.

Jeffery, L. H. (1955) 'Further comments on archaic Greek inscriptions', *BSA* 50: 67–84.

Jennings, H. (1985) *Pandemonium: The Coming of the Machine as Seen by Contemporary Observers, 1660–1885.* New York.

Jockey, P. (1998) 'Neither school nor *koine*: the local workshops of Delos and their unfinished sculpture', in Palagia and Coulson 1998: 177–84.

Johnson, M. (2000) 'Self-made men and the staging of agency', in Dobres and Robb 2000: 212–31.

   (2004) 'Agency, structure and archaeological practice', in Gardner 2004a: 241–7.

Johnston, S. I. (1999) *Restless Dead: Encounters Between the Living and the Dead in Ancient Greece.* Berkeley.

   ed. (2004) *Religions of the Ancient World: A Guide.* Cambridge, Mass.

   ed. (2005) 'Introduction: divining divination', in *Mantikê: Studies in Ancient Divination*, ed. S. I. Johnston and P. T. Struck: 1–28. Leiden.

Jones, A. H. M. (1957) *Athenian Democracy.* Oxford.

Jones, C. P. (1993) 'Greek drama in the Roman Empire', in *Theater and Society in the Classical World*, ed. R. Scodel: 39–52. Ann Arbor.

Jones, N. (2004) *Rural Athens under the Democracy.* Philadelphia.

Jordan, D. R. (1980) 'Two inscribed lead tablets from a well in the Athenian Kerameikos', *MDAI(A)* 95: 225–39.

   (1985) 'Fourteen defixiones from a well in the SW corner of the Athenian agora', *Hesperia* 54: 205–55.

   (1988) 'New archaeological evidence for the practice of magic in classical Athens', in *Praktika of the 12th International Congress of Classical Archaeology* IV. 273–7. Athens.

   (1989) 'A note on a gold tablet from Thessaly', *Horos* 7: 129–30.

   (1999) 'Three curse tablets', in Jordan *et al.* 1999: 115–24.

Jordan, D. R., Montgomery H., and Thomassen, E., eds. (1999) *The World of Ancient Magic: Papers from the First International Samson Eitrem Seminar at the Norwegian Institute at Athens, 4–8 May 1996.* Bergen.

Joyce, A. (2000) 'The founding of Monte Albán: sacred propositions and social practices', in Dobres and Robb 2000: 71–91.

Just, R. (1989) *Women in Athenian Law and Life.* London.

Kagarow, E. G. (1929) *Griechische Fluchtafeln* (= *Eos* Suppl. 4). Leopoli.

Kahn, C. H. (1993) 'Proleptic composition in the *Republic*, or why Book I was never a separate dialogue', *CQ* 43: 131–42.

(1996) *Plato and the Socratic Dialogue: The Philosophical Use of a Literary Form.* Cambridge.

Kallet, L. (1993) *Money, Expense, and Naval Power in Thucydides' History 1.–5.24.* Cambridge.

(2001) *Money and the Corrosion of Power in Thucydides: The Sicilian Expedition and Its Aftermath.* Berkeley.

Kallipolitis, V. (1978) 'I basi tou agalmatos tis Ramnousias Nemesis', *ArchEph* 1978: 1–90.

Kanellopoulos, C. (2006) 'The tholos at Epidauros and Vitruvian resonating chambers', <www.archaeological.org/webinfo.php?page=10248&searchtype= abstract&ytable=2006&sessionid= 4D&paperid=775> (6 January 2006).

Karageorghis, V., and Taifacos, I., eds. (2004) *The World of Herodotus.* Nicosia.

Kearns, E. (1990) 'Saving the city', in Murray and Price 1990: 323–44.

Keesling, C. (1999) 'Endoios' painting from the Themistoklean wall: a reconstruction', *Hesperia* 68: 509–48.

(2003) *The Votive Statues of the Athenian Acropolis.* Cambridge and New York.

(2004) 'The Hermolykos/Kresilas base and the date of Kresilas of Kydonia', *ZPE* 147: 79–91.

(2007) 'Early hellenistic portrait statues on the Athenian Acropolis: survival, reuse, transformation', in Schultz and von den Hoff (2007).

Kemp, W. (1998) 'The work of art and its beholder: the methodology of the aesthetics of reception', in *The Subjects of Art History*, ed. M. A. Cheetham: 180–96. London.

Kennedy, G. A. (1994) *A New History of Classical Rhetoric.* Princeton.

Kjellberg, E. (1926) *Studien zu den attischen Reliefs des V. Jahrhunderts.* Uppsala.

Kleingünther, A. (1933) ΠΡѠΤΟΣ ΕΥΡΕΤΗΣ: *Untersuchungen zur Geschichte einer Fragestellung* (= *Philologus* Suppl. 26.1). Leipzig.

Kluge, K., and Lehmann-Hartleben, K. (1927) *Die antiken Grossbronzen.* Berlin.

Knell, H. (1978) 'Die Gruppe von Prokne und Itys', *AntP* 17: 9–19.

Knox, B. (1979) *Word and Action: Essays on the Ancient Theatre.* Baltimore and London.

Konstan, D., and Dillon, M. (1981) 'The ideology of Aristophanes' *Wealth*', *AJP* 102: 371–94.

Korres, C., and Tomlinson, R. A. (2002) 'Sphettia Hodos: part of the road to Kephale and Sounion', in Goette 2002: 43–60.

Kossatz-Deissmann, A. (1997) 'Tragodia', *LIMC* 8.1: 48–50.

Krahmer, G. (1923/4) 'Stilphasen der hellenistischen Plastik', *RM* 38/9: 138–84.

Krauss, B. (1972) 'Zum Asklepios-Kultbild des Thrasymedes in Epidauros', *AA*: 240–57.

Kraut, R. (1988) 'Reply to Clifford Orwin', in Griswold 1988: 177–82.

Kreis, S. (2001) 'Christianity as cultural revolution', *The History Guide: Lectures on Ancient and Medieval European History*, Lecture 15. <www.historyguide.org/ancient/lecture15b.html>.

Krober, A. ed. (1953) *Anthropology Today: An Encyclopedic Inventory.* Chicago.

Kroll, J. H. (1972) *Athenian Bronze Allotment Plates.* Harvard.

Kron, U. (1976) *Die zehn attischen Phylenheroen: Geschichte, Mythos, Kult und Darstellungen* (= *MDAI(A)* Beiheft 5). Berlin.

Krumeich, R. (1997) *Bildnisse griechischer Herrscher und Staatsmänner im 5. Jahrhundert v. Chr.* Munich.

Kuch, H. (1993) 'Continuity and change in Greek tragedy under postclassical conditions', in Sommerstein *et al.* 1993: 545–57.

Kyrieleis, H. (1986) *Archaische und Klassische griechische Plastik: Akten des internationalen Kolloquiums vom 22.–25. April 1985 in Athen.* Mainz am Rhein.

Lada-Richards, I. (2002) 'The subjectivity of Greek performance', in Easterling and Hall 2002: 395–418.

Lalonde, G. V. (1968) 'A fifth-century hieron southwest of the Athenian Agora', *Hesperia* 37: 123–33.

Lalonde, G. V., Langdon, M. K., and Walbank, M. B. (1991) *Agora* xix: *Inscriptions: Horoi, Poletai Records, Leases for Public Land.* Princeton.

Lambert, S. D. (1996) 'Notes on two Attic *horoi* and some corrigenda to *The Phratries of Attica*', *ZPE* 110: 77–83.

(2002) 'The sacrificial calendar of Athens', *BSA* 97: 353–99.

Lanni, A. M. (1997) 'Spectator sport or serious politics? οἱ περιεστηκότες and the Athenian lawcourts', *JHS* 117: 183–9.

Lapatin, K. (1992) 'A family gathering at Rhamnous? Who's who on the Nemesis base', *Hesperia* 61: 107–19.

(2001) *Chryselephantine Statuary in the Ancient Mediterranean World.* Oxford.

Lape, S. (2004) *Reproducing Athens: Menander's Comedy, Democratic Culture and the Hellenistic City.* Princeton.

Lapini, W. (1997) 'Les hoplites athéniens de 431 (Thuc. 2.13.6)', *Mnemosyne* 50: 257–70.

Lauter, H. (1980) 'Zur wirtschaftlichen Position der Praxiteles-Familie im spätklassischen Athen', *AA* 95: 525–31.

Lawton, C. L. (1995) *Attic Document Reliefs: Art and Politics in Ancient Athens.* Oxford.

Lazzarini, L. ed. (2002) *Interdisciplinary Studies on Ancient Stone* (= *ASMOSIA* 6). Padua.

Le Guen, B. (2001) *Les associations de technites dionysiaques à l'époque héllenistique.* Nancy.

Legrand, Ph.-E. (1932) *Hérodote: Introduction.* Paris.

Levendi, I. (2003) *Hygieia in Classical Greek Art* (= *Archaiognosia* Suppl. 2). Athens.

Lewis, D. M. (1967) 'A note on *IG* i² 114', *JHS* 87: 132.

Lewis, D. M., and Stroud, R. S. (1979) 'Athens honours King Euagoras of Salamis', *Hesperia* 48: 180–93.

Liddel, P. (2003) 'The places of publication of Athenian state decrees from the fifth century BC to the third century AD', *ZPE* 143: 79–93.

Lippold, G. (1954) *Leda und Ganymedes.* Munich.

Lloyd, G. E. R. (1979) *Magic, Reason and Experience: Studies in the Origin and Development of Greek Science.* Cambridge.

Lobel, E. (1936) 'A tragic fragment', in *Greek Poetry and Life: Essays Presented to Gilbert Murray.* Oxford.

Lohmann, H. (1993) *Atênê: Forschungen zu Siedlungs- und Wirtschaftsstruktur des klassischen Attika.* Cologne.

Löhr, C. (2000) *Griechische Familienweihungen: Untersuchungen einer Repräsentationsform von ihren Anfängen bis zum Ende des 4. Jhs. v. Chr.* (= *Internationale Archäologie* 54). Rahden.

Long, C. (1958) 'Greeks, Carians and the purification of Delos', *AJA* 62: 297–306.

Loomis, W. (1995) 'Pay differentials and class warfare in Lysias' *Against Theozotides*: two obols or two drachmas?', *ZPE* 107: 230–6.

(1998) *Wages, Welfare Costs and Inflation in Classical Athens.* Ann Arbor.

López Jimeno, M. del Λ. (1991) *Las Tabellae Defixionis de la Sicilia Griega.* Amsterdam.

Loraux, N. (1986) *The Invention of Athens: The Funeral Oration in the Classical City.* Cambridge, Mass.

(1993) 'Autochthonous Kreousa: Euripides, *Ion*', in *The Children of Athens*, trans. C. Levine: 184–236. Princeton.

Lord, A. B. (2000) *The Singer of Tales*, 2nd edn. Cambridge, Mass.

Lorenz, K. (2006) 'Im Sog der Bilder: Bilddesign und Theaterdramaturgie im späten 5. Jahrhundert v. Chr.', in *Kulturen des Bildes*, ed. B. Mersmann and M. Schulz: 419–33. Munich.

Low, P. (2002) 'Cavalry identity and democratic ideology in early fourth-century Athens', *PCPS* 48: 102–22.

Luhrmann, T. (1989) *Persuasions of the Witch's Craft: Ritual Magic and Witchcraft in Present-Day England.* Oxford.

Luraghi, N. (2000) 'Author and audience in Thucydides' *Archaeology*', *HSCP* 100: 227–39.

(2006) 'Meta-*historiê*: method and genre in the *Histories*', in *The Cambridge Companion to Herodotus*, ed. C. Dewald and J. Marincola: 76–91. Cambridge.

MacDonald, B. (1981) 'The emigration of potters from Athens in the late fifth century and its effects on the Attic pottery industry', *AJA* 85: 157–68.

MacDowell, D. M. (1975) 'Law-making in Athens in the fourth century BC', *JHS* 95: 62–74.

(1995) *Aristophanes and Athens: An Introduction to the Plays.* Oxford.

(2004) 'Epikerdes of Kyrene and the Athenian privilege of *ateleia*', *ZPE* 150: 127–33.

McGlew, J. F. (2002) *Citizens on Stage: Comedy and Political Culture in the Athenian Democracy.* Ann Arbor.

Macleod, C. (1983) *Collected Essays.* Oxford.

Maehler, H. (1997) *Die Lieder des Bakchylides*, II: *Dithyramben und Fragmente.* Leipzig.

Maidment, K. J. (1935) 'The later comic chorus', *CQ* 29: 1–24.

Maloney, E. P. (2003) 'Theatre for a New Age: Macedonia and Ancient Greek Drama.' PhD dissertation, University of Cambridge.

Manakidou, F. (1993) *Beschreibung von Kunstwerken in der hellenistischen Dichtung.* Stuttgart.

Mann, C. (2002) 'Aristophanes, Kleon und eine angebliche Zäsur in der Geschichte Athens', in *Spoudaiogeloion: Form und Funktion der Verspottung in der aristophanischen Komödie (= Beiträge zum antiken Drama und seiner Rezeption 11)*, ed. A. Ercolani: 105–24. Stuttgart.

Mannack, T. (2001) *The Late Mannerists in Athenian Vase Painting.* Oxford.

Marcadé, J. (1953–7) *Recueil de signatures de sculpteurs grecs,* 2 vols. Paris.

    (1986) 'Les sculptures décoratives de la tholos de Marmaria à Delphi: Etat actuel du dossier', in Kyrieleis 1986: 169–73.

Marchant, E. C. (1905) *Thucydides Book 1.* London.

Margolis, J., ed. (1978) *Philosophy Looks at the Arts.* Philadelphia.

Marinatos, N., and Rawlings, H. R. (1978) 'Panolethria and divine punishment: Thuc. 7.87.6 and Hdt. 2.120.5', *PP* 33: 331–7.

Markle, M. M. (1985) 'Jury pay and assembly pay at Athens', in Cartledge and Harvey 1985: 265–97.

Marshall, M. (1990) 'Pericles and the plague', in *Owls to Athens: Essays on Classical Subjects Presented to Sir Kenneth Dover,* ed. E. Craik: 163–70. Oxford.

Marwick, A. (1998) *The Sixties: Cultural Revolution in Britain, France, Italy and the United States.* Oxford.

Mastronarde, D. J. (1990) 'Actors on high: the *skênê* roof, the crane, and the gods in Attic drama', *CA* 9: 247–94.

    (1994) *Euripides, Phoenissae.* Cambridge.

Mattingly, H. B. (1988/96–7) 'Review discussion: Develin, *Athenian Officials*', *AJAH* 13: 139–53.

Mattush, C. (1998) 'Rhodian sculpture: a school, a style, or many workshops?', in Palagia and Coulson 1998: 149–56.

Melina, D. (2002) *Breaking the Frame: Metalepsis and the Construction of the Subject.* Columbus, Ohio.

Menn, S. (2005) 'On Plato's πολιτεία', *Proceedings of the Boston Area Colloquium in Ancient Philosophy* 21: 1–55.

Meritt, B. D. (1946) 'Greek inscriptions', *Hesperia* 15: 169–253.

    (1960) 'Greek inscriptions', *Hesperia* 29: 1–77.

Meyer, E. A. (1993) 'Epitaphs and citizenship in classical Athens', *JHS* 113: 99–121.

Meyer, E. A., and Lendon, J. E. (2005) 'Greek art and culture since *Art and Experience in Classical Greece*', in Barringer and Hurwit 2005: 255–76.

Meyer, M., and Mirecki, P., eds. (1995) *Ancient Magic and Ritual Power.* Leiden and New York.

Mikalson, J. (1984) 'Religion and the plague in Athens, 431–423 BC', in Rigsby 1984: 217–25.

Miles, M. M. (1980) 'The date of the temple on the Ilissos River', *Hesperia* 49: 309–25.

    (1989) 'A reconstruction of the temple of Nemesis at Rhamnous', *Hesperia* 58: 131–249.

Miller, M. C. (1997) *Athens and Persia in the Fifth Century* bc: *A Study in Cultural Receptivity.* Cambridge.

Millett, P. (1998) 'Encounters in the Agora', in *Kosmos: Essays in Order, Conflict and Community in Classical Athens*, ed. P. A. Cartledge, P. Millett, and S. von Reden: 203–28. Cambridge.

Mills, S. (1997) *Theseus, Tragedy and the Athenian Empire.* Oxford.

Mitchel, F. (1973) 'Lykourgan Athens: 338–322', in *Lectures in Memory of L. T. Semple. Second series, 1966–1970*, ed. E. Sjöqvist and C. G. Boulter: 163–214. Norman, Okla.

Mitsos, M. (1967) 'Epigraphika ex Asklepieiou Epidauros', *AE*: 1–28.

Moles, J. L. (1996) 'Herodotus warns the Athenians', *PLLS* 9: 259–84.

Momigliano, A. (1944) 'Sea power in Greek thought', *CR* 58: 1–7.

Monoson, S. S. (2000) *Plato's Democratic Entanglements: Athenian Politics and the Practice of Philosophy.* Princeton.

Moon, W., ed. (1995) *Polykeitos, the Doryphoros and Tradition.* Madison.

Moraux, P. (1960) 'Une défixion judiciaire au musée d'Istanbul', *Mémoires Académie Royale de Belgique* 54.2: 3–61. Brussels.

Morgan, J. (2002) 'A badly restored sculptor's name in the Erechtheion accounts', in *The Archaeological Institute of America 103rd Annual Meeting Abstracts 25*: 125. Boston.

Morgan, K. (2002) 'Comments on Gill', in Annas and Rowe 2002: 173–87.

Morris, I. (1998) 'Beyond democracy and empire: Athenian art in context', in Boedeker and Raaflaub 1998: 59–86.

   (2000) *Archaeology as Cultural History.* Oxford.

   ed. (1994) *Classical Greece: Ancient Histories and Modern Archaeologies.* Cambridge.

Most, G. (1997) 'Hesiod's myth of the five (or three or four) races', *PCPS* 43: 104–27.

   (1999) 'From *logos* to *mythos*' in *From Myth to Reason: Studies in the Development of Greek Thought*, ed. R. Buxton: 25–47. Oxford.

   (2000) 'Generating genres: the idea of the tragic', in Depew and Obbink 2000: 15–35.

Müller, H. (1988) 'Praxiteles und Kephisodot der Jüngere – zwei griechische Bildhauer aus hohen Gesellschaftsschichten?', *Klio* 70: 346–61.

Muller-Dufeu, M. (2002) *La sculpture grecque: sources littéraires et épigraphiques.* Paris.

Munson, R. V. (2001) *Telling Wonders: Ethnographic and Political Discourse in the Work of Herodotus.* Ann Arbor.

Murphy, N. R. (1951) *The Interpretation of Plato's Republic.* Oxford.

Murray, O. (1966) Ὁ ἈΡΧΑΙΟΣ ΔΑΣΜΟΣ', *Historia* 15: 142–56.

   (1990) 'Cities of reason', in Murray and Price 1990: 1–25.

Murray, O., and Price, S., eds. (1990) *The Greek City from Homer to Alexander.* Oxford.

Murray, P., ed. (1996) *Plato on Poetry.* Cambridge.

(2002) 'Plato's Muses: the goddesses that endure', in *Cultivating the Muses: Struggles for Power and Inspiration in Classical Greek Literature*, ed. E. Spentzou and D. Fowler: 29–46. Oxford.

Murray, P., and Wilson, P., eds. (2004) *Music and the Muses: The Culture of Mousike in the Classical Athenian City.* Oxford.

Myres, J. L. (1906) 'The list of thalassocracies in Eusebius', *JHS* 26: 84–130.

Nagy, G. (2002) *Plato's Rhapsody and Homer's Music.* Athens.

Neer, R. (2002) *Style and Politics in Athenian Vase Painting: The Craft of Democracy, 530–460 BC.* Cambridge.

Nehamas, A. (1998) *The Art of Living: Socratic Reflections from Plato to Foucault.* Berkeley.

Neils, J. (1983) 'A Greek nativity by the Meidias painter', *Bulletin of the Cleveland Museum of Art* 70: 274–89.

Nelson, R., and Shiff, R., eds. (2003) *Critical Terms for Art History.* Chicago.

Nesselrath, H.-G. (1990) *Die attische mittlere Komödie: Ihre Stellung in der antiken Literaturkritik und Literaturgeschichte.* Berlin.

(2000) 'Eupolis and the periodization of Athenian comedy', in Harvey and Wilkins 2000: 233–46.

Nicolai, R. (2001) 'Thucydides' *Archaeology*: between epic and oral traditions', in *The Historian's Craft in the Age of Herodotus*, ed. N. Luraghi: 263–85. Oxford.

Nightingale, A. W. (1995) *Genres in Dialogue: Plato and the Construct of Philosophy.* Cambridge.

Norden, E. (1913) *Agnostos Theos.* Leipzig.

Nussbaum, M. C. (1980) 'Aristophanes and Socrates on learning practical wisdom', *YCS* 26: 43–97.

Oakley, J. H. (2004) *Picturing Death in Classical Athens: The Evidence of the White Lekythoi.* Cambridge.

Ober, J. (1985) *Fortress Attica: Defense of the Athenian Land Frontier, 404–322 BC.* Leiden.

(1989a) 'Defense of the Athenian land frontier, 403–322 BC', *Phoenix* 43: 294–301.

(1989b) *Mass and Elite in Democratic Athens: Rhetoric, Ideology, and the Power of the People.* Princeton.

(1998) *Political Dissent in Democratic Athens: Intellectual Critics of Popular Rule.* Princeton.

Oddy, W. A. (1985) 'Vergoldungen auf prähistorischen und klassischen Bronzen', in *Archäologische Bronzen, Antike Kunst, Moderne Technik*, ed. H. Born: 64–70. Berlin.

(1990) 'The gilding of bronze sculpture in the classical world', in *Small Bronze Sculpture from the Ancient World*, ed. M. True and J. Podany: 103–24. Malibu.

(1991) 'Gilding: an outline of the technological history of the plating of gold on to silver or copper in the Old World', *Endeavor* 15: 29–33.

Oddy, W. A., Vlad, L. B., and Meeks, N. D. (1979) 'The gilding of bronze statues in the Greek and Roman world', in *The Horses of San Marco, Venice*: 182–6. Rome.

Ogden, D. (1999) 'Binding spells: curse tablets and voodoo dolls', in *Witchcraft and Magic in Europe*, II: *Ancient Greece and Rome*, ed. B. Ankarloo and S. Clark: 1–90. London.

Oliver, G. J., ed. (2000a) *The Epigraphy of Death: Studies in the History and Society of Greece and Rome*. Liverpool.

  (2000b) 'An introduction to the epigraphy of death: funerary inscriptions as evidence', in Oliver 2000a: 1–23.

  (2006) 'Artists and artisans: the economies of architectural sculpture and sculptors in classical and hellenistic Greece', <www.ascsa.edu.gr/conferences /Dito.htm#15> (6 January 2006).

Olson, S. D. (1987) 'The identity of the *despotes* at *Ecclesiazusae* 1128f.', *GRBS* 28: 161–6.

  (1991) 'Anonymous male parts in Aristophanes' *Ecclesiazusae* and the identity of the *despotes*', *CQ* 41: 36–40.

  (2002) *Aristophanes, Acharnians: Edited with Introduction and Commentary.* Oxford.

Olson, T. (2002) *Poussin and France: Painting, Humanism, and the Politics of Style.* New Haven.

Onians, J. (1999) *Classical Art and Cultures of Greece and Rome.* New Haven.

Osborne, M. J. (1981–2) *Naturalization in Athens*, 2 vols. Brussels.

Osborne, R. (1985) *Demos: The Discovery of Classical Attika.* Cambridge.

  (1990) 'The *demos* and its divisions in classical Athens', in Murray and Price 1990: 265–93.

  (1991) 'The potential mobility of human populations', *OJA* 10: 231–52.

  (1992) '"Is it a farm?" The definition of agricultural sites and settlements in ancient Greece', in Wells 1992: 21–7.

  (1993) 'Competitive festivals and the polis: a context for dramatic festivals at Athens', in Sommerstein *et al.* 1993: 21–37.

  (1994) 'Looking on – Greek style. Does the sculpted girl speak to women too?', in Morris 1994: 86–91.

  (1996) *Greece in the Making, 1200–479 BCE.* London.

  (1997a) 'The ecstasy and the tragedy: varieties of religious experience in art, drama, and society', in Pelling 1997: 187–212.

  (1997b) 'Review of Lohmann (1993)', *Gnomon* 69: 243–7.

  (1998) *Archaic and Classical Greek Art.* Oxford.

  (2000) 'The art of personification on Athenian red-figure pottery', *Apollo* 7: 9–14.

  (2003) 'Changing the discourse', in *Popular Tyranny: Sovereignty and Its Discontents in Ancient Greece*, ed. K. A. Morgan: 251–72. Austin, Tex.

  (2004a) *Greek History.* London.

  (2004b) *The Old Oligarch: Pseudo-Xenophon's Constitution of the Athenians. Translation, Introduction and Commentary.* London.

  (2006) 'Introduction', in Goldhill and Osborne 2006: 1–9.

Osborne, R., and Hornblower, S., eds. (1994) *Ritual, Finance, Politics: Athenian Democratic Accounts Presented to David Lewis.* Oxford.

Ostwald, M. (1986) *From Popular Sovereignty to the Sovereignty of Law: Law, Society and Politics in Fifth-Century Athens*. Berkeley and Los Angeles.

Overbeck, J. (1868) *Die antiken Schriftquellen zur Geschichte der bildenden Künste bei den Griechen*. Leipzig.

Owen, G. E. L. (1965) 'The place of the *Timaeus* in Plato's dialogues', in Allen 1965: 313–38.

Page, D. (1934) *Actors' Interpolations in Greek Tragedy*. Oxford.

ed. and trans. (1942) *Greek Literary Papyri*, I. Cambridge, Mass, and London.

Palagia, O. (1980) *Euphranor* (= *Monumenta Graeca et Romana* 3). Leiden.

(1993/8) *The Pediments of the Parthenon*. Leiden.

(2000) 'Meaning and narrative techniques in statue bases of the Pheidian circle', in Rutter and Sparkes 2000: 53–78.

(2006a) 'Classical Athens', in Palagia 2006b: 119–62.

ed. (2006b) *Greek Sculpture: Function, Materials and Techniques in the Archaic and Classical Periods*. Cambridge.

(2006c) 'Marble carving techniques', in Palagia 2006b: 243–79.

Palagia, O., and Coulson, W., eds. (1998) *Regional Schools in Hellenistic Sculpture: Proceedings of an International Conference Held at the American School of Classical Studies at Athens, March 15–17, 1996*. Oxford.

Palagia, O., and Pollitt, J. J., eds. (1996) *Personal Styles in Greek Sculpture*. Cambridge.

Parker, R. (1996) *Athenian Religion: A History*. Oxford.

(2005) *Polytheism and Society at Athens*. Oxford.

Parkin, T. (1992) *Demography and Roman Society*. Baltimore.

Paton, J. M., *et al.* (1927) *The Erechtheum*. Cambridge, Mass.

Patterson, C. (1981) *Pericles' Citizenship Law of 451–450 BC*. New York.

Patterson, O. (1982) *Slavery and Social Death: A Comparative Study*. Cambridge, Mass.

Peek, W. (1941) *Inschriften, Ostraka, Fluchtafeln* (= *Kerameikos* 3). Berlin.

Pelling, C., ed. (1997) *Greek Tragedy and the Historian*. Oxford.

Persson, K. (1988) *Pre-industrial Economic Growth: Social Organisation and Technical Progress in Europe*. Oxford.

Petropoulakou, M., and Pentazos, E. (1973) *Attike: Oikistika Stoicheia, Prote Ekthese*. Athens.

Pfuhl, E. (1930) 'Ikonographische Beiträge zur Stilgeschichte der hellenistischen Kunst', *JdI* 45: 1–61.

Picon, C. (1993) 'The Oxford maenad', *AntP* 20: 89–104.

Podlecki, A. (1971) 'Cimon, Skyros and "Theseus' bones"', *JHS* 91: 141–3.

Pollitt, J. J. (1972) *Art and Experience in Classical Greece*. Cambridge and New York.

(1974) *The Ancient View of Greek Art*. New Haven.

(1986) *Art in the Hellenistic Age*. Cambridge.

(2000) 'The phantom of the Rhodian School of sculpture', in de Grummond and Ridgway 2000: 92–110.

Pollitt, J. J., and Palagia, O., eds. (1996) *Personal Styles in Greek Sculpture*. Cambridge.

Pomeroy, S. (1989) 'Slavery in the light of Xenophon's *Oeconomicus*', *Index* 17: 11–18

(1994) *Xenophon Oeconomicus: A Social and Historical Commentary.* Oxford.

Porter, J. I., ed. (2005a) *Classical Pasts: The Classical Traditions of Greece and Rome.* Princeton.

(2005b) 'What is "classical" about classical antiquity?', in Porter 2005a: 1–65.

Posch, W. (1991) 'Die *typoi* des Timotheos', *AA*: 69–73.

Postan, M. (1973a) *Essays on Medieval Agriculture and General Problems of the Medieval Economy.* Cambridge.

(1973b) *Essays on Medieval Trade and Finance.* Cambridge.

Preisendanz, K. (1972) 'Fluchtafel (Defixion)', *RAC* 8: 1–29.

Press, G. A., ed. (2000) *Who Speaks for Plato? Studies in Platonic Anonymity.* Lanham, Md.

Price, T., and Feinman, G., eds. (1995) *Foundations of Social Inequality.* New York.

Pritchett, W. K. (1974) *The Greek State at War*, II. Berkeley.

(1975) *Dionysius of Halicarnassus: On Thucydides.* Berkeley.

Raab, I. (1972) *Zu den Darstellungen des Parisurteils in der griechischen Kunst.* Frankfurt am Main.

Raaflaub, K. A. (1987) 'Herodotus, political thought, and the meaning of history', *Arethusa* 20: 221–47.

(2002) 'Philosophy, science, politics: Herodotus and the intellectual trends of his time', in *Brill's Companion to Herodotus*, ed. E. Bakker *et al.*: 149–86. Leiden.

Radermacher, L. (1951) 'Artium Scriptores (Reste der voraristotelischen Rhetorik)', *Österreichische Akademie der Wissenschaften* 227: 3.

Raeck, W. (1984) 'Zur Erzählweise archaischer und klassischer Mythenbilder', *JdI* 99: 1–25

Randall, R. H. (1953) 'The Erechtheum workmen', *AJA* 57: 199–257.

Real, W. (1973) *Studien zur Entwicklung der Vasenmalerei im ausgehenden 5. Jhr.* Münster.

Reckford, K. J. (1987) *Aristophanes' Old-and-New Comedy.* London.

Reed, C. M. (2003) *Maritime Traders in the Ancient Greek World.* Cambridge.

Reeve, C. D. C. (1988) *Philosopher-Kings: The Argument of Plato's Republic.* Princeton.

Reuterswärd, P. (1960) *Studien zur Polychromie der Plastik: Griechenland und Rom.* Stockholm.

Revermann, M. (1999–2000) 'Euripides, tragedy and Macedon: some conditions of reception', *ICS* 24–5: 451–67

Rhodes, P. J. (1972) *The Athenian Boule.* Oxford.

(1979–80) 'Athenian democracy after 403 BC', *CJ* 75: 305–23.

(1981) *A Commentary on the Aristotelian* Athenaion Politeia. Oxford.

(1988) *Thucydides, History II.* Warminster.

(1991) 'The Athenian code of laws, 410–399 BC', *JHS* III: 87–100.

(1992) 'The Athenian Revolution', in *The Cambridge Ancient History*, V: *The Fifth Century BC*, ed. D. M. Lewis, J. Boardman, J. K. Davies, and M. Ostwald: 62–95. Cambridge.

(1993) *A Commentary on the Aristotelian* Athenaion Politeia, 2nd edn. Oxford.

Rhodes, P. J., and Osborne, R. (2003) *Greek Historical Inscriptions, 404–323 BC.* Oxford.

Ridgway, B. S. (1969) 'Stone carving', in Roebuck 1969: 96–117.

(1981) *Fifth-Century Styles in Greek Sculpture.* Princeton.

(1990) *Hellenistic Sculpture*, I. Madison.

(1995) '*Paene ad exemplum*: Polykleitos' other works', in Moon 1995: 177–99.

(1997) *Fourth-Century Styles in Greek Sculpture.* Madison.

(1999) *Prayers in Stone: Greek Architectural Sculpture.* Berkeley, Los Angeles, and London.

(2004) *Second Chance: Greek Sculptural Studies Revisited.* London.

Rieche, A. (1972) 'Die Kopien der Leda des Timotheos', *AntP* 17: 21–55.

Riethmüller, J. W. (2005) *Asklepios: Heiligtümer und Kulte* (= *Studien zu antiken Heiligtümern* 2). Heidelberg.

Rigsby, K. J., ed. (1984) *Studies Presented to Sterling Dow on His Eightieth Birthday* (= *GRBS* Monographs 10). Durham, North Carolina.

Robert, C. (1881) *Bild und Lied: Archäologische Beiträge zur Geschichte der griechischen Heldensage.* Berlin.

Robertson, C. M. (1992) *The Art of Vase Painting in Classical Athens.* Cambridge.

Robertson, N. (1990) 'The laws of Athens, 410–399 BC: the evidence for review and publication', *JHS* 110: 43–75.

Robinson, E. W. (1997) *The First Democracies: Early Popular Government Outside Athens* (= *Historia* Einzelschriften 107). Stuttgart.

Robinson, R. (1953) *Plato's Earlier Dialectic.* Oxford.

Roebuck, C., ed. (1969) *The Muses at Work: Arts, Crafts and Professions in Ancient Greece and Rome.* Cambridge, Mass., and London.

Rolley, C. (1999) *La sculpture grecque 2: la période classique.* Paris.

Roochnik, D. L. (1987) 'The erotics of philosophical discourse', *HPhQ* 4: 117–30.

(2003) *Beautiful City: The Dialectical Character of Plato's Republic.* Ithaca.

Roos, E. (1951) 'De exodi Ecclesiazusarum fabulae ratione et consilio', *Eranos* 49: 5–15.

Rosen, R. M. (1988) *Old Comedy and the Iambographic Tradition.* Atlanta.

(1995) 'Plato comicus and the evolution of Greek comedy', in Dobrov 1995a: 119–37.

Rosen, R. M., and Marks, D. R. (1999) 'Comedies of transgression in gangsta rap and ancient classical poetry', *New Literary History* 30: 897–928.

Rosewarne, D. (1994) 'Estuary English: tomorrow's RP?', *English Today* 37.10 no. 1: 3–9.

Rothwell, K. S. (1990) *Politics and Persuasion in Aristophanes' Ecclesiazusae.* Leiden.

(1992) 'The continuity of the chorus', *GRBS* 33: 209–25.

Roux, G. (1961) *L'Architecture de l'Argolide aux IVème et IIIème siècles avant J. C.* Paris.

Rowe, C. J. (1993) *Plato, Phaedo.* Cambridge.

(1998) *Plato, Symposium* Warminster.

(2006) 'The literary and philosophical style of the *Republic*', in Santas 2006: 7–24.

Rubel, A. (2000) *Stadt in Angst: Religion und Politik in Athen während des peloponnesischen Krieges*. Darmstadt.

Rubinstein, L. (1993) *Adoption in Fourth-Century Athens*. Copenhagen.

(1999) 'Adoption in classical Athens', in *Adoption et fosterage*, ed. M. Corbier: 45–62. Paris.

Rutherford, R. B. (1995) *The Art of Plato*. London.

(2002) 'Comments on Nightingale', in Annas and Rowe 2002: 249–62.

Rutter, N., and Sparkes, B., eds. (2000) *Word and Image in Ancient Greece*. Edinburgh.

Saïd, S. S. (1979) '*L'Assemblée des femmes*: les femmes, l'économie et la politique', in *Aristophane, les femmes et la cité*, ed. J. Bonnamour and H. Delavault: 33–69. Fontenay-aux-Roses.

Sakellariou, M. (1990) *Between Memory and Oblivion: The Transmission of Early Greek Historical Traditions*. Athens.

Sallares, R. (1991) *The Ecology of the Ancient Greek World*. London.

Salviat, F. (1979) 'Vedettes de la scène en province: signification et date des monuments chorégiques de Thasos', *Thasiaca* (= BCH Suppl. 5): 155–67. Athens.

Santas, G. ed. (2006) *The Blackwell Guide to Plato's Republic*. Oxford.

Sassaman, K. (2000) 'Agents of change in hunter-gatherer technology', in Dobres and Robb 2000: 148–68.

Saxonhouse, A. W. (1978) 'Comedy in Callipolis', *American Political Science Review* 72: 888–901.

(1992) *Fear of Diversity: The Birth of Political Science in Ancient Greek Thought*. Chicago.

Schapiro, M. (1953) 'Style', in Krober 1953: 287–303.

Schaps, D. (1977) 'The woman least mentioned: etiquette and women's names', *CQ* 27: 323–30.

Scheidel, W., ed. (2001) *Debating Roman Demography*. Leiden.

(2002) 'A model of demographic and economic change in Roman Egypt after the Antonine plague', *JRA* 15: 97–114.

(2003) 'The Greek demographic expansion: models and comparisons', *JHS* 123: 120–40.

Schlörb, B. (1965) *Timotheos* (= *JdI* Ergänzungsheft 22). Berlin.

Schlörb-Vierneisel, B. (1964) 'Zwei klassische Kindergräber im Kerameikos', *MDAI(A)* 79: 85–113.

Schmitz, W. (1988) *Wirtschaftliche Prosperität, soziale Integration und die Seebundpolitik Athens: Die Wirkung der Erfahrungen aus dem ersten attischen Seebund auf die athenische Aussenpolitik in der ersten Hälfte des 4. Jh v. Chr.* Munich.

Schofield, M. (1993) 'Plato on the economy', in Hansen 1993: 183–96.

(1999) *Saving the City: Philosopher Kings and Other Classical Paradigms*. London.

Schöne, A. (1987) *Der Thiasos: Eine Ikonographische Untersuchung über das Gefolge des Dionysos in der attischen Vasenmalerei des 6. und 5. Jhs v. Chr.* Göteborg, Sweden.

Schuchhardt, W. (1930) 'Die Entstehung der Parthenonfrieses', *JdI* 45: 218–80.

Schultz, P. (2001) 'The akroteria of the temple of Athena Nike', *Hesperia* 70: 1–47.
(2003a) 'Kephisodotos the younger', in *The Macedonians in Athens, 322–229 BC*, ed. O. Palagia and S. Tracy: 186–93. Oxford.
(2003b) 'Review of Brouskari 1999', *AJA* 107: 29–30.
(2004) 'Review of Touloupa 2002', *AJA* 108: 648–9.
Schultz, P., and Hoff, R. von den, eds. (2007) *Early Hellenistic Portraiture: Image, Style, Context.* Cambridge.
Scodel, R. (1984) 'The irony of fate in Bacchylides 17', *Hermes* 112: 137–43.
Scott, D. (1999) 'Plato's pessimism and moral education', *OSAP* 17: 15–36.
Scranton, R. (1969) 'Greek building', in Roebuck 1969: 2–34.
Sealey, R. (1987) *The Athenian Republic: Democracy or the Rule of Law?*, University Park, Penn.
(1990) *Women and Law in Classical Greece.* Chapel Hill.
Snyder, J. M. (1989) *The Woman and the Lyre.* Bristol.
Sedley, D. N. (2003) *Plato's Cratylus.* Cambridge.
Seibert, G. (1978) 'Signatures d'artistes, d'artisans et de fabricants dans l'antiquité classique,' *Ktema* 3: 111–31.
Seiler, F. (1986) *Die griechische Tholos.* Mainz.
Sesonske, A. (1961) 'Plato's *Apology: Republic* I', *Phronesis* 6: 29–36.
Sewel, W. H., Jr (1992) 'A theory of structure: duality, agency and transformation', *American Journal of Sociology* 98: 1–29.
Shanks, M., and Tilley, C. (1992) *Re-constructing Archaeology: Theory and Practice.* London and New York.
Shapiro, H. A. (1993) *Personifications in Greek Art: The Representation of Abstract Concepts, 600–400 BC.* Kilchberg.
(1994) *Myth into Art: Poet and Painter in Classical Greece.* London.
Shear, I. M. (1999) 'The western approach to the Athenian Akropolis', *JHS* 119: 86–127.
Shear, J. L. (2001) 'Polis and Panathenaia: The History and Development of Athena's Festival'. PhD dissertation, University of Pennsylvania.
(2003) 'Atarbos' base and the Panathenaia', *JHS* 123: 164–80.
(forthcoming) 'The oath of Demophantos and the politics of Athenian identity', in *Horkos: The Oath in Greek Society*, ed. A. H. Sommerstein and J. Fletcher. Exeter.
(in preparation) *Polis, Demos, and Revolution: Responding to Oligarchy in Athens, 411–380 BC.*
Shear, Jr., T. L. (1970) 'The monument of the Eponymous Heroes in the Athenian Agora', *Hesperia* 39: 145–222.
(1971) 'The Athenian Agora: excavations of 1970', *Hesperia* 40: 241–79.
(1973) 'The Athenian Agora: excavations of 1972', *Hesperia* 42: 359–407.
(1984) 'The Athenian Agora: excavations of 1980–1982', *Hesperia* 53: 1–57.
(1993) 'The Persian destruction of Athens: evidence from Agora deposits', *Hesperia* 62: 383–482.
(1994) 'Ἰσονόμους τ' Ἀθήνας ἐποιησάτην: the Agora and democracy', in *The Archaeology of Athens and Attica Under the Democracy*, ed. W. D. E. Coulson et al.: 225–48. Oxford.

(1995) 'Bouleuterion, Metroon and the archives at Athens', in *Studies in the Ancient Greek Polis* (= *Historia* Einzelschriften 95), ed. M. H. Hansen and K. A. Raaflaub: 157–90. Stuttgart.

Shefton, B. (1962) 'Herakles and Theseus on a red-figured louterion', *Hesperia* 31: 330–68.

Shimron, B. (1973) 'πρῶτος τῶν ἡμεῖς ἴδμεν', *Eranos* 71: 45–51.

Sickinger, J. P. (1999) *Public Records and Archives in Classical Athens*. Chapel Hill.

Sidwell, K. (2000) 'From Old to Middle to New? Aristotle's *Poetics* and the history of Athenian comedy', in Harvey and Wilkins 2000: 247–58.

Sifakis, G. M. (1967) *Studies in the History of Hellenistic Drama*. London, Toronto, and New York.

Silk, M. S. (1993) 'Aristophanic paratragedy', in Sommerstein *et al.* (1993) 477–504.
(2000) *Aristophanes and the Definition of Comedy*. Oxford.

Sinclair, A. (2000) 'Constellations of knowledge: human agency and material affordance in lithic technology', in Dobres and Robb 2000: 196–212.

Sinclair, R. K. (1988) 'Lysias' speeches and the debate about participation in Athenian public life', *Antichthon* 22: 54–66.

Slater, N. W. (1989) '*Lekythoi* in Aristophanes' *Ecclesiazusae*', *Lexis* 3: 43–51.
(1995) 'The fabrication of comic illusion', in Dobrov 1995a: 29–45.
(1997) 'Waiting in the wings: Aristophanes' *Ecclesiazusae*', *Arion* 5: 97–129.
(2002) *Spectator Politics: Metatheatre and Performance in Aristophanes*. Philadelphia.

Slings, S. R. (2003) *Platonis Rempublicam*. Oxford.

Smart, J. (1977) 'Review article: *The Athenian Empire*', *Phoenix* 31: 245–57.

Smith, A. C. (1993) 'Athenianizing associations in the sculpture of the temple of Asklepios at Epidauros', *AJA* 97: 300.

Snodgrass, A. (1964) 'Carian armourers – the growth of a tradition', *JHS* 84: 107–18.

Söldner, M. (1999) 'Erzählweise auf spätklassischen Vasen als Deutungsfalle: zur Relevanz ikonographischer Hermeneutik', in *Classical Archaeology Towards the Third Millennium, Reflections and Perspectives: Proceedings of the XVth International Congress of Classical Archaeology, Amsterdam, July 12–17, 1998*, I, ed. R. Docter and E. Moormann: 393–7. Amsterdam.

Sommerstein, A. H. (1984) 'Aristophanes and the demon Poverty', *CQ* 34: 314–33.
(1998) *Aristophanes, Ecclesiazusae*. Warminster.

Sommerstein, A., Halliwell, S., Henderson, J., and Zimmermann, B., eds. (1993) *Tragedy, Comedy and the Polis: Papers from the Greek Drama Conference, Nottingham, 18–20 July 1990*. Bari.

Sourvinou-Inwood, C. (1990) 'The cup Bologna PU 273: a reading', *Metis* 5: 137–55.

Spence, I. (1993) *The Cavalry of Classical Greece: A Social and Military History with Particular Reference to Athens*. Oxford.

St Clair, W., and Picken, R. (2004) 'The Parthenon in 1687: new sources', in Cosmopoulos 2004: 166–95.

Stafford, E. (2000) *Worshipping Virtues: Personification and the Divine in Ancient Greece*. London.

Stais, B. (1887) 'Agalmatia Athinas ex Akropoleos', *ArchEph* 5: cols. 31–4.

Stansbury-O'Donnell, M. D. (1999) *Pictorial Narrative in Ancient Greek Art*. Cambridge.

Stears, K. (2000) 'The times they are a' changing: developments in fifth-century funerary sculpture', in Oliver 2000a: 25–58.

Stephanis, I. E. (1988) *Dionysiakoi Technitai*. Heracleion.

Stevens, P. T. (1976) *Colloquial Expressions in Euripides* (= *Hermes* Einzelschriften 38). Wiesbaden.

Stewart, A. (1977) *Skopas of Paros*. Park Ridge, New Jersey.

(1979) *Attika: Studies in Athenian Sculpture of the Hellenistic Age*. London.

(1982) 'Dionysos at Delphi: the pediments of the sixth temple of Apollo and religious reform in the age of Alexander', in *Macedonia and Greece in Late Classical and Early Hellenistic Times* (= Studies in the History of Art 10), ed. B. Barr-Sharrar and E. Borza: 205–27. Washington, DC.

(1990) *Greek Sculpture: An Exploration*. New Haven.

(1995) 'Notes on the reception of the Polykleitan style: Diomedes to Alexander', in Moon 1995: 246–61.

(1997) *Art, Desire and the Body in Ancient Greece*. Cambridge.

Storey, I. C. (1995) '*Wasps* 1284–91 and the portrait of Kleon in *Wasps*', *Scholia* 4: 3–23.

Strasburger, H. (1958) 'Thukydides und die politische Selbstdarstellung der Athener', *Hermes* 86: 17–40.

Strauss, B. S. (1986) *Athens After the Peloponnesian War: Class, Faction and Policy, 403–386 BC*. London.

(1993) *Fathers and Sons in Athens: Ideology and Society in the Era of the Peloponnesian War*. London.

(1997) 'The problem of periodization: the case of the Peloponnesian War', in *Inventing Ancient Culture: Historicism, Periodization, and the Ancient World*, ed. M. Golden and P. Toohey: 165–75. London.

Strauss, L. (1964) *The City and Man*. Chicago.

Strocka, V. M. (1975) 'Athens Kunst im Peloponnesischen Krieg', in *Krisen in der Antike*, ed. G. Alföldy *et al.*: 46–61. Düsseldorf.

Stroud, R. S. (1971) 'Greek inscriptions: Theozotides and the Athenian orphans', *Hesperia* 40: 280–301.

(1979) *The Axones and Kyrbeis of Drakon and Solon* (= *University of California Publications: Classical Studies* 19). Berkeley.

(1998) *The Athenian Grain-Tax Law of 374/3 BC* (= *Hesperia* Suppl. 29). Princeton.

Strubbe, J. H. M. (1991) 'Cursed be he that moves my bones', in Faraone and Obbink 1991: 33–60.

Studniczka, F. (1887) 'Agalmatia Athinas ek tis Athinon Akropoleos', *ArchEph* 5: cols. 133–54.

Stupperich, R. (1977) 'Staatsbegräbnis und Privatgrabmal im klassischen Athen'. PhD dissertation, Westfälischen Wilhelms Universität, Munster.

Sutton, D. F. (1987) 'The theatrical families of Athens', *AJP* 108: 9–26.

(1990) 'Aristophanes and the transition to Middle Comedy', *LCM* 15: 81–95.

Symeonoglou, S. (2004) 'A new analysis of the Parthenon frieze,' in Cosmopoulos 2004: 5–42.

Taaffe, L. K. (1993) *Aristophanes and Women*. London.

Tanner, J. (2006) *The Invention of Art History in Ancient Greece*. Cambridge.

Taplin, O. (1993) *Comic Angels and Other Approaches to Greek Drama through Vase-Painting*. Oxford.

(1999) 'Spreading the word through performance', in Goldhill and Osborne 1999: 33–57.

Tausend, K. (1989) 'Theseus und der Delisch-Attische Seebund', *RhM* 132: 225–35.

Taylor, C. (2005) *A New Political World: Changing Patterns of Participation in Athenian Democracy*. PhD dissertation, University of Cambridge.

Taylor, M. C. (2002) 'One hundred heroes from Phyle', *Hesperia* 71: 377–97.

Taylor, M. W. (1991) *The Tyrant Slayers: The Heroic Image in Fifth-Century* BC *Athenian Art and Politics*, 2nd edn. Salem, New Hampshire.

Themelis, P. (1996) 'Damophon', in Palagia and Pollitt (1996) 154–85.

(2000) *Hiroes kai Hiroa stin Messini*. Athens.

(2003) *Ancient Messene*. Athens.

Thesleff, H. (1989) 'Platonic chronology', *Phronesis* 34: 1–26.

Thomas, C. (2005) *Finding People in Early Greece*. Columbia, Miss.

Thomas, R. (1992) *Literacy and Orality in Ancient Greece*. Cambridge.

(1993) 'Performance and written publication in Herodotus and the sophistic generation', in *Vermittlung und Tradierung von Wissen in der griechischen Kultur*, ed. W. Kullmann and J. Althoff: 225–44. Tübingen.

(1994) 'Law and lawgiver in the Athenian democracy', in Osborne and Hornblower 1994: 119–33.

(2000) *Herodotus in Context: Ethnography, Science, and the Art of Persuasion*. Cambridge.

(2003) 'Prose performance texts: *epideixis* and written publication in the late fifth and early fourth centuries', in Yunis (2003): 168–88.

Thompson, H. A. (1940) *The Tholos of Athens and its Predecessors* [=*Hesperia* Suppl. 4]. Princeton.

(1968) 'Activity in the Athenian Agora: 1966–1967', *Hesperia* 37: 36–72.

Thompson, H. A., and Wycherley, R. E. (1972) *Agora* xiv: *The Agora of Athens: The History, Shape, and Uses of an Ancient City*. Princeton.

Tiberios, M., True, M., Tsiaphaki, D., and Walter-Karydi, E., eds. (2002) *Color in Ancient Greece: The Role of Color in Ancient Greek Art and Architecture, 700–31* BC. Thessaloniki.

Todd, S. C. (1990a) 'Lady Chatterley's lover and the Attic orators: the social composition of the Athenian jury', *JHS* 110: 146–73.

(1990b) 'The purpose of evidence in Athenian courts', in *Nomos: Essays in Athenian Law, Politics and Society*, ed. P. A. Cartledge, P. Millett, and S. Todd: 19–40. Cambridge.

(1993) *The Shape of Athenian Law.* Oxford.

(1996) 'Lysias against Nikomakhos: the fate of the expert in Athenian law', in Foxhall and Lewis 1996: 101–31.

Tomlin, R. S. O. (1988) *Tabellae Sulis: Roman Inscribed Tablets of Tin and Lead from the Sacred Spring at Bath* (= *Oxford University Committee for Archaeology Monographs* 16.1). Oxford.

Touchette, L. A. (1995) *The Dancing Maenad Reliefs: Continuity and Change in Roman Copies* (= *Institute of Classical Studies Bulletin* Suppl. 62). London.

Touloupa, E. (2002) *Ta enaetia glupta tou naou tou Apollonos Daphniphorou stin Eretria* (= Library of the Athenian Archaeological Society no. 220). Athens.

Townsend, R. F. (1995) *Agora* XXVII: *The East Side of the Agora: The Remains Beneath the Stoa of Attalos.* Princeton.

Tracy, S. V. (1984) 'Hands in fifth-century BC Attic inscriptions', in Rigsby 1984: 277–82.

Traill, J. S. (1975) *The Political Organisation of Attica: A Study of Demes, Trittyes and Phylai and Their Representation in the Athenian Council.* Princeton.

Travlos, J. (1971) *Pictorial Dictionary of Ancient Athens.* London.

(1988) *Bildlexicon zur Topographie des antiken Attikas.* Tübingen.

Trevett, J. (1992) *Apollodorus the Son of Pasion.* Oxford.

Trumpf, J. (1958) 'Fluchtafel und Rachpuppe', *MDAI(A)* 73: 94–102.

Ussher, R. G. (1969) 'The staging of the *Ecclesiazusae*', *Hermes* 97: 22–37.

(1973) *Aristophanes, Ecclesiazusae: Edited with Introduction and Commentary.* Oxford.

Valakas, K. (2002) 'The use of the body by actors in tragedy and satyr play', in Easterling and Hall 2002: 69–92.

van Wees, H. (2004) *Greek Warfare: Myths and Realities.* London.

Vanderpool, E. (1950) 'The apostle Paul in Athens', *Archaeology* 3: 34–7.

(1969) 'A *palaistra* in Kephissia', *ArchDelt* 24 (A): 6–7.

(1974) 'Victories in the anthippasia', *Hesperia* 43: 311–13.

(1978) 'Roads and forts in northwestern Attica', *CSCA* 11: 227–45.

Vernant, J.-P. (1962) *Les origines de la pensée grecque.* Paris.

Versnel, H. S. (1991) 'Beyond cursing: the appeal to justice in judicial prayers', in Faraone and Obbink 1991: 60–106.

Vidal-Naquet, P. (1960) 'Temps des dieux et temps des hommes: essai sur quelques aspects de l'expérience temporelle chez les Grecs', *Revue de l'histoire des religions* 159: 55–80.

Vierneisel-Schlörb, B. (1979) *Klassische Skulpturen des 5. und 4. Jahrhunderts v. Chr.* Munich.

von Reden, S. (1995) *Exchange in Ancient Greece.* London.

von Reden, S., and Goldhill, S. (1999) 'Plato and the performance of dialogue', in Goldhill and Osborne 1999: 257–89.

Voutiras, E. (1998) ΔΙΟΝΥΣΟΦΩΝΤΟΣ ΓΑΜΟΙ: *Marital Life and Magic in Fourth-Century Pella*. Amsterdam.

   (1999) 'Euphemistic names for the powers of the nether world', in Jordan *et al.* 1999: 73–82.

Waldera, L. (2001) 'Cultural revolution', *Fast Company*, January. <www.fastcompany.com/articles/archive/lwaldera.html>.

Walker, W., and Lucero, L. (2000) 'The depositional history of ritual and power', in Dobres and Robb 2000: 130–47.

Wallace, R. W. (1989) *The Areopagos Council, to 307 BC*. Baltimore.

   (1994) 'Private lives and public enemies: freedom of thought in classical Athens', in *Athenian Identity and Civic Ideology*, ed. A. L. Boegehold and A. C. Scafuro: 127–55. Baltimore.

   (2004) 'Damon of Oa: a music theorist ostracized?', in Murray and Wilson 2004: 249–67.

Walsh, G. (1978) 'The rhetoric of birthright and race in Euripides' *Ion*', *Hermes* 106: 301–15.

Webster, T. B. L. (1956) *Art and Literature in Fourth-Century Athens*. London.

   (1967) *Hellenistic Art*. London.

   (1970) *Studies in Later Greek Comedy*, 2nd edn. Manchester.

Wells, B., ed. (1992) *Agriculture in Ancient Greece: Proceedings of the Seventh International Symposium at the Swedish Institute at Athens, 16–17th May 1990*. Stockholm.

West, M. L. (1981) 'The singing of Homer and the modes of early Greek music', *JHS* 101: 113–29.

   (1992) *Ancient Greek Music*. Oxford.

Westlake, H. (1969) 'Ὡς εἰκός in Thucydides', in *Essays on the Historians and Greek History*: 153–60. New York.

Whitehead, D. (1983) 'Competitive outlay and community profit: *philotimia* in democratic Athens', *C&M* 34: 55–74.

   (1986) *The Demes of Attica, 508/7–ca. 250 BC*. Princeton.

   (1993) 'Cardinal virtues: the language of public approbation in democratic Athens', *C&M* 44: 37–75.

   (1998) Ὁ ΝΕΟΣ ΔΑΣΜΟΣ: "tribute" in Classical Athens', *Hermes* 126: 173–88.

Whitley, J. (1991) *Style and Society in Dark Age Greece: The Changing Face of a Pre-literate Society, 1100–700 BC*. New York and Cambridge.

Wickkiser, B. L. (2003) 'The Appeal of Asklepios and the Politics of Healing in the Greco-Roman World'. PhD dissertation, University of Texas at Austin.

Wilhelm, A. (1904) 'Uber die Zeit einiger Attischen Fluchtafeln', *JÖAI* 7: 105–26.

Williams, B. A. O. (1973) 'The analogy of city and soul in Plato's *Republic*', in *Exegesis and Argument: Studies in Greek Philosophy Presented to Gregory Vlastos* (= *Phronesis* Suppl. 1), ed. E. N. Lee, A. P. D. Mourelatos, and R. M. Rorty: 196–206. Assen. (Reprinted in B. A. O. Williams, *The Sense of the Past: Essays in the History of Philosophy*, ed. M. Burnyeat: 108–17. Princeton, 2006.)

   (2002) *Truth and Truthfulness*. Princeton.

Wilson, P. J. (1991) 'Demosthenes 21 (Against Meidias): democratic abuse', *PCPS* 37: 164–95.

(1999) 'The *aulos* in Athens', in Goldhill and Osborne 1999: 58–95.

(2000) *The Athenian Institution of the Khoregia*. Cambridge.

(2002) 'The musicians among the actors', in Easterling and Hall 2002: 39–68.

Wimsatt, W., and Beardsley, M. (1978) 'The intentional fallacy', in Margolis 1978: 293–306.

Winkler, J. J., and Zeitlin, F. I., eds. (1990) *Nothing to Do with Dionysos? Athenian Drama in Its Social Context*. Princeton.

Wobst, H. M. (2000) 'Agency in (spite of) material culture', in Dobres and Robb 2000: 40–50.

Worth, K. (2004) 'Greek notes in Samuel Beckett's theatre art', in Hall *et al.* 2004: 265–83.

Wüst, E. (1968) 'Der Ring des Minos', *Hermes* 96: 527–38.

Wycherley, R. E. (1957) *Agora* III: *Literary and Epigraphical Testimonia*. Princeton.

Xanthakis-Karamanos, G. (1979) 'The influence of rhetoric on fourth-century tragedy', *CQ* 29: 6–76.

(1980) *Studies in Fourth-Century Tragedy*. Athens.

Yalouris, N. (1992) *Die Skulpturen des Asklepiostempels in Epidauros* (= *AntP* 21). Berlin.

Young, J. (1955) 'Greek roads in south Attica', *Antiquity* 30: 94–7.

Yunis, H., ed. (2003) *Written Texts and the Rise of Literate Culture in Ancient Greece*. Cambridge.

Zanker, G. (2004) *Modes of Viewing in Hellenistic Poetry and Art*. Madison.

Zeitlin, F. I. (1986) 'Thebes: theater of self and society in Athenian drama', in *Greek Tragedy and Political Theory*, ed. J. P. Euben: 101–41. Los Angeles. (Reprinted in Winkler and Zeitlin 1990: 130–67.)

(1994) 'The artful eye: vision, *ekphrasis* and spectacle in Euripidean theatre', in *Art and Text in Ancient Greek Culture*, ed. S. Goldhill and R. Osborne: 138–96. Cambridge.

(1999) 'Aristophanes: the performance of utopia in the *Ecclesiazousae*', in Goldhill and Osborne 1999: 167–200.

Ziebarth, E. (1899) 'Neue attische Fluchtafeln', *GöttNachr*: 1028–32.

(1934) 'Neue Verfluchungstafeln aus Attika, Boiotien und Euboia', *Sitzungs-berichte der preussischen Akademie der Wissenschaften, Phil.-hist. Klasse* 33: 1022–50.

Zielinski, T. (1925) *De trimetri Euripidei evolutione* (= *Tragodumenon Libri Tres*, book I). Krakow.

Index